A THEORY OF COGNITIVE AGING

ADVANCES
IN
PSYCHOLOGY
28

Editors

G. E. STELMACH

P. A. VROON

NORTH-HOLLAND
AMSTERDAM · NEW YORK · OXFORD

A THEORY OF COGNITIVE AGING

Timothy SALTHOUSE
Department of Psychology
University of Missouri-Columbia
Columbia, MO, U.S.A.

1985

NORTH-HOLLAND
AMSTERDAM · NEW YORK · OXFORD

ISBN: 0 444 87827 0

Publishers:
ELSEVIER SCIENCE PUBLISHERS B.V.
P.O. Box 1991
1000 BZ Amsterdam
The Netherlands

Sole distributors for the U.S.A. and Canada:
ELSEVIER SCIENCE PUBLISHING COMPANY, INC.
52 Vanderbilt Avenue
New York, N.Y. 10017
U.S.A.

PRINTED IN THE NETHERLANDS

Table of Contents

Chapter   Title

Acknowledgments

I would like to thank a number of people who were of great help in the preparation of this monograph. Lynn Saults did many of the technical illustrations, and Don Kausler and Reinhold Kleigl made valuable comments on draft versions of many of the chapters. Paul Baltes and his colleagues at the Max Planck Institute for Human Development and Education in Berlin provided a very congenial environment for the final revisions of the manuscript, and a Research Career Development Award from the National Institute on Aging provided the freedom from normal teaching responsibilities to work on this project.

Introduction

In beginning this monograph I feel somewhat like the speaker who was introduced by the phrase "Nobody understands this complex field, but our next speaker is nevertheless willing to tell you all about it." Because of an understandable reluctance to be considered naive or foolish in attempting to explain what may not yet be explainable, this introductory chapter briefly describes the motivation and purpose for writing a book such as this at the current time.

As indicated by the title, the topic of the present monograph concerns a theory proposed to account for age differences in cognitive functioning. Actually, there are four goals of the monograph. The first is to advocate a more explicitly theoretical approach to research in the area of cognitive aging. I suspect that progress in this field has been impaired, and that which has been achieved is not easily recognized, because of the absence of systematic and integrative theories. Presenting one theoretical perspective is quite often the most effective way of encouraging the development of alternative perspectives, and thus greater sensitivity to theoretical issues might result as a reaction to the current effort. A second goal is to outline three important dimensions along which it is argued that any theory of cognitive aging phenomena must take a position, and the third goal is to evaluate empirical evidence relevant to specific positions along those dimensions. Other researchers may well evaluate this evidence differently, but identification of major developmental issues in terms of the three theoretical dimensions may provide a focus for subsequent research, and facilitate the organization of prior literature. The fourth goal of the monograph is to summarize the major concepts of the current theory, and to describe its application to selected findings in the research literature.

It is my hope that this effort will at least be judged successful with respect to the first three goals because of

a conviction that research in the field of aging and cognition
needs the structure and direction provided by coherent theories.
I am not nearly so confident that the particular theory I
am proposing is going to provide that structure and direction,
but it seems to be the best available at the current time.

The age range of primary interest in this monograph is
between 18 and 70, which includes the large majority of the
working years during adulthood, but specifically excludes
very old ages in which the incidence of diseases makes it
difficult to distinguish the effects of 'normal aging' from
the effects of disease-induced pathologies. In this respect,
the focus here is on the process of **aging**, and not merely
on the **aged** as a distinct segment of the population. Moreover,
unless otherwise indicated, the research findings and conclusions
derived from them will be based upon observations of relatively
healthy, non-institutionalized adults thought to be generally
comparable to one another in most respects other than chronological
age.

Cognitive aging encompasses an extremely large range
of topics since in its broadest sense it refers to the effects
of aging on all aspects of cognition, ranging from pathological
or abnormal cognition to social cognition. In this monograph
the term cognition will be restricted to the processes of
mental or intellectual functioning observed in normal adults,
and thus will follow the dominant usage of the term in contemporary
human experimental psychology. However, even this limited
definition of cognition is too broad from the perspective
of a theory of cognitive aging because there is now considerable
evidence that aging has differential effects on different
aspects of cognition. Some of this literature has been reviewed
in an earlier monograph (Salthouse, 1982), and it can be briefly
summarized by stating that age effects are generally greatest
on tasks requiring the acquisition or transformation of information
(sometimes referred to as fluid intellectual activities),
but are minimal to non-existent on tasks involving the retrieval
or utilization of previously acquired information (sometimes
designated as crystallized intellectual activities). At the

very least, therefore, a theory of cognitive aging should
make a distinction between the two types of cognition, and
either propose different theoretical mechanisms for the two
types, or restrict the theory to the age-sensitive aspects
of cognition on the grounds that abilities unaffected by age
do not require an explanation in a theory of age-related phenomena.

For the most part, the latter perspective is followed
in the current monograph in that it is assumed that understanding
of the processes of aging is likely to progress more rapidly
by studying those aspects of behavior exhibiting the greatest
effects of aging. This orientation is likely to result in
what some observers would characterize as an overly negative
or pessimistic view of mental aging because it deliberately
ignores all those aspects of cognitive functioning which remain
stable or improve with increased age (but see Chapter 5 for
a discussion of the positive effects of experience). Critics
might well argue that we don't need any more information about
the range or cause of the debilities associated with age until
such time that remediations or prosthetic devices are developed
for impairments that are already well-recognized. Possibly
even more compelling is the objection that a balanced assessment
of the capabilities of older adults requires a focus on the
ecological validity of the tasks used to assess cognitive
functioning. In other words, finding that a particular cognitive
ability is extremely sensitive to increased age may have little
relevance for the functional effectiveness of older adults
if that ability is not representative of those required in
real-life (i.e., extra-laboratory) situations.

While these arguments are reasonable, particularly if
one is attempting to assess the overall cognitive competence
of adults of varying ages, they can be considered misdirected
in that they tend to shift the focus away from the primary
issue of this monograph, namely, what is responsible for the
effects of aging on cognitive functioning? In this respect,
therefore, pointing out that there are many aspects of cognition
which do not exhibit very pronounced effects of aging, or
raising questions about the ecological validity of the tasks

in which large age effects are commonly obtained, are both
irrelevant if one is attempting to understand why age differences
occur in those tasks in which they are commonly reported.
These other issues are clearly important and deserve consideration
in any overall appraisal of cognitive functioning in adulthood,
but they are deliberately excluded from the scope of the present
monograph.

Very little attempt is made to summarize or review earlier
research, but instead the intent is to try to impose an organizational structure upon empirical results in the field of
cognitive aging. As stated above, a major purpose is to develop
an agenda for future research efforts, one that will be more
systematic and prove more fruitful than that characteristic
of past research on the topic of aging and cognition.

The volume begins with a brief overview of the function
and nature of theories, in which a five-part distinction among
theoretical levels is introduced and discussed. The next
chapter proceeds to discuss the unique requirements of a developmental theory, and proposes three dimensions useful in characterizing potential determinants of development. Chapter
4 consists of a discussion of the information-processing perspective, which is viewed as a framework rather than a theory
because it provides a large number of concepts which can be
interrelated in diverse ways. Chapters 5 and 6 summarize some
of the major qualifications on the literature considered relevant
for the current theory. The first of these chapters deals
with the contributions of experience and expertise in modifying
developmental patterns, thereby potentially distorting the
'true' effects of aging. Chapter 6 continues this restricting
process by discussing several methodological issues that complicate
the interpretation of age differences (or lack of age differences)
in empirical research. Major themes of these chapters are
that the importance of experience is often underestimated
in research on aging, and that valid generalizations about
patterns of aging must be based on a careful understanding
of how experience and a variety of methdological factors might
attenuate or accentuate true developmental trends. Another

concern is with apparent misuse and abuse of the statistical interaction procedure in analysis of variance designs as the exclusive means of attempting to localize aging effects in a specific process or component.

Chapter 7 outlines the arguments for, and summarizes the evidence relevant to, the general properties considered necessary in an adequate theory of cognitive aging. The importance of processing speed in general cognition is discussed in Chapter 8, and the effects of age on measures of speed are documented in Chapter 9. Chapter 10 outlines the basic theory, while Chapters 11 through 13 deal with the application of the theory to three substantive domains or 'realms of ability,' in each case by means of a selective review of the relevant literature. These three ability areas -- memory, perceptual-spatial, and reasoning -- are considered to encompass, or be relevant to, the major cognitive phenomena pertinent to aging, and thus any adequate theory of cognitive aging should account for important findings within at least these domains. The monograph concludes with a summary chapter containing a brief discussion of desirable directions for future research.

Writing this monograph has been an extremely humbling experience, both as a participant in the emerging discipline of cognitive gerontology and as an individual scholar. The experience has been discouraging from the perspective of the entire field because I have come to appreciate how little is definitively known about the causes of cognitive aging. It led to even more chagrin when I attempted to offer speculations in the face of this absence of concrete knowledge. Many of the theoretical hypotheses discussed in the monograph are admittedly quite preliminary, and I would not be surprised to find that many of them fail to receive confirmation in subsequent research. However, by making my position vulnerable in this manner I hope to be contributing to the stimulation of research that will eventually lead to an advancement of knowledge about the nature and cause of cognitive aging. Although it may prove embarrassing to have my assertions demonstrated to be incorrect, at the present state of knowledge

it may be nearly as useful to find out what is not true about
aging and cognition as it is to find out what is true.

I have an acquaintance who has the habit of introducing
his spouse as 'my current wife,' despite the fact that he
has never been married before and has no plans of getting
divorced and remarried. His explanation for this rather unusual
(and admittedly facetitious) behavior is a desire to keep
reminding his wife that marital status is fragile and could
change at any moment. Although this attitude is arrogant
and sadistic in the context of human relationships, it is
probably appropriate for scientific theories. I therefore
introduce this monograph with the qualification that the proposal
in the later chapters is 'my current theory,' and with the
expectation, and indeed desire, that it will soon be superceded
by a more suitable replacement.

The Nature and Function of Theories

As indicated in the previous chapter, the goal of the current monograph is to describe a theory of age-related cognitive functioning. The lack of testable theories about the nature and cause of adult age differences in cognitive abilities has frequently been lamented (e.g., Baltes & Labouvie, 1973; Baltes & Willis, 1977; Birren, 1960a; Birren, Cunningham, & Yamamoto, 1983; Birren & Renner, 1977; Birren, Woods, & Williams, 1979, 1980; Charles, 1973; Horn & Donaldson, 1980; Riegel, 1973; Welford, 1958), and a primary purpose of the present monograph is to begin to remedy that deficiency. In this chapter a fairly general introduction to the purpose, terminology, and influence of theories is presented. The following chapters become progressively more specific, with the basic theory outlined in Chapter 10, and its application to various ability domains discussed in Chapters 11 through 13. While not intended to be particularly profound, these early chapters are considered useful to set the context for the later discussion of theoretical issues. Because many theoretical disputes probably arise from subtle differences in background assumptions, it is desirable to begin as early as possible in the attempt to make one's perspective explicit.

Purpose of Theories

Imagine being asked to search for "something valuable," but with no other instructions concerning the identity, size, shape, color, or even the approximate location of the target item. Furthermore, assume that you are being asked to conduct this search in an unfamiliar environment with a culture considerably different from your own. What would you look for first, how would you delimit your search to regions that exhibit the greatest likelihood of success, and most importantly, how would you determine what is valuable and what is worthless? In the absence of additional information to guide answers to these questions one possible strategy might be to attempt

to bring as many miscellaneous objects to the attention of
the designated value assessors, and then to focus one's later
search efforts on the objects deemed most valuable by those
arbiters of worth. Of course, if there is not a single arbiter
but instead a constantly changing panel or committee of appra-
isors, the value standards may not be easily discernible,
or even remain consistent across time. This will have the
consequence of introducing a certain amount of randomness
in the value criteria, but a diligent object-gatherer could
still be successful if a substantial proportion of the objects
collected are judged of acceptable worth by a majority of
the value referees.

Many people would probably feel uncomfortable in this
activity of collecting objects almost haphazardly in the hopes
that some might be considered valuable by other people according
to standards that are never explicitly defined, and which
cannot be counted upon to be the same from one occasion to
the next. In fact, it might be argued that this is a singularly
meaningless squandering of human energy since, with the exception
of the possible accumulation of "value points" on the part
of the individual object-collectors, this activity seems to
result in little or no contribution of significance to society.
Eventually it would probably be treated as nothing more than
an elaborate game, and, particularly if the value decisions
appear to be inconsistent from one occasion to the next, most
participants would probably resort to a strategy of convenience
-- collecting only those objects similar to those acquired
in the past or those that can be obtained with minimal expenditure
of effort.

In many respects the preceding description might be said
to reflect the current state of research in psychological
gerontology. It may be only slightly exaggerating to suggest
that at the present time nearly all facts are deemed equally
meaningful and relevant, and that the search for facts is
consequently proceeding in an almost random fashion, or equally
bad, dictated by mere convenience or historical tradition.
Without some means of organizing the facts and establishing

their intrinsic importance independent of what might be somewhat
capricious judgments of the value referees, contemporary gerontological psychology could be considered little more than
fact gathering.   It is true that an impressive amount of facts
has been accumulated, but it is disputable whether this compendium
of facts is contributing to true knowledge about mechanisms
of cognitive aging.

A minimum requirement for knowledge is organization of
information such that the facts are meaningfully related to
one another.   The organizational structure not only provides
a framework within which the various facts can be integrated,
but it also serves as a basis for assigning differential importance
to the set of possible observations.   Without such a meaningful
structure, facts cannot be assimilated and there will be little
discernible accumulation of information in the field.   Moreover,
some means of distinguishing relevant from irrelevant observations
is necessary because irrelevant observations are often not
simply neutral, but can actually be a hindrance to advancing
scientific knowledge in that they obscure the clarity with
which reality can be interpreted and communicated.

How can this structure be achieved?   What is it that
converts facts into knowledge, and establishes the significance
of potential observations so that new and existing facts can
be properly assimilated, and the most promising directions
for new observations can be identified?   In some cultures
Gurus serve in this role, but in the scientific culture it
is theories that impose structure and organization on one's
observations by expressing the relationships among concepts
in the form of theoretical hypotheses.   These hypothesized
relationships serve to determine which observations are pertinent
and which are merely curious anomalies, and also serve to
integrate observations into a coherent structure.

In addition to the critical integrative and predictive
functions of theories, some gerontological theorists have
claimed that theories should also lead to optimization of
the phenomena of interest (e.g., Baltes, Reese, & Nesselroade,
1977; Baltes & Willis, 1977).   In other words, a psychological

theory, in addition to its organizing and directing role in research, is presumed to suggest a means of modifying behavior to a more desirable form. Although modification is often possible once a suitable theory is available, it is debatable whether optimization should be considered a prerequisite for an adequate scientific theory.

One reason why optimization may not be a necessary criterion for a satisfactory theory is that in some fields there is no possibility of intervention or modification and yet perfectly acceptable scientific theories have been developed. For example, astronomy is surely a science with a number of well-defined theories, but it is absurd to think that the solar system could be rearranged to produce a more optimal configuration.

Optimization also seems unsuitable as a function for theories because while theories are predictive about future behavior, they are not prescriptive. That is, theories can predict, but they cannot prescribe unless they also incorporate a set of values which distinguish between optimal and non-optimal forms of behavior. For example, assume that a theory is developed to explain the age-related decline in psychometric intelligence, and that it is now to be used for purposes of optimization. In what direction should behavior be optimized? Most people would probably argue that it is desirable to maintain intellectual functioning at high levels throughout adulthood, and therefore the theory should presumably indicate how proficient levels of functioning can be maintained. However, it is important to realize that this judgment implies acceptance of a value system in which maintenance is considered a desirable goal. It could just as easily be argued that it is more beneficial for society as a whole to have a gradual diminution of mental capacity with increased age in order to allow dominance and power in the society to pass over to younger people with new, and possibly superior, ideas. To a person with this latter perspective, attempting to maintain intellectual functioning at high levels throughout adulthood would clearly not be optimal. These two considerations indicate that while the capability of modification is often a byproduct of an adequate theory, actual implementation of that modifiability in a particular direction requires something more than the theory itself.

The major purposes of a scientific theory are therefore to integrate facts into a coherent system of knowledge and to generate predictions that can serve to direct future research. Mandler and Kessen (1959) have pointed out that in these respects a theory functions somewhat like a map. It indicates the relationships among phenomena, but because it is more abstract than the phenomenon it is designed to explain, it provides a broader and more integrated perspective of the field. This allows 'the forest to be seen despite the trees' since theories are concerned with larger substantive issues and not simply restricted to specific observations. Details are not ignored, however, because the directive nature of theories often results in the research becoming much more focused and able to pursue selected phenomena with greater thoroughness than would be likely without this explicit direction.

Another advantage of the integrative and abstract character-istics of theories is that:

> ...the structure and discipline of theory helps
> to reduce the triviality and isolated, unrelated
> nature of much research (Charles, 1973, p. 37).

The structure will be imposed on the phenomena from above, in a top-down manner, rather than attempting to achieve inductive generalities from the bottom-up starting from the entire assortment of diverse observations. A suggestion by Marx (1970) that theories may be viewed as both a **tool** for the purpose of knowledge generation, and as an ultimate **goal** of science as the ideal representation of knowledge, is relevant in this connection. The relative youth of research in gerontological psychology makes it unrealistic to aspire towards an ultimate form of knowledge at this time, but use of theories as a tool for the systematic acquisition of information seems both feasible and necessary in order to acquire true knowledge.

Some observers have suggested that the existence of many plausible alternative interpretations of aging phenomena means that researchers in the psychology of aging must be able to

tolerate much ambiguity. However, there is a difference between
tolerance for ambiguity and tolerance of chaos, and between
the need for structure and the need for certainty. It is
highly desirable to have an organization imposed in the field
to allow important issues to be identified and examined in
a systematic fashion, even if those issues are not immediately
resolved. While it may not be possible to determine the ultimate
direction of the research, the structure at least allows one
to be confident that the same path is not being repeatedly
traversed.

The Hierarchical Organization of Theories

One probable reason for the reluctance of many researchers
to embrace theoretical perspectives is the bewildering terminology that pervades many theories. At least until the theoretical
systems are well understood, it often appears that the same
terms have more than one referent, with only a few of them
having the same usage as that in normal language. Furthermore,
when different theories address the same phenomena they frequently
use different terms to label their concepts, or the terms
seem to be used in an inconsistent, or even contradictory,
fashion.

The confusing multiple usage of scientific terms can
be illustrated by considering some of the different ways in
which the term 'model' has been used in connection with scientific
theories. First, it has been used in a rather general sense
as a synonym for analogy, as in the statement that the particle
theory of light relies upon a billiard-ball model of light
elements. The specific relationship of the model to the theory
has also varied, however, and some writers describe a model
as though it were more general than the theory, almost a macro-
theory, while others refer to it as more specific than the
theory, like a type of micro-theory. Model also refers to
the use of different species in the study of a particular
phenomenon, as in the phrases 'rat model of aging' or 'chinchilla
model of hearing.' Still another context in which the term
model has been used is in experimental design where it can
refer to a data-analytic strategy (e.g., the analysis of variance

model), or to an expected pattern of data (e.g., a stability or decrement model of aging).

In view of the inconsistency of past usages of this and other theoretical terms, it is important to try to make unambiguous distinctions among the various concepts in any theoretical system. We will begin this effort by first discriminating five levels of theoretical discourse. These levels are outlined in Table 2.1, but it should be emphasized that the boundaries between adjacent levels are loosely defined and should not be considered rigid or fixed. A major reason for presenting this taxonomy is to provide a means of identifying, and more precisely characterizing, the nature of differences among alternative theoretical perspectives. That is, two rival interpretations may be rather similar and differ only at the model or theory level, or they could be based on fundamentally different assumptions at the level of the world view or framework.

The broadest or most general level of theory is the world view, sometimes called the world hypothesis (Pepper, 1942), the scientific paradigm (Kuhn, 1962), or the metamodel (Overton & Reese, 1973). As indicated in Table 2.1, the world view consists of the set of beliefs or assumptions that the theorist holds about the nature of reality. These implicit views tend to become assimilated as one receives training in a particular discipline, and while they influence the way in which problems are formulated and the types of explanations considered for those problems, they are seldom questioned and cannot be subjected to empirical verification. Alternative world views therefore cannot be distinguished on the basis of truth or falsity, but rather must be evaluated in terms of their usefulness in attempting to understand the world.

Most scientists probably think very little about world views, and tend to accept the assumptions of the world view dominant in one's scientific culture in the same unquestioning manner that one receives religious beliefs or the norms of the society in which one is raised. Moreover, because of their general and implicit nature, world views are most often discussed by philosophers of science instead of practicing

Table 2.1

Hierarchical Levels of Theoretical Discourse

Level	Content
World View	Assumptions about reality and the nature of man
Framework	Loose collection of concepts and general principles
Theory	Statement of relationships among selected concepts
Model	Implementation of theory to explanation of specific phenomenon
Phenomena	Systematic observations a limited aspect of reality

researchers in a particular discipline. These philosophical treatments often refer to alternative world views in terms of their "root metaphors" (Pepper, 1942), which are simplistic expressions of the key concepts in each perspective, often in the form of a base analogy.

Three dominant world views and their corresponding root metaphors are **mechanism** based on the metaphor of a machine, **organicism** based on the metaphor of the living organism, and **contextualism** derived from the metaphor of the historical event. Each of these world views is presumed to embody a set of assumptions about the fundamental nature of reality, including the properties considered intrinsic and those which must be derived or explained. For example, a pure mechanistic perspective would view the world and its contents as an elaborate machine, with identification of the forces acting upon that machine and description of the processes by which they exerted their effects as the goals of scientific investigation.

The organismic world view is based on the notion that reality is dynamic and purposeful in the manner of a living organism, and consequently the question of the nature of the external forces acting upon the system is not as meaningful as the issue of how the structure of the system changes as it evolves and develops. Moreover, because dynamism is accepted as an intrinsic property of organic systems, the concept of change is a priori and not something that needs to be explained with the introduction of external forces.

Change is also an a priori concept in the contextualistic world view since the emphasis here is upon acts or events that by their very nature are continuously changing. This perspective is known as contextualism in part because the meaning or significance of the activity is dependent upon the context in which it occurs; there are thus no absolute or universal properties which exist independent of a dynamic and interactive context.

Only capsule descriptions of these world views are presented because very little is yet known about the structure and extent of these implicit belief systems. It is clear, however, that

the metaphors are oversimplifications and that it is unlikely
that a given individual's set of implicit assumptions incorporates
all aspects of one of these analogies. That is, stating that
the root metaphor is a machine implies that the universe is
thought to share some of the properties of a machine (e.g.,
that it is primarily activated by external forces), but other
properties are assumed to be completely irrelevant (e.g.,
the use of metal in most machines, and the necessity of lubrication
as well as energy), and consequently are not incorporated
as part of the analogy. A problem with the use of metaphors
in categorizing different world views is therefore that the
boundaries between the relevant and irrelevant properties
of the metaphor are seldom stated, and consequently the resulting
descriptions are often vague and imprecise.

The next level in the theoretical hierarchy is what will
be called a framework, following the usage of Anderson (1983,
p. 12). A framework consists of a collection of concepts
and principles that can be used in attempting to understand
a particular domain, but which are not tied together to allow
specific predictions. Stimulus-response psychology might
be considered such a framework in that the concepts of stimuli,
responses, and associations between stimuli and responses
served as the primary terms in a large number of theoretical
proposals. More recently, the loosely defined area of information-
processing psychology can be categorized as a framework because
the conceptualization of humans as processors of information
provides an array of concepts such as capacity, structures,
and stages that can be used to construct theories of specific
behavior. (The information-processing framework will be discussed
in considerable detail in Chapter 4). Because frameworks,
like world views, are not directly linked to empirical observations, they cannot be evaluated in terms of truth or falsity
but must be judged by criteria such as fertility or usefulness.

The next level in the hierarchy of theoretical terms
is the theory. In the present context theories are considered
to be statements of the relationships among concepts, and
are more precise and explicit than a framework. It is therefore

quite possible for strikingly different theories to be generated within the same framework by simply altering the direction of causal relationships between concepts. Moreover, because the application of a theory to a particular phenomenon is expressed in the form of a model, the next level in the hierarchy, it is also possible for the same general theory to have somewhat different manifestations depending upon either the interpreter of the theory, or the phenomenon to which it is applied. Both theories and models are therefore connected to the empirical phenomena, although a model may be incorrect and the larger theory still valid because of flaws in the specific application of the theory. The final level in the hierarchy outlined in Table 2.1 represents the phenomena which are abstracted from systematically collected observations of behavior.

Another way of viewing the relationship between models and theories as conceptualized here is to suggest that models attempt to characterize the task environment, while theories are concerned with broader, trans-situational issues. That is, models are proposed to explain how a particular task is performed and the nature of the variables thought to contribute to variations in performance, while theories are designed to integrate a number of broad principles that have applicability in a variety of task domains.

Traditionally, theories and models are evaluated by the criteria of accuracy, simplicity, and fertility. Accuracy is self-evident because the theory would be useless if it did not provide a plausible and internally consistent explanation of the major phenomena of interest. Simplicity is also a straightforward criterion in that, other things being equal, the least complex and most parsimonious interpretation of a phenomenon is to be preferred. Fertility is somewhat more complex because while it is desirable that a theory encompass a broad range of phenomena, all theories are necessarily limited in scope and should not be expected to handle all relevant phenomena. Mandler and Kessen (1959) expressed this point quite clearly in suggesting that the expectation of omniscience in a scientific theory is

> ...rather like saying of Beethoven: His work is
> allright as far as it goes, but his handling of
> comic opera is pitifully inadequate (Mandler & Kessen,
> 1959, p. 151).

Limiting one's expectations for the range of theories may
be particularly appropriate in the field of aging because
of the relatively small amount of previous theoretical work
in this area. As long as the phenomena addressed by the theory
are representative of the total set of cognitive processes,
nearly any plausible theory should be useful in advancing
knowledge about the effects of aging on cognition.

The preceding taxonomy is relatively loose, and it is
likely that many writers would prefer to make more rigorous
distinctions, or to substitute alternative terminology with
qualifying prefixes such as proto-, meta-, pre-, macro-, or
micro-. Nevertheless, the taxonomic categories listed in
Table 2.1 appear to encompass most of the activities that
can be considered theoretical, and are useful for distinguishing
among the various approaches to theory.

Theoretical Relativism

One of the major reasons for an interest in the hierarchy
of theoretical levels, and particularly in those levels above
the formal theory, is that each of these sets of assumptions
guides and influences the activity of the research scientist.
Metaphysical commitments bias the researcher towards certain
kinds of problems and modes of explanation, and these dispositions
are no less potent when only tacit and not openly recognized
rather than explicitly considered and consciously adopted.
This type of bias was colorfully described by Sarason (1984)
as follows:

> There is a limitation to the human mind that is
> as fascinating as it is ignored, as fateful for
> the future as it has been for the understanding
> the past, and as much a source of optimism as of
> pessimism...Briefly put, the limitation is that
> each of us possesses a world view much of which,
> by virtue of the socialization process, we never

> have to articulate and therefore do not have reason
> to challenge. More accurately, we are possessed
> by our world view as much as we possess it (Sarason,
> 1984, p. 477).

The conceptual issues considered important, the kinds of theoretical perspectives adopted, and even the specific methods
employed to investigate phenomena are all severely restricted,
if not completely determined, by these implicit beliefs about
the nature of the world and the kinds of concepts that are
likely to be most useful in attempting to understand it.

Moreover, theoretical relativism is not simply a property
of world views, but instead is a characteristic evident at
all levels in the theoretical hierarchy. To be convinced
of this point, one merely needs to think of how it is that
only a minute fraction of the totality of behavior is ever
examined by a given psychologist. Even if it is admitted
that for reasons of practicality a researcher must restrict
his or her focus to a relatively narrow aspect of behavior,
why is one aspect of behavior selected and not some other?
Often the reasons are primarily related to convenience and
tradition, but ideally this selection is determined on the
basis of theoretical considerations. Frameworks and theories
serve to distinguish central from peripheral issues, thereby
restricting the infinite set of conceivable observations one
could make into those that are potentially meaningful, and
those that can be ignored because they are either trivial
or unlikely to yield valuable information. Models further
limit the scope of inquiry by specifying which particular
aspects of a given behavior (i.e., which dependent variables)
are likely to yield the most information about the hypothesized
mechanisms.

Theoretical relativism also has its negative aspects.
For instance, because theories are necessarily of rather limited
scope, and serve to establish a particular weighting of the
relative importance of various classes of observations, they
can be considered to exert a blinding effect on other phenomena.
That is, because some phenomena are not considered significant

or relevant from a given theoretical perspective, researchers committed to that perspective would be unlikely to discover or investigate those phenomena. This is probably the greatest disadvantage of a theoretical approach to science in that it makes it difficult to recognize and appreciate phenomena that fall outside the scope of the theory within which one is working.

Because of the blinding effect of theories, some researchers have argued that a theoretical approach is desirable only when there is enough information available to establish at least the initial plausibility of the theory. The reasoning is that an invalid theory is worse than no theory because it channels research along unproductive directions and consequently results in a waste of valuable resources. A reasonable reaction to this argument can be expressed by paraphrasing an old adage, "tis better to have theorized and failed than never to have theorized at all." In other words, there is a value in theory-guided research even if the theory is eventually discovered to be unsatisfactory. At minimum, researchers in the discipline will have learned why theories of that type are inadequate. More generally, knowledge is likely to progress more rapidly from directed inquiry based on asking systematically related questions, **regardless of the answers to those questions**, than from a strategy of not posing questions and passively waiting for knowledge to accumulate.

Background Assumptions

The discussion of theoretical relativism makes it clear that one's theoretical perspective, including implicit assumptions at the world-view level, exert a substantial influence on every aspect of research. In fact, the same terms may have quite different meanings in different theories, and consequently even the most basic definitions are at least partly specific to a given theoretical context. It is therefore highly desirable to be as explicit as possible about the nature of one's theoretical perspective before attempting to apply that system to the interpretation of empirical phenomena. We will thus end this chapter by summarizing some of the major convictions and predispositions of the current perspective. Because the theory to be advocated falls within the information-processing framework, many of these preconceptions will be identical to those outlined by Lachman, Lachman, and Butterfield (1979). The interested reader may therefore wish to consult that source for further discussion of this topic.

It is clearly unrealistic to attempt to list all of the assumptions that influence one's mode of thinking, both because some of those assumptions are probably unrecognizable, and because their number is so large that an exhaustive list would be impractical. Nevertheless, this effort is useful in allowing the current perspective to be positioned with respect to a number of important theoretical dimensions, and to set the context for subsequent discussion of theoretical concepts.

One assumption of the current perspective, which is probably shared by the majority of contemporary psychological researchers, is empiricism, in the sense that observation is recognized as the primary source of information and the ultimate means of resolving scientific disputes. Rational arguments are of course necessary in any theoretical system, but observation is accorded a higher status as a means of acquiring knowledge than self-reflection by most scientists at the current time.

Perhaps the most fundamental commitment underlying the present orientation is determinism -- the belief that all behavior has causes which can ultimately be identified. It is unlikely that the goal of discovering the causes of all behavior will be achieved in the near future, but it nonetheless seems a worthy aspiration, and even partial successes may result in considerable advances in knowledge.

Accompanying the assumption of determinism is a belief in reductionism, the doctrine that higher levels of activity should be explained in terms of more basic levels. However, in order to keep the discussion within reasonable bounds, the reductionism is limited to proximal and not distal causes. In other words, while it may eventually be feasible to explain all aspects of cognition and other complex forms of behavior in terms of the collective activity of individual neurons,

it will suffice if primitive explanations within a given level
of analysis can be plausibly related to processes at the same,
or an immediately lower, level of analysis. Proximal reductionism
also applies to hypothesized social and cultural determinants
of cognitive aging phenomena in that the socio-cultural (distal)
factors must be translated into plausible psychological (proximal)
variables and then those variables demonstrated to be causally
related to the phenomena of interest. Limiting the principle
of reductionism in this manner eliminates the necessity of
elaborating an almost endless sequence of progressively more
distal causal mechanisms extending well beyond an individual
researcher's realm of expertise. Restricting reductionism
to a single level also allows for the possibility of emergent
phenomena which can only be understood within a particular
level of analysis. The best example of such an emergent phenomenon
may be the familiar traffic jam, in which neither a thorough
understanding of the physics and mechanics of individual automobiles, nor of the physiology and anatomy of individual human
operators can explain why the automobiles are not functioning
at optimum speeds. Insistence on a rigorous reductionism
would make the investigation of phenomena such as the traffic
jam exceedingly difficult if not impossible, and therefore
it seems more reasonable to seek explanations in terms of
a set of primitives within the same general level of analysis.

It is important to note that the principle of determinism
implies that all phenomena should be explainable, even those
sometimes postulated to be intrinsic or otherwise a priori.
This specifically includes the concept of change or development,
which according to the current perspective is as much in need
of explanation as any other behavioral phenomenon. Because
the organismic and contextualistic world views accept the
concept of change as a given which may need no further explanation,
some philosophically-inclined observers would probably categorize
the current perspective as more consistent with a mechanistic
world view. However, no specific causal categories are ruled
out in the search for determinants of change, and therefore
genetic and biological factors should be considered along

with external forces. In this respect the mechanism label
is rather misleading because internal and interactive factors
are considered as plausible as external factors in determining
the course of development.

A third general principle that serves to establish the
context for the approach to theories taken in the present
monograph is nomotheticism. This means that the primary concern
is with average or group trends, and not with variations unique
to particular individuals. Certain researchers have been
so impressed with the variability exhibited across individuals
in the magnitude of aging effects that they have tended to
overlook the fact that there are nevertheless quite substantial
differences in the average performance of groups of individuals
of different ages. From the current perspective, the average
trends are the primary phenomena to be explained, and only
after adequate explanations are available to account for group
results should attention be directed to the apparent exceptions
to these prototypical patterns.

There are two reasons for this nomothetic bias. The
first is simply that it is difficult to determine whether
individual results represent an interesting exception to the
general pattern until sufficient data are available to firmly
establish the nature of that general pattern. That is, unless
one has some idea as to the average trends to be expected,
and at least some of the reasons for those trends, it may
be fruitless to spend time attempting to derive separate and
independent explanations for each individual pattern. The
second reason is that a certain amount of variability is to
be expected in all processes with multiple determinants, and
a preoccupation with the variability around the trends rather
than the trends themselves may be premature at this stage
of limited understanding.

It is almost certainly the case that greater predictability
would be possible if all sources of individual differences
were well understood because age generally accounts for a
relatively small proportion of the total variance in any given
behavior. Nevertheless, the age-associated variance is nearly

always significantly greater than zero, and thus reliable age patterns are discernable and require explanation even if they are sometimes small relative to other determinants of performance. Ultimately one would hope that all individual differences could be interpreted within a single theory, but at the present time even a theory sufficient to account for only the age-related differences in cognition seems quite ambitious.

Summary

It is often said that science advances by replacing old theories with superior theories, but it is not always recognized that without a theory to replace there may be little or no possibility of progress. Theories provide needed structure and organization in an area, and function like a map in charting the territory worth further exploration. At least five levels of theoretical discourse can be identified, ranging from implicit world views to general frameworks to explicit theories and specific models and empirical phenomena. Adoption of a particular theoretical perspective does entail certain risks, but the advantages appear to far outweigh the disadvantages. Assumptions influencing the theory to be advocated in later chapters are empiricism, determinism, reductionism, and nomotheticism.

Development of Theories of Development

This chapter begins by defining what is meant by the term aging. The preceding chapter was necessary before attempting to provide such a definition because it was first important to discuss the concept of theoretical relativism, and briefly outline philosophical commitments implicit in the current perspective. Without such a background one might fail to appreciate the difficulty of selecting a definition sufficiently precise to delimit the phenomenon, but not too restrictive as to exclude a variety of important theoretical perspectives. Birren and Renner (1977) may have been the most successful in this effort because they explicitly sought a definition which:

> ...does not imply an exclusively biological, environmental, or social causality, and keeps the door open for the study of incremental as well as the decremental changes in functions which occur over the life span (Birren & Renner, 1977, p. 4).

Their definition was that:

> Aging refers to the regular changes that occur in mature genetically representative organisms living under representative environmental conditions as they advance in chronological age (Birren & Renner, 1977, p. 4).

Although this definition has been carefully formulated and would probably be acceptable to most gerontological researchers, it can still be faulted from certain theoretical perspectives. For example, by using the phrase 'representative environmental conditions' instead of 'optimal environmental conditions,' some theorists might argue that the preceding definition tends to minimize the potential contribution of environmental influences by explicitly linking the concept of aging to existing characteristics of the environment. According to this view, the term aging should be restricted to those changes observed only in ideal environments in order to rule out all extrinsic determinants of development regardless of their representativeness or pervasiveness. This objection is mentioned merely to indicate that it is unlikely that any definition of such a complex phenomenon as aging will be found to be satisfactory to a wide variety of theoretical perspectives, however, and the Birren and Renner definition will suffice for the current purposes.

The key term in this definition, and in nearly all definitions of aging, is the word changes. Change indicates that it is the dynamic transitions between states that are of interest, and not simply the contrast between initial and terminal states. Some comparison is therefore implied by the term aging, either involving the same individual at two points in time, or otherwise similar individuals at different ages, but in each case it is the inferred change rather than the observed differences that are of primary interest. Aging is therefore viewed as the process (or processes) responsible for converting one 'product' into another, and it will consequently be necessary for any theory of aging to incorporate some form of change mechanism into its theoretical structure.

Further clarification of the concept of aging comes from an examination of the differences between common definitions of child development and aging. Many of the definitions of development in childhood stress growth characteristics such as inevitability, magnitude, unidirectionality, within-species uniformity, and irreversibility (e.g., Flavell, 1970), while definitions of aging seem much more vague with respect to many of these properties. The notion of an ultimate end-state is also a distinguishing feature of the two classes of phenomena in that development is generally considered a progression towards the mature form of whatever characteristic is under investigation, while aging represents the changes occurring after the attainment of maturity. Some writers have therefore suggested that the term development is inappropriate for the adult portion of the lifespan, and is best restricted to the

period from conception to maturity. This argument is rejected
here because of the need for a broad inclusive term to refer
to all of the changes that occur across the adult years, and
not simply those ultimately attributable to intrinsic maturational
processes often implied by the term aging. The word development
serves this purpose as it denotes time-dependent changes in
a particular system, without regard to the cause of these
changes. Because time for a given individual is represented
by his or her chronological age, we will simply define behavioral
development in the present context as any age-related changes
in behavior. The advantage of this definition is that it
does not imply any ultimate end-state, and encompasses a wide
variety of potential determinants. That is, while the developmental changes are age-related, they could originate from
ontogenetic maturational processes, influences of the biophysical
environment, sociocultural factors, or a number of other miscellaneous sources such as cumulative learning.

The term 'maturation' will be used broadly to refer
to intrinsically-based (endogenous) determinants of development.
It will therefore be used in contrast to extrinsic (exogenous)
determinants of development such as those due to influences
of the physical and social environment.

Status of Developmental Theories

The field of gerontological psychology has been criticized,
and justly in my opinion, for being preoccupied with "counting
and classifying the wrinkles of aged behavior (Kastenbaum,
1968, p. 280)," to the neglect of seeking explanations for
the causes of those wrinkles. In other words, researchers
in the psychology of aging seem to have been content to expand
and refine the entries in a catalog of age-related behavioral
deficiencies, but have exhibited little concern with discovering
the reasons for those deficiencies. Baltes and Willis (1977)
expressed this distinction between description and explanation
succinctly in the following passage:

   ...if much of gerontological research does not intend
   to explicate a process of development, then aging

subjects continue to be experimental constants leading
to a parametric variation of principles formulated
within a framework of general experimental psychology
rather than to a psychology of aging. On the contrary,
the focus of explanatory aging research is on change
in both the antecedent and consequent variables
and attention must be given to the formulation of
explanatory processes which are intrinsically change-
oriented (Baltes & Willis, 1977, p. 144).

Of course, it is unrealistic to expect a relatively new
field to be concerned with explanation before the phenomena
that will need to be explained have been adequately described.
Much of the early work in any discipline is necessarily explor-
atory, and devoted to characterizing the natural history of
the phenomenon under investigation. Nevertheless, the notion
of theoretical relativism discussed in the previous chapter
suggests that even the description will be at least partly
influenced by one's theoretical perspective, and attempts
to conduct atheoretical research can be characterized as little
more than chaotic fact-gathering. It is therefore desirable
that theories be used to help organize and direct research
as soon as is feasible in a given topic area.

Why hasn't cognitive aging research placed greater reliance
upon theoretical systems in formulating research questions
and interpreting research results? One possible reason is
that some researchers may feel that because they have relied
upon a theoretical model to localize a source of the age differences in a particular domain of activity, they have thereby
'explained' those differences. This strategy has received
many alliterative labels such as "characterizing the change,"
"defining the difference," "differentiating the deficit,"
"localizing the loss," and "particularizing the process."
However, despite the impressive-sounding terminology, the
strategy can be criticized for not being truly explanatory.
That is, while the use of a theoretical system to identify
the critical process clearly makes the procedure theoretical

and therefore somewhat speculative, the theoretical system is typically inadequate as an explanation of the age-related change since it rarely includes a change process.

This point can be elaborated by considering an interpretation of adult age differences in memory that was popular several years ago (although very similar reasoning is evident in much contemporary research). The interpretation was based on a theoretical distinction between tasks in which the remembered information was recalled, and otherwise similar tasks in which the information was recognized. It was hypothesized that both recognition and recall tasks involved components of encoding and storage, but because the response alternatives are present in the test of recognition and not in the test of recall, only the recall task was thought to involve the component of retrieval. Given this characterization of the two tasks, it was a simple matter to administer both recognition and recall tasks to adults of various ages to determine whether the age differences were substantially greater in the recall task (postulated to contain the component of retrieval as well as the encoding and storage components), than in the recognition task (in which there was presumably little or no involvement of the retrieval component). To the extent that this is the case, and the evidence on this issue is rather mixed (see Burke & Light, 1981, and Salthouse, 1982, for reviews), the researcher might feel justified in concluding that the age differences in memory were explained by problems of retrieval.

Figure 3.1 illustrates this reasoning in an abstract form. The distinction between the tasks, in particular the identity of the deleted component, is supplied by a theoretical model and therefore any inferences from such a study are completely dependent upon the validity of the assumptions underlying that model. In this respect the research is clearly theoretical in nature. It is probably theory at this model level to which Giambra and Arenberg (1980) were referring in their statement that:

...it is of little use to look at age differences

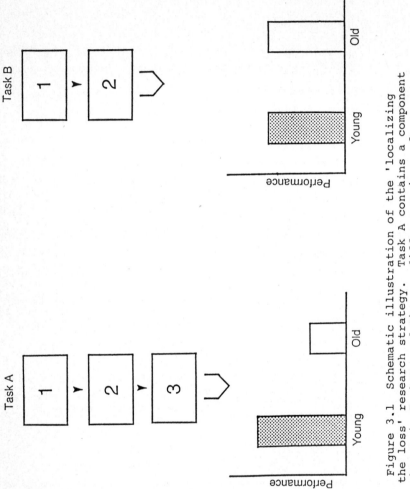

Figure 3.1 Schematic illustration of the 'localizing the loss' research strategy. Task A contains a component absent in Task B, and the age difference in performance in larger in Task A. The apparent implication is that age differences are "explained" in terms of the added component.

or changes...if no sufficiently powerful and explicit
theory exists to account for the performance on
that task of the 'standard' young adult group (Giambra
& Arenberg, 1980, p. 257).

According to the theory, component 3 in Figure 3.1 is
absent in task B but present in task A, and therefore a discovery
that age differences are greater in task A than in task B
would imply that component 3 is particularly susceptible to
the effects of aging. To some researchers this discovery
is equivalent to stating that the age differences in this
aspect of behavior are accounted for by impairments in Component
3, and therefore the effects of aging are "explained" in terms
of a reduction in the efficiency of Component 3.

While the strategy outlined above may be reasonable
for identifying age-sensitive components (but not necessarily,
as discussed in Chapter 6), it fails to provide any explanation
of why or how that particular component was affected by aging.
The discovery that the magnitude of the age differences varies
across tasks, i.e., that there is a statistical interaction
of age and task, is useful in providing a potentially more
precise specification of the difference to be explained, but
it does not by itself constitute an explanation of that difference. We would now know that the age differences in various
forms of behavior originate because of age differences in
specified components or processes, and in this respect we
have clarified exactly what needs to be explained. However,
we still have no information about why that particular component
or process changed with age, and why other components did
not. The approach is theoretical in that it relies on a model
to relate observations to theoretical concepts, but unless
there is a mechanism to account for the dynamic transition
from one state or configuration to the next it is inadequate
as a theory of development.

Consider the functions portrayed in Figure 3.2. The
solid line represents the inferred function for component
3, while the dashed lines illustrate the presumed age relationships

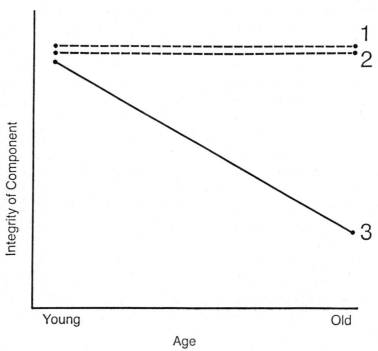

Figure 3.2 Hypothetical age functions for three
processing components. Age effects are clearly more
pronounced in Component 3, but the reason for the
negative age relationship in that component is still
not apparent.

for components 1 and 2. Taken together, these functions indicate an ideal outcome from an age-by-task manipulation of the type described above. Clearly, component 3 is 'where the action is' with respect to the effects of aging on this task because it exhibits a much more dramatic change with advancing age than either components 1 or 2. However, expressing the results in this fashion merely emphasizes the point that we have not progressed beyond description because age on the abscissa has not been replaced by a truly explanatory mechanism.

This objection to the localizing the loss strategy also applies to sophisticated correlation-based conceptualizations of adult cognitive abilities. For example, Horn (1980, 1982a) has proposed a model of the organization of intellectual abilities in which some abilities are presumed to decline with age while others improve with age. The goal of such models is to characterize the structure of intelligence, and thus they can be considered as attempts to develop maps of the interrelationships of cognitive abilities. However these static characterizations often tend to ignore the dynamic processes responsible for that configuration and thus may be inadequate from an explanatory perspective.

The absence of an explanatory mechanism can be illustrated by imagining the alternative perspectives of a city provided by a geographer and a historian. The geographer, like the analyst of ability structures, will be able to provide a map of the territory and thus will be able to tell us, for example, that the density of schools and single-family residences are positively correlated, while the density of schools and the density of factories are negatively correlated. Although clearly informative, this structure could be produced by many sets of dynamic processes. For example, the schools may have come first because the earliest teachers were pioneers and sought out desirable locations to 'school-stead' in a manner analogous to homesteading. Once these schools were established they may have then attracted families with children who needed residences with convenient access to the schools. And finally,

the factories may have come last, and hence were forced to
locate in regions dictated by the desire of the residents
to avoid having factories located close to schools and residences.
Alternatively, of course, the factories could have come first,
and then the residences for the people working in the factories,
and then the schools for the children of the workers. The
historian and the temporal perspective he or she could provide
is therefore desirable to determine which of several possible
change patterns was actually responsible for the present structure. In an analogous fashion, a transitional or dynamic
perspective is needed in cognitive development to help understand
how one organizational configuration or structure gradually
evolved into another one.

A minimum requirement for a developmental explanation
is an indication of what happened during the interval between
the two measurement periods that contributed to the observed
difference. It is also necessary to describe how and why that
particular change occurred. Baltes and Willis (1977) emphasize
this point as follows:

> ...process-oriented explanatory analysis has to
> incorporate a perspective of change not only with
> regard to the behavior change to be explained but
> also with regard to the class of antecedent variables
> and their interlocking functional relationships
> (Baltes & Willis, 1977, p. 141).

Without some dynamic mechanism to account for the systematic
alteration in the parameters or components under investigation,
i.e., an attempt to address the questions of how and why and
not merely the question of what, the type of model-dependent
research described above has all of speculative weaknesses
of theory along with the impotency and purposelessness of
mere description.

Rabbitt (1981a) summarized the present issue with admirable
clarity in the following paragraph, which also contains sentiments
on the importance of theory similar to those advocated in
the previous chapter:

A survey of the gerontological literature immediately
suggests that most studies are simply replications
of briefly fashionable experimental paradigms on
old and young subjects. The models from which these
paradigms are derived are seldom discussed and,
in any case, are usually not sufficiently developed
to permit interpretation of the "age differences"
that are invariably found...No experimental paradigm
can be said to be "theoretically neutral," and unless
we relate our experimental comparisons to clearly
specifiable models of performance and in particular
of performance **change**, we deceive ourselves and
waste our time (Rabbitt, 1981a, p. 556-557).

Where is the Why?

If it is accepted that explanatory theories of aging
need to incorporate some type of change mechanism, the question
then becomes at what level in the theoretical hierarchy should
the change concept be formulated? As noted earlier, some
writers (e.g., Hultsch & Hickey, 1978; Reese, 1976) have implied
that the world view is the logical place for such a fundamental
concept. In fact, it has even been argued that because of
the central status of change in the organismic and contextualistic
world views, they are the preferred world views in developmental
disciplines. However, by incorporating change as an a priori
concept one runs the risk of accepting the whole phenomenon
of development as a given, with the research enterprise largely
limited to descriptions of structural characteristics at various
periods of development. This seems unsatisfactory because
in order to answer the question of why, the dynamic mechanisms
must themselves be subject to investigation and analysis,
and not merely embedded as assumptions about the nature of
reality.

Change mechanisms could be incorporated at the framework
level, but again this appears to be too broad a perspective
for the generation of productive hypotheses. The framework
contains the concepts to be used in the theoretical formulations,

and therefore it is essential that the necessary concepts to be used in the explanation of change exist, or can be derived, within that framework. However, frameworks do not by themselves contain statements of the relationships among concepts, and therefore they seem inadequate as the locus for the dynamic mechanisms needed in a developmental theory.

Of the remaining two levels in the theoretical hierarchy, theory and model, models may be too specific to incorporate adequate change mechanisms because they represent the application of a given theory to a particular experimental task or phenomenon. Models are clearly necessary, but to rely on them for specifying the nature of the change mechanisms will likely result in very limited generality because there may well be a different model for every task.

Using models as the primary means of expressing the how and why of developmental change also runs the risk of what might be termed 'issue isolationism' -- the treatment of each empirical phenomenon as a separate issue warranting its own independent interpretation of change. Considering various age-related phenomena as separate and autonomous may eventually be dictated by empirical observations, but the issue isolationism philosophy can be criticized for being conceptually myopic and unparsimonious. Failure to consider related aspects of aging which might serve to integrate and simplify the explanations is clearly a short-sighted perspective. Moreover, the attempt to seek a separate explanation for each phenomenon is also not a very parsimonious way to formulate theoretical systems. An empirical literature based on an assemblage of independent mechanisms with little or no connection to one another will be too fragmented to provide a basis for integrating diverse findings into a coherent system. A broader, synthesizing conception of development seems desirable to achieve deeper, and more complete, understanding. (Birren and Renner [1977] have expressed similar views about the impediments created by what they term 'research sectarianism.')

The preceding considerations lead to the conclusion

that the most appropriate location for change mechanisms is
at the level of the theory. World views and frameworks are
too broad and not explicitly tied to observations, while models
lack the across-task generality necessary for a primary developmental process. The change mechanisms will probably be expressed
as relationships among concepts available at the framework
level, and they will be interpreted in the context of specific
tasks in the form of models. However, in order to be both
explicit and general, it is suggested that theories are the
most appropriate level for the explanation of change processes
associated with adult development. Models will be useful
for specifying the precise nature of the differences needing
explanation, and theories will provide a statement of the
origin of those differences.

Why versus When

Much of the contemporary research in cognitive aging
seems to be concentrated on identifying the factors responsible
for the appearance and disappearance of age differences in
cognitive performance. This research can be characterized
as focusing on the question of **when** age differences occur
by manipulating factors which minimize or maximize the magnitude
of the age differences one observes. An alternative research
strategy is to attempt to minimize the influence of other
contributing factors in order to investigate **why** the age differences occur. Both of these approaches are quite legitimate,
although the former may be easier to pursue and probably yields
greater immediate benefits than the latter.

A similar distinction between possible research strategies
is evident in the field of professional achievement. Intellectual ability almost certainly contributes to variations
in professional accomplishments, but by no means is it the
only determinant. There are many relevant factors such as
context, connections, motivation, external support, personal
style, etc. Moreover, some researchers interested in professional
achievement tend to focus on a variety of factors which serve
to moderate the influence of intellectual ability in achievement

while others are more interested in the causes of variations in intellectual ability. Based on the long history of research on intellectual ability, it seems likely that identification of moderating variables will be easier, and probably have quicker practical applications for the purpose of maximizing achievement than specification of causal factors responsible for age-related variations in intellectual ability.

Despite the short-term advantages of the strategy of determining when differences occur, it is nevertheless important to attempt to explain why differences are consistently found in certain basic abilities. Explanation, of the type provided by an answer to the question of why and not just when, is desirable not only on scientific grounds, but also offers the best opportunity for successful intervention or remediation in the long-term.

What is the Why?

I have previously (Salthouse, 1982) suggested that most of the theoretical perspectives in gerontological cognitive psychology can be distinguished by their relative positions on three separate, and largely orthogonal, dimensions. For convenience, the combination of these dimensions is illustrated in the cube in Figure 3.3, although it is recognized that the dimensions may not be truly orthogonal and hence the cubical representation could be somewhat misleading.

The x or horizontal axis represents a continuum from maturational or intrinsic factors to environmental or extrinsic factors as the primary cause of the observed aging phenomena. Of course, both nature and nurture are required for the maintenance and development of any living organism, but the issue of the relative importance of the two factors for cognitive aging phenomena is still a meaningful one. For example, if virtually identical developmental trends were observed across a wide range of physical and social environments then it would seem reasonable to suggest that the environmental factor is relatively unimportant for the age-related changes in that particular variable. A theory would be placed near the left edge of

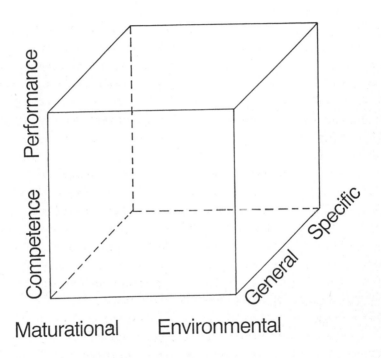

Figure 3.3 Schematic representation of three conceptual dimensions considered relevant in the characterization of theories of cognitive aging. Because the dimensions define a space, it is presumed that alternative theories are located in different regions in accordance with their positions on each dimension.

the horizontal axis in Figure 3.3 if it assumed that maturational factors related to the biological integrity or efficiency of the nervous system were primarily responsible for the developmental trends in the relevant aspects of cognitive behavior. On the other hand, the theory would fall on the right edge if it postulated that factors outside the individual, in the surrounding environment, were the major contributors to the observed developmental trends.

The vertical or y axis refers to whether the theory assumes that the observed behavior reflects the individual's true competence, or whether it is more appropriately interpreted as mere performance. In the latter case, no inferences are possible about basic capacities since there are assumed to be a number of extraneous factors that lead to a discrepancy or gap between what the individual actually does, and that which he or she is capable of doing. However, if the theory postulates that the phenomena accurately reflect the individual's competence, or at least does so to an equivalent extent for all age groups, then one can use the results as a basis for inferences about relatively stable abilities.

The diagonal or z axis in Figure 3.3 indicates whether the theory relies upon a mechanism with generality across a variety of situations and tasks, or postulates a highly specific mechanism limited to a particular type of situation. A theory (or model) formulated to account for a single phenomenon, with little or no attempt to explain other phenomena, would be placed at the far edge of this continuum. On the other hand, a theory relying upon a general mechanism to account for many different phenomena would be assigned a position at the near edge of the continuum.

It is important to recognize that although these three dimensions are each theoretical, many discussions of aging phenomena implicitly assume positions on each dimension. One of the most striking illustrations of this tendency to accept positions as fact instead of recognizing that they are merely hypotheses is evident in the Recommendations to

the White House Conference on Aging from the 1971 APA Task
Force on Aging (Eisdorfer & Lawton, 1973). In the first section,
with the auspicious title of "Alleged Loss of Intellectual
Functioning," it is stated that:

> For the most part, the observed decline in intellectual
> functioning among the aged is attributable to poor
> health, social isolation, economic plight, limited
> education, lowered motivation, or other variables
> not intrinsically related to the aging process.
> Where intelligence scores do decline, such change
> is associated primarily with tasks where speed of
> response is critical (Eisdorfer & Lawton, 1973,
> p. ix).

Although statements of this type might be justified for
purposes of influencing public policy, and may even reflect
the views of the majority of gerontologists, they can be criticized
from a scientific perspective because they portray hypotheses
as established facts. In particular, statements such as these
suggest that there is no controversy with respect to the three
theoretical dimensions outlined above. Developmental trends
are presumed to be attributable to extrinsic rather than intrinsic
factors, they are claimed to be largely due to performance-limiting
factors such as poor motivation rather than reflections of
true competence, and they are assumed to be attributable to
specific mechanisms such as a slower speed of response instead
of a more general mechanism. A major thesis of the current
monograph is that these issues are not only debatable, but
that reasonably convincing arguments can be presented for
diametrically opposed positions on each of these dimensions.
In fact, the theory to be advocated in later chapters is based
on the ideas that the adult developmental trends in many cognitive
tasks are due to intrinsic biologically-based age changes
that result in fairly general alterations in competence, not
merely performance-limiting processes restricted to a few
specific tasks or abilities.

Some extremism of the type reflected in the quotation

presented above is perhaps understandable in light of the
perception that:

> ...there has been a tendency to be too ready to
> attribute an impairment to maturational factors
> without seriously considering the possibility of
> environmental deficits, or the operation of performance-
> inhibitory behavior components that have developed
> in response to, and are maintained by, environmentally
> based contingencies (Baltes & Labouvie, 1973, p.
> 186).

Nevertheless, it is desirable if not essential in scientific
writing to preserve the distinction between what is known
and what is merely assumed.   This is an explicit goal in the
present monograph, and much of the discussion in Chapter 7
will focus on an evaluation of the available evidence pertaining
to these theoretical issues.

Summary

Theories of development need to incorporate a developmental
mechanism responsible for converting the behavior characteristic
of one developmental period into that characteristic of a
later developmental period. Identifying the theoretical process
which may account for the behavioral differences is a first
step, but the reasons for that change in process must then
be specified in order to produce a satisfactory explanation.
Because of the different functions of world views, frameworks,
theories, and models, it is suggested that developmental mechanisms
are best incorporated at the level of theory.   It is also
proposed that the possible mechanisms will likely vary in
three dimensions -- maturational versus environmental, performance
versus competence, and general versus specific -- and that
any localization within these dimensions implies the acceptance
of a particular set of theoretical assumptions.

The Information-Processing Framework

In recent years the dominant metaphor for explaining behavior in cognitive psychology has been the digital computer and what has come to be known as the information-processing perspective. One of the appeals of the computer analogy is that computers are capable of a broad range of powerful accomplishments, and yet are based upon a limited number of fairly simple processing operations. It is therefore reasonable to suggest that information-processing concepts may be useful in attempting to understand and explain some of the enormous complexity of human cognitive activity. The current chapter presents a brief overview of the information-processing framework, followed by an examination of the implications of this perspective for research investigating the effects of aging on cognitive functioning.

One of the attractions of the information-processing perspective is that it is considered valuable as an important level of analysis between phenomenology and physiology (Estes, 1978; Newell & Simon, 1972; Sternberg, 1977). Unlike the phenomenological approach, complex behavior is subjected to detailed analysis in the hopes of discovering fundamental explanatory mechanisms. However the mechanisms need not be physiological, and thus the reductionism is not complete. There are three common justifications for this limited reductionism in the study of cognition. One is a belief that the current state of knowledge in physiology, neurology, and biochemistry is still inadequate to account for even fairly simple aspects of behavior, and that it will be many years or possibly even decades before complex behavior will be explainable by such reductionistic mechanisms. A second reason is that even if such explanations were available, it is likely that they will be extremely complicated and clumsy since much of the regularity of complex behavior may only be evident at higher levels of analysis. The third reason for accepting a limited reductionism in cognitive information processing is based on the belief that the functional relationships among processes are what is important, and not the specific medium or substance in which those processes happen to be implemented.

Actually, it is somewhat misleading to refer to the information-processing perspective as though it represented a single level of analysis because there are many levels possible between physiology and phenomenology, and different information-processing researchers tend to operate at different levels. For example, some researchers consider short-term memory to be composed of a number of operations such as encoding, storage, and rehearsal, while other researchers prefer to view all of short-term memory as a single elementary operation. In the following discussion examples will be freely borrowed from many different levels in the information-processing literature in an attempt to illustrate the broad utility of these concepts. Examples might be fewer, but it is believed that the same arguments would apply if only a single level were considered.

Lachman, Lachman, and Butterfield (1979) have written a fascinating book detailing the background and major characteristics of the information-processing approach to cognition. According to these authors, cognitive psychologists within the information-processing paradigm:

> ...have defined the area of study as the way man collects, stores, modifies, and interprets environmental information or information already stored internally. They are interested in knowing how he adds information to his permanent knowledge of the world, how he accesses it again, and how he uses his knowledge in every facet of human activity. Information-processing-oriented cognitive psychologists believe that such collection, storage, interpretation, understanding, and use of environmental or internal information **is cognition** (Lachman, Lachman, & Butterfield, 1979, p. 7).

Lachman, et al. (1979) also point out that the major intellectual antecedents of the information-processing perspective in psychology are communication theory and computer science. Communication theory provided important concepts such as the notion that anything which reduced uncertainty could be considered information, and the fact that all information-processing channels have some limit on their transmission capacity. The field of computer science exerted a pervasive effect by supplying a new and powerful machine that could function as an analogy for understanding complex mental processes.

Throughout recorded history there have been attempts by scientists to attempt to explain complex biological or psychological phenomena by means of analogies with machines thought to be relatively well understood. For example, it has been proposed that humans are like hydraulic systems in which activity is determined by the flow of some vital substance from one structure to another, like simple levers in which action in one location causes a predictable change in another location, and like telephone switchboards in which a large number of possible stimuli can be mapped into a large number of possible responses. (My favorite machine analogy is the use of the toilet to explain the functioning of the nerve cell based on the common principles of all-or-none action and a refractory period between successive excitations.)

The advantage of general-purpose computers as the machine analogy for understanding the functioning of the human mind is that extremely impressive accomplishments can result from combinations of fairly simple elements. Indeed, the term 'artificial intelligence' indicates that intelligent behavior is no longer a distinguishing characteristic of humans, and implies that it is now necessary to discriminate between natural intelligence and intelligence produced by artificial machines. The fruitfulness of the computer metaphor will eventually be exhausted, but at the current time it still appears useful to look to such a versatile machine for many explanatory concepts in attempting to understand the complex phenomena of human cognition.

However, it is important to point out that the key feature
of the information-processing approach is not the computer
metaphor, but rather an emphasis on analyzing the processes
thought to be responsible for the behavior under investigation.
Detterman (1980) illustrated this distinction in the following
passage:

> It is most fashionable to consider cognitive models
> in terms of computer analogies, but I prefer an
> analogy to a factory. A factory is composed of
> machines that take raw materials and transform them
> into finished products. The products actually produced
> will depend on the raw materials supplied to the
> factory and the machines used in the manufacturing
> process. What we would like to understand about
> these factories is why some are more efficient than
> others...First, we logically analyze the finished
> product to determine what steps must have gone into
> its manufacture. Then we develop raw materials
> which represent various stages of completion of
> the finished product. We then deliver a complete
> set of these materials to each of the factories
> we are interested in studying and return home to
> await delivery of the finished products. As the
> finished products arrive we note their quality of
> construction and the time required for delivery.
> We also note which factories fail to deliver...From
> these data, we develop a model of the processes
> used in the factories to produce the final product...Note
> that we describe only the processes used by the
> machine. We do not know the machine's structure,
> its location in the factory, its capacity, or any
> other details about its operation (Detterman, 1980,
> p. 589).

Another characteristic of the information-processing
perspective is that because it attempts to account for all

phases of processing involved in mental activity, it offers
a more integrated and less compartmentalized approach to understanding behavior than most alternative approaches. Norman
and Bobrow (1975b) summarized this characteristic as follows:

>   The phenomena of attention, perception, memory,
>   and cognition are interrelated -- intertwined might
>   be a better word -- and the explanation for one
>   set of phenomena helps to elucidate the others (Norman
>   & Bobrow, 1975b, p. 114).

Unlike earlier researchers who often made rigid distinctions
between subdisciplines concerned with perception, verbal learning,
thinking, etc., (and frequently tended to denigrate the contributions from other subdisciplines), the information-processing
researcher believes that the task of understanding will be
greatly facilitated by an awareness of the raw materials and
products of other aspects of cognition.

Examples of Two Information-Processing Models

In order to demonstrate how the information-processing
approach has actually been implemented in cognitive psychology,
it is instructive to consider two prototypical applications
of this perspective. Both of these models are classics in
the field, although subsequent developments have led even
the authors to favor modifications of the original proposals.

The first model to be discussed, and one of the first
to use information-processing concepts in a deliberate attempt
to account for selected aspects of human cognition, was proposed
by Broadbent (1958) to explain certain phenomena related to
attention. The main aspects of his model are illustrated
in Figure 4.1, which is an adaptation of the flow chart Broadbent
used to summarize his proposals.

It is particularly useful to contrast this scheme with
the earlier 'black-box' approach of stimulus-response behaviorism
in which it was assumed that stimuli entered one end of the
box and responses were emitted at the other end of the box,
but with little concern about the internal processes responsible
for the connection. Notice that although it is still assumed

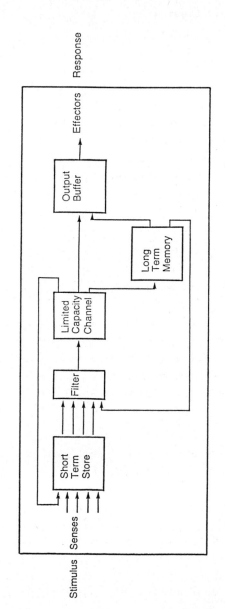

Figure 4.1 Representation of Broadbent's (1958) information-processing model of cognition. Each box was presumed to represent a distinct processing component, with the flow of information between components indicated by the direction of the arrows.

that stimuli enter the system at one end and responses leave
the system at the other end, Broadbent was not content for
the 'box' to remain black and mysterious but instead attempted
to speculate about what was happening inside the box or system.
In particular, he proposed that the stimuli were received
by the appropriate senses and then temporarily placed in a
small-capacity memory store. Because there was assumed to
be a limit on the amount of information that could be handled
at any given time in the central channel, a selective filter
was postulated to reduce the amount of information propagated
to the central processor. Some transformed version of the
information was then sent via the response buffer to the response
systems, or was first directed to the long-term memory system.
An important aspect of Broadbent's model was that it outlined
a plausible flow of information across structures specialized
for particular operations, from which one could infer the
temporal relationship among various operations (e.g., the
filter was located prior to long-term memory and the output
buffer, and thus had its effects relatively early in the processing
sequence).

The specific details of Broadbent's model are not of
concern here, in part because they have largely been supplanted
by later models, but the model is significant because it was
one of the first systematic attempts to speculate about the
temporal relations among the internal operations of the human
mind. By specifying a particular series of structures and
operations thought to be sufficient to account for the behavior
of interest, this information-processing model stimulated
many possibilities for research that were not even considered
from earlier perspectives. It is too much to claim that the
black box of the mind was opened and its contents revealed,
but the work of Broadbent and other early information-processing
psychologists (e.g., Miller, Galanter, & Pribram, 1960) did
convey a spirit in which this might not be a completely unrealistic
goal.

The second classic information-processing model to be

discussed is the product of a collaborative effort by Atkinson and Shiffrin (Atkinson & Shiffrin, 1968; Shiffrin & Atkinson, 1969). The major ideas are summarized in the flow diagram in Figure 4.2. Two features of this model were important when it was introduced. One was the distinction among three types of memory stores; a sensory register responsible for maintaining a very rich and detailed representation of the stimulus for up to several seconds, a short-term store of severely limited capacity in which most conscious mental operations were performed and intermediate results held, and the long-term store containing relatively permanent information. The second major characteristic of the Atkinson and Shiffrin model was the distinction between structural features and control processes, expressed by the authors as follows:

> The permanent features of memory, which will be referred to as the memory structure, include both the physical system and the built-in processes that are unvarying and fixed from one situation to another. Control processes, on the other hand, are selected, constructed, and used at the option of the subject and may vary dramatically from one task to another even though superficially the task may appear very similar (Atkinson & Shiffrin, 1968, p. 90).

Atkinson and Shiffrin explicitly acknowledged the influence of concepts from computer science in formulating their theory as they state:

> If the memory system is viewed as a computer under the direction of a programmer at a remote console, then both the computer hardware and those programs built into the system that cannot be modified by the programmer are analogous to our structural features; those programs and instruction sequences which the programmer can write at his console and which determine the operation of the computer, are analogous to our control processes. In the sense that the computer's method of processing a given batch of data depends

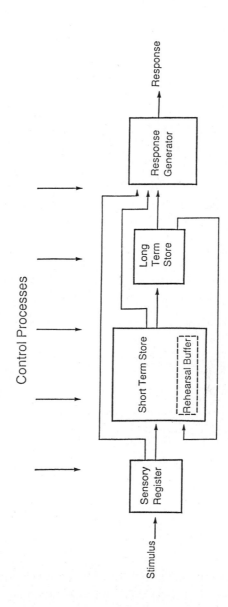

Figure 4.2 Representation of the Atkinson and Shiffrin (1968) information-processing model of cognition. Notice the distinction among three types of memory stores, and the presence of control processes which influence the processing carried out within, and between, different components.

on the operating program, so the way a stimulus
input is processed depends on the particular control
processes the subject brings into play. The structural
components include the basic memory stores; examples
of control processes are coding procedures, rehearsal
operations, and search strategies (Atkinson & Shiffrin,
1968, p. 90).

The introduction of control processes greatly expanded
the potential scope of theories within the information-processing
framework because they were no longer exclusively passive
and reactive. By deliberately emphasizing the possibility
that humans can exert an influence on the direction and nature
of their cognitive processes, the Atkinson and Shiffrin model
epitomizes what has come to be a major focus of the information-
processing perspective -- the active involvement of humans
in their own cognition. This characteristic is evident in
the extensive research concerned with aspects of encoding,
organization, and various types of rehearsal in the domain
of memory, and it has similar manifestations in other activity
domains. Acceptance of the idea that humans are active participants in their own information processing is one of the reasons
why it is difficult to categorize the information-processing
framework within either the mechanistic or organismic world
views; many of the concepts are derived from the general-purpose
computer which is a machine, but the system is inherently
active as proposed by the organismic world view.

The Broadbent (1958) and Atkinson and Shiffrin (1968)
models illustrate how some of the ideas and concepts from
communication theory and computer science have been incorporated
into theorizing about psychological phenomena. Many more
models have been proposed since these were introduced, and
therefore they should not be interpreted as reflecting the
current state of thinking in the information-processing perspective. However, these are clearly two of the most influential
models in this area and thus they serve to indicate the general
character of models within the information-processing perspective.

(It is an interesting footnote in the history of the information-processing perspective that one of the first models utilizing ideas from computer science and expressed in the form of a flowchart appeared in a 1954 article by Birren, Allen, and Landau concerned with aging. In attempting to account for age differences observed in addition tasks, these authors proposed a model that included such now-familiar concepts as short-term memory, long-term memory, and coded representations.)

Criticisms of Information-Processing Models

Although the information-processing perspective has been extremely influential in contemporary cognitive psychology, it has not been without its critics. Some of the criticisms are specific to particular models and thus are not of central interest here. However, a number of more general objections have also been raised, and it is valuable to consider them before attempting to develop a theory within the information-processing framework.

One very prevalent criticism relates to the penchant of many information-processing researchers to express their theoretical ideas in the form of flow charts. This tendency is so common that some observers have even referred to information-processing psychologists as boxologists in that they appear to be fixated upon the drawing of boxes and arrows. The mere fact that information-processing researchers might be claimed to have a box fetish does not disturb these critics, but they do object to the implication that a process has been explained simply by localizing it within a box that has a distinctive label. In other words, flow charts are useful to illustrate the general relations among structural elements in a theoretical system, but they cannot be used as a substitute for the detailed specification of operations and mechanisms. Stated bluntly, opening the black box of the mind to reveal nothing more than a constellation of many smaller, but nevertheless still-mysterious, boxes constitutes only minimal progress in theoretical understanding.

This criticism is well-taken in that it is probably true

that boxes and arrows have sometimes been offered in place
of explanation. However, it should be recognized that flow
charts are primarily designed for purposes of communication,
and their inappropriate use as explanations is a function
of the individual investigator rather than an intrinsic feature
of the information-processing approach.

Another frequently raised criticism is that portraying
human cognition in terms of a sequence of separate processes
implies both a discreteness and a linearity that is misleading
and artificial. That is, representing two operations in separate
boxes at minimum connotes some degree of functional independence,
and may even suggest distinct anatomical loci. Because there
is seldom any evidence that the hypothesized stages of processing
are truly independent, and almost no evidence that they are
located in different regions of the cortex, information-processing
models have been criticized for conveying a deceptive sense
of precision. The idea that information flows in a strictly
linear sequence, with the processing from one component fully
completed before information is passed to the next component,
is also considered an indefensibly strong assumption.

This criticism may be somewhat overstated in that most
researchers utilizing the information-processing framework
realize that flow charts and other means of communicating
the hypothesized sequence of information, are merely organizational
devices. They serve to illustrate the functional components
of the proposed system, but are not generally interpreted
to have uniquely specified temporal or spatial characteristics.
On the other hand, it is quite true that some theorists interpret
the linear, independent, and serial processing connotations
literally, and thus these characteristics should be subjected
to empirical verification and not simply incorporated as a
priori assumptions. Furthermore, in recent years several
promising interactive parallel models of information processing
have been proposed (e.g., McClelland & Rumelhart, 1981; Rumelhart,
1977), and thus linearity and seriality are not necessary
characteristics of information-processing models.

A third criticism of the information-processing approach
is that there has been very little attempt to integrate the
processes postulated in different models. For example, what
one researcher considers encoding may be more analogous to
the component of rehearsal or storage in another researcher's
model. The issue of common processes is seldom addressed
directly because there are few studies in which a variety
of alternative tasks have been administered to the same individuals
so that correlations among parameters could be examined.
(But see Lansman, 1981, for a notable exception.) The existence
of such a simple means for determining isomorphism of processes
across different models suggests that while the criticism
of poor integration is valid, the problem is clearly not insurmountable and may be resolved once larage-scale correlational
research is undertaken.

A fourth criticism of many information-processing models
is that they rely upon a central executive or decision-maker
that is not an intrinsic part of the model. For example,
Atkinson and Shiffrin state that control processes are 'selected,
constructed and used' by the subject, but it is never specified
how and where the subject is incorporated into the model.
Critics have therefore argued that models of this type are
little more than sophisticated homunculus theories since all
of the intelligent action is handled by invoking an intelligent
agent rather than attempting to explain it directly. Again,
this criticism is frequently justified, but in defense it
should be pointed out that any theory is necessarily of limited
scope. To expect a single theory to handle all aspects of
cognition is probably unrealistic, and whether the phenomena
outside its scope are attributed to the subject, to a black
box, or to some metaphysical object, should be irrelevant
with respect to how well the model handles the phenomena within
its intended domain.

A fifth objection, directed primarily against those models
implemented as computer simulations, is that information-processing
researchers are often content to demonstrate that their specu-

lations are capable of accounting for the behavior, and are
less concerned about whether those particular mechanisms are
the ones actually employed. Because the goal of many information-
processing models is to specify a sequence of operations that
can account for the transformations of known input into observable
output, a paramount consideration has been whether the postulated
mechanisms are sufficient to produce the necessary transformations.
The issue raised by some critics is essentially that the sufficiency criterion is not sufficient. That is, merely demonstrating
that the desired output could be produced from the relevant
input within a particular sequence of processing operations
does not indicate that humans actually employ that specific
processing system. What is necessary, but often omitted,
is to indicate how it could be established that that specific
sequence of processing operations, and not some functionally
equivalent alternative sequence, was responsible for the relevant
aspects of human behavior.

This criticism is complex and cannot be easily dismissed
or accepted. On the one hand, it is true that information-
processing researchers are often negligent in explicitly relating
theoretical concepts to empirical observations. As a consequence,
there has been an alarming proliferation of models proposed
for the same or similar phenomena with few hints as to how
they might be distinguished. (In fact, it is sometimes lamented
that anyone can create his or her own information-processing
model by merely relabeling the boxes or altering the direction
of a few arrows from an earlier model.) It is almost as discouraging to be confronted with too many explanations for
a phenomenon as it is to be without a single explanation.
On the other hand, it is also true that considerable knowledge
is gained by discovering the sufficient conditions to produce
complex behavior. Furthermore, after a number of different
proposals have been evaluated, it should eventually be possible
to identify the necessary conditions as well, at which point
there are numerous constraints on the types of explanations
that need to be explored. It may not be feasible to specify

the detailed mechanisms uniquely responsible for producing
a particular class of behavior, but examination of the different
proposals sufficient to produce that behavior will surely
result in an advancement of knowledge.

A final criticism of the information-processing perspective,
and the major one of concern in the present context, is that
there has been little or no attention devoted to the types
of mechanisms that could account for differences or changes
in information-processing efficiency (e.g., Rabbitt, 1979a,
1979b, 1981a, 1981b, 1982a, 1982b). In fact, despite application
to an enormous range of phenomena, there has been relatively
little systematic work concerned with identifying possible
sources of any type of individual differences, either those
existing between people (inter-individual), or those that
occur over time in the same individual (intra-individual).

While it is true that factors responsible for individual
differences in speed or accuracy of performance have largely
been neglected within the information-processing framework,
there are a number of means by which such differences might
be manifested. The next section outlines several of these
possibilities and briefly describes the nature of each.

A Taxonomic Scheme

The taxonomy employed here is a synthesis of speculations
proposed by a number of information-processing researchers
(e.g., Butterfield, 1981; Calfee & Hedges, 1980; Carroll &
Maxwell, 1979; Chi & Glaser, 1980; Hunt, 1978, 1983; Pellegrino
& Glaser, 1979; Simon, 1976; Snow, 1979, 1981; Sternberg,
1977, 1978, 1980). No claim is made that the present system
is exhaustive, but it was deliberately designed to encompass
most of the dimensions proposed to characterize individual
differences in various aspects of human information processing.
Some of the entries in this system have little empirical support
at the current time, but all appear plausible as potential
sources of individual differences in a variety of behavioral
activities.

The taxonomy is outlined in Table 4.1. Following the

Table 4.1

Sources of Individual Differences in Cognition
from an Information-Processing Perspective

Process Characteristics

Level	Specific Difference
Component	Efficiency and/or Effectiveness
	Identity
Sequence	Order
	Mode
	Availability
Executive	Sequence Repertoire
	Sequence Selection
	Sequence Assembly

Resource Characteristics

Type	Specific Difference
Structural	Space (Working Memory Capacity)
	Contents
	Knowledge Representation
	Knowledge Quality
	Knowledge Quantity
	Knowledge Organization
Dynamic	Arousal Level
	Attentional Capacity
	Basic Operation Time

general information-processing perspective, cognition is assumed
to occur as a sequence of components (i.e., elementary processes
or basic operations) that progressively transform input information
into various internal representations, or into overt responses.
These representations are assumed to be maintained in memory
stores of either short duration and small capacity, or long
duration and large capacity. The process-resource distinction
in this scheme is somewhat arbitrary, but broadly refers to
a contrast between the dynamic operations of processing and
the miscellaneous factors which set limits or constraints
on the amount of processing that can be carried out. In other
words, behavior is produced by processes drawing upon resources.

Level entries under the process category refer to progressively larger (or hierarchically superior) dynamic units.
The structure entries under the resource category refer to
relatively static resources related to the capacity or contents
of memory, while the dynamic entries indicate more fluid or
labile resources. Entries under the Specific Differences
column indicate the detailed manner in which individual differences
are hypothesized to be manifested.

At the component level, individual differences can be
exhibited either in the efficiency (i.e., speed or duration)
or effectiveness (i.e., quality or accuracy) of separate components, or in the identity of the specific components employed
(e.g., components ABC vs. components ABD). Several researchers
(e.g., Carroll, 1976; Newell & Simon, 1972; Rose, 1980) have
proposed sets of component operations which, when properly
combined, are presumed to account for performance of a large
number of cognitive tasks. For example, Rose (1980) has suggested
that eight operations can be identified as contributing to
the performance of a large number of cognitive activities:
encoding, constructing, transforming, storing, retrieving,
searching, comparing, and responding. Individual differences
could exist in the duration (efficiency) of any one of these
operations, or in the quality of the product (effectiveness)
resulting from that operation.

It is also possible that different people use different operations at particular positions in the sequence, e.g., one person might encode, construct, and search, while another might encode, transform, and search. A difference of this type would be characterized in the present taxonomy as a discrepancy in the identity of specific components.

Order and mode of the sequence of components reflect the manner in which the individual components are organized and combined, and thus function as the control structure or strategy for a given cognitive activity. Individual differences may be evident in the serial arrangement of components (e.g., sequence ABC vs. sequence ACB), and in the temporal (e.g., serial vs. parallel) or informational (e.g., dependent or contingent vs. independent or non-contingent) relation among components. Also included within this category would be variations in the rule by which components are combined to produce the dependent variable (e.g., additive, multiplicative, determined by the slowest or least efficient component, etc.). In addition, sequences might differ in their availability, with some procedural sequences executed as though they were in a compiled state rather than each processing component being separately and sequentially interpreted. Availability in this context may therefore be somewhat analogous to the distinction between effortful or controlled processing on the one hand, and automatic or resource-independent processing on the other hand.

Individual differences at the executive level could be evident in the number of alternative processing sequences (i.e., strategies) that one can employ (e.g., only one possible sequence vs. many alternative sequences), the effectiveness of matching strategy to situation (e.g., in terms of available resources or in terms of likelihood of success), and the ease with which new processing sequences or strategies can be constructed and assembled. Taken together, these factors at the executive level may be considered to comprise the individual's strategic or procedural knowledge.

Figure 4.3 summarizes the various types of process differences

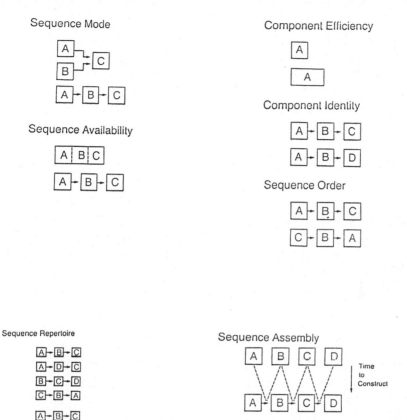

Figure 4.3 Schematic illustration of alternative means by which individual differences might be manifested in process aspects of information processing.

in a schematic fashion. In all cases it is assumed that the
representation in the top of each panel results in a different
level of performance than that based upon the second representation.

Resource characteristics include a range of variables
linked only by their adherence to Navon's (1984) definition
of a resource as:

> ...any internal input essential for processing...that
> is available in quantities that are limited in any
> point in time (Navon, 1984, p. 217).

This definition emphasizes the fact that a dominant concern
in the information-processing approach has been the identification
of factors responsible for imposing limits on human performance.
That is, all cognitive behavior has certain measurable boundaries,
and a major research emphasis has been to specify the nature
of these restricting conditions for a broad variety of mental
tasks.

Two categories of internal inputs or resources can be
identified following the distinction between structural and
dynamic aspects of capacity proposed in an earlier monograph
(Salthouse, 1982):

> This structural-dynamic distinction is roughly analogous
> to the different ways one might speak of the capacity
> of a banquet hall as opposed to the capacity of
> a fast food restaurant. In the case of the banquet
> hall one is primarily interested in the total number
> of seats available in order to assess the maximum
> number of diners that can be accomodated at one
> time. However, with a fast food restaurant it is
> probably more meaningful to speak of capacity in
> terms of the number of meals that can be served
> in a given period of time (Salthouse, 1982, p. 180-181).

Structure entries therefore include the number of storage
slots in the rapid-access short-term memory (working memory
capacity), and several characteristics of the contents of
the long-term memory system. This latter memory system is

assumed to be so large that individual differences in its
capacity are probably not meaningful, but the information
within it is postulated to vary in mode (representational
form), accuracy (quality), amount (quantity), and accessibility
(organization).

Dynamic entries include energizing aspects such as arousal
or attention, and the temporal factor of how long it takes
to perform basic processing operations, or to execute the
transition between operations. The arousal and attention
concepts probably reflect total amount available for processing,
but they could also be interpreted in terms of the efficiency
with which a given amount is allocated for processing. The
resource conceptualization of time is a somewhat different
perspective on time than the prevailing view in cognitive
psychology because here temporal variables are assumed to
function as a cause of altered efficiency, and not simply
as a dependent variable indexing that efficiency. The closest
analogy is probably to the cycle time of a computer in that
newer generations of computers with shorter cycle times for
basic operations have superior performance capabilities to
older and slower computers even when executing the same programs
(e.g., Birren, 1965; Hunt, Frost, & Lunneborg, 1973).

What is the Critical Resource?

As mentioned earlier, a persistent theme of the information-
processing approach to cognition has been the search for factors
responsible for limitations on human performance. Although
the search has often focused on specific process aspects such
as the efficiency of selected components or the effectiveness
of a given sequence of components, it has frequently been
considered necessary to invoke a more general concept of the
type categorized here as a resource. For example, performance
generally deteriorates as a given task is made more complex,
and yet this increased complexity is often accomplished without
any apparent alteration in the identity or sequence of components.
In a situation such as this it seems necessary to postulate
the existence of a rather general, finite-capacity, processing

resource. Experiments involving the performance of two concurrent
tasks have also been considered strong evidence for a general
resource limitation since there is often interference in the
performance of the two tasks independent of the similarity
of the tasks.   For example, simple reaction time has little
or no apparent features in common with, say, a free recall
memory task, and yet performance of one or both tasks is often
found to suffer compared to when the tasks are performed in
isolation.   The dominant interpretation of this phenomenon
has been that both tasks make demands upon a common resource
which is limited in its availability.   Performance on one
or both tasks is consequently degraded to the extent that
the demands for that resource are not satisfied.

Five categories of resources were outlined in Table 4.1,
but the knowledge resources can be ignored in this context
because they are primarily relevant in semantically-rich activity
domains, and would be expected to exert little or no influence
on many of the simple and abstract tasks frequently examined
in the cognitive psychology laboratory.   Moreover, because
the arousal and attention concepts are often used interchangeably
(e.g., Kahneman, 1973), and may not be easily distinguished
on operational grounds, they may be considered together as
exemplars of an energy conceptualization of resources.   The
idea of resources as energy, together with the space (working
memory), and time (basic operation time or processing rate)
interpretations leads to three presumably distinct conceptualizations of the entity responsible for general limitations
on performance.   Actually there are probably many more categories
that could be distinguished because each of these could be
sub-divided with respect to the type of fuel, the specialization
of the space, etc., but the broad categories of space, energy,
and time appear to encompass most of the proposals that have
appeared in the cognitive psychology literature.

The conceptualization of resources in terms of space
in the form of a limited-capacity working memory system is
probably the most popular interpretation at the present time,

perhaps because of the dominance of spatial metaphors for memory in the research literature (Roediger, 1980). A defining attribute of this perspective is the notion that there is a limit in the size or volume of some hypothesized container that functions as the central workspace for most cognitive operations. Broadbent (1971) used the analogy of a desktop, while Klatzky (1980) suggested a carpenter's workbench, but regardless of the specific metaphor it is assumed that there is a finite space within which items can be considered to be attended or in conscious awareness. If most processing operations require access to that central workspace for their successful completion, then the size of the workspace will obviously impose constraints on the amount and level of processing which can be appropriately executed. A small workspace will severely restrict the number of operations that can be carried out simultaneously, and may require frequent time-consuming, and error-prone, exchanges of information to and from the largercapacity long-term storage system. On the other hand, if a large workspace is available, it should be possible to perform even fairly complex operations, or combinations of simple operations, without having to deposit and retrieve intermediate products in larger-capacity storage systems.

The conceptualization of processing resources as a form of mental energy has been growing in popularity in recent years, as reflected in the increasing usage of such metaphorical terms as 'resource reservoir,' 'pool of capacity,' and the 'channeling,' 'expenditure,' or 'draining' of resources. The basic idea in this perspective is that certain mental operations are presumed to require a finite amount of some energizing or vitalizing commodity for their successful completion. Although Kahneman (1973) is generally credited with instigating the contemporary renaissance of this perspective, Spearman (1923, 1927) was one of the first to promote the notion of finite amounts of mental energy in human cognition. Because Spearman's ideas are still remarkably current it is worth quoting some of them in this context:

This continued tendency to success of the same person
throughout all variations of both form and subject-matter
-- that is to say, throughout all conscious aspects
of cognition whatever -- appears only explicable
by some factor lying deeper than the phenomena of
consciousness. And thus emerges the concept of
a hypothetical general and purely quantitative factor
underlying all cognitive performances of any kind...The
factor was taken to consist in something of the
nature of an "energy" or "power"...But if, thus,
the totality of cognitive operations is served by
some general factor in common, then each different
operation must necessarily be further served by
some specific factor peculiar to it...These would
thus function as alternative "engines" into which
the common supply of "energy" could be alternatively
distributed (Spearman, 1927, p. 5-6).

Kahneman's (1973) proposal that human information processing
was limited by the amount of available energy in much the
same way that an electrical generator can only supply a finite
amount of power to the operations it supports, can therefore
be considered only a recent reincarnation of the resources
as energy viewpoint. From either Spearman's or Kahneman's
perspective, varying amounts of this mental or attentional
energy would lead to both quantitative and qualitative differences
in performance since many activities would have to operate
at less than optimum efficiency, or not at all, when the demands
for energy exceed the available supply.

As noted earlier, the time conceptualization of resources
is relatively novel in the information-processing literature,
although there has been some theoretical and empirical interest
in the concept of speed of processing in the psychometric
intelligence literature (see Chapter 8). Fundamental to the
notion of temporal resources is the idea that people might
differ in the speed with which they carry out most processing
operations. A faster speed of processing is postulated to

be advantageous in many situations because more operations
can be completed in the same period of time, or later operations
can be executed before the products of the earlier operations
are lost, and thus the rate of performing mental operations
is assumed to be a potentially important processing resource.

The preceding discussion suggests that restrictions of
space, energy, and time could all contribute to reduced performance
on a great variety of cognitive tasks.   Indeed, in light of
the arguments outlined above it would be very surprising that
if suitable investigations were to be conducted they did not
yield evidence documenting the influence of each class of
resources.   In this sense each of these resources is 'critical'
because altered levels would likely reduce performance for
all activities which make demands upon resources.   The more
interesting question, to be addressed in Chapters 7, 8, and
9, is which of these resources is primarily affected by processes
of aging, and can be considered critical not for limitations
of performance found in all humans, but for the reductions
in performance associated with increased age.

Quantifying Resources

Some form of limited-capacity general processing resources
is now so entrenched in the information-processing perspective
that the tendency for performance on many tasks to be positively
correlated with one another has been attributed to a common
reliance on the same limited-capacity resource, and it has
even been suggested, following Spearman (1923, 1927), that
the resource concept is analogous to the g-factor in intelligence
(e.g., Hunt, 1980b; Hunt & Lansman, 1982).   There is clearly
considerable power in the notion of a single entity whose
quantitative variation is responsible for both quantitative
and qualitative differences in performance, but it is important
not to rely upon the notion of general-purpose limited resources
as an explanatory concept not itself amenable to further analysis
or explanation.   Despite its recent popularity, the idea of
limited processing resources actually has a very questionable
logical status.   Allport (1980), Baddeley (1981), Navon (1984),

Reisberg (1983), and Wessels (1982) have all pointed out that
it is circular to attribute decrements in performance to limitations in amount of resources, and to explain the absence
of decrements by the absence of limitations, unless there
is independent converging evidence concerning the amount of
resources available and the amount required by particular
tasks. Unfortunately, evidence relevant to the quantity of
processing resources has been very difficult to obtain for
any of the resource concepts and consequently the notion of
general-purpose processing resources remains highly speculative
and largely unverified.

        Consider how one might obtain evidence about the quantity
of processing resources available to the individual. A technique
sometimes proposed for assessing the capacity or resource
demands of various tasks relies on what is known as the secondary
task procedure. This situation consists of the subject performing
a number of different primary tasks, each in combination with
the same secondary task. For example, a recall memory task
and a recognition memory task might each be performed together
with a simple reaction time task. The reasoning is that the
resource requirements of the primary tasks can be assessed
by examining performance on the secondary task because more
demanding primary tasks result in a smaller residual amount
of resources available for the secondary task. The primary
task which yields the superior performance in the secondary
task can therefore be interpreted as requiring fewer resources
for its successful execution than the other task. Underwood
(1976) has characterized this reasoning as relying upon the
Archimedes Displacement Principle in that the quantity is
assessed indirectly by noting the amount of disruption or
displacement which occurs when the to-be-measured entity is
inserted into some known 'container'.

        Unfortunately there are a number of problems with the
secondary task procedure that limit its usefulness for purposes
of quantifying amount of resources in research on individual
differences. For example, the extent of interference may

vary with the competition for specific processing structures
in addition to general resources, and the amount of overhead
necessary for coordinating the two concurrent tasks may be
greater for some task combinations than for others. An even
more serious problem from the perspective of attempting to
assess the quantity of available resources is that the secondary
task procedure yields only ordinal measures at best, expressed
in the rather arbitrary units of the secondary task. That
is, because there is no way to assure that a constant allocation
of attention or effort is devoted to the secondary task in
each condition, only broad qualitative statements can be made
about the relative difficulty of various task combinations.

Many of these difficulties can also be expressed in terms
of the Archimedes Displacement Principle analogy mentioned
above. Imagine that two individuals are each attempting to
measure the volumes of objects in their possession by determining
the amount of liquid displaced when the objects are placed
in a container. However, in addition to potential variation
in the size of the to-be-measured objects, let us also assume
that the two people are using containers filled to different
proportions (e.g., 80% vs. 50% of capacity), and that the
liquids in the containers have different degrees of viscosity
(e.g., water vs. heavy-weight oil). Under these circumstances
it is clear that the measurements from the two individuals
would not be comparable because the amount of displaced liquid
will be determined by the residual volume of the container
and the elasticity or 'displaceability' of the liquid. An
even more extreme possibility, perhaps analogous to structural
interference between two tasks, could be imagined in which
there was a chemical reaction between the object and the liquid
such that the composition of both the object and the liquid
changed when they were brought together. The point is that
we may be in a comparable position when applying the dual-task
procedure in individual differences research because there
is no guarantee that the conditions of measurement are comparable
across the various individual difference categories.

Secondary task procedures, or assorted divided-attention variants of them, therefore seem to be flawed as a means of quantifying the amount of processing resources available to an individual. They are also inadequate from an analytical perspective since space, energy, and time conceptualizations of resources would all predict decrements in performance from the requirement to perform two concurrent activities, and consequently the procedure would not be informative about which resource was responsible. This latter consideration suggests that it is probably useful to examine how each particular type of resource might be quantified rather than attempting to devise a procedure to measure resources in general.

Measurement of Specific Resources

Although the space conceptualization of resources has enjoyed great popularity over the last 10 to 20 years, there has not yet been any consensus with respect to how the amount of available space, or short-term storage capacity, might be measured. One problem with reaching such agreement has been that the two measures most frequently proposed as indices of the size of working memory yield substantially different estimates of capacity. That is, the common memory span, reflecting the number of unrelated items that can be immediately repeated in the original order, typically averages between five and nine items, while the recency segment from the serial position curve in free recall generally averages only between two and four items.

To illustrate, Parkinson, Lindholm, and Inman (1982) obtained measures of memory span with both digits and words and several estimates of working memory capacity from the recency segment of free recall for both young and old adults. Their results, displayed in Table 4.2, indicate that the magnitudes clearly differ across the span and recency-based procedures. These authors also reported that the two types of measures were only moderately correlated ($r = .39$ to $r = .58$) with each other among the older adults, and not significantly correlated ($r < .32$) among the young adults.

Table 4.2

Working Memory Estimates of Young and Old Adults
Data from Parkinson, Lindholm, & Inman (1982)

Measure	Group	
	Young	Old
Digit Span	6.8	5.8
Word Span	5.4	4.4
Primary Memory		
Estimate A	2.9	2.3
Estimate B	2.7	2.1
Estimate C	2.6	2.1
Estimate D	2.7	2.2
Estimate E	3.4	2.7

Of course, one could argue that only one of these measures accurately reflects working memory capacity (e.g., Baddeley & Hitch, 1974), but at the present time there is little agreement with respect to which measure should be considered to provide the better estimate. Craik and Rabinowitz (1984) have proposed that the term working memory applies only when the materials must be manipulated, transformed, or recombined, and that the term primary memory be applied when the material is passively maintained in an untransformed fashion. This distinction is useful, but it still fails to yield a quantitative estimate of the size of working memory because the nature and magnitude of the manipulations and transformations are left unspecified. For example, simply reversing the order of the input items as in the case of backwards digit span involves transforming the material, but it seems unlikely that the reversal transformation would be equivalent in its effects to a manipulation consisting of recoding the digits into letters according to the sequential position in the alphabet. To the extent that different types of manipulations and transformations yield different estimates of working memory size, therefore, distinguishing between primary and working memory seems to offer little advantage for the purpose of quantifying capacity.

No unambiguous techniques have been devised to measure the amount of mental energy available to an individual, or required by a task, and therefore this conceptualization of resources has not yet proven to be empirically testable. It has been speculated that physiological measures related to pupil dilation, rate of metabolism, electro-encephalogram activity, etc., might serve as the observable indicants of mental energy (e.g., Kahneman, 1973), but the correspondence of physiological quantity to cognitive effectiveness has not yet been convincingly established for most measures.

Temporal resources have seldom been precisely defined, but at least some theorists have suggested that they might be assessed with the use of very simple speeded tasks such as reaction time. The reasoning, which is elaborated in much greater detail in Chapter 8, is that an individual's characteristic rate of performing mental operations can be inferred from the time required to perform extremely simple tasks which are presumably independent of possible variations in strategy.

Although these different resource conceptualizations are discussed as though they were distinct and independent, it should be realized that they may be related, and possibly even interchangeable. For example, if working memory is dynamic and needs periodic refreshing, then the capacity of working memory will be determined by the time or energy available for refreshing. Conversely, if the amount of workspace available for computation is limited, more swapping of information to and from long-term memory will be necessary and the time for most activities will increase. In a similar manner, time and energy may be interchangeable because increased energy may contribute to faster time, and vice versa.

There are two ways in which this interchangeability of resource concepts may be viewed. One is with despair in that it might prove impossible to identify which type of resource is primarily responsible for widespread limitations of human performance. Such a reaction is understandable if the goal is to localize suspected causes in clearly distinct compartments, and one discovers that the causal factor appears to take different forms in different situations. However, an alternative interpretation might be that the interrelatedness of the concepts suggests that something very important and fundamental in human information processing is involved, regardless of its specific manner of expression. That is, the discovery that the concepts of energy, space, and time may be translatable to one another may be interpreted as an indication that whatever its manifestation in a specific context, there is something crucial about the central and general limits on cognitive operations. We will return to this issue in Chapter 7.

Methodological and Theoretical Complications

The preceding sections have indicated that the information-processing perspective provides a rich set of possibilities

for conceptualizing specific factors responsible for individual differences in cognitive performance. Moreover, many
likely sources of individual differences have been virtually
unexplored and appear to be promising areas for aging (and
other individual difference) research. Notable examples are
sequence repertoire, sequence selection, and sequence assembly,
although few facets of information processing can be considered
so extensively researched that they are well understood.
One quite reasonable strategy that could be employed is to
attempt to determine the effects of aging on each entry in
a catalog such as that presented in Table 4.1. In fact, it
may be argued that this is precisely what is occurring at
the current time, although unsystematically and with little
recognition of the efforts outside one's own particular problem
area.

     On the other hand, the existence of such a large number
of mechanisms as plausible determinants of individual differences
in information processing is not without disadvantages. A
major difficulty is that because any complex processing system
must be highly integrated, with multiple lines of communication
and feedback, a change in one aspect of the system is likely
to result in readjustments of the entire system. In other
words, a difference in one mechanism may either attenuate
or accentuate performance differences produced by another
mechanism. A consequence of these complex interrelationships
is that there is often a problem of attribution in identifying
which particular mechanism is the true cause of the observed
phenomenon. Indeed, the possible interactive effects among
various aspects of the processing system are so great that
it may be impossible to study individual differences in a
single mechanism without making fairly strong explicit, or
implicit, assumptions about the absence of differences in
other mechanisms (cf., Baron, 1978; Baron & Trieman, 1980;
Butterfield, 1981; Carroll, 1980; Hitch, 1980; Hunt & MacLeod,
1979; Sternberg, 1978). At times one may even question whether
the assumptions are more critical and important than the specific

hypotheses being investigated.

A few examples will help illustrate these interactive effects. Several years ago, Hunt, Frost, and Lunneborg (1973) found that college students with high verbal ability exhibited less clustering of words according to semantic category than otherwise comparable students with low verbal ability. It was consequently inferred that, contrary to one's intuitions, high verbal students used an organizational strategy in memory recall less frequently than low verbal students. However, Hunt (1980a) later described results by Schwartz which indicated that this difference in strategy was only evident in the items recalled from working memory. This led to the inference that the high-verbal individuals had larger or more efficient working memories than low-verbal individuals, and could therefore recall recent items without relying on an organizational strategy. Taken together, these studies can thus be interpreted as suggesting that the difference in working memory capacity (i.e., a structural resource) was at least partially responsible for the differences in organizational strategy (i.e., the sequence of information-processing components).

Sternberg (1977) has also reported a paradoxical pattern in the relation between durations of specific processing components in tasks of reasoning and performance on tests of general intelligence. The expected finding that high intelligence was associated with faster component execution was obtained for most components, but the component concerned with encoding exhibited the opposite relationship -- more intelligent individuals were actually slower at encoding the stimuli than less intelligent individuals. Sternberg's interpretation of this latter result was that the longer time spent in encoding the stimuli served to facilitate the execution of subsequent processing components. In other words, efficiency of different components interact in a complex fashion to contribute to overall task performance, and quite misleading inferences might be derived by focusing on only a single component.

Although these examples of interactions among various

aspects of information processing are taken from research with young adults, it is reasonable to expect that even more interactions would be evident across adulthood as age-related changes in one aspect lead to adjustments, compensations, and optimizations in other aspects. If for no other reason than the fact that the changes evolved gradually over an extended period of time, one would anticipate great difficulties in localizing differences in performance within a single aspect of the processing system because the interdependencies almost guarantee that differences in one aspect would eventually propagate to differences in other aspects.

In the face of these complicated interconnections among elements of the information-processing system, it may be reasonable to reexamine the feasibility of information-processing techniques for investigating individual differences, and particularly age-related differences, in cognition. Specifically, one might ask what options are available to deal with the complexity of so many possible sources of performance differences? Three alternatives can be identified at the current time.

One potential strategy is simply to abandon the information-processing perspective on the grounds that the multiplicity of mechanisms to account for individual differences indicates that this approach has outlived any usefulness it may once have had. To adherents of the computer metaphor in psychology this is clearly a radical alternative, but it is an understandable reaction to the tremendous complexity of potential explanations revealed by the preceding discussion. Indeed, it could be argued that the aforementioned difficulties are signs of a paradigm shift in Kuhn's (1962) sense of the phrase, and that the information-processing approach is about to be replaced by a more powerful set of assumptions about the nature of human cognition. While conceivable, no clearly formulated alternatives have yet captured the attention of a sizable number of researchers, and thus the new paradigm that might replace the information-processing perspective is still not obvious. Until such time that an alternative set of guiding

principles are developed and accepted, therefore, it appears
that the information-processing approach will continue to
provide a meaningful framework within which cognitive researchers
can plan and interpret their research.

A second option for dealing with the large number of
potential information-processing mechanisms is to proceed
as in the past, although perhaps with somewhat greater sensitivity
to the possibility of alternative mechanisms contributing
to some of the observed behavioral differences. The dominant
mode of carrying out information-processing research on individual
differences has been to focus on a specific mechanism, and
then to attempt to isolate its effects by suitable experimental
manipulations. When appropriately conducted, this type of
research can be very informative about the sensitivity of
the mechanism of interest to the type of individual difference
being investigated. Moreover, while no single research study
can hope to provide a definitive conclusion about the nature
of any individual difference classification, a reasonable
understanding may be possible from the aggregate results of
many studies, each investigating a different possible mechanism.

It might be difficult to develop procedures to assess
every conceivable determinant, particularly since one can
never be certain that all possible mechanisms have been identified,
but to the extent that several determinants have been investigated
and relevant individual differences found in only one, a theorist
can be fairly confident that a major determinant of the individual
differences has been isolated. Even if more than one individual
difference is detected, many more will have been ruled out
and some degree of isolation will have been achieved. The
only real disadvantages to this all-inclusive approach are
that it is an extremely inefficient and cumbersome means of
isolating the principal differences between individuals, and
that interesting and important causal links among mechanisms
may not be detected because of the focus on single mechanisms.
This is the danger of 'issue isolationism' mentioned in Chapter
3, and Newell (1973), Ridgway (1981), and Sternberg (1977)

have all lamented the lack of theoretical and empirical interrelationships across tasks and phenomena resulting from this
type of focus upon specific paradigms rather than more encompassing
theoretical perspectives.

A third strategy that might be pursued to cope with the
large number of potential determinants of individual differences
in cognitive tasks is to adopt a particular theoretical perspective
concerning the etiology of the individual differences. The
interpretation may be at any level from social or cultural
to physiological or biochemical, but will serve a useful purpose
as long as it narrows the range of possible mechanisms that
are implicated in the individual differences. Moreover, the
most useful theories will not only indicate the origin of
the individual differences but will also incorporate dynamic
mechanisms to explain how the present configuration of information
processing evolved from a former state. It is towards this
topic that we now turn.

Dynamic Mechanisms

The discussion in the earlier sections of this chapter
has focused on descriptions of static differences that might
exist between individuals in different classification categories,
but there has been no mention of the dynamic processes responsible
for the transition from one information-processing configuration
to another. In a sense, these static descriptions can be
considered analogous to before and after portrayals, but the
nature of the transition between states has generally been
neglected. Rabbitt (e.g., 1979b, 1981a, 1982a) has been a
particularly strong advocate for the view that change mechanisms are needed in any truly satisfactory model of human
cognition. With some types of individual differences (e.g.,
sex, race) the question of how the differences emerged from
a prior state are not particularly meaningful from a psychological
perspective. However, with intra-individual differences such
as cognitive development in childhood, skill, aging, and disease-
-induced performance pathology, the change processes are of
considerable interest. It is therefore in these areas that

detailed theories with specific predictions as to the types of changes that are occurring, and the mechanisms that are most directly affected, will likely be of the greatest value.

Knowledge about the manner in which differences have evolved is surely a more complete form of understanding than simple awareness of end states. In fact, it can even be argued that much of the organization and coherence of behavior is apparent only from a dynamic perspective. That is, the present configuration of process and resource characteristics may best be understood by determining the mechanisms responsible for transforming them from the earlier configuration. In view of what seems to be an unmanageably large set of potential sources of individual differences in information processing, a focus on change mechanisms might provide the integrating concepts needed to account for the multiple manifestations of change.

Others have taken a similar view in suggesting that the most fruitful approach to understanding the organization and nature of behavior at any point in time might be to study how the behavior changed from an earlier form (e.g., Hunt, 1976; Norman, 1980; Rabbitt, 1981a; Ridgway, 1981). The major problem at the present time is that there are few theories

...of the genesis of individual differences...(which)

...tell us where to look for differences in cognition

(Hunt, 1976, p. 242).

Nevertheless, there are at least three sources of theoretical speculations that could be used to guide the investigation of the evolution of behavior over time. Each entails some risk because there is no assurance that the theory from which the assumptions are derived is valid, but with appropriate cautions they can serve to provide a meaningful and coherent framework for organizing one's research efforts.

One source is a set of theoretical assumptions about the most plausible change mechanisms in the domain of interest. The theory can be of any level of detail, but generally will be helpful as long as it includes proposals about what it

is that is changing over time. For example, one might argue
that many of the adult age differences in memory efficiency
are attributable to the lack of recent practice with active
memorizing because of the greater time that has elapsed since
older adults were in school compared to young adults. The
scope of mechanisms to be investigated in attempting to characterize the exact nature of the age-related memory differences
could therefore be greatly restricted by adhering to a theoretical
position such as this. A researcher adhering to the disuse
perspective would probably be interested in hypotheses related
to effects of practice on component efficiency, sequence availability, etc., and issues related to the repertoire and selection
of mnemonic strategies, but not in presumably unmodifiable
processing characteristics such as the size of working memory,
the amount of attentional capacity, etc. It is true that
other mechanisms might be involved in contributing to the
observed differences across individuals, and that the theoretical
perspective consequently might not be sufficient to account
for all mechanisms that could be identified. Nevertheless,
the short-term advantages of providing a coherent frame of
reference for the planning and interpretation of research
may substantially outweigh the negative aspects of incompleteness,
and warrant the use of this approach in many situations.

A second type of speculation might limit the focus of
investigation by offering speculations about the causal nature
of particular kinds of influences. Knowledge of the likely
cause of the individual difference could thus suggest the
most reasonable mechanisms affected by that causal factor.
An example of this kind of postulation is Hunt's assertion
that:

> Physical influences such as heredity, nutrition,
> and brain damage, must exert their influence through
> alteration of mechanistic processes. Educational
> and cultural influences must exert their influence
> through changes in representations and strategies
> (Hunt, 1983, p. 146).

It is clear that if one accepts these propositions, certain mechanisms need not be examined with particular kinds of individual differences (e.g., the strategic variable of sequence repertoire with racial differences, the mechanistic property of component efficiency with cultural differences). Instead, the research efforts could be concentrated on those aspects of processing predicted to be most susceptible to the presumed etiology of the individual difference (e.g., component efficiency, attentional capacity, or cycle time with brain damage, sequence repertoire or knowledge quantity with socio-economic class differences). This approach is also not fail-safe, and grossly misleading conclusions can be reached if the initial presumptions are later proved incorrect. However, it should be fairly easy to check on the validity of one's assumptions, and the advantage of providing an organizational framework for guiding and interpreting research results is by no means trivial.

The third type of theoretical speculation about dynamic mechanisms that can help delineate the specific processes and/or resources responsible for particular categories of individual differences in cognition are proposals about the pattern of adjustments or interactions in the processing system that are likely to result given the existence of one or more specific mechanisms. If there is a rational explanation as to how a variety of processes should be affected by a difference in a presumably fundamental mechanism, then the research can be focused on the target processes and individual differences in other aspects of processing can be temporarily ignored.

This class of theorizing can be illustrated by anticipating the discussion of Chapters 9 and 10 and considering the view that many adult age differences in cognitive functioning are attributable to a slower rate of processing nearly all types of information. The slower processing rate could occur because of the following plausible sequence of events. First, the gradual constriction of cerebral arteries due to cardiovascular diseases such as arteriosclerosis can reduce the oxygen flow to the brain, thereby damaging or destroying many nerve cells.

The decreased number of functioning neurons might then lead
to a diminished level of neural signals relative to the background
noise activity. And finally, in order to compensate for the
reduced signal-to-noise ratio, it need only be assumed that
the nervous system integrates over a longer period of time
in much the same way that statistically-sophisticated researchers
increase the size of their samples to overcome the noise preventing
the attainment of statistical significance. The net effect
of all of this could very well be a slower rate of performing
nearly all elementary operations within the central nervous
system.

A difference at this general level (basic operation time)
can be assumed to result in the following second-order differences
in other processing mechanisms: (a) lower component efficiency
because every operation is executed at a slower rate; (b)
possible shift in the identity of specific components or in
the sequence of components as a means of adapting to the reduced
efficiency with the original processing sequences; (c) potential
differences in the type of representation to maintain compatibility
with any altered sequences of processing operations; (d) likely
reduction in the number of alternative processing sequences
employed (sequence selection), and therefore inferred to be
within the individual's capability (sequence repertoire);
(e) less efficient construction of new sequences of components
because assembly processes are slower; and (f) smaller amounts
of new knowledge because of slower encoding and rehearsal
processes. Greater efficiency of nearly all processing operations
might also result in fewer computational demands upon working
memory which in turn "...could be functionally equivalent
to a larger storage capacity (Daneman & Carpenter, 1980, p.
451)".

It might also be expected that a difference in the speed
of processing information would have consequences in more
complex aspects of behavior. For example, Welford (1963)
has suggested that a tendency for rigidity to increase with
age might be explained by assuming that older people "reacted

to a reduced speed in decision making by increasing their reliance on standard solutions and standard routines (p. 121)." That is, because a slower rate of processing impairs the speed of devising new solutions to problems, an older adult who is slowing down may appear rigid because of a failure to construct appropriate responses to new situations as rapidly as necessary.

It is by no means established that the age differences in cognition are attributable to mechanisms such as those outlined above. However it does seem necessary to impose some type of dynamic perspective on the research findings in the area of age and cognition because an approach based on an exhaustive cataloging of age-related differences in information processing is not only extremely formidable, but seems unlikely to result in integrative understanding. Arguments and empirical evidence relevant to different types of dynamic perspectives will therefore be examined in the chapters that follow.

Summary

The information-processing approach provides a framework, loosely based on an analogy with computers, for conceptualizing the nature of human cognition. It has been a powerful influence for nearly 30 years, but is not without critics. Among the objections most relevant in connection with aging is that information-processing researchers have exhibited little concern for within-individual changes in performance. Individual differences can be attributed to a broad variety of process or resource entities, although inferences of resource limitations must necessarily be based on indirect evidence. However, the enormous number of possibilities to account for differences in performance, together with the realization that a difference in one component of the system will likely result in differences in other components, suggests that it is impractical to attempt to construct an exhaustive catalog of information-processing components which do, and do not, exhibit sensitivity to increased age. A more feasible approach seems to involve the adoption of a theoretical perspective capable of accounting for the transition between cognitive states of young and older adulthood.

Experience and Expertise

It might seem strange to include a chapter on the topic of experience and expertise in a monograph concerned with cognitive aging, but there are actually three very important reasons for this inclusion. The first is that because both aging and the acquisition of expertise are within-individual changes that take place over an extended period of time, it may be informative to look for the possibility of common mechanisms of change or adaptation. That is, the development of skill within a given domain involves a dynamic alteration of the behavioral capacities of an individual, and as such might provide a valuable source of ideas about the nature and consequences of changes in information processing that occur as a function of increased age.

A second reason for examining the literature on experience and expertise is that a frequently invoked explanation of developmental trends in behavior is what has been called the disuse theory, i.e., the idea that older adults perform at lower levels than young adults on a particular task because they are out of practice with the ability relevant for that task. I have previously characterized the two major assumptions of this approach as:

> ...that practice or experience is necessary for
> an ability to develop or be maintained; without
> such use, a function will atrophy in the same manner
> as a muscle which has been incapacitated...(and
> that)...young adults(s), perhaps because of recent
> exposure to the educational system...(are)...equally
> practiced or experienced in nearly all abilities,
> and that as (they begin)...to develop special skills
> for particular vocations certain of these abilities
> are used more frequently than others. Over a period
> of many years this differential frequency of usage
> is thought to be responsible for the decline in

unused abilities reflected in age-related performance
decrements observed in psychometric tests and psychological experiments (Salthouse, 1982, p. 47-48).

Explanations based on the disuse concept therefore assume
that young adults are rather general experts, or at least
extremely competent novices, while older adults have become
very selective experts. However, in order for this interpretation
to be convincing it must be demonstrated that the differences
between young and old adults are qualitatively similar to
the types of differences evident between novices and experts
in the relevant ability domain. Examination of the effects
of experience and expertise is therefore useful as a means
of determining the plausibility of a particular class of theoretical explanation for behavioral development patterns.
(Actually the disuse issue is best addressed by examining
parallels between aging and the deterioration of performance
that results from the lack of practice of a previously acquired
skill, but there is almost no relevant data of this type.)

A third major reason for discussing the topic of experience
and expertise in a monograph on aging and cognition is that
it is likely that differential amounts of experience contribute
to discrepancies among age trends in different types of behavior,
and between the age trends observed in the laboratory and
those evident in the real-world. That is, for most activities
in daily life, increased age is positively correlated with
experience, and therefore contrasts with behaviors differentially
represented in daily experience, or between functioning in
the laboratory and in the real-world, involves a probable
confounding of age and expertise.

The natural correlation of age and experience is likely
to be particularly relevant in measures that reflect the cumulative
knowledge of an individual. Many earlier writers, in attempting
to characterize the intellectual abilities of older adults,
have acknowledged a distinction between current or raw capacities
and the aggregate attainments from earlier exercising of these
capacities (e.g., Birren, 1952, 1964; Birren & Morrison, 1961;
Botwinick, 1967, 1975; Bromley, 1974; Cattell, 1963, 1971;

Denney, 1984; Foulds & Raven, 1948; Fozard & Thomas, 1975; Gilbert, 1935; Horn, 1975, 1978, 1980, 1982b; Horn & Cattell, 1966, 1967; Jones, 1955, 1959; Jones & Conrad, 1933; Reed & Reitan, 1963; Wechsler, 1958; Welford, 1958). However, the dichotomy has largely remained speculative because of incomplete information about how experience alters performance. A major goal of the current chapter is to attempt to remedy this defect by reviewing the empirical literature on the effects of experience and the nature of expertise.

The argument about the confounding of age and expertise has two far-reaching implications. The first is that comparisons of behavioral competence across the adult years in activities performed as part of one's daily life must be very cautiously interpreted because of the potential confounding of developmental and experiential determinants of performance. Of particular importance in this context are situations in which the developmental trend suggests stability or enhancement of the ability across the adult lifespan because of the possibility that the positive contributions of experience overshadowed any potential negative effects of aging on efficiency of functioning. Jones (1956) has even argued that many standardized intellectual tests favor older adults because the content is more dependent on experience than ability and thus the results from such tests 'give an impression of a smaller decrement than is actually the case (p. 158).'

A second implication of the confounding of age and expertise is that the results of laboratory studies may not be very generalizable to well-practiced activities performed outside the laboratory. That is, if abilities studied in the laboratory involve minimal amounts of practice while those used in one's daily life are extremely practiced, and if practice contributes to changes in the efficiency of performance, then it may be impossible to predict real-world functioning on the basis of laboratory performance.

An example of the discrepancy between findings in the laboratory and performance of real-life, highly practiced, activities was described by Salthouse (1984) in a study of age and skill effects in transcription typing. The interval between successive keystrokes was measured in a serial reaction time task of the type frequently studied in the laboratory, and in the activity of transcription typing. Typists between the ages of 18 and 72 years of age were found to exhibit sizable age-related slowing in the reaction time task, while the rate of typing was completely independent of age. Because the reaction time and typing tasks are structurally very similar, it seems reasonable to conclude that the older typists had developed a compensatory mechanism which allowed them to maintain a high level of typing proficiency despite apparent declines in the speed of basic perceptual and motor processes.

These typing results provide a concrete example of the potential discrepancy between observations in the laboratory and those in daily life, but concern about the limited relevance of laboratory results for understanding age trends in real-world functioning has been raised many times in the gerontological literature. To illustrate, the following four quotations are representative of many that have been concerned with this issue:

Physiological age exacts its tax year by year as the individual grows older; but psychological age adds to the personal capital stock of experience and bonds of association as real assets to be drawn upon (Miles, 1935, p. 82).

Age alone is an insufficient factor by which to judge one's efficiency in his own particular work, especially if we consider the practice and judgment acquired through the years and the possible compensation in age for weaker sensory perceptions and slower grasp and learning by better integration of knowledge in the light of past experience and practice (Gilbert, 1935, p. 42).

A man's reaction time may have dropped and his physical

strength diminished, but he may still be able to outdistance his younger fellows because he has learned the tricks of the trade and because he uses the strength and speed that he has more efficiently...The point is that, even if we isolate all the biological and psychological variables that influence performance and simply add scores, we may do the older man a great injustice (Kaplan, 1951, p. 301).

Consideration only of the internal capacities of the individual would neglect the fact that skilled performance over a lifetime is a continuing process of adaptation in which the individual develops work methods and tempo in relation to his particular limitations or capacities. Measurements of physical and psychological capacities, while essential, do not lead directly to estimation of how well individuals, given a period of learning and adaptation, will perform at tasks (Birren, 1964, p. 133-134).

A common theme in these passages is the view that there are grounds for a very optimistic perspective on the real-world consequences of aging since positive effects of experience can often be assumed to overshadow any potentially negative effects associated with aging. In fact, some researchers (e.g., Baltes, Dittmann-Kohli, & Dixon, 1984; Baltes & Willis, 1982; Charness, 1982) have even attempted to establish the correspondence between practice and aging by determining how much practice on a task is needed to bring the performance of the older adults to the initial level of the young adults. The point of this exercise is not necessarily to suggest that the same mechanisms are involved in the two types of behavioral change, but rather to indicate the small size of the age effects relative to the amount of change induced by increased experience.
    Although frequently invoked in discussions of real-world functioning, the notion of experience-based compensation for age-related decrements in ability has never been thoroughly

investigated. (However, the previously cited typing research
and work by Charness in the domains of chess and bridge represents
an intriguing beginning, e.g., 1979, 1981, 1983). The major
reason for this omission is that, as noted above, there has
been surprisingly little systematic information available
on how experience leads to improved performance across a variety
of psychological tasks. The following sections are devoted
to surveying the literature on how experts at any age differ
from novices in order to begin to understand what changes
with experience and, wherever possible, how it changes.

The Nature of Skill and Expertise

Skill and expertise are terms used to refer to the most
admired (e.g., fastest, most efficient, most consistent) forms
of behavior in a given activity domain. Regardless of the
type of activity -- perceptual, motoric, or cognitive, the
skilled or expert individual exemplifies an exquisite adaptation
of human capacities to environmental requirements and demands.
Unlike ability, which is assumed to be cross-situational and
largely hereditary or at least biologically determined, skill
is considered to be experientially-based and fairly task-specific.
Indeed, skilled individuals are typically defined solely in
terms of greater performance proficiency in a particular domain
of behavior. Proficiency is manifested in a number of alternative
ways, however, and it is useful to review some of the more
specific characteristics associated with skilled performance.

Above all, skilled behavior is said to possess the qualities
of speed, accuracy, and adaptability that are missing, or
at least less prominent, in unskilled behavior. Skilled performers
exhibit economy of effort and yet are consistently able to
produce very precise behavior. This is not to say that experts
never make errors, but rather that experts are quicker to
detect and correct errors when they occur. Adaptability is
an important characteristic of expertise because the skilled
individual is able to produce comparable forms of behavior
under widely varying conditions, but is flexible enough to
adjust and modify molecular approaches to the task in order
to maintain the same molar level of performance. Much of

the behavior of experts is also apparently executed with fewer attention demands, thereby allowing skilled performers to be more resistant to distraction from external sources, or conversely, to be better able to handle other activities simultaneously.

Although the preceding description conveys many of the important qualities of skilled performance, it is deficient in not suggesting the specific means by which these characteristics are achieved. In order to be more analytical about the precise nature of skill or expertise, one must adopt a theoretical perspective with the potential for decomposing complex forms of behavior into a more restricted set of heuristically useful explanatory mechanisms. The taxonomy outlined in Table 4.1 appears ideally suited for this purpose, and consequently it will be used to organize the analytic examination of the nature of skill and expertise.

While most of the taxonomic categories of Table 4.1 appear reasonable as possible factors contributing to skill differences, the experimental research has been unequally distributed across the various entries. For example, until quite recently the majority of studies from the information-processing perspective focused upon parameters of discrete components, with very little effort directed at investigating other potential sources of individual differences. The emphasis upon processing components or elementary operations is so strong that Posner and MacLeod (1982, p. 478) have recently suggested that the primary goal of information-processing research is "...the identification of fundamental operations that can be used to characterize the human mind," and several theorists have even proposed inventories or catalogs of components presumed to be sufficient to explain most cognitive activity (e.g., Carroll, 1976, 1980; Newell & Simon, 1972; Rose, 1980; Shuell, 1980). This bias toward the investigation of the most elementary aspects of information processing has also been carried over into the study of skilled behavior, and thus only a few of the taxonomic entries of Table 4.1 have a large number of empirical studies relevant to the issue of skill. Nevertheless each of the

theoretical entities will be discussed from the perspective
of skill and expertise to determine the likelihood that at
least some of the variations in experience-based proficiency
are attributable to that particular aspect of information
processing.

A wide range of activities will be considered in the
following discussion in an attempt to provide the broadest
possible conception of skill and expertise. However, by not
restricting the coverage to a particular task only a rather
abstract outline of the nature of skill can be provided, and
exact details will have to be filled in when referring to
a specific activity. This type of broad overview is nevertheless
considered useful because the fact that only a limited number
of mechanisms can be investigated in a single experiment means
that a somewhat narrow, and possibly distorted, picture of
the nature of expertise may be emerging from individual studies.

Component Efficiency At the level of individual components
one could look for skill differences in the time required
to complete a given processing operation, or in the quality
of the product of that operation. It is clear that if behavior
is the outcome of a series of processing components it will
be produced faster, and perhaps be of a higher level of quality,
the greater the efficiency and/or effectiveness of individual
components. Ample evidence is now available documenting the
existence of substantial practice-related improvement in elementary
components (see Salthouse & Somberg, 1982a, for a review of
much of this literature), and thus this class of interpretation
has a priori plausibility as a determinant of skilled behavior.

Examples of research on skill differences focusing on
parameters of individual components are available in numerous
contrasts of skilled and less-skilled readers. As an illustration,
Jackson and McClelland (1979) examined measures of sensory
and cognitive components in skilled and average readers and
found that the former were quicker than less proficient readers
in a component concerned with activating name codes from visual
stimuli. A similar skilled reader advantage in this and other
processing components has been reported in many different

studies (e.g., Gilbert, 1959; Graesser, Hoffman, & Clark, 1980; Jackson, 1980; Jackson & McClelland, 1975; Mason, 1978; Palmer, MacLeod, Hunt, & Davidson, 1985; Perfetti & Lesgold, 1977). The evidence is now so great that it is indisputable that readers of varying levels of proficiency systematically differ in the efficiency of executing specific information-processing components. It is never clear from correlational results such as these whether the expertise is the consequence or the cause of the more efficient component execution time, but the substantial practice-related reductions in component duration suggest that greater component efficiency is a contributing factor to skill in at least some ability domains.

Component Identity   Differences at the level of component identity would be evident if skilled individuals substitute a new component in the otherwise unchanged processing sequence used by unskilled individuals. Some of the qualities of skilled behavior might be mediated by this shift in components, particularly if the new component has advantages in shorter time, increased precision, or reduced demands for attention.

An example of a possible shift in the identity of a single component with increased skill is the feedback component in typewriting. Coover (1923), Diehl and Siebel (1962), West (1967) and others have suggested that as typists become more skilled there is a shift from reliance upon visual to kinesthetic information in monitoring the correctness of keystroke responses. Eccles (1978) has also speculated that dentists undergo a similar shift from reliance upon visual information to kinesthetic information as they become more experienced, and Fitts and Posner (1967), Singleton (1978), and Summers (1981) have hypothesized that this type of shift underlies many kinds of skill. Alteration of the type of feedback information would be classified as a change in component identity if the feedback substitution is achieved without otherwise altering the nature of the relevant information processing. It is unclear to what extent skill variations in other tasks are primarily attributable to a change in a single processing component, but such a mechanism is at least a plausible determinant of some kinds of skilled performance.

<u>Sequence Order</u> A common theme in much of the older literature on skilled performance is that skilled individuals often employ what appears to be a different strategy of performing the task than do less proficient individuals. In the present scheme a strategy is nothing more than a particular sequence of processing components, and therefore differences in the strategy of performance are classified under the heading of sequential order of components. This category is distinguished from the preceding one in that the skill-related difference is assumed to involve more than one processing component; either the order of component execution is altered, or an entirely new sequence of processing components is involved.

One rather clear example of a skill difference of this type is apparent in a recent study by Salthouse and Prill (1983). The task in these experiments was to launch a projectile at the correct moment to intersect a moving target. A processing model was first developed to represent how subjects performed the task, and the model then guided a series of analyses conducted to determine the locus of performance differences associated with overall task proficiency. The results indicated that there were little or no skill effects on measures of individual component effectiveness, but the better-performing subjects appeared to employ a strategy of updating their initial estimates while poorer-performing subjects followed a more passive strategy involving only a single intersection estimate.

Despite relatively few concrete demonstrations of strategy differences contributing to variations in skill, it is almost certainly the case that strategic factors are responsible for proficiency differences in many activity domains. One of the things learned with extensive experience is surely the most effective or efficient method of performing a task, and it is reasonable to expect that skilled performers would employ the best method they are capable of executing.

<u>Sequence Mode</u> Skilled and unskilled individuals might also differ in the mode of executing the processing components. Experts, by virtue of their greater task-specific knowledge,

might execute certain processing components only after particular outcomes of prior components (i.e., in an information-dependent mode), or, because of their presumed greater residual attentional capacity, experts might be able to execute two or more components simultaneously (i.e., in a parallel-processing mode).

It is likely that expert diagnosticians differ from novices in employing a dependent, or contingent, series of inquiries based upon their extensive knowledge of the interrelationship of symptom states and particular diseases. Empirical support for this speculation has been provided by Kleinmuntz (1968) who concluded that:

> The more experienced neurologist's overall search strategy is guided by a maximization principle in which he radically reduces his problem environment with each question until he has zeroed-in on a differential diagnostic judgment (Kleinmuntz, 1968, p. 181-182).

Leaper, Gill, Stanisland, Horrocks, and de Dombal (1973) also reported that inexperienced physicians conducted more stereotyped interviews than experienced physicians, who were more adaptable in fitting their interview questions to the individual case. Less experienced diagnosticians presumably engage in an unsystematic non-contingent search in which successive questions are only marginally guided by prior information. Therefore, even if expert and novice diagnosticians eventually consider the same symptoms (i.e., proceed through the same sequence of components), the experts will have an advantage if they progress through the sequence in a contingent rather than random fashion. This advantage may be even greater if experts are better Bayesian processors than novices, by more appropriately revising their prior judgments in light of new information.

A shift from serial to parallel processing of components with greater expertise is evident in anecdotal reports of people learning to drive an automobile. When first beginning to drive, the demands of operating the vehicle cannot be interspersed with conversation, and consequently talking is often restricted to periods of waiting at stop signs and lights, i.e., conversation and driving are serial operations. However, after a moderate amount of experience most drivers are simultaneously able to control the moving vehicle and still contribute their share of a conversation, i.e., conversation and driving have become parallel activities.

An especially intriguing laboratory demonstration of an apparent shift from serial to parallel processing was reported by Hirst, Spelke, Reaves, Caharack, and Neisser (1980). These investigators examined the effects of practice on simultaneous reading and writing from dictation. Early in practice the concurrent performance of the two activities was very poor, but eventually each task could be performed together as effectively as when performed by itself. Other examples of skill differences associated with changes in the mode of sequence execution could be described, but it seems clear that at least some of the attributes of skilled behavior listed earlier may be related to factors of this type. For example, the characteristic of experts appearing to waste little time or effort when performing tasks in their area of expertise may be due to a greater reliance upon contingent and dependent operations. And as suggested by the Hirst, et al. (1980) study, the ability of highly skilled individuals to perform more than one activity at the same time may be due to a form of parallel processing developed through extensive experience with the task.

Sequence Availability   The idea that people might differ in the availability of their information-processing sequences is relatively new, and primarily based upon an analogy to computer programs that have been compiled for more efficient operation. It is assumed that a sequence of procedural components which has become automatic and largely independent of conscious control has many advantages over a sequence in which each individual component is separately and effortfully interpreted. For example, by not making demands upon the limited processing resources, more of the attentional capacity can be devoted to the monitoring or facilitation of other component operations, or to receiving additional external stimulation, that could lead to improved levels of performance.

The development of automatic processing sequences may be a key factor in the ability of skilled individuals to maintain consistent levels of performance despite varying environmental conditions. What were previously laborious analytical 'solutions' gradually become converted into habitual routines or paths through the state space for a given problem. As these paths become more direct and efficient they lead to the activation of higher levels of abstraction or integration. It is likely that this type of mechanism is responsible for the phenomenon described by Norman (1980) whereby novices seem to focus on the mechanics of each specific act necessary to carry out a complex behavior, while experts are apparently able to concentrate on more global goals and higher-order purposes. Larkin, McDermott, Simon, and Simon (1980) have also suggested that master physicists derive at least some of their expertise from automated action sequences that require less monitoring than consciously controlled sequences to ensure successful completion. Once automated, these sequences might also function as subroutines, and thus serve as building blocks in the hierarchical organization of progressively more complex activity. Moreover, since the automated sequences are no longer a part of conscious thought, their functioning may contribute to the impression that experts often seem to perform in an intuitive or holistic manner in contrast to the deliberate and analytical approach characteristic of novices.

Perhaps the most convincing demonstration of automated processing sequences comes from the series of experiments reported by Schneider and Shiffrin (1977; Shiffrin & Schneider, 1977). Extensive practice at classifying the same set of stimulus elements led to quantitative (faster) and qualitative (independence of reaction time from set size) differences in performance that were interpreted as the result of unconscious, resource-independent, activation of elements in long-term memory.

Additional suppport for the view that well-practiced information-processing tasks make fewer demands upon some

limited processing resource such as attention is available
in studies in which secondary task performance is examined
after different amounts of experience on a primary task.
This procedure has obvious limitations as discussed in the
previous chapter, but at least six studies (e.g., Bahrick,
Noble, & Fitts, 1954; Crosby & Parkinson, 1979; Johnston,
Wagstaff, & Griffith, 1972; Logan, 1978, 1979; Salthouse &
Somberg, 1982a) have been reported in which increased experience
was associated with better performance of either the primary
task, the secondary task, or both tasks. Results such as
these can be interpreted as suggesting that the processing
demands of the primary task are reduced with increased practice,
presumably because the task is executed in an increasingly
automatic fashion.

 Sequence Repertoire   Certain expert craftsmen are almost
legendary for their ability to accomplish the same molar activity
with a wide variety of different procedures. These procedures
can be considered analogous to alternative solution sequences
through the task or problem space, and it is clear that someone
with a greater repertoire of possible pathways to the same
goal will frequently produce performance superior to that
of a person with only a single, fixed, method of performing
the task. Further, much of the flexibility and adaptability
of skilled performers may be due to the greater number of
processing sequences available to experts relative to those
available to novices.

 Because no two surgical operations are exactly the same,
skilled surgeons probably owe some of their expertise to a
larger repertoire of possible processing sequences (i.e.,
alternative surgical techniques) compared to novice surgeons.
A given surgical outcome can be achieved in many different
ways, and the physician capable of executing more of those
ways in a competent fashion will, other things being equal,
be considered more skilled than a physician capable of fewer
operative procedures. Despite the intuitive reasonableness
of this suggestion there appears to be little laboratory-based
research documenting the relationship between level of expertise

and capability of achieving the same global activity in a variety of different ways.

Sequence Selection   Another important characteristic of highly skilled individuals is that they almost always seem to adopt a procedure optimally suited to the particular problem at hand. This ability to match processing sequences or strategies to problem states or stimulus conditions is an advantage only with moderately complex tasks that allow for a range of different component sequences to perform the task. However, since this includes all but the simplest of human activities, variations in the effectiveness of sequence selection is likely an important factor in many types of skill. Welford has even suggested that "the efficiency of strategy is the mark and measure of what we call skill (1980, p. 107)."

One illustration of skill relying upon sequence selection may be the expert personnel manager who is sensitive to the varying needs and talents of the people under his or her super-vision. Each employee can be considered a different stimulus situation, with the different personnel strategies representing alternative processing sequences. The most skilled manager is the one best able to match management strategy to particular employee in order to maximize total output with minimum expenditure of resources.

A concrete example of this phenomenon was provided by Charness (1979, 1983) in studies of skilled bridge players. Charness found that more skilled players selected better bids than less skilled players even when confronted with unfamiliar configurations of cards. Because the bridge hands were novel to all players, the advantage of the skilled player is presumably attributable to better evaluation and more appropriate matching of alternative actions to potential consequences. This phenomenon of increased skill associated with better solution selection was also confirmed in domain of chess by Charness (1981) and Holding and Reynolds (1982).

Sequence Assembly   In addition to the executive features of sequence repertoire and sequence selection, experts in a given domain are probably more effective than novices at

devising and constructing optimal sequences of processing
components. These novel strategies might provide unique solutions
to familiar problems, or may lead to greatly improved levels
of achievement by overcoming previous performance limitations.
In either case, the person better able to assemble and integrate
unique processing sequences will often have an advantage over
someone with less of this assembly ability.

The ability to assemble new sequences of processing components
is likely to be an important factor in skills emphasizing
creative and innovative activities. For example, a highly
developed ability to organize and integrate simple components
(i.e., words or line segments) into unique combinations may
be a critical feature in the success of many writers and artists.
Even with much simpler tasks, the construction of more efficient
procedures for executing repetitive activities is likely to
be an important factor contributing to skilled performance.
For example, Anderson (1982) has identified assembly processes
of composition (compilation) and proceduralization (specific
parameterization) that would both lead to more efficient performance of a variety of skills through the development of what
could be considered new sequences of processing operations.
Book (1908) referred to a similar concept many years ago when
he suggested that one of the things acquired with practice
on a task was the 'shortcircuiting' of the processing elements.

It is difficult to identify a laboratory-based example
of skill-related differences in sequence assembly because
most of the research has focused on changes with experience
in the performance of the same processing sequence. Moreover,
in order to interpret the results of studies examining the
efficiency of assembling new processing sequences one must
pay careful attention to the possibility of both negative
and positive transfer attributable to previously learned sequences. Nevertheless, it seems reasonable to speculate that
efficient construction of effective strategies is correlated
with expertise in many ability domains.

Working Memory Capacity   To many contemporary researchers,
the most plausible general mechanism responsible for individual

differences in information-processing effectiveness is the size of working memory. As discussed in the previous chapter, working memory is postulated to be the place where all processing operations are executed, and in which the intermediate results of prior operations are deposited. A smaller store for maintaining currently active information would be a handicap for most processing activities since more swapping operations would be needed to and from long-term memory, which would increase both the time of the activity and the risk of some type of error.   The size of working memory could therefore influence the efficiency of a variety of tasks, and might be an important determinant of many types of individual differences.

However, it seems unlikely that experience with a particular task results in an increase in an individual's basic working memory capacity, but instead probably improves the efficiency with which information may be coded in that limited-capacity system. For example, what might be considered a classic finding in the recent literature on expertise is that experts and novices differ much more in their memory for material meaningful in the relevant domain than for other types of material. Chase and Simon (1973), Chi (1978), De Groot (1978), Frey and Adesman (1976), and Lane and Robertson (1979) have all reported that expert chess players are superior to less proficient chess players in the recall of meaningful (i.e., plausible) configurations of chess pieces, but are equivalent in their recall of random, nonmeaningful, configurations. Similar patterns of results have been reported in the field of bridge (e.g., Charness, 1979; Engle & Bukstel, 1978), music (Halpern & Bower, 1982), the game of Go (Reitman, 1976), and with technical electronic drawings (Egan & Schwartz, 1979). Because the experts were superior only with the material that was meaningful for their domain, their advantage could not be attributed to a superior working memory capacity. Instead it appears that the amount and organization of information possessed by the individual affects the efficiency with which material can be entered and retrieved from the long-term storage system.

<u>Knowledge Representation</u>   In recent years a number of

researchers have hypothesized that expert problem solvers
are expert in part because they construct superior internal
representations of the initial problem (e.g., Chase & Chi,
1981; Chi, Feltovich, & Glaser, 1981; Chi & Glaser, 1980;
Glaser, 1980; Greeno, 1980; Simon & Simon, 1978; Voss, Tyler,
& Yengo, 1983). By embodying major principles and important
relationships among relevant task elements, these high-quality
representations are likely to suggest appropriate action sequences
in progressing towards the ultimate task solution.

The form in which information is represented internally
may also have important implications for a variety of perceptual
and cognitive tasks. For example, imagining alternative perspectives of a physical object is likely to be much easier
when the object is internally represented in a spatial rather
than verbal form. Hatano and Osawa (1983) have also demonstrated
that mental abacus experts apparently represent digits in
a visual-spatial format, which may contribute to their amazing
proficiency at mental computation. The flexibility of the
representation, or the appropriateness with which representations
are matched to the situation, may therefore be a distinguishing
characteristic of skill in certain domains.

Knowledge Quality In some activity domains experts may
be distinguished from novices more by the type or accuracy
of their knowledge than by its sheer quantity. The skilled
individuals may have more finely differentiated information,
or their information may be more veridical than that of their
less-skilled counterparts. For example, Lesgold (1984) has
reported that expert radiologists compared to novices have
more specialized (i.e., refined and elaborated) schemata for
diagnosis, and more precise localization of anatomical structures.

Higher-quality knowledge is particularly likely when
performance is dependent upon highly accurate conditional
probabilities relating actions to consequent external states.
Many of the remarkable competence of skilled equipment operators
may be due to their more accurate knowledge of the capabilities
and limitations of their equipment. Indeed, some writers
have speculated that one concomitant of skill is a detailed

internal model or mental picture of the dynamics of the mechanical system developed with experience on the system (e.g., Kelley, 1968). Master chefs also probably owe some of their expertise to a finely developed sensitivity to the eventual taste consequences of varying amounts of spices and seasonings. Moreover, a greater quality of knowledge about geometrical relationships on the billiard table may be a major factor in the skill of superb pool players.

Knowledge Quantity Perhaps the most intuitively obvious characteristic of skilled individuals is the quantity of their domain-specific knowledge. Experts generally possess much more of the information relevant to their particular specialty than do novices, and it is difficult to overestimate the importance of this greater quantity of knowledge. The larger information base may contain more details about problem states and action consequences, or might simply consist of greater awareness of the interrelations of task elements or problem states. In either case, individuals with the larger store of information will be in a better position to handle nearly all aspects of information processing, including the assembly, compilation, and execution of sequences of processing components.

A series of studies by Voss and his colleagues (Chiesi, Spilich, & Voss, 1979; Spilich, Vesonder, Chiesi, & Voss, 1979; Voss, Vesonder, & Spilich, 1980) have provided an illustration of some of the advantages of increased knowledge in the domain of baseball. College students selected on the basis of high or low knowledge of baseball were asked to perform a variety of comprehension, generation, and recall tasks involving material relevant to baseball. The results indicated that, compared to low-knowledge people, the high-knowledge people: (a) were more sensitive to critical details in recognition; (b) had better preservation of sequence order; (c) were better at anticipating future states; and (d) had superior recall of baseball information but not other information of comparable complexity. It therefore appears that knowledge quantity, providing that it is organized into integrated structures, has a substantial influence on many aspects of information processing.

Superior knowledge quantity is likely to be a factor
contributing to skill in all semantically-rich domains (cf.,
Simon, 1979). This obviously includes all intellectual tasks,
most professional-level activities, and a large number of
miscellaneous vocational and avocational pursuits. Quantity
of knowledge is probably also important even in relatively
simple pattern recognition tasks where much of the skill is
based on knowing the particular aspects of the stimulus to
which one should attend. An example of this is the finding
by Elstein, Shulman, and Sprafka (1978) and by Sterling (1982)
that skilled physicians request more meaningful symptom information
in a diagnostic situation than do novices. Expert wine tasters
able to make subtle distinctions along dimensions not even
recognized by most non-experts may be another illustration
of this phenomenon. Simply knowing what is relevant in a
given task may be a large determinant of successful performance
on that task. Moreover, unless one has extracted the appropriate
information from the task environment, all further processes
concerned with that information may be meaningless.

<u>Knowledge Organization</u> It is almost a truism that information
is useless if it is not accessible, and expertise may be at
least partially attributable to a knowledge organization that
facilitates the retrievability of relevant information. Welford
expressed this view in the following manner:

> Probably the most important and beneficial effects
> of experience lie not in the widening of factual
> knowledge, but in its coordination and ordering...An
> important part of this process seems to consist
> of recognizing ways in which groups of objects and
> sequences of events hang together...Events of both
> perception and action are thereby "coded" into larger
> units, and, by dealing with the codes as unitary
> wholes instead of with the individual details summed
> up in them, the "mental load" upon the subject is
> lightened (Welford, 1962, p. 338).

In a later source, Welford (1963) elaborated these ideas by

suggesting that

> ...dealing in larger units of data and action makes
> possible a wider grasp and broader scale of concept-
> ualization ...(which leads to)...breadth of vision
> and depth of understanding (Welford, 1963, p. 121).

It seems clear that improved organization of one's knowledge
may be a major factor in many forms of expertise.

Experts appear to have their domain-specific knowledge
organized according to structural principles or functional
relationships which allows more efficient and deeper comprehension
of intermediate problem states. Johnson, Duran, Hassebrock,
Moller, Prietula, Feltovich, and Swanson (1981) have suggested
that an important characteristic of experienced medical diagnosticians is a hierarchically-organized and well-differentiated
system of disease knowledge efficiently 'tuned' to the symptoms
of most diseases, and which can then be used to facilitate
the diagnostic process. Superior organization may also be
a factor enabling more efficient 'chunking' of information
into working memory, and thus contribute to higher levels
of performance in a great variety of domain-relevant activities.

A qualitative difference in knowledge organization as
a function of expertise has been demonstrated in sorting and
recall tasks by Chi, Feltovich, and Glaser (1982) in a study
of physicists, by Sterling (1982) in a comparison of radiologists
and non-radiologists, by Schoenfeld and Herrmann (1982) in
an examination of mathematicians, and by Adelson (1981, 1984)
in studies of computer programmers. In all cases the experts
grouped domain-specific information according to semantic
or 'deep-structure' principles, while novices organized according
to more superficial 'surface' features. These results can
be interpreted as suggesting that the domain-relevant knowledge
of experts is organized in a more meaningful, principle-based,
manner than that of novices.

Arousal Level   It is sometimes said that the true mark
of a master athlete is that he or she rises to the occasion
with what seems to be a super-human effort. A heightened
level of arousal is probably responsible for many of these

impressive athletic accomplishments, as well as contributing
to the very intense periods of concentration characteristic
of masters in many intellectual activities. Still unclear
is whether the effects of arousal are best conceived as specific
to a few tasks or processing operations, or more general with
pervasive effects throughout the system.

Paradoxically, the greater efficiency of information-
processing associated with expertise may also lead to a reduction
in the level of arousal needed to maintain satisfactory performance
on a given task. Ahearn and Beatty (1979) presented an example
of this type of relationship in an analysis of the magnitude
of pupil dilation (often used as an index of arousal level)
in college students of high and lower intellectual ability
while they were solving mental arithmetic problems. As expected
by an arousal interpretation, pupil size increased for both
groups of subjects with increases in the difficulty of the
problems. However, there was a smaller increase across all
three levels of problem difficulty for the more intelligent
subjects. Because intelligence might be considered analogous
to mental skill, these results can be interpreted as suggesting
that the more skilled individuals exhibited lower levels of
arousal during the performance of the tasks than did the less
skilled individuals.

Attentional Capacity It is possible that some types
of individual differences are due to the better-performing
individuals possessing a greater capacity for attentive processing
of information than lower-performing individuals. Because
attentional capacity is presumed to be quite general, a smaller
amount of attentional capacity should result in the superiority
being evident on all information-processing activities which
place a demand on attention. Skill is defined as task-specific
proficiency, however, and therefore it is unlikely that expertise
is associated with alterations in the amount of attention
capacity generally available to the individual. Increased
efficiency and automaticity of tasks within the domain of
expertise may reduce the attention demands of the relevant
activities and thus free more for the performance of concurrent

tasks, but it seems unreasonable to suggest that experience increases an individual's general attentional capacity.

Basic Operation Time   The final characteristic of information processing to be considered is the basic time for elementary operations within the nervous system. If, like in a computer, all processing operations are executed at multiples of the basic cycle time, individuals differing in their rate of processing would likely produce varying levels of performance even if all other aspects of information processing were identical. As is the case with working memory size and attentional capacity, however, a difference in cycle time would likely be manifested in a great variety of tasks and not restricted to a single activity domain as would be required if this were a concomitant of practice-related skill.   Moreover, although skill-related differences in other aspects of processing might have consequences similar to a reduced basic operation time (e.g., improved component or sequence efficiency), experience seems unlikely to modify an individual's general rate of processing information.

Can Aging be Characterized as Lack of Expertise?

One of the reasons for examining the effects of experience and expertise in a monograph concerned with cognitive aging was to determine whether, at a qualitative level, the (predominantly positive) effects of experience were similar to the (largely negative) effects of aging.   A discovery that the same configuration of information-processing differences served to distinguish novices from experts as older adults from young adults would be consistent, although certainly not conclusive, evidence for the disuse interpretation of age differences in cognition.

Unfortunately the anecdotal and formal evidence surveyed in the preceding sections suggests that this type of configurational comparison will not be feasible, at least at an abstract level, because effects of skill and expertise appear to be evident in nearly all aspects of information processing that have been identified.   Without a clearly defined pattern of differential effects of experience, an experience-based analogy could be found for age differences in virtually any aspect

of information processing. The strategy of comparing configurations of skill effects and age effects may still be possible
within certain domains if the skill effects can be localized
in specific characteristics of information processing. However,
this will require multivariate comparisons (in order to allow
evaluation of more than one information-processing aspect)
of exactly the same task at several levels of practice, and
in two or more age groups. Few, if any, studies of this type
are yet available and thus this approach to investigating
the disuse hypothesis of age-related cognitive impairment
must await further research.

Conceptualizing the Change Process

A second reason for considering the effects of experience
in a monograph on aging was to explore the possibility that
the change mechanisms responsible for converting novices into
experts are similar to those which occur over the adult lifespan.
An obvious prerequisite for this type of analysis is an adequate
understanding of how skill or expertise is acquired. However,
before attempting to review some of the speculations about
the nature of skill acquisition, it is necessary to delimit
the range of discussion so as not to attempt to cover all
aspects of learning. Skill and expertise can clearly be considered
to be end products of learning, but it is neither practical
nor desirable to try to examine the entire field of learning
from this perspective. Instead we will simply focus on the
major mechanisms proposed in the literature on skill acquisition
to account for the transition from novice to expert levels
of performance.

One of the most influential descriptions of skill learning
was by Fitts (1964) who made a distinction among three phases
of skill acquisition -- cognitive, associative, and autonomous. More recently, Anderson (1982) has elaborated this
distinction and expressed the dominant operations within each
phase in information-processing terminology. The first phase
involves a sequence of information-processing components conceptualized verbally, in the form of declarative propositions.
This is where the task is understood and the individual identifies

information-processing components necessary for the performance of the task.   At least in the domain of motor skills, however, the understanding is 'in the mind and not the muscles' and therefore performance in the cognitive phase is generally slow, tentative, and often inaccurate or imprecise.

The second phase consists of translating the verbal or declarative knowledge of the task into a sequence of action processes or procedures. Fitts (1964) called this the associative phase because it involves the association of previously independent procedures into a single integrated sequence.   These procedures are initially executed in a slow interpretive fashion, but with practice the sequences become progressively more efficient by restructuring and short-circuiting of the constituent processes.

The third and final phase in Fitts' categorization of skill learning is the autonomous phase in which the sequences become increasingly automatic and independent of conscious direction or attention.   In terms of a computer metaphor, the task-specific programs that were constructed and debugged in the associative phase now function as they are compiled rather than executed in a step-by-step interpretive manner. After sufficient practice, these autonomous procedural sequences may even serve as the units in the construction of more complex activities, thereby facilitating the development of hierarchically organized patterns of complex behavior.   The importance of achieving progressively more abstract levels of control or understanding in a problem domain was recognized many years ago in the pioneering work of Bryan and Harter (1899), and has remained a key factor in nearly all conceptualizations of skill since that time.

What parallels might be drawn between processes of aging and processes of skill acquisition? The lack of more detail in the characterization of how skill in general is acquired clearly limits the number of hypotheses that can be generated about change mechanisms associated with aging, but at least two possibilities can be identified. One is that processing sequences may be 'decompiled,' and revert back into a more primitive interpreted mode of performance.   The following

statement of Eliot at the age of 84 reported by Miles (1933)
is an example of how previously routine and unconscious activities
may require more attention with increased age:

> If I lift a glass of water I must now keep watch
> on it or the glass may slip from my hand. A few
> years ago the hand itself would entirely take care
> of such a matter (Miles, 1933, p. 120).

A second hypothesis for age-related changes suggested
from an analogy with skill acquisition is that processing
sequences may become 'unassembled' with increased age. That
is, portions of a processing sequence may flow smoothly, but
there may be occasional hesitations or pauses which might
suggest that the 'glue' holding the components together is
weakening or disintegrating with age.

Both of these suggestions imply that aging results in
a loss of behavioral organization. This is an intriguing
idea, and would lead to the expectation that the most organized
or complex behavior would be most vulnerable to the effects
of aging, an expectation which has largely been confirmed,
as we will see in Chapter 7. The major problem with this
characterization is that it is only descriptive, and offers
no explanation as to why or how such behavioral disorganization
might have occurred. That is, even if the effects of aging
can be accurately characterized as a loss of behavioral organization, we would not be able to explain these aging effects
unless fundamental mechanisms responsible for the organization
and disorganization can be identified. In this respect, it
appears that there is presently little advantage of attempting
to incorporate the change mechanisms developed in the field
of skill and expertise into proposals designed to explain
cognitive aging phenomena.

Importance of Experience in Age Comparisons

The preceding sections have demonstrated that the effects
of experience are widespread and not easily localized in a
particular aspect of information processing. Because experiential
consequences are not only extensive, but nearly always positive
in direction, they can be summarized by the function illustrated

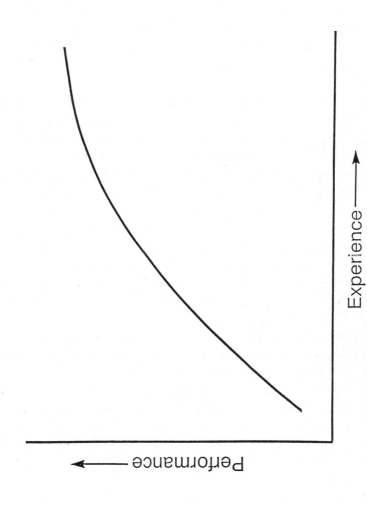

Figure 5.1 Hypothesized function relating performance to experience.

in Figure 5.1. That is, performance is expected to improve montonically with increased experience on a given activity, although probably at a negatively accelerated rate.

Now consider what would happen if the experience function is superimposed upon a function indicating declining proficiency with increased age. As illustrated in Figure 5.2, the specific level of performance would be nearly impossible to predict because of the enormous number of possible combinations produced by different ages of initiation of the experience and different durations of the experience. An additional complicating factor completely ignored in this diagram is the possibility that the efficiency of learning varies across the lifespan such that the slope of the experience function depends upon the age at which the experience begins. It is clear that the combination of age-related declines and experience-related improvements is unlikely to result in simple patterns of performance.

Recognition of the joint effects of aging and experience has led several writers to argue that neither age nor experience is sufficient by itself to predict an individual's competence in many abilities. For example, McFarland asserted that:

> ...one of the most important questions in the field
> of job placement and aging is as follows: "When
> in the aging process is physiological and psychological
> deterioration no longer compensated for by past
> experience?" (McFarland, 1956, p. 235).

This question obviously cannot be answered in the abstract, but to the extent that older adults continue to benefit from experience, one would expect the fact that experience is generally positively correlated with increased age to favor the older adults in many situations. Welford (1958) has suggested this relation between age and experience is responsible for the observation that increased age is often associated with wisdom and good judgment because their extensive experience in certain matters has allowed them to have ready access to an extensive, highly organized, body of knowledge.

While Figure 5.2 illustrates that the mixture of age

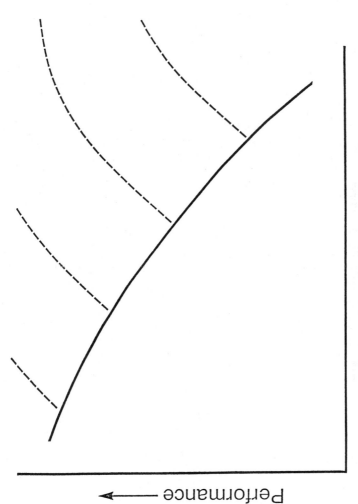

Age/Experience ⟶

Performance ⟵

Figure 5.2 Illustration of possible consequences if an incremental experience-performance function is superimposed on a decremental age-performance function. Notice that virtually any level of performance might result.

and experience may lead to virtually any relation between age and performance, it is important to recognize that expertise in any given domain requires an enormous commitment of time and energy. This means that there will necessarily be only a limited number of ability domains in which a given individual can be considered an expert. With increased age and experience people can therefore be considered to have become selective experts, even though as novices in other domains their levels of ability may have declined. Young adults because of their limited opportunities for acquiring expertise are probably experts in very few domains, and perhaps only in the area of academic skills (which, possibly not coincidentally, most resemble many of the tasks used in the laboratory). However, their novice levels of performance are presumably quite competent.

This selective expertise notion is similar to ideas of Baltes, Dittmann-Kohli, and Dixon (1984), Baltes and Willis (1982), Birren and Morrison (1961), and Denney (1984), and was popularized by Cattell (1971) in his investment theory of intelligence. According to Cattell, crystallized intelligence is the trustee of the gains from the investment of fluid intelligence in specific domains.

The basic premise of the selective expertise concept is that the relation between performance and chronological age will vary with the amount of experience people at each age have had exercising the relevant ability. An important implication of this proposal is that meaningful reflections of 'basic' or 'pure' aging processes must either be based on novice levels of performance, or great care must be taken to ensure that experience is equated across age groups. To the extent that cumulative experience is allowed to vary with age, it is inevitable that complicated and confusing developmental trends will be obtained (cf., Birren & Morrison, 1961; Cattell, 1963; Horn, 1975; Horn & Donaldson, 1980; Thorndike, Bregman, Tilton, & Woodyard, 1928; Welford, 1958).

How can experience be equated across individuals? There is no simple answer to this question because of the impracticality of rigorously controlling life experiences, and because the

effects of experience have been demonstrated to be ubiquitious,
and evident in nearly all aspects of information processing.
However, experience can be expected to have a major influence
on tasks which involve substantial amounts of previously acquired
knowledge.   It may therefore be unreasonable to expect to
obtain accurate reflections of developmental changes in cognition
with tasks in which increased age is associated with vastly
greater opportunities for acquiring the relevant knowledge.

     Some estimates of experience-independent cognitive proficiency
might be derived by examining the rate of increase in cumulative
knowledge at different ages.   That is, rather than relying
upon the absolute amount of information available at each
age, one could focus on the rate of growth of information
as a function of age. Since knowledge is presumably cumulative,
the function relating age to knowledge will not be negative,
but the rate of increase for each additional period of exposure
might vary across ages.   Unfortunately, two problems with
this procedure limit its usefulness. These are that meaningful
comparisons depend upon the assumptions: (a) that the processes
of acquisition are independent of the current level of knowledge;
and (b) that the opportunities for acquisition of new knowledge
remain constant.   The first assumption does not appear plausible
because the development of superior organization, which occurs
with experience, is likely to facilitate the ease of subsequent
acquisition.   The second assumption can also be questioned
since the occupational specialization and gradual narrowing
of interests which often accompany increased age will tend
to restrict exposure to new sources of information.   There
are clearly individuals who continually seek new stimulation,
and age comparisons in acquisition rate might be possible
with samples of this type, but in the population at large
it is probably the case that the opportunities for new knowledge
become increasingly more limited with age.

     In light of these considerations, it is perhaps most
meaningful to examine aging effects on basic capacities only
on tasks which can be presumed to be minimally influenced
by experience, either because the material is novel, or so

simple and common that it is highly overlearned by virtually
everyone in the culture. This conclusion is in striking contrast
to Charness's suggestion that:

> To provide valid generalizations about aging, it
> is necessary to use the tasks that people engage
> in on a day to day basis (Charness, 1982, p. 22).

A difference in perspective is probably responsible for these
different claims in that Charness was apparently interested
in maximizing ecological validity, while the primary concern
here is with the nature and cause of age differences in basic
or elementary processes.

A variety of terminology has been proposed to characterize
the distinction between abilities thought to be independent
of, or dependent upon, experience, e.g., ability versus achievement, process versus product, and potential versus realized,
but the fluid versus crystallized dichotomy proposed by Cattell
(1963, 1971) and Horn (e.g., 1970, 1978, 1980, 1982a; Horn
& Cattell, 1966, 1967) is the best known and has the greatest
amount of empirical evidence. According to Cattell:

> fluid ability...is due to an influence present and
> operative at the time of the experiment, whereas
> crystallized ability has a form determined by, and
> representing, history (Cattell, 1963, p. 5).

As one would expect from the preceding arguments, increased
age has been demonstrated to result in an increase in measures
reflecting crystallized abilities, but to be associated with
a decrease in measures reflecting fluid abilities (e.g., Horn
& Cattell, 1966, 1967; Horn, Donaldson, & Engstrom, 1981).
Although logical considerations about the confounding of age
and experience motivated the present concern, whereas theoretical
speculations supported by empirical patterns of correlations
justified the Horn and Cattell proposal, the contrast between
fluid and crystallized abilities seems to capture the intended
distinction and thus it will be used in the present context.
That is, the focus in the remaining chapters will be on the
nature and causes of age-related differences in several forms
of fluid cognitive abilities. In particular, we will attempt

to investigate reasons for the age-related declines in three
domains concerned with memory abilities, perceptual-spatial
abilities, and abstract reasoning abilities.

It is critical to point out that the decision to concentrate
only on measures thought to be relatively free of experiential
influences is based on a desire to examine presumably basic
aging processes, and not because of a belief that such measures
provide the best or most valid means of assessing cognitive
functioning and intellectual ability. In fact, a strong argument
can be made that fluid abilities decrease in importance with
age as one's occupation becomes fixed and interests are channeled
in specific directions such that cumulative knowledge plays
an increasingly greater role in one's activities.

It is also important to note that it is not assumed that
practice or specific experience has no effect on performance
of fluid ability tests. Rather, it is postulated that abilities
assessed by tests of this type are typically not differentially
exercised by members of one age group or another. This assumption
would obviously be challenged if it were discovered that different
patterns of life experiences substantially altered performance
on tests of this type, or that members of certain age groups
benefit considerably more than members of other groups with
specific practice on the abilities.

Summary

Increased experience has been found to exert beneficial
effects on nearly every aspect of information processing that
has been examined. While the pervasiveness of the effects
offers little basis for comparing lack of practice with increased
age on specific processes, the fact that age is generally
associated with greater experience means that many age-related
declines may be obscured by the confounding contribution of
differential experience. This suggests that an accurate appraisal
of the effects of aging on cognitive abilities requires that
only measures be examined which can be reasonably argued to
be minimally influenced by experience. However, it is important
to emphasize that the focus is on cognitive abilities and
not cognitive capabilities, with the latter based on the inter-

action of current abilities and cumulative knowledge. The
relation between age and cognitive capability is not well-
documented, but it is certainly not identical with the age-
cognitive ability relationship, and cognitive capability might
well be presumed to either increase or remain stable during
the adult working years for many activity domains.

General Methodological Issues

The introductory chapters on theory were deliberately placed before the current one on methodology to emphasize that theoretical issues should dictate one's methods rather than vice versa. An anecdote often related in courses on experimental methodology clearly describes the absurdity of method or tool determining issue or product. It seems that a policeman encountered an inebriated citizen crawling around on the front porch of his house, and when asked what he was doing the drunk replied "looking for the keys to my house." The policeman joined in the search, but when he too was unable to find the keys, the drunk was asked whether he was certain that he had lost the keys on the porch. The reply was "No, I lost them out on the street, but there is no light out there and so I am looking on the porch where there is light." Of course, the point of this story is that one should not be so enamored of a particular methodological procedure or technique because of its convenience, simplicity, or elegance that the focus on major issues is lost.

Experimentally-oriented psychologists are sometimes criticized for substituting method for substance in this manner by focusing on very minute procedural details to the neglect of consequential issues. This criticism may frequently be justified, but it is at least as bad to think that the quality of one's answers is independent of the methods used to ask the questions. Whether we like it or not, methodological factors are an essential part of research and need to be considered as much in the evaluation of research as in its design and execution.

It is therefore useful to examine a number of general methodological issues before proceeding to the discussion of the current theoretical position and evaluation of the evidence relevant to it. Several of these issues pertain to the difficulties of interpreting age-by-treatment interactions, which are among the most desired outcomes in research on psycho-

logical aging. These problems tend to pervade many different
domains and thus they will be discussed in the present chapter
instead of separately, and redundantly, in the various chapters
devoted to specific content areas.

It is important to emphasize that issues related to identifying the true cause of age-related phenomena are of only
minor interest in this context because categorization of a
variable as causal or extraneous is dependent upon one's theoretical perspective. Theoretical issues of the type discussed
in the following chapter clearly have methodological implications,
but we will not be concerned with those topics in the present
context.

Representativeness of Samples

An issue invariably raised whenever one describes research
with individual difference variables such as age is how can
it be determined that the behavior one observes in various
groups is determined by the variable of interest, and not
by other potentially relevant variables. The answer to this
question, at least for the variable of age in which random
assignment of individuals to groups is impossible, is that
it cannot be determined with absolute certainty. Because
the members of different age groups are 'placed' in these
groups on other than a random basis, they can easily differ
on a number of variables besides age itself. Since it is
obviously impractical to attempt to equate intact groups on
all conceivable variables, other considerations must dictate
which variables need to be controlled and which can safely
be ignored. For example, examination of the prior literature
will indicate which variables are likely to influence the
phenomenon, and should either be controlled or systematically
manipulated. One's theoretical perspective will further delimit
the range of potentially relevant variables by suggesting
those which should be held constant and those which might
be worth incorporating as a manipulated factor by controlled
variation.

Another more limited aspect of representativeness concerns
the extent to which the individuals in each age group exhibit

performance consistent with that expected in the overall population. One way this question can be phrased is, are the
data of the current samples typical of that reported in other
studies in the past? To the extent that they are, one has
evidence that the samples in the study are very similar to
what one would expect from the general population, or at least
the population easily accessible to psychological researchers.
In this respect, therefore, the samples in each age group
can be considered equally representative of their respective
populations. Reference to the normative trends would also
allow the relative representativeness of samples from different
studies to be determined, thereby providing a basis for evaluating
reasons for potential discrepancies across studies. For example,
if two studies produce contradictory results and one is found
to have absolute levels of performance markedly different
from the values reported in other studies while the other
has quite typical results, it may be reasonable to infer that
an unusual sample or research participants contributed to
the inconsistency.

One technique that could be used to assess this aspect
of representativeness is to administer a standard task in
each aging study in addition to the tasks of primary interest.
The standard task would have to be specific to a given ability
domain, but once identified, it could be incorporated in all
studies in that domain. Salthouse and Kausler (1985) listed
four criteria for such a standard task: (a) at least moderate
reliability; (b) quick and easy administration to allow adequate
time for the primary task; (c) suitability for the development
of age-specific norms based on results from large representative
samples; and (d) intrinsic relationship with a variety of
performance measures in the ability domain of interest.

In many respects, the most important criterion is the
last one, which can be considered equivalent to the concept
of validity. Unless performance on the standard task is known
to be related to the dependent variable, there may be little
value in reporting the scores of the samples from the various
age groups on that task. To illustrate, many researchers

commonly report the scores of their participants on psychometric variables such as score on a standardized vocabulary test, or on demographic variables such as years of education. These data do serve to describe the gross characteristics of the samples, but because they are of unknown relevance for most cognitive tasks they lack validity in specific domains. It is therefore quite possible for two studies, each comprised of samples at each age group having comparable values on these psychometric or demographic variables, to yield widely discrepant age trends on two slightly different versions of a particular task. Without more information about the comparability of the samples on dimensions relevant to performance in the context of interest, it will be impossible to determine whether any differences in results were attributable to characteristics of the procedure or to characteristics of the samples.

A more satisfactory approach to the problem of represent- ativeness is the use of a limited number of standard tasks deliberately selected to have empirically-established relevance to many variables within the given domain. Because the standard task provides a common, and relevant, basis for comparison across studies, the investigator is in a position to directly determine whether differential representativeness was a factor contributing to any discrepancies in the observed pattern of results. Candidates for standard tasks have been the score on the digit symbol subtest from the Wechsler Adult Intelligence Test in the domain of speeded performance (Salthouse, 1985), and a version of the paired-associate memory task in the domain of memory (Salthouse & Kausler, 1985).

Reliance upon standard tasks is obviously not an ideal solution to the problem of ensuring representativeness of one's samples, but it does provide a means of establishing that different investigators are dealing with the same phenomenon, at least with respect to the comparability of the samples. The question of whether the people who typically participate in research projects concerned with aging and cognitive processes are equally representative of their respective age groups is more complicated, and cannot be easily answered with this,

and perhaps with any other, technique. However there are
some grounds for believing that age trends may often be underestimated because the members of the older groups in many
research studies are frequently healthier, better educated,
and more intelligent (at least in certain dimensions) than
their age peers who do not participate in such studies. It
is still not clear whether the degree of selectivity is greater
among older adult subjects than among young adult subjects,
who are often college students, but it is certainly possible
that somewhat misleading estimates of the true magnitude of
age relationships in cognitive functioning may be emerging
from current studies.

Statistical Power

Since there is enormous variability across people in
nearly all behavioral characteristics, researchers in behavioral
science frequently have to rely upon statistical inference
to establish that the phenomena under investigation are not
merely attributable to chance fluctuations. However, in order
to use statistical techniques appropriately, one must ensure
that conditions are reasonable for accurately distinguishing
between systematic and unsystematic variance. This is the
issue of statistical power, and it has several aspects relevant
to research on aging. The three topics discussed in this
section concern the strengths of the independent variable
manipulations, the stability of the performance estimates
within each age group, and the precision of the measurements
derived from each individual subject.

The concern about the strength of effects of the primary
variable can be easily illustrated by assuming that the overall
age trend is for performance on a given measure to decline
at a rate of approximately 5% per decade. If the precision
of measurement is limited to 20%, (e.g., the combination of
within-subject and between-subject variability results in
a 95% confidence interval of plus or minus 20% the observed
value), it would be very difficult to detect a difference
between age groups separated by only 10 years. On the other
hand, age groups separated by 50 years should be easily distin-

guished with reasonably sized samples. Because the expected
magnitude of the difference between age groups is 50% with
a separation of 50 years but only 5% with a separation of
10 years, the latter contrast will generally be more powerful,
and consequently have a greater chance of detecting any differences
that might exist, than the former. It is primarily considerations
of this type which have led most researchers with limited
research resources (i.e., time, money, subject availability)
to rely on extreme-group research designs in which a group
of older adults is contrasted with a group of young adults.

The strength aspect of power is also important in attempting
to assess the relative contributions of two or more factors
on a particular dependent variable. For example, Botwinick
and Arenberg (1976) have criticized certain studies by Schaie
and his colleagues on the grounds that the factors being compared
had disparate strengths, i.e., the range of historical time
was only 7 years compared to a chronological age range of
50 years. Actually, this criticism is valid only if one assumes
that time has the same meaning for the factor (presumably
biocultural environmental change) indexed by historical time,
and for the factor (presumably maturation) indexed by chronological
age (cf., Chapter 7). Without further information about the
relative slopes of the time-variable functions, however, it
is probably safest to assume that the functions are comparable,
and thus to attempt to equate the intervals used to index
the two factors.

Perhaps the aspect of statistical power most familiar
to many researchers is that related to sample size -- that
is, the number of individuals required in each age group to
reduce effective variability to a level where there is a reasonable
probability (power) of detecting a difference between groups
if one actually existed. This aspect of power is widely recognized
at the current time, and is often documented by formal computations
of the likelihood of being able to detect a difference of
a given magnitude with the existing levels of variability
and sample sizes.

Another related aspect of statistical power deals with

the appropriateness of the power for the intended purpose. In many studies the researcher was content (probably implicitly rather than explicitly) with a level of power adequate to yield a reasonable probability of detecting a statistically significant age difference. Because the age differences in many performance variables are substantial, the precision of the measurement may have been quite low. This usually doesn't present problems for the original study, but it can be a difficulty in subsequent attempts at conducting quantitative meta-analyses where a greater degree of precision is desirable, or when one attempts to examine age differences among subsets defined on the basis of individual characteristics such as strategy usage. For example, if the average difference between a young and an old age group is 30 units of the dependent variable, the original investigator may be content with statistical power sufficient to have a moderately high probability of detecting a difference of 20 units. However, this rather gross assessment can be deceptive if a later researcher attempts to use that data to estimate parameters within each age group to a precision of 5 or 10 units.

This latter usage is becoming more prevalent in the efforts to obtain exact quantitative descriptions of the age functions for different variables. What is often ignored when using data in this manner is that while the statistical power may have been adequate to yield statistically significant differences between the groups, the interval for a given level of confidence around each value may still be extremely large. Members of a particular age group are not so homogeneous that they can be accurately described with a single measure of central tendency of the scores, and this is particularly true when there are relatively small samples (e.g., less than 30 individuals) available from each age category. Therefore if the meta-analyst treats the data as exact point values rather than as broad intervals, the mathematical descriptions could be quite misleading.

The problem with conducting analyses on subsets of the sample, e.g., only those individuals determined to have used a particular strategy, is that although the power to detect a difference may have been respectable for the entire sample, it will typically be quite low for the reduced sample. One obvious way to avoid this difficulty is to attempt to replicate with a larger sample any finding of no age differences in a small sample suspected to have low power.

A third aspect of statistical power concerns the reliability of the dependent measures. Stated simply, it is unrealistic to expect to be able to detect a difference between two groups if one does not have confidence that the same results would be obtained from a repetition of the test in the same individuals. Horn and Donaldson (1980) have considered the reliability issue so important, and neglected in cognitive aging research, that they suggested that:

> ...the conclusions of many studies should not be
> accepted because the evidence for reliability is
> not sufficient to support the claims on which the
> conclusions are based (Horn & Donaldson, 1980, p. 482).

These authors also pointed out that it is helpful to think of age effects in terms of the correlation between age (possibly coded dichotomously in a point-biserial correlation) and the variable of interest. In this manner it becomes obvious that the size of the correlation is limited by the reliability of the dependent variable, i.e., only the systematic variance is available for partitioning into segments related, and unrelated, to age. If the reliability of the measure is low, there will be little systematic variance and the best one could hope for would be small to moderate correlations with age.

There are at least three features that contribute to high reliability. One is unrestricted range of variation in that the magnitude of the correlation between two sets of scores is directly dependent upon the dispersion of each set of scores. Reliability is therefore likely to be lower in a homogeneous group of individuals than in a more heterogeneous group simply because the homogeneous sample has a smaller range of scores. This principle also operates in the opposite direction, however, in that reliability may be overestimated when data are collapsed across groups with different average levels of performance. Figure 6.1 illustrates that combining data in this fashion results in a moderately high, but artificially inflated, overall correlation between the two measurements even if there is no correlation within each group.

One possible strategy to avoid incorporating age effects into the estimates of measurement reliability is to use partial correlations in which the age variable has been statistically removed from the reliability coefficient. That is, since the reliability coefficient is a correlation between two scores, each of which is likely to be related to age, an estimate of the correlation independent of age could be obtained by partialling age out of the reliability coefficient. For instance, if age is correlated .7 with each of the two measures for a variable and they are correlated .7 with each other, the best estimate of reliability might not be .7, but instead .41, the correlation after partialling out the contribution of the age variable.

There is obviously a tradeoff between excessive homogeneity, which produces spuriously low estimates of reliability, and misleading heterogeneity, resulting from the incorporation of group differences into the measure's variability, but it is important to be sensitive to both types of distortions when interpreting estimates of reliability. Whenever possible, it is probably best to provide separate estimates of reliability for all dependent variables within each age grouping included in the study.

The second and third requirements for high reliability are stability of the phenomenon and consistency of its measurement. If the phenomenon is not stable and fluctuates markedly from one occasion to the next, it may yield low measurement reliability regardless of the sensitivity or consistency of the measurement (cf., Nesselroade, 1977). Examples often used to illustrate lack of stability are blood sugar level or body temperature over a period of hours. Even the most precise measurements of these characteristics will be unreliable if evaluated with test-retest or alternate-forms indexes of reliability since it is their nature to exhibit widely varying

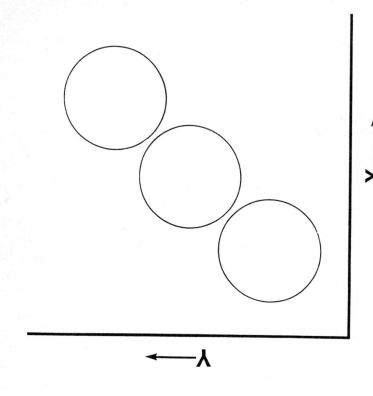

Figure 6.1 Illustration of how spurious correlations can result from the aggregation of data from groups with different mean levels on each variable.

levels. Behavioral measures may also have low stability,
particularly if the variable of interest is influenced by
the utilization of one of several alternative strategies,
and different strategies are employed in each encounter with
the task.

Another form of reliability assessment may be employed,
e.g., the split-half or concurrent reliability technique,
but it will still be the case that the phenomenon is inherently
unstable. A concurrent index of reliability may therefore
be misleading when contrasting within-task correlations with
between-task correlations, and could result in inappropriate
conclusions about the reasons for low correlations across
different dependent measures. That is, since between-task
correlations are necessarily also across-time correlations,
it is desirable that the correlations used to assess the consistency of measurement within the same task also be across-time
in order to allow any potential instability of the phenomenon
to be manifested. This is especially the case when variations
in one's approach to the task, which could reasonably be expected
to change from one occasion to the next, are suspected to
affect the dependent variable. Even if the dependent variable
is internally consistent at a given time, one cannot infer
that an enduring, trait-like property of the individual is
being assessed because adoption of an alternative approach
to the task might result in quite different performance at
another time.

It is therefore argued that since the split-half form
of reliability is relatively insensitive to behavioral instability,
it fails to provide an appropriate basis for evaluating the
likelihood of obtaining similar results on a subsequent occasion.
Because this is often an implied comparison in assessing the
magnitude of correlations between two variables, it is recommended
that other forms of reliability assessment be used in which
there is a time interval between the two measurements which
corresponds at least approximately to the interval between
the measurements of different variables.

Measurement Equivalence

Another important methodological issue concerns the extent to which a variable reflects the same phenomenon in the same manner at all measurement occasions. There are at least two situations in which measurement equivalence can be called into question. One is when considerable time has elapsed either between measurements, or between the time at which different individuals received comparable experiences. It is sometimes suggested that the meaning of the variable may change across adulthood as interests, experience, and other features of the individual change. For example, a task designed to assess learning ability may truly reflect one's competence at acquiring new knowledge among adolescents and young adults because of the great variety of learning experiences recently received in the process of formal education. However, because older adults are typically far removed from the period of formal education, they may approach the task differently and perhaps view it as a puzzle-like game or even a disguised test of emotional stability. The meaning of one's score may therefore be influenced by the manner in which the task was perceived.

One method of addressing the question of measurement equivalence is by examination of the pattern of correlations between the dependent variable and a variety of other variables. To a certain extent it can be argued that the meaning of a measure is established by its pattern of correlations with other measures. The reasoning is essentially the same as that used in the assessment of construct validity in that the meaning of the construct is determined by its correlational pattern. In other words, the critical dependent measure (e.g., score on the test of learning ability) should be correlated with presumably similar measures (e.g., other scores of learning ability) and should not be correlated with presumably irrelevant measures (e.g., measures reflecting dimensions of personality). However, if this correlational pattern shifts from one age group to another it would suggest that the dependent variable may not reflect the same processes in each group. There are

apparently few situations where measurement equivalence across
the adult life span has been investigated in this manner,
but inspection of the correlational pattern is a fairly straightforward technique to employ whenever one suspects that the
meaning of one's measures might be different in different
age groups.

A second, less recognized, aspect of measurement equivalence
relates to the meaning of the score across the entire range
of the dependent variable.   The question here is whether the
same mechanisms are responsible for performance not simply
across different groups of subjects, but across different
levels of the dependent variable.   One possibility is that
a threshold mechanism exists which triggers a change in the
underlying processes when a specified level of performance
is achieved. In other words, at low levels of performance
one set of processes is used to perform the task, while at
higher levels a different set of processes is used. The development of reading speed might be an example of this type because
reading speed is initially limited by processes of letter
perception and identification that become relatively unimportant
at higher levels of skill.   Therefore even though the dependent
variable has ostensibly remained the same, its meaning, in
terms of the processes upon which it is based, may change
dramatically. This is likely to be a particularly severe problem
in aging studies when different groups of individuals are
performing at different levels of the dependent variable.
Other interpretation problems associated with non-equivalent
baseline levels of performance are discussed later in this
chapter.

The Process-Variable Relationship

The purpose of psychological research can be described
as attempting to understand the mechanisms or processes responsible
for behavioral activity.   Specific aspects of behavior are
isolated and measured under various conditions in the hopes
that they will be informative about the processes underlying
the relevant behavior.   An assumption generally implicit in
most behavioral research is that there is a simple linear

relationship between the magnitudes of the inferred psychological
process and the observed behavioral variable. In other words,
if a manipulation results in a behavioral change of X magnitude
in the relevant dependent variable, the change in the critical
internal process is assumed to be directly proportional to
X.

What is often not recognized is that it is only an assumption
that the process-variable function is linear, or even uniformly
monotonic. As Loftus (1978) clearly pointed out, there are
an enormous number of possibilities for the process-variable
function, and knowledge of the particular shape of the function
is critical for the proper interpretation of statistical interactions. Since a major methodological tool of gerontological
psychologists is the age-by-treatment interaction (where treatment
can refer to any type of contrast or manipulation present
in all age groups), the issue of the process-variable relationship
is of obvious relevance to researchers in the psychology of
aging. (See Labouvie, 1980, for additional discussion of
this topic, which he refers to as concept-metric inconsistency.)

The process-variable issue can be illustrated with the
aid of Figure 6.2, which portrays a hypothetical function
relating process along the abscissa to dependent variable
along the ordinate. Points A and B represent the familiar
case of a floor effect in the variable, while points E and
F indicate a ceiling effect. Obviously in both the floor
and ceiling situations the dependent variable is completely
insensitive to variations in the underlying process, but relative
degrees of insensitivity can occur throughout the entire range
of the dependent variable. In this respect, measurement floors
and ceilings can be considered special, and extreme, cases
of deviations from linearity or monotonicity in the functions
relating process to variable. For example, points B, C, D,
and E are nearly equally spaced along the process axis, but
they result in strikingly unequal differences along the dependent
variable axis. The difference in performance between C and
D is greater than that between D and E and between B and C,
even though the intervals along the process axis are all equal.

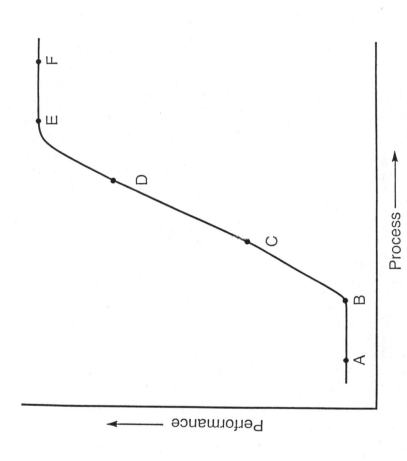

Figure 6.2 Schematic illustration of a process-variable relationship. The x-axis is assumed to represent progressively more reliance upon, or utilization of, the underlying psychological process, while the y-axis represents magnitude of the dependent variable used to assess performance.

The situation portrayed in Figure 6.2 is hypothetical, and
it may never be possible to obtain direct measures of the
process to allow functions such as these to be evaluated.
Nevertheless, it is important to realize that most psychological
research is based on the assumption that the relation between
the underlying process is not only monotonic, but uniformly
linear.   Since there is seldom any basis for verifying this
assumption, it is incumbent upon researchers to be cautious
in their inferences about underlying processes on the basis
of observed variations in the dependent variable. This warning
is particularly pertinent when making comparisons across age
groups because the various groups are likely to be performing
at different regions along the process-variable function.
If this is the case, a manipulation that produces a large
difference in one group (e.g., from C to D) and a small difference
in another group (e.g., from D to E), might still have comparable
effects on the underlying psychological process.   The point
of this discussion is that interactions of age and some manipulation can be unambiguously interpreted only by making largely
unverifiable assumptions that the process-variable function
is not only monotonic, but uniformly linear.

A second important issue related to process-variable
relationships is the extent to which the functions in different
age groups are comparable.   Figure 6.3 illustrates one manner
in which process-variable functions might differ in two groups
of individuals.   There are any number of reasons for differences in the functions, but one means by which the function
on the right could be produced is if a critical level of a
process is reached and it then ceases to produce variations
in the dependent variable. Because quite different levels
of the dependent variable could be produced in the two functions
with exactly the same difference along the process axis, there
is clearly a potential for grossly misleading inferences of
empirical interactions.

A distinction by Norman and Bobrow (1975a) between resource-
limited functions and data-limited functions is relevant in
this context.   In the data-limited region of the function,

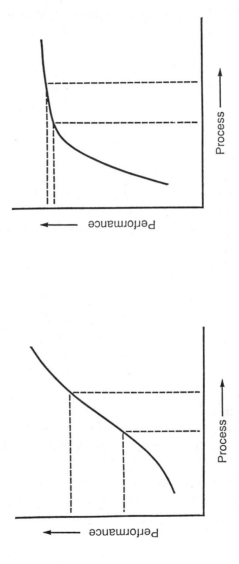

Figure 6.3 Illustration of possible differences in the nature of the function relating process to variable. Although the variation along the process dimension is equivalent in the two panels, strikingly different shifts in performance are produced because of the different process-variable functions.

which might be produced when sensory or memory defects limit
the quantity or quality of information available for processing,
variations in the process cease to have corresponding effects
on the dependent variable. Because increased age is often
associated with sensory and memory impairments, it is at least
conceivable that the process-variable functions in young and
old adults differ in the manner illustrated in Figure 6.3.
Regardless of the specific shape of each function, however,
it is clear that the validity of interpretations of age by
manipulation interactions will be impaired whenever there
is a difference between age groups in the nature of the function
relating process to variable.

The distinction between data-limited and resource-limited
segments of the process-variable function is also important
in emphasizing that there are likely to be multiple determinants
of any given phenomenon. Merely because performance is no
longer limited by one determinant does not mean that other
determinants will also be without influence. Moreover, recognition
of the existence of several determinants of a phenomenon raises
the possibility that ceiling effects can occur even at performance
much below the maximum possible level because other determinants
serve as data-limiting processes even after the manipulated
variable is beyond its region of resource limitation. Age-by-
treatment interactions might therefore be spurious because
the performance of one group is data-limited while the performance
of the other group is still resource-limited.

The Problem of Different Baselines

Much of the preceding discussion is related to the pervasive
problem of how one is to interpret the results of specific
manipulations when the groups being compared perform at different
absolute levels of the dependent variable. Still another
problem with the interpretation of interactions related to
non-equivalent baselines concerns differences in discriminability
at different portions in a variable's range. Generally speaking,
the greatest discriminability is in the middle of a variable's
range because it is in that region where there is maximum
potential for variation. As the average level of performance

approaches either extreme, there is a greater likelihood of
artificial curtailment of values and thus a smaller range
of possible variation. (See Figure 6.4 for an illustration
of this phenomenon).   The consequence of this measurement
artifact is that the sensitivity to nearly any manipulation
will be greatest at intermediate values of the dependent variable.
In other words, interactions of age and some manipulation
may be produced simply because the level of performance for
one age group was closer to the middle of the variable's range
than that for the other age group.

The previous sections have indicated that the results
of specific manipulations from groups of individuals performing
at different absolute levels of the dependent variable cannot
be unambiguously interpreted without making a number of strong
assumptions about the equivalence of measurement throughout
the variable's entire range, and about the exact form of the
process-variable function in each age group. When the problem
of differential sensitivity throughout the range of the variable
is added to this list, it becomes obvious that the existence
of different baseline levels of performance is a serious compli-
cation in the interpretation of statistical interactions.
There is a familiar caveat in statistics to the effect that
the presence of a statistical interaction qualifies the interpretation of any main effects.   In light of the preceding
discussion, this caveat may well be reversed by suggesting
that the presence of a main effect serves to qualify the interpretation of any interactions.

Unfortunately, while several alternatives have been proposed
to solve the problem of interpreting results with different
baseline levels of performance in the various groups being
compared, none is completely satisfactory and each must be
considered a compromise in one fashion or another.   In the
following paragraphs the rationale for each proposed solution
is discussed, along with some of the criticisms directed at
each.

Perhaps the simplest solution to the problem of unequal
baselines is to attempt to impose some type of transformation

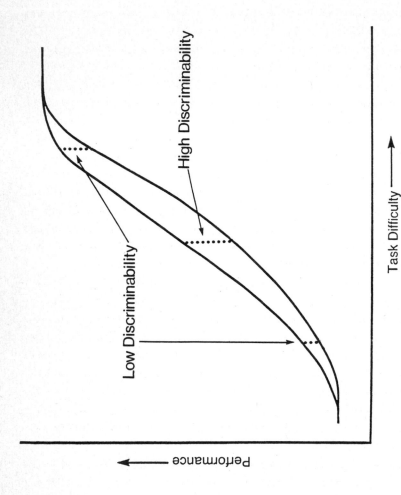

Figure 6.4 Illustration of how differences in performance vary as a function of the level of task difficulty. Discrepancies between the lines are barely noticeable at extreme levels, but become quite pronounced as the values approach the middle of the measurement range.

on the dependent variable that will minimize the suspected difficulties. For example, the arcsin transformation is often used to stretch the differences in a variable at the extremely low and high ends to minimize restriction of range near the floor and ceiling of measurement. Another type of transformation with more profound implications is to shift from consideration of absolute differences to relative differences when the baselines differ across two or more groups. That is, instead of interpreting an increase from 20 to 30 units as equivalent to an increase from 50 to 60 units, the former would be considered 2.5 times the magnitude of the latter because the proportional increase was 50% compared to 20%. As Arenberg (1982) discusses, absolute and relative measures imply quite different conceptualizations of change, and thus it is not surprising that this type of switch in measurement can radically alter the pattern of results.

The problem with relying upon transformations of the dependent variable to eliminate difficulties associated with unequal baseline levels of performance is that this procedure is only defensible if one knows the exact form of the process-variable relation. Without such information it is quite likely that an inappropriate transformation would be imposed, in which case completely meaningless results would be obtained. Moreover, since we seldom if ever have accurate information about even the gross shape of the process-variable function, much less its detailed parameters, the use of transformations for the purpose of eliminating possible artifacts associated with differential baseline levels of performance is generally not advisable. Transformations can sometimes be justified on theoretical grounds, as when one postulates a process expected to produce proportional output, but they should always be used with extreme caution, and never without an awareness of the implications of an inappropriate transformation.

A second possible solution to the problem of unequal baselines is to attempt to select members of each group who perform at comparable levels in some version of the task. By specifically excluding individuals who perform outside a narrow range of the dependent variable, it may be possible to obtain samples of individuals from different age groups who do not differ in their baseline level of performance. Great care must be taken to ensure that the measures of performance are highly reliable because low reliability may lead to a regression-to-the-mean phenomenon in which subsequent measurements result in the samples performing at levels more characteristic of their respective populations. In other words, although the samples were matched on the basis of the first measurement, they may no longer be matched on subsequent occasions of measurement. One means of checking this possibility is simply to repeat the measurements of the matching variable to determine whether the groups are still equivalent on a later assessment. Of course if they are not then the matching procedure will have been unsuccessful and some other procedure must be attempted.

While the matching strategy eliminates the problem of unequal baselines, it raises the question of the degree to which the resulting samples are representative of their respective age groups. It may be argued that if the effects of aging are universal they should be evident in all individuals at a given age, regardless of their specific levels of performance. From this perspective, therefore, the strategy of solving the problem of different baselines by judicious selection of subjects within each age group may be justifiable. However, it seems just as plausible to argue that aging effects are variable in their manifestations across individuals, and that people found to be relatively insensitive to some of those effects may also be insensitive to other effects. Stated more bluntly, it is probably not reasonable to attempt to investigate one aspect of a phenomenon by studying people deliberately chosen because they do not exhibit another aspect of the phenomenon.

A third possible solution to the problem of unequal baselines is to change the conditions of the task in different groups of subjects in order to achieve comparable levels of performance. A variety of manipulations could be used to adjust the level of performance, but in all cases an attempt is made to manipulate a variable unrelated to the process under investigation. For example, the perceptibility of the stimuli might be adjusted in a group of young subjects to result in levels of performance on a memory task equivalent to that of a group of older subjects. In this case, the perceptibility manipulation is assumed to be independent of the processes involved in the memory task, and therefore overall levels of performance can be equated in the two groups. An unacceptable manipulation would be one that affects the process under investigation, as would be the case if the two groups were contrasted on a memory task at two different retention intervals. Because the processes contributing to poorer performance with longer retention intervals are unlikely to be completely independent of the other processes involved in the memory task, using this method of equating performance would introduce a confounding which would preclude simple interpretation of any results that might be obtained. Attempts to control for amount of initial learning in memory tasks may also be criticized on these grounds because it is conceivable that the effects of repetition are not always reflected in the performance scores used to assess learning. That is, four repetitions of a task may lead to qualitatively different consequences than two repetitions regardless of the level of performance achieved in an immediate assessment.

The strategy of attempting to equate the performance of different groups by manipulating conditions of the task is generally done by administering the same levels of the condition factor to all members of a given group. However, a somewhat more sophisticated version of the strategy consists of adjusting task conditions separately for each individual subject in each age group (e.g., Salthouse, Rogan, & Prill, in press; Somberg & Salthouse, 1982). This generally results in somewhat more precise equating of performance, but the basic reasoning is the same as that described above for the group version of the strategy.

The principal objection to the equating strategy is that one runs the risk that the manipulation used to adjust the level of performance also affected the process under investigation

(cf., Long, 1984). The technique is seldom employed if there
is direct evidence that the manipulated process and the process
under investigation interact with one another, but the possibility
of such an interaction can never be completely ruled out.
If there is an interaction among processes, and individuals
in different groups received different values of the manipulation,
it will be difficult if not impossible to interpret the resulting
data.   For this reason, the equating solution to the problem
of unequal baselines should also be used cautiously, and with
recognition of the dangers of unknown interactions contaminating
the results.

The last technique to be discussed for dealing with the
problem of unequal baselines, although by no means a panacea,
is probably the best procedure available at the current time.
This strategy, termed the method of control by systematic
variation by Baltes, Reese, and Nesselroade (1977, p. 218),
involves the administration of several levels of a relevant
variable to the samples of each age group. Focus would then
be on the similarity of the functional relationships of the
dependent variable to the independent variable within each
age group, rather than upon the absolute level of performance.
The advantage of this approach is that the investigator can
examine the entire function to determine whether the manipulated
variable had similar effects in the various age groups. Moreover,
to the extent that the functions are similar, it might then
be possible to make comparisons at selected values of the
independent variable across the two age groups, thus equating
for level of performance on a rational basis.   In any event,
however, the availability of the complete function allows
a more thorough comparison of qualitative and quantitative
aspects of a phenomenon across various age groups.

The major disadvantage of the systematic variation procedure
is, of course, the much more extensive data collection required
to determine the dependent variable at many levels of the
manipulated variable. In effect the investigator has to conduct
several simultaneous experiments instead of just one because
the new manipulated variable must be crossed with each of

the variables of primary interest. This additional effort may be necessary in light of the previous discussion, however, and thus we might expect to see more research reported in which many levels of the independent variable are examined in each age group.

Summary

The purpose of this chapter was to discuss several problems that prevent the meaningful interpretation of results from studies of cognitive aging. Because many studies in the literature can be criticized one or more of these grounds, all research findings should be carefully scrutinized before accepting them as relevant to important theoretical issues. In particular, one should examine studies reporting the absence of age differences to make sure that the samples were representative, the measures reliable, and the statistical power reasonably large. Statistical interactions suggesting differential effects of aging at various levels of the treatment variable also need to be interpreted conservatively because of the many alternative determinants of interaction patterns. It is too much to suggest that no statistical interactions can be meaningfully interpreted when the groups being compared are performing at different initial levels, but skepticism, or at least caution, should be the rule rather than the exception when confronted with results of this type.

Requirements of a Cognitive Aging Theory

In this chapter empirical evidence will be reviewed relevant to the three theoretical dimensions introduced in Chapter 3 and considered critical for distinguishing among theories of cognitive aging. A primary goal of this evaluation is an approximate localization within the three-dimensional theory space (Figure 3.3) of the most plausible theory of cognitive aging. The process of deciding among alternative regions in the theory space necessarily involves an examination of many of the rival hypotheses proposed to account for phenomena of adult cognition. In this respect, therefore, the present chapter can be considered to consist of a critical review of several alternative theoretical positions that could be proposed to account for results in the area of aging and fluid cognitive abilities. The conclusions from this review are in the form of hypotheses, but the derivation of the hypotheses is made explicit by describing the evidence upon which they are based.

Maturation vs. Environment

The first theoretical dimension to be examined is the continuum reflecting maturational versus environmental factors as the principal determinants of adult developmental trends in cognitive functioning. The discipline of psychology has always been concerned with the nature-nurture issue, but it is particularly important in developmental psychology because:

> (s)ince the nurturing environment is changing as
> the hereditary nature of the individual evolves,
> it is often difficult to determine whether observed
> age differences are not actually manifestations
> of environmental changes (Salthouse, 1982, p. 25).

Maturational and environmental determinants of development are therefore often confounded, particularly if one takes a broad view of environment as encompassing a variety of social and cultural characteristics in addition to purely physical

ones. An adequate theory of cognitive aging must indicate
the relative importance of these factors for producing adult
developmental trends in cognition, however, and thus the evidence
relevant to each needs to be examined and evaluated.   Note
that it is the relative importance of maturation and environment
that is of concern, and not the overly simplistic issue of
whether all age differences are attributable either to maturational
or to environmental factors.   Both are clearly necessary,
but they may differ in their degree of influence on age-related
cognitive functioning in normal environmental conditions and
it is the question of how much influence each factor exerts
that is of primary interest in this context.

     The intrinsic relationship between age and potential
environmental change is illustrated in Figure 7.1.   Because
increased age necessarily occurs across historical time, there
is a distinct possibility that factors related to historical
time, such as a change in the bio-cultural environment, contribute
to the developmental trends one observes.   This potential
contribution of the environmental factor is emphasized in
subsequent figures by representing each age as a single point
along the diagonal, and indicating the duration of environmental
exposure with horizontal lines.

Cross-Sectional versus Longitudinal Research Designs

     To many researchers the issue of maturational versus
environmental determinants of development seems easily resolvable
by a comparison of the results of cross-sectional and longitudinal
research designs employing the same dependent measures and
comparable samples of individuals.   For example, if development
is primarily determined by maturation, then it shouldn't matter
whether the various ages are represented by different people
at the same point in time (the cross-sectional method illustrated
in Figure 7.2a), or by the same people at different points
in time (the longitudinal method illustrated in Figure 7.2b).
In other words, both of the methods portrayed in Figure 7.2
should yield equivalent results if the primary cause for developmental trends is related to intrinsic maturational processes,
i.e., if maturation is synonymous with age then only the vertical

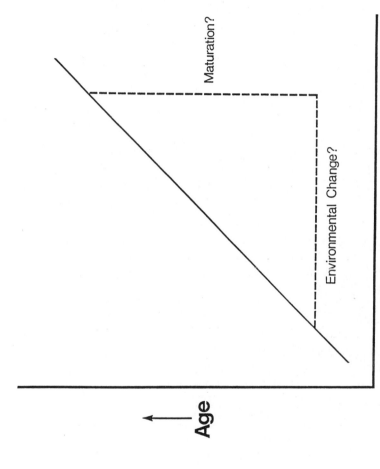

Figure 7.1 Illustration of the inevitability of a correlation between historical time (during which the environment may be changing) and age (which is presumably associated with maturation of the individual).

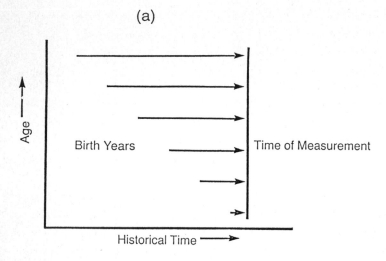

(a)

Age

Birth Years

Time of Measurement

Historical Time

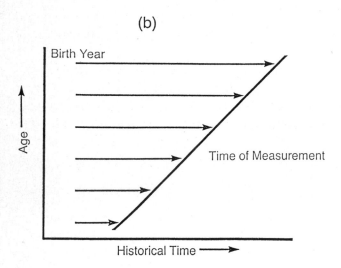

(b)

Birth Year

Age

Time of Measurement

Historical Time

Figure 7.2 Diagram of the relationship between age and historical time in cross-sectional (a), and longitudinal (b) research designs.

axis in the figures will be relevant. (The preceding statement does need some qualifications, e.g., that there is no effect on the behavioral measure of repeated assessment in the longitudinal method and that the attrition in the longitudinal sample is random, but the general point is still valid.)

On the other hand, if development is a function of both maturation and the specific socio- or bio-cultural environment one has experienced in the formative childhood years, the two research designs might be expected to result in different developmental patterns. That is, because relevant aspects of the environment may have changed in significant ways over time, people born in certain periods (i.e., a given birth cohort) could have a different course of development than people born in other periods (i.e., different birth cohorts). For this reason, the single-cohort longitudinal design (Figure 7.2b), which controls for early-environment experiences, might yield somewhat different results than the multiple-cohort cross-sectional design (Figure 7.2a).

Unfortunately, interpretations become quite complicated when outcomes of each design are examined more closely in terms of the possible role of environmental and maturational factors. One of the major considerations contributing to ambiguity of interpretation is that even though the two designs differ with respect to the number of cohorts involved, the factor of environmental change cannot be ruled out in either design. This point is evident in Figure 7.2 where the relationship between age and historical time (which can serve as a crude index of environmental change) is illustrated in both cross-sectional and longitudinal designs.

Notice that in the cross-sectional design (Figure 7.2a), individuals at different ages at the time of test are also at different ages during previous environmental periods. In other words, all individuals experienced the same environment at the time of testing, but experienced different environments as they were growing up. However, because the same individuals are assessed at different ages in the longitudinal design (Figure 7.2b), the environment was constant at any given age, but varied systematically across different ages. Therefore while everybody grew up in the same period of historical time, and hence presumably experienced similar environments as they were maturing, each age assessment was carried out in a different environmental period.

Because neither design completely eliminates he possible influence of environmental factors, it may be impossible to reach conclusions about the relative contribution of maturation or environment to development simply from a comparison of the results obtained in cross-sectional and longitudinal designs. The problem becomes even more complex when additional issues related to the nature of the environmental influence are considered.

For example, one important issue is whether the environmental influence is ageindependent or age-dependent, and if the latter, which segment of the life span is most susceptible to the environmental influence. (See Kausler, 1982, for related discussion of this issue.) Age-independent influences are those that can be assumed to affect all ages in the population by nearly the same amount. For example, altered composition of pollutants in the air, increased ambient noise level, widespread technological innovations such as television, and certain political or cultural events might be expected to exert a nearly equivalent effect on all age groups in the population. Figure 7.3 illustrates the effects of an age-independent environmental change with the assumptions that there is no maturational trend and that the environmental influence abruptly lowers performance by a fixed amount. Notice that an age-independent environmental change would distort the developmental patterns obtained from longitudinal studies, but would merely shift the overall level, leaving the same relation of age to performance, in cross-sectional studies.

Age-dependent environmental changes are those shifts in the physical or social environment whose impact is selective on particular age groups in the population. The educational practices of a society is the best example of this type of age-specific change in the general environment since changes

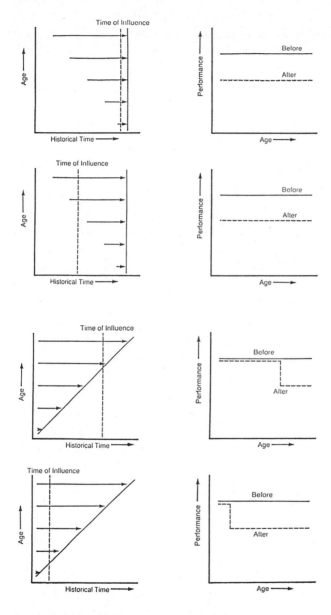

Figure 7.3 Illustration of possible consequences of a sudden age-independent shift in the environment producing a drop in performance.

in the method or content of schooling will most likely affect
only those members of the population who are of school age.
The specific age range of susceptibility can vary across the
entire lifespan, however, and is not necessarily the first
segment of life.   For example, changes in societal attitudes
towards the elderly may affect the behavior of older adults,
but are unlikely to lead to substantial changes in the behavior
of children or young and middle-aged adults.   Figure 7.4 illustrates a few of the many outcomes possible in cross-sectional
and longitudinal studies under the assumptions that there
is no influence of the maturational component but that the
environmental component results in abrupt declines in performance,
and that the maximum susceptibility to environmental influence
ie either in the first or last 20 years of life.   Although
clearly quite complex, these outcomes are merely a small subset
of the many that could occur if other patterns of maturational
and environmental influence, or other periods of sensitivity
to environmental influence, were considered.

     It may be possible to reduce this complexity somewhat
by specifying the region of the lifespan most likely to be
susceptible to environmental influences, and then restricting
one's analyses to outcomes pertinent to that region.   Unfortunately, there is little agreement at the present time about
the portion of the lifespan most sensitive to external influences.
Some writers (e.g., Flavell, 1970; Schaie, 1973, 1975) have
suggested that experiential factors are more important than
maturational factors in adults rather than children, while
others have proposed just the opposite (e.g., Kuhlen, 1963).
Three reasons Kuhlen (1963) provided for why older people
may be less influenced by cultural change than their younger
counterparts were:

> ...(a) because of reduced need or motivation to
> learn (reflecting the decreased demand of the culture
> that they learn), (b) because of pressure of the
> work-a-day-world, which denies the adult opportunities
> to interact with his broader environment, and (c)
> because of the tendency of older persons to insulate

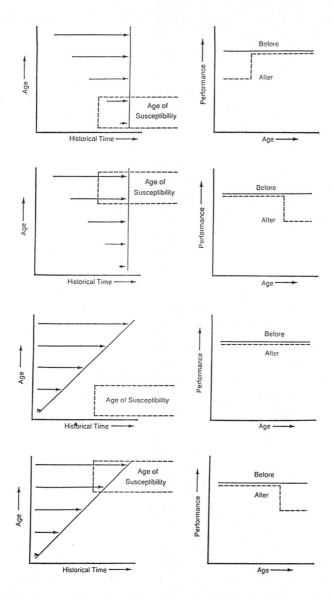

Figure 7.4   Illustration of possible consequences of a
sudden age-specific shift in the environment producing
a drop in performance.

themselves psychologically from new features of
their environment (Kuhlen, 1963, p. 118-119).
However, because equally compelling arguments could probably
be generated for the assertion that environmental influences
are greatest in the period of middle and old age, this issue
cannot simply be resolved on a priori grounds.

It could be argued that the examples illustrated in Figures
7.3 and 7.4 are unrealistic because environmental influences
are probably not discrete and abrupt, but instead continuous
and gradual. Actually, however, examination of the consequences
of variations in the temporal pattern of the environmental
influence tends to strengthen, rather than weaken, the conclusion
that a contrast of the results from cross-sectional and longitudinal designs is a poor means of attempting to evaluate
the relative importance of environmental and maturational
factors in development.

First consider what would happen if the environmental
influence was completely unsystematic and discontinuous.
For example, climatological patterns and world political or
economic crises are presumably characteristics of the physical-
cultural environment which change over time, but it would
be difficult to account for a monotonic developmental trend
on the basis of chaotic and nearly random fluctuations of
the type these variables are likely to exhibit. On the other
hand, if the relevant environmental characteristics varied
in a completely regular and uniform manner, they might not
result in any distortion of the developmental trends because
they would be effectively constant for individuals of all
ages. That is, a variable exhibiting an invariant rate of
change is unlikely to result in a differential effect on any
particular age group because the magnitude of the change is
equivalent at each age.

Rate of variation of the environmental influence over
time is also important because if the relevant characteristics
of the environment change very slowly, e.g., result in a noticeable
change only over a period of more than 100 years, then it
is improbable that environmental changes contribute to the

developmental trends that might be observed within given individuals. Most advocates of the environmental-shift position tend to assume that "...changes in the physical and social environment are faster and more dramatic than those that individuals may undergo (Riegel, 1976, p. 11)," but in fact we really don't know much about the rates of change among relevant characteristics of the environment. Moreover, unless those rates are at least as fast as any that might occur within the individual, the plausibility of environmental factors as a determinant of behavioral development within the individual must remain suspect.

In light of the preceding discussion, it seems reasonable to suggest that distinguishing between the factors of maturation and environment as contributors to patterns of adult development is not practical on the basis of an examination of results from cross-sectional and longitudinal research designs. There are still reasons for preferring one design over another, e.g., cross-sectional designs for the rapid assessment of age-related differences and longitudinal designs for the investigation of individual patterns of development, but the question of the relative importance of maturation and environment for adult development does not appear resolvable with such designs.

Sequential designs involving time-lagged repetitions of cross-sectional or longitudinal designs (see Figure 7.5) offer a means of determining the time course of relevant environmental factors, and thus may allow a more precise characterization of any generation-specific (i.e., cohort) influences that might exist. As the interval between extreme measurement periods approaches the human lifespan, sequential methods can also provide an indication of the generality of the developmental trends across different time periods (cf., subsequent discussion of cross-time comparisons). However, the primary focus of the sequential designs has been to evaluate effects of birth cohort, and not of a changing environment per se. A cohort is simply one configuration of age – historical time pairings, represented in Figures 7.1 through 7.5 as one of a nearly infinite set of possible diagonal lines. Therefore

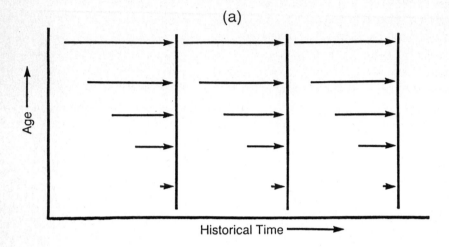

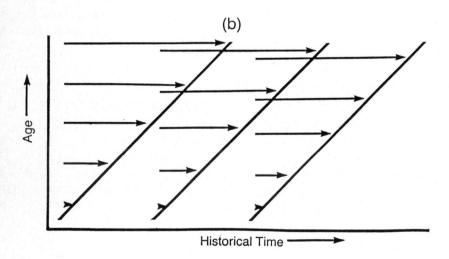

Figure 7.5 Time-lagged extension of cross-sectional (a), and longitudinal (b) procedures to produce sequential designs.

because cohort effects involve a mixture of maturational and
environmental change factors, they are of indeterminate origin
and cannot be interpreted as only reflecting the role of environmental influences.

The preceding discussion leads to the implication that
it is unlikely that definitive conclusions can be reached
concerning the relative importance of maturational and environmental factors in development from an examination of results
from cross-sectional, longitudinal, or even sequential research
designs. Fortunately other techniques are available for examining
the relative importance of environment and maturation as factors
in adult development, several of which are considered in the
following sections.

Cross-Time Comparisons

One technique for determining the contribution of the
environmental factor to patterns of adult development in cognitive
performance is to examine age trends in a similar test administered
to people of a variety of ages at widely spaced points in
time. The reasoning is that if comparable age patterns are
evident across the different time periods then it must either
be concluded that the environmental factor is relatively unimportant, or that it has been changing in a similar fashion
throughout the entire historical period examined.

One source of evidence relevant to the issue of cross-time
comparability of age trends in mental functioning is available
in references to cognitive characteristics of older adults
in historical material. The following quotations represent
some of those preserved from earlier eras.

Old men are children for a second time (Aristophanes,
423 B.C., **Clouds**, 1, 1417).

An old man can no more learn much than he can run
fast (Plato, ca., 390 B.C., **Republic**, VII, 536).

A good old man, sir; he will be talking: as they
say, when the age is in, the wit is out (Shakespeare,

1598, **Much Ado about Nothing**, III, v. 36).

> Outside of their own business, the ideas gained
> by men before they are twenty-five are practically
> the only ideas they shall have in their lives.
> They <u>cannot</u> get anything new. Disinterested curiosity
> is past, the mental grooves and channels set, the
> power of assimilation gone. Whatever individual
> exceptions that might be cited to these are of the
> sort that 'prove the rule' (James, 1893, **Principles
> of Psychology, Vol. 2,** p. 402).

Of course, there is no way of knowing the exact ages of the
people characterized as old, or the health status of the individuals that formed the basis of these observations, but it
is nevertheless interesting to note that impressions of age-related
impairments in cognitive functioning are not unique to modern
periods which have undergone rapid physical and cultural changes.
        Somewhat more systematic observations date back to at
least 1842 when Quetelet, anticipating a procedure later used
extensively by Lehman (1953), reported analyses of the age
at which playwrights produced their best work. His conclusions
were that:

> ...dramatic talent scarcely begins to be developed
> before the 21st year; between 25 and 30, it manifests
> itself very decidedly; it continues to increase,
> and continues vigorous, until towards the 50th or
> 55th year; then it gradually declines, especially
> if we consider the value of the works produced (Quetelet,
> 1842, p. 75).

More objective data concerning age-related declines in
various aspects of cognitive functioning have been reported
in numerous studies of the relationship between age and intelligence originating in the 1920s (e.g., Foster & Taylor, 1920;
Jones & Conrad, 1933; Mursell, 1929; Yerkes, 1921). There
have also been several reports of similar age trends in the
same test administered at different points in time, although

the time intervals have generally been quite small relative to the adult lifespan and thus are probably of limited value in this context. As noted earlier in this chapter, one can only speculate about the amount of time needed for significant environmental changes to occur. Schaie (1958) implied that an interval of more than 20 years might be necessary because when discussing a difference between the results reported in 1958 and those found in studies of the 1930s he suggested that:

> ...not enough time seems to have elapsed...to attribute these differences entirely to cultural changes (Schaie, 1958, p. 24).

However, in later studies Schaie and his colleagues (e.g., 1975) have been willing to infer the existence of environmental changes over a period of only seven years, and thus there seems to be little agreement (even within the same investigator) about the time course of relevant environmental characteristics.

Data spanning an interval of approximately 40 years, which is presumably long enough for most important shifts in the relevant environmental characteristics to be manifested, can be obtained from the standardization samples for the Wechsler Intelligence tests in 1939, 1955, and 1981. Figure 7.6 illustrates data of this type from the Block Design Test. Notice that although there are differences in absolute scores (likely due in part to slight changes in the test and the sampling procedures employed), the pattern for increased age to be associated with lower performance is evident in each of these time periods. Similar trends are evident in the scores from other subtests in the Wechsler battery, and in most other data involving the same test administered at different periods of time (e.g., Arenberg, 1974; 1978; Schaie, 1983).

It is sometimes argued that the factors responsible for producing the shifts in absolute level of performance across time periods also contribute to the age differences that are observed. While clearly conceivable, at the present time there is apparently little direct evidence for this interpretation. Moreover, in order to be seriously considered, an explanation

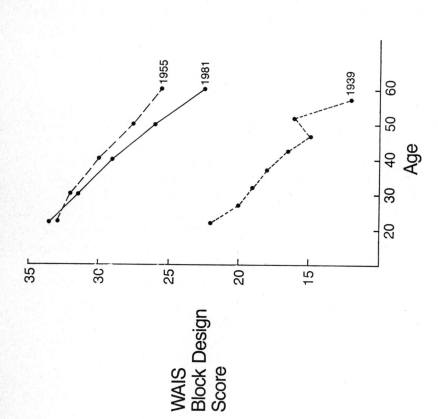

Figure 7.6 Age-performance functions on the Wechsler
Block Design Test at three different time periods. Data
from Wechsler (1939, 1955, 1981).

should be provided for why the same developmental pattern
seems to be evident at each measurement period, and this issue
has seldom been addressed when speculating about the possibility
of shifting environmental influences contributing to developmental
trends in behavior.

Cross-Cultural Comparison

An alternative technique for investigating the relative
importance of maturational and environmental factors in aging
phenomena is cross-cultural comparison. The reasoning here
is that different cultures at the same point in time presumably
differ on the relevant environmental dimensions at least as
much as the same culture at different points in time.

Although there do not appear to be any systematic cross-
cultural comparisons of age trends in cognitive functioning,
some indications of the potential magnitude of such cultural
variations are available by examining the age patterns in
the same test administered to populations from different cultural
contexts. Figure 7.7 illustrates age trends on the WAIS Block
Design test from large representative samples in the US (Wechsler,
1958), Puerto Rico (Green, 1969), and India (Ramalingaswami,
1975). There are clear differences in absolute level of performance across cultures, but the important point is that a similar
age pattern seems to be evident in each culture. (The data
from India may represent a possible exception, but the unavailability of measures for older age groups precludes a definite
resolution of this question.) Comparable patterns of cross-
cultural similarity of age trends were also apparent with
data from other WAIS subtests. These results therefore suggest
that the effects of aging on certain aspects of mental functioning
may be relatively independent of the socio-cultural environment
in which they are assessed. It would obviously be more convincing
if data were available from more diverse cultures, but the
range of cultural variation is necessarily limited because
the meaning of the test may be at least partially dependent
upon one's culture. The important point, however, is that
the data of the type illustrated in Figure 7.7 do not indicate
that there is substantial variation in adult cognitive develop-

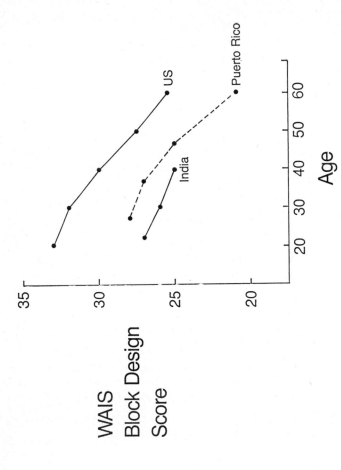

Figure 7.7 Age-performance functions on the Wechsler Block Design Test in three different cultures. Data from Green (1969), Ramalingaswami (1975), and Wechsler (1955).

mental trends across cultural contexts.

It seems reasonable to argue that environmental differences should also be evident across subcultures within the same society, such as urban versus rural residents. That is, in many respects the differences in 1985 between, for example, Los Angeles, California and Columbia, Missouri, may be as great as the differences between Los Angeles in 1965 and Los Angeles in 1985. If so, and if the environmental factor is an important determinant of adult developmental trends in cognition, one might expect to find different age-related patterns in data collected from residents of small towns and data collected from residents of large cities. An impression based on evaluating research originating from different regions of the United States is that this hypothesis is not supported, but unfortunately, there doesn't appear to be any relevant systematic data on this issue.

There have been some studies which addressed the question of the effects of life experiences on developmental trends in cognition, and because those experiences might be considered equivalent to a specific cultural context, they are also pertinent in this context. The goal of much of this research has been to give credence to Anastasi's (1973, p. v) claim that "There is less emphasis on how long the person has lived and more on what he has been doing during those years." One of the most explicit statements of this position was provided by Schaie:

> If we wish to understand the behavior of the aged, we must understand the particular kind of life exper-iences they have had. Different age groups must have had different life experiences, and it is frequently more plausible to argue that people of different ages differ on a given characteristic because they belong to a different generation, rather than because they differ in age (Schaie, 1975, p. 113).

Unfortunately, the evidence on this topic is both inconsistent and methodologically flawed, and thus it does not yet seem possible to reach a definitive conclusion with respect to

the influence of life experiences on patterns of cognitive
aging. One problem is that many of the 'experience' variables
are correlated with level of cognitive ability and thus it
is difficult to draw causal inferences about the direction
of the relationship. For example, amount of formal education
and socio-economic status or occupational level are sometimes
considered categories of life experiences, but a minimum amount
of fluid intellectual ability is probably necessary for entry
into successive levels of education or occupation. Therefore
unless there is some way to determine that the individuals
receiving the different experiences were of equivalent fluid
intellectual levels before receiving those experiences, it
is impossible to interpret contrasts of this type. In other
words, a meaningful test of the 'Use it or lose it' hypothesis
can only be provided if one is fairly certain that all individuals
once had 'it.'

A second problem with many of the 'life experience' studies
is that the measures of cognitive ability were of the crystallized
type (e.g., specific knowledge, vocabulary, etc.), which would
obviously be expected to exhibit effects of specific experience.
Because age effects are typically small to non-existent on
experience-dependent measures, they are not particularly interesting in the present context. Measures reflecting cognitive
style or self-assessed cognitive functioning are also inappropriate
for the purpose of demonstrating effects of specific experience
on age-related changes in fluid cognitive abilities.

And finally, still another problem associated with interpreting studies of the effects of varying experience on age-related
cognitive changes is that a third variable, such as health
status, could have mediated both activity restriction or life
style and cognitive decline. Potential confoundings of this
type need to be eliminated, e.g., by partialling out measures
of health status, before results from differential experience
studies can be meaningfully interpreted.

Cross-Species Comparison

A third method of investigating the relative contributions
of environmental and maturational determinants of development

is to examine the age trends in what are thought to be similar tasks with lower species. The advantage of using non-human subjects is that the shorter lifespan and more rigid control of the environment makes it reasonable to argue that the environment has not changed in significant ways throughout the individual organism's lifetime. Therefore, by ruling out the possibility of change in the physical or cultural environment, any observed developmental differences can presumably be attributed solely to maturational factors.

One task which appears to assess memory aspects of cognition is the passive avoidance task. This task consists of administering electric shock to animals when they enter a chamber, and then determining how long they avoid the shock chamber at a later time. Better memory should therefore be reflected in a longer latency to enter the chamber on a second placement in the apparatus. Several studies employing mice (e.g., Bartus, Dean, Goas, & Lippa, 1980) and rats (e.g., Gold, McGaugh, Hankins, Rose, & Vasquez, 1981) have reported that older animals exhibit poorer memory, that is, shorter latency to enter the shock chamber, than younger animals. Similar age-related decrements are also evident in a variety of other tasks that could be argued to involve some form of cognition (e.g., for reviews see Arenberg & Robertson-Tchabo, 1977; Bartus, 1980; Campbell, Krauter, & Wallace, 1980; Davis, 1978; Dean, Scozzafava, Goas, Regan, Beer, & Bartus, 1981; and Goodrick, 1980). There are often factors of motivation, activity level, and motor speed that complicate interpretations of age trends in animal studies, but it does not appear to be the case that age decrements in 'cognitive' performance are simply confined to humans living in a continuously changing environment.

Assessing the Maturational-Environmental Dimension

Although the comparisons across time periods, cultures, and species are not definitive in isolation, when considered together they seem to provide a reasonably sound basis for inferring that environmental factors probably play a rather minor role in the age-related declines observed in many mental abilities. Horn (e.g., 1975, Horn & Donaldson, 1976) reached a similar conclusion on the basis of the relative magnitudes of aging effects on crystallized and fluid intelligence abilities. It is the fluid abilities that exhibit the greatest declines with age and yet the crystallized abilities are presumed to be more dependent upon environmental characteristics because they represent accumulated knowledge acquired through interactions with one's culture.   There is a risk of circularity in this argument unless one has independent and unambiguous definitions of fluid and crystallized abilities, but it is obviously inconsistent with an environmental interpretation to find that those measures exhibiting the least sensitivity to cultural exposure are the ones with the greatest sensitivity to aging.

Notice that it is not the existence of effects on absolute level of performance attributable to time of measurement or socio-cultural environment that is in dispute, but rather that the age trends in performance are in some fashion an artifact of those factors.   The evidence reviewed above suggests that while the former may be true, there appears to be little basis for believing the latter.   Contrary to the reservations expressed by some writers (e.g., Baltes & Labouvie, 1973; Schaie, 1965, 1967), therefore, the available evidence, although admittedly limited, seems to suggest that age-performance functions can be safely generalized across a variety of cultures, generations, and even species.

Performance versus Competence

The issue of whether observed age differences in behavior are reflections of true competence or simply represent performance limited by a variety of extraneous factors is an important, and not surprisingly, a controversial, topic in cognitive gerontology. It is certainly reasonable to speculate that such variables as unfamiliarity, appropriateness of set or attitude, amount of recent practice, level of motivation, and the like are greater in some age groups than in others, and that it is these variables which are responsible for any developmental trends observed in the relevant behavior.   However the viability of these or any other hypotheses must be determined by evaluation against the empirical evidence and not simply accepted or rejected on the basis of mere speculation.

One category of research relevant to the performance-competence issue has focused on the changeability or plasticity of the behavior of older adults. For example, a training program might be administered to a group of older adults and performance on the relevant variable contrasted either before and after training for the same individuals, or after relevant training and after irrelevant training for different individuals. The manipulated variable (e.g., training) has often been found to be effective in altering performance, and in some cases the magnitude of the effect was as large or larger than the age effects typically observed across the adult lifespan. An inference often implicit in this type of research is that because the manipulated variable has been demonstrated to have a substantial effect in a group of older adults, who typically perform at lower levels than young adults on those behavioral measures, it is that variable which is responsible for the commonly reported age differences. In other words, the argument is that age trends in the targeted behavior merely reflect performance that is restricted below the level of competence by the manipulated variable.

(In fairness, it should be mentioned that the focus in several of these studies was not to evaluate the role of performance versus competence as determinants of observed age differences in cognitive functioning. For example, Baltes and Willis [1982] acknowledged many of the criticisms discussed below, but argued that they were irrelevant when the concern was with demonstrating the existence of plasticity or behavioral reserve in older adults.)

There are three fundamental objections to this reasoning (see Arenberg, 1982, Donaldson, 1981, and Horn and Donaldson, 1976, for related criticisms). One is that the research seems designed to attack a strawman position. That is, much of the 'plasticity' research was apparently motivated by a desire to counteract a stereotype that as one grows older there is no longer a capacity to benefit from experience. It is not clear who is currently assumed to hold this extreme position

because few contemporary researchers in the area of learning
and memory would deny that learning can occur at all ages.
For example, Arenberg and Robertson-Tchabo (1977) introduced
their review of much of this literature with the following
statement:

> If the adage, "You can't teach an old dog new tricks,"
> was not buried in the previous handbook...the research
> reported since then should complete the internment
> (Arenberg & Robertson-Tchabo, 1977, p. 421).

For most researchers, therefore, the question is not whether
any learning can occur in older adulthood, but rather whether
the efficiency of learning varies across different ages.
Because the issue is a relative and not an absolute one, research
based on a single group seems of little value in attempting
to explain, or even more precisely describe, the behavioral
differences found to be related to adult age.

The second objection to the training research with only
a single, typically older, group of adults is that the demonstration that the observed behavior of one group of adults
does not reflect their optimal level, i.e., that their performance
is less than their competence, says nothing about the presence
or absence of such a performance-competence gap in other groups
of adults. It may very well be the case that a similar, or
even larger, performance-competence gap exists in adults of
other ages, and if so, the plausibility of the manipulated
variable as a determinant of observed age differences in behavior
is severely reduced. Unfortunately, many of the studies investigating behavioral plasticity examined only a single (older-adult)
group, and thus they are clearly inadequate as a basis for
concluding that age differences in behavior are attributable
to performance-limiting factors unrelated to competence.

A reasonable first step if one suspects that the measurement
process is unfair or biased for one segment of the population
relative to other segments is to demonstrate that such bias
or unfairness does in fact exist. For example, if when measuring
the heights of groups of people it is discovered that one
group was measured while standing in a depression or ditch,

one cannot then immediately attribute any height differential that might be observed to the fact that one group was evaluated under disadvantageous conditions. What is necessary before making such an inference is to ensure that members of other groups were not also being measured while standing in holes or depressions. Because relatively few studies in this area have included more than one age group in their investigation of performance-limiting variables, they are of little or no value for addressing the question of whether the age differences typically observed are primarily reflections of true competence or mere performance.

The third flaw in the reasoning derived from studies of behavioral plasticity in adulthood is that even if it were demonstrated that the performance-competence gap was larger in one age group than another, it by no means follows that the variables found to minimize that gap are also responsible for the observed age differences. In other words, even if there is a relation between age and variables found to limit performance below competence, this correlation does not imply a pattern of causation. To use a somewhat absurd example, testing older adults on visually presented reasoning tests with and without their corrective spectacles would probably reveal that performance improves with greater visibility, but one cannot then conclude that impaired vision is the cause of the age differences in reasoning. In order to establish the causal linkage, at minimum it should be established that age differences in the relevant behavioral measure are eliminated or greatly reduced when the performance-limiting variable is the same in all age groups. Only after the sufficiency of the explanation was verified in this manner could one begin to ascertain the causal priority of the relevant variables.

An implication of the preceding discussion is that an interpretation of the observed age differences in cognition based upon a greater gap between performance and competence with increased age requires the satisfaction of two criteria. First, it must be demonstrated that the performance-competence gap is in fact larger in the poorer-performing age groups.

And second, it must be demonstrated that the manipulations used to establish the existence of the performance-competence gap are causally related to the observed developmental trends. Because there is little point in pursuing the second requirement before the initial condition has been satisfied, we will first examine the empirical evidence relevant to the existence of a greater discrepancy between cognitive performance and cognitive competence with increased age.

Although many hypotheses about factors responsible for a suspected performance-competence gap have been proposed, few have been subjected to definitive investigation. Nevertheless, at least two speculations concerning the postulated gap between performance and competence have been reasonably well-investigated. These are the proposals that older adults perform at less than their true capabilities because the tasks are unfamiliar to them, or because they are insufficiently motivated to perform at their maximum levels.

Familiarity as a Performance-Limiting Variable

First consider familiarity. Because many of the subjects in the young-adult groups in studies of aging are college students, it is sometimes suggested that they are highly practiced in most cognitive tasks and thus have an advantage over older adults because of greater familiarity with the tasks and materials. Indeed, Cornelius (1984) has reported that older adults rate tasks assessing fluid reasoning skills as less familiar to them than do young adults. However, because the ratings were obtained after performing the tasks, it is possible that they were at least partially influenced by the individual's self-evaluation of his or her performance. In fact, older adults did rate tasks in which they performed relatively poorly as more difficult than tasks in which they performed relatively better. Additional support for this interpretation is the finding by Lachman and Jelalian (1984) that young and old adults did not differ in their predicted levels of performance before engaging in a task, but self-efficacy judgments did vary with age after having performed the task. On the basis of results such as these it is not clear whether age differences

in rated familiarity should be interpreted as a cause, or
as a consequence, of the age-related reductions in cognitive
functioning.

It is also important to recognize that the plausibility
of the unfamiliarity argument clearly depends upon the specific
nature of the tasks and materials. For example, differential
familiarity seems unlikely to be a major factor in fluid cognitive
tasks deliberately selected to be free of experiential influences.
Even the students on my college campus, who have a reputation
for engaging in strange and unusual activities, particularly
on weekends, are seldom observed practicing the recall of
unrelated words, interpreting distorted pictures, guessing
the next letter in a series, etc. On the other hand, if the
familiarity is hypothesized to be based on similar, but not
necessarily identical, activities, then adults of all ages
may have received equivalent amounts of experience remembering
items in a shopping list, putting together objects from assembly
instructions, anticipating whether a bicyclist will weave
in front of one's car, etc. The point is that a priori speculations are not sufficient; empirical evidence is needed to
demonstrate the validity of the hypothesis that differential
familiarity on the part of young adults contributes to the
age differences typically observed in measures of fluid cognitive
functioning.

It is not clear exactly how much exposure is necessary
to overcome the presumed lack of familiarity or recent practice,
but an interpretation of this type certainly becomes less
plausible as the amount of experience with the task increases.
The fact that age trends in a variety of mental or cognitive
tasks have been found to be quite consistent across many repeated
sessions therefore weakens the unfamiliarity argument.

Perhaps the most extensive data relevant to the effects
of experience on age trends in behavior are shown in Figure
7.8. The data in this figure were obtained in a study reported
by Salthouse and Somberg (1982a), in which young and old adults
reported to the laboratory for 51 experimental sessions.
The results displayed here are from a memory-scanning reaction

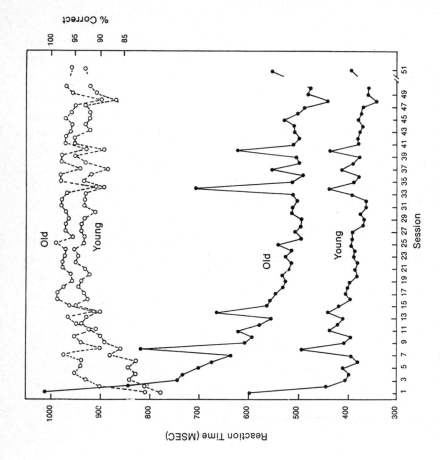

Figure 7.8 Choice reaction time (solid lines) and accuracy (dotted lines) of young and old adults as a function of experimentally controlled practice.

time task in which the subject was to decide as fast as possible
whether a symbol was presented in an earlier set. (Similar
results, although sometimes complicated by a measurement ceiling,
were evident in the other measures in the study.) The important
point is that the differences between the young and old age
groups remained relatively constant throughout 50 sessions
of practice. It is impossible to predict whether the age
differences might eventually be eliminated with even greater
practice, but the data in Figure 7.8 suggest that both age
groups achieved at least a relatively asymptotic level of
performance.

A similar pattern of relatively constant age differences
across moderate (more than 1 hour) amounts of practice has
been reported in an assortment of perceptual-motor tasks (e.g.,
Baron, Menich, & Perone, 1983; Beres & Baron, 1981; Berg,
Hertzog, & Hunt, 1982; Leonard & Newman, 1965; Madden, 1983;
Madden & Nebes, 1980; Noble, Baker, & Jones, 1964; Plude &
Hoyer, 1981; Plude, Kaye, Hoyer, Post, Saynisch, & Hahn, 1983;
Rabbitt, 1964), and in a number of other tasks such as memory
span (e.g., Taub, 1973; Taub & Long, 1972), and intelligence
tests (e.g., Kamin, 1957). It therefore seems reasonable
to conclude that age trends in at least some types of mental
functioning are not easily eliminated by moderate practice.
This conclusion actually should not be too surprising because
Birren long ago pointed out that "...adaptations which occupy
many years of the life span may not be readily reversible
(1960a, p. 321)," but it is obviously desirable to have direct
evidence for such an important inference.

Motivation as a Performance-Limiting Variable

Motivation clearly influences the expression of one's
competence, and it is reasonable to speculate that age-associated
differences in motivation contribute to some of the declines
in performance observed with increased age. Two basic categories
of motivational explanation have been proposed, one based
on task-specific motivational differences, and the other on
general or task-independent differences in motivation. We
will first consider an example of the task-specific difference

in motivation as a possible determinant of age-related reductions in cognitive performance.

Critics frequently claim that because many of the tests used by cognitive psychologists were originally developed to assess children, they may be perceived by older adults as silly and meaningless. Moreover, if the tests are not taken seriously, at least some of the age declines in performance might be attributable to diminished motivation to perform tasks of this type. Although a reasonable hypothesis, empirical data are needed for this speculation to be considered plausible, and the little which is available has largely been inconsistent with expectations from this perspective.

One means of evaluating the possibility that older adults perform poorly because of lack of interest in child-oriented tasks is to examine age trends on tasks deliberately designed to be meaningful to adults. For example, concept identification tasks have been presented in the context of discovering which foods were poisoned after a meal in a restaurant (e.g., Arenberg, 1968b; Hartley, 1981; Hayslip & Sterns, 1979), critical thinking ability has been assessed in the form of questions about inter- pretations of newspaper-like stories (e.g., Cohen & Faulkner, 1981; Friend & Zubek, 1958), and memory ability has been assessed with items from a fictitious shopping list (McCarthy, Ferris, Clark, & Crook, 1981), with coherent stories and recipes (e.g., Cohen & Faulkner, 1984; Dixon, Simon, Nowak, & Hultsch, 1982; Gilbert & Levee, 1971; Meyer & Rice, 1981; Moenster, 1972; Taub, 1975, 1979) and by asking questions about recently viewed motion pictures (e.g., Jones, Conrad, & Horn, 1928). These particular tasks are clearly oriented towards adult activities and interests, and thus a motivation-based interpretation would predict little or no age differences in performance. In fact, however, each of the studies cited above reported markedly poorer performance with increased age, and thus this evidence does not support a task-specific motivational difference as the cause of the age differences in cognition.

Before discussing the status of a general motivational deficit accounting for age differences in cognition, it is

useful to point out that some writers have disputed the interpretation that a difference in general motivation should be
considered a performance, rather than competence, factor.
For example, Jones (1959) suggested that:

> To the extent that loss of intellectual interest
> is generalized, a lagging test performance may be
> a valid rather than invalid indicator of actual
> abilities. Even if we can succeed in altering the
> motivational pattern in a person who has lost interest
> in intellectual activities, we may not be able to
> reverse the changes which have occurred in his mental
> functioning (Jones, 1959, p. 718).

It may therefore be plausible to argue that a motivational
deficit which cannot be overcome by relatively simple manipulations
is equivalent to a difference in competence and not simply
performance.

One of the earliest general motivational hypotheses was
proposed by Thorndike, Bregman, Tilton, and Woodyard (1928)
who suggested that learning has little adaptive value for
adults because they have already learned about as much as
they have any need to know. These authors thus argued that
motivation of adults in learning tasks might be expected to
be fairly low, particularly compared to children.

The role of general motivation as a factor contributing
to the poorer performance of older adults relative to young
adults can be investigated in studies manipulating the monetary
payoffs associated with accurate performance. If older adults
perform below their level of competence because they are less
motivated than young adults, then increasing their motivation
by providing sufficient monetary compensation might result
in the elimination of the performance-competence gap. Moreover,
if an age-related increase in the performance-competence gap
is responsible for the observed age differences, greater motivation
should also result in the elimination of the age differences
in performance.

One of the best studies of this type was reported by
Hartley and Walsh (1980). These researchers compared adults

with a mean age of 21 years and adults with a mean age of
69 years on a memory task under three incentive conditions
involving 0, 5, and 50 cents for each correctly recalled word.
Since there were 24 words in each list and the total time
required for a list was less than 5 minutes, the compensation
possible in the high incentive condition was as much as $12.00
for 5 minutes, which is equivalent to an hourly rate of $144.00
an hour! It seems unlikely that this level of compensation
was not motivating for participants of all ages. Nevertheless,
the results from this study indicated that motivation had
very little effect on the age differences in memory performance. The pattern of results is illustrated in Figure 7.9,
where it can be seen that the group with an average age near
70 performed at only about 50% to 60% the level of the group
with an average age of near 20 across all motivational conditions.

     Similar findings of roughly comparable effects of motivation
(manipulated either by instructions, incentives, or penalties)
across young and old groups of adults have been reported in
perceptual-motor tasks (e.g., Botwinick, Brinley, & Robbin,
1958; Grant, Storandt, & Botwinick, 1978; Salthouse, 1978a,
1979; Salthouse & Somberg, 1982a), and in a variety of cognitive
tasks (e.g., Ganzler, 1964; Hulicka, Sterns, & Grossman, 1967).
It has also been reported that the pattern of age differences
is quite similar even when the subjects in the studies were
college professors, who are presumably highly motivated and
experienced with mental tasks (e.g., Perlmutter, 1978; Schaie
& Strother, 1968; Sward, 1945).

     Actually, because many of the studies of aging on cognitive
abilities involve older volunteers and young 'draftees' conscripted
from an introductory psychology class to satisfy a course
requirement, it is possible to argue that the motivation level
is generally higher among the older participants. Systematic
data are not available on this issue, but experimenters (e.g.,
Birren, 1960b; Davies & Griew, 1965; Welford, 1957, 1958)
often report that motivation and cooperation was at least
as great among the older adults in their studies. Post-exper-
imental questionnaires (e.g., Mueller, Kausler, & Faherty,

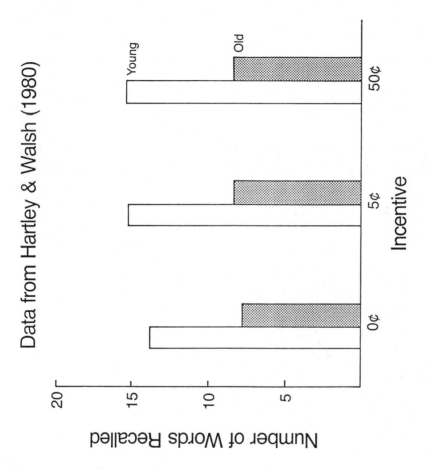

Data from Hartley & Walsh (1980)

Figure 7.9 Recall performance of young and old adults
with monetary incentives of 0¢, 5¢, and 50¢ for each
correctly recalled word.

1980; Mueller, Kausler, Faherty, & Olivieri, 1980; Mueller, Rankin, & Carlomusto, 1979; Perlmutter, 1978) and anecdotal reports (e.g., Birren, 1964) also suggest that, contrary to some speculations, older adults do not have higher levels of anxiety than young adults, and may even be less anxious about their performance because they are no longer as concerned about how they are evaluated or perceived by others. Some of the preceding observations are not well-documented, but the available evidence seems fairly convincing in suggesting that differential motivation plays a very minor role, if any, in the age-related declines in observed in cognitive functioning.

Another argument against a motivational interpretation of the age differences in cognition is that older adults are often found to perform less accurately than young adults on tasks of incidental learning such as recalling the names of activities one has recently performed (e.g., Bromley, 1958; Kausler & Hakami, 1983a; Peak, 1968, 1970). Because this information was acquired unintentionally, it seems unlikely that motivation could have influenced performance, and yet the level of performance on such measures is typically found to decrease with increased age.

Assessing the Performance-Competence Dimension

Results such as those described with respect to familiarity and motivation support the hypothesis that developmental trends in cognitive functioning are not primarily attributable to a larger discrepancy between performance and competence with increased age. The existence of such a performance-competency gap in many ability domains is not disputed, but the available evidence does not appear to indicate that the gap is any greater for older adults than for younger ones. Another way of stating this conclusion is that age differences in cognition seem to be due to inefficiencies in processing and not simply to deficiencies in production. A reasonable theoretical position on the performance-competence dimension is therefore that many of the observed age differences in cognitive functioning generally reflect true variations in actual competence, and not merely the effects of extraneous performance factors.

Specific versus General

The third dimension for theoretical variation is the general versus specific dimension. Expressed in the terminology of Table 4.1, this issue is whether the cause of the age-related differences are best characterized as differences in specific processes or as differences in general resources. Because it is unrealistic to expect to resolve the issue of whether age differences are best characterized as specific or general from a single empirical study, a combination of logical argument and patterns of empirical results will be considered.

One argument for favoring a position on the general end of this dimension is related to the concern about issue isolationism discussed in Chapter 3. That is, it is more parsimonious to assume the existence of a single general mechanism rather than having to postulate separate and independent explanations for each phenomenon related to mental aging. A specific mechanism implies that only a narrowly defined ability is affected, and yet examination of the literature reveals that age-related performance impairments have been reported in an enormous number of seemingly unrelated activities. Instead of attempting to review this literature, we will simply examine a sample of the 'explanations' or hypothesized causes proposed to account for age-related differences observed in specific studies. Table 7.1 contains an assortment of such explanations, although this list should neither be considered exhaustive nor representative. The purpose of tabulating these proposed explanations for age differences in cognition is simply to illustrate the concern about issue isolationism. The entries vary in degree of specificity and therefore it is possible that some of them represent overlapping hypotheses, but few observers would contend that this compilation is a parsimonious means of characterizing and explaining age differences in cognition.

It seems very unlikely that independent mechanisms are responsible for all of the behavioral differences reported between young and older adults, and yet the entries in Table 7.1 indicate that many phenomena are being treated as though they were unrelated to one another because of the specificity

Table 7.1

Proposed Hypotheses for Age Differences in Cognition

Age-Related Impairments are Attributable to:	Source:
Decline in Organization	Denney, 1974; Hultsch, 1971
Decline in Logical Classification	Denney & Denney, 1973
Decreased Proficiency of Elaborative Rehearsal	Kausler & Puckett, 1979
Decrement in Memory-Driven Attentional Selectivity	Rabbitt, 1979b
Decreasing Use of Effective Strategies	Perlmutter & Mitchell, 1982
Deficiencies at Both Input and Retrieval	Till & Walsh, 1980; Craik, 1968
Deficit in Attending to Relevant Information	Madden, 1983
Deficit in Coding Sequential Material	Taub, 1974; Craik & Masani, 1967
Deficit in Encoding or Registration	Botwinick & Storandt, 1974; Craik & Masani, 1967; Taub, 1979
Deficit in Inference Making	Cohen, 1981
Deficit in Retrieval	Craik & Masani, 1969; Schonfield & Robertson, 1966
Deficit in Short-Term Storage	Craik, 1965, 1968; Drachman & Leavitt, 1972; Gordon & Clark, 1974; Inglis & Ankus, 1965; Welford, 1958
Difficulty in Abstraction and Generalization	Bromley, 1963
Difficulty in Identifying or Utilizing Hierarchical Structure	Dixon, Simon, Nowak, & Hultsch, 1982

Table 7.1 (Continued)

Difficulty in Integration and Recoding of Information	Craik, 1968
Excessive Cautiousness	Botwinick, 1966; Korchin & Basowitz, 1957
Faster Decay of Immediate Memory	Fraser, 1958
Failure to Elaborate and Integrate Specific Context	Craik & Rabinowitz, 1984
Failure to Integrate and Extract General Rules	Rabbitt, 1965
Failure to Utilize Information Redundancy	Rabbitt, 1968
Failure to Use Context at Encoding and Retrieval	Shaps & Nilsson, 1980
Greater Susceptibility to Interference	Caird, 1966; Craik & Masani, 1967; Talland, 1968; Welford, 1958
Greater Susceptibility to Set	Heglin, 1956
Inability or Disinclination to Concentrate	Horn, 1979
Inability to Cross-Index Information	Rabbitt, 1981a
Inability to Develop and Utilize Mediators	Canestrari, 1968
Inability to Form or Retain Sets	Rabbitt, 1965
Inability to Ignore Irrelevant Information	Hoyer, Rebok, & Sved, 1979; Rabbitt, 1965
Inability to Maintain Activity with New Input	Canestrari, 1968
Inability to Maintain and Retrieve Meaningful Materials	Taub, 1979
Inability to Modify Ongoing Activity	Botwinick, Brinley, & Robbin, 1958b.

Table 7.1 (Continued)

Inability to Recode, Integrate or Chunk Verbal Material	Craik & Masani, 1967
Inability to Reorganize Percepts	Botwinick, Robbin, & Brinley, 1959
Inconsistent Associations	Perlmutter, 1978
Ineffective Control of Cognitive Sets	Brinley, 1965
Ineffective Use and Production of Retrieval Cues	Perlmutter, 1979
Inefficient Spontaneous Use of Encoding and Retrieval Strategies	Perlmutter & Mitchell, 1982
Inefficient Strategies	Sanders, Murphy, Schmitt, & Walsh, 1980
Less Distinctive Encoding	Hess & Higgins, 1983
Less Inhibitory Control	Birren, 1956
Lessened Integrative Ability	Basowitz & Korchin, 1957; Welford, 1958
Loss of Differentiation and Hierarchic Integration	Friedman, 1974
Loss of Flexibility of Active Control	Rabbitt, 1982b
Mediation Deficiency	Canestrari, 1968; Hulicka, Sterns, & Grossman, 1967
Reduced Ability To Generate Problem Representations	Hartley & Anderson, 1983
Redundant Processing	Jerome, 1962; Rabbitt, 1968
Weak Performance Evaluation	Bromley, 1956

of the proposed explanations. Of course it may eventually
be established that separate and independent explanations
are necessary for many age-related phenomena, but until that
time a more integrated and parsimonious approach seems preferable.

     Another argument against a position on the specific end
of the general-specific continuum is that many of the reports
claiming to have localized age-related difficulties in specific
processing components were flawed by inappropriate interpretations
of age-by-treatment (or condition) interactions. An extended
discussion of some of the assumptions necessary to interpret
interactions appropriately was presented in Chapter 6, and
because most of these are unverified, the resulting interactions
may well be questioned. In particular, measurement unreliability,
possible shifts in the process-variable relation across ages
or treatments, and group differences in absolute level of
performance plague many of the studies in which age effects
were purported to have been localized in one particular process
or component. It is also possible that some of the apparent
localizations were produced by inadvertent confounding of
amount of experience with various tasks such that relative
familiarity rather than the manipulation of interest was the
true cause of the observed differences. To the extent that
one or more of these factors was operative in a given study,
the results from that study are open to question.

The Complexity Effect

     One of the most compelling reasons for favoring a general,
as opposed to a specific, localization is that many of the
results interpreted as evidence for a specific mechanism could
also be produced with a single, general mechanism. To illustrate,
assume that the absolute magnitude of the age difference in
performance increases with increased task complexity, perhaps
defined in terms of the number of mental operations presumed
necessary to perform the task. This trend is schematically
represented in Figure 7.10. Notice that if this illustration
is representative, virtually any manipulation that produces
a sufficiently large change in the level of task complexity
will also tend to result in an interaction between age and

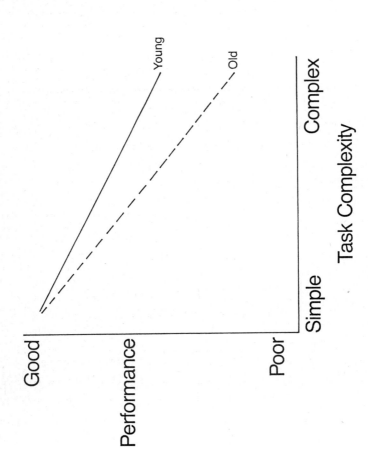

Figure 7.10 Schematic illustration of the complexity effect.
Notice that the magnitude of the age differences increase as
the task becomes more complex.

that manipulation. Many researchers would probably interpret the interaction as reflecting the operation of an age-specific process, but it could simply be that more complex tasks exhibit greater absolute differences between age groups, regardless of the particular manipulation employed. That is, the major determinant of the magnitude of most aging effects may be the complexity of the task rather than its specific content. A similar viewpoint was expressed by Kay (1959) in the following passage:

> There are examples in aging experiments where different results have been attributed to assumed differences in psychological processes, but it would appear that often what is in fact contributing to the discrepancy in the results are the very different degrees of difficulty of the two tasks (Kay, 1959, p. 647).

Gross differences between tasks have precluded a single index of task complexity, but it is often possible to use performance of the young adults as an inverse reflection of complexity on the assumption that increases in complexity reduce the performance of young adults. Reliance upon level of performance as the index of complexity has obvious limitations because other factors such as sensory requirements, retention interval, and similarity of response alternatives also affect performance (see the complexity-difficulty distinction in Chapter 8), but it does offer a crude means of making across-task comparisons of age trends. A complexity effect would therefore be demonstrated if the magnitude of the differences between age groups is inversely proportional to the absolute level of performance of the young adults, i.e., age differences increase as the performance of the young adults decrease.

Patterns of this type are extremely common in the empirical literature on age and cognition, and have been noted by many observers (e.g., Birren, 1965; Brinley, 1965; Crowder, 1980; Jones, 1959; Welford, 1958, 1965), including those focusing on research with animals (e.g., Arenberg & Robertson-Tchabo, 1977; Goodrick, 1972). A few examples will be briefly described to illustrate how the complexity effect has been manifested in different aspects of behavior.

One study illustrating the complexity effect was a card-sorting experiment reported by Botwinick, Robbin, and Brinley (1960). Three levels of complexity were established by varying the nature of the rule governing the sorting of cards into slots; the lowest complexity involved a decision based on a single aspect (number), the next level involved two aspects (number and color), and the highest complexity required a decision based on three aspects (number, color, and odd/even). Time to sort the cards increased across complexity conditions for both young and old adults, but the amount of increase was much greater for the older adults, indicating that the magnitude of the age differences increased with greater task complexity.

A demonstration of the complexity effect in the area of perception is evident in a study by Wallace (1956) in which subjects attempted to identify visual figures displayed sequentially behind a narrow slit. The major results of this study were that young and old adults were nearly comparable with very simple drawings, but the overall performance decreased, and the magnitude of the age differences increased, as the drawings were made more complicated by using silhouettes and intricate drawings.

Kirchner (1958, also see Kay in Welford, 1958) reported a complexity effect in a task involving memory. The simple version of the task involved the subject pressing the key corresponding to the light just presented, while in more complex versions the response was to the light which occurred two or three lights previously. As expected from the complexity hypothesis, the age differences increased substantially as the memory demands of the task became greater. Botwinick and Storandt (1974) reported a similar trend of larger age differences with increased memory demands in a task they termed Following Instructions, and Brinley and Fichter (1970) and Wright (1981) have also confirmed that age differences increase with the magnitude of the memory demands.

A variety of miscellaneous findings in the literature

in memory and aging can also be interpreted in terms of the complexity effect. For example, items with little pre-experimental association strength will presumably require more mental activity to associate than those with high pre-experimental association value. The results that age differences are greatest in paired associates learning with unrelated pairs (e.g., Botwinick & Storandt, 1974; Canestrari, 1966; Kausler & Lair, 1966) is therefore consistent with the complexity phenomenon. Botwinick (1984), McNulty and Caird (1966), and Salthouse (1982) have pointed out that the tendency for the magnitude of age differences to be greater for recall tests than for recognition or cued recall tests could be explained on the basis of the former requiring more cognitive operations, i.e., involving greater complexity, than the latter. Whether the additional operation is termed retrieval or something else, the fact that the task with the presumed greater number of necessary operations also exhibits the greatest age differences suggests that this phenomenon can be considered another illustration of the complexity effect. The finding (e.g., Erber, Herman, & Botwinick, 1980; Eysenck, 1974; Mason, 1979; Simon, E., 1979) that age differences often increase when the stimuli are to be processed at the 'deepest' level (e.g., by determining the meaning of the word compared to judging the presence or absence of a specific letter) is also consistent with the complexity effect phenomenon. Deeper levels of processing probably consist of additional cognitive operations performed on the stimuli, and as noted above, complexity is readily defined in terms of the number of mental operations.

An example of the complexity effect in verbal comprehension is available in the results of a study by Cohen (1979). Subjects in this experiment were presented brief passages and then asked verbatim questions which merely required reproduction of presented information, or inferential questions which required an inference from the available information. Age differences were largest with the inferential questions, which clearly required more mental operations to answer successfully than the verbatim questions.

And finally, a problem-solving study by Clay (1954, 1957)

required adults of varying ages to place numbers in cells
of a matrix such that the sums across rows and columns would
equal specified values. Complexity of problems such as these
varies directly with the size of the matrix, and Clay found
that the age differences in solution accuracy increased dramatically as the matrix increased from 3-by-3 to 4-by-4 to 5-by-5
and finally to 6-by-6.

     The common finding that older adults suffer greater perfor-
mance impairments than young adults under conditions of divided
attention (e.g., Broadbent & Gregory, 1965; Broadbent & Heron,
1962; Talland, 1962) can also be considered a manifestation
of the complexity effect. That is, the number of required
cognitive operations increases when two tasks have to be performed
concurrently compared to when they are performed in isolation,
and thus the cause of the divided attention impairment may
simply be that more mental activity is required in nearly
the same amount of time.

     No exhaustive review of the literature has been undertaken
with respect to the consistency of the complexity effect,
but there appear to be relatively few exceptions to this trend.
Moreover, those which do exist often had floor or ceiling
effects in the measurement, or had a restricted range of task
complexity across experimental conditions which obscured the
phenomenon. It therefore seems reasonable to suggest that
the complexity effect, i.e., the tendency for age differences
to increase with task complexity, is a well-established phenomenon
in the cognitive aging literature. When viewed from the perspective of the complexity effect, the entries in Table 7.1
might therefore simply represent different manifestations
of complexity, and not necessarily descriptions of different
types of specific deficits associated with increased age.

     It should also be noted that the definition of complexity
in terms of the number of mental operations required to perform
the task can also be related to the interpretation of complexity
as abstractness. As Horn (1978) stated:

          In some tests level of complexity corresponds roughly
          to the number of relationships that one must perceive

and resolve in order to comprehend a pattern that inheres in relationships (Horn, 1978, p. 226).

Perception and resolution of a given relationship may take a variable number of mental operations, but on the average the number of operations will tend to be proportional to the abstractness of the relationship. Greater levels of abstractness are therefore likely to be associated with increased amounts of complexity.

Although the complexity concept has numerous manifestations, it is not necessarily equivalent to the psychometric notion of difficulty. In the context of testing, an item's difficulty is assessed in terms of the proportion of individuals from a specified population who provide the correct answer. As will be discussed in Chapter 8, there are many possible reasons for a failure to solve a given item successfully, and consequently it should not be assumed that a high failure rate is necessarily attributable to a greater number of mental operations.

What type of mechanism or mechanisms might be responsible for the complexity effect? At least two possibilities can be readily identified -- a weakness at a superordinate level responsible for the monitoring and control of information processing, and an impairment at a subordinate level concerned with the supply of an 'ingredient' essential for most aspects of information processing. Although the notion of an executive processor is intriguing, attempting to explain the complexity effect by invoking this concept, along with the assumption that the executive becomes less effective with increased age, has the limitation of still requiring an explanation for why that executive becomes less effective with increased age. Simply shifting the hypothesized source of the deficit to a higher level leaves unexplained the origin of the deficit at that level. If the presumed cause of the managerial inefficiency does not itself arise at the managerial level, there seems to be little gain by postulating a weakness in executive-level processing. A more promising approach may be to examine the possibility of differences at a more basic or fundamental level, in the form of a reduction in available processing resources.

Limited Processing Resources

A complexity effect evident across a great variety of
dependent variables is obviously inconsistent with a specific
locus for age-related cognitive impairments because it seems
to suggest that the important question is not **which processes**
were involved, but rather, **how much processing** was required.
A single, general mechanism can account for the complexity
effect if one merely assumes that the resources necessary
for the performance of most mental activities become less
available with increased age, as illustrated in Figure 7.11.
Because more complex tasks would be expected to make greater
demands on the limited resources, and since the quantity of
resources is presumed to diminish with age, age differences
in performance would be largest with more complex tasks, as
portrayed in Figure 7.12. This latter figure also illustrates
the expectation that if the task placed little or no demand
upon the processing resources, then performance should remain
invariant across most of the adult years (cf., Hasher & Zacks,
1979).

A limited-resource theory is also consistent with the
suggested localizations along the theoretical dimensions of
maturation-environment and competence-performance. Because
the processing resources are presumed to be biologically based,
they are most likely determined by maturational factors.
And because they set limits on the individual's potential,
a resource theory emphasizes competence and not merely performance. These theoretical positions, in addition to the general
rather than specific bias, serve to define the major characteristics of the theory advocated in later chapters.

Quantity of Resources or Efficiency of Allocation?

An alternative version of the resources perspective is
that the total amount of processing resources does not decline
with age, but that the efficiency with which those resources
can be allocated or deployed to various information-processing
activities does decline. For example, the suggestion that
age deficits in performance can be 'repaired' with appropriate

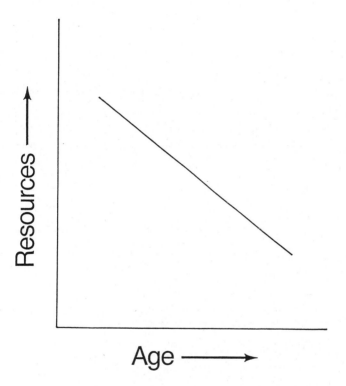

Figure 7.11 Hypothesized negative relation between adult age and availability of processing resources.

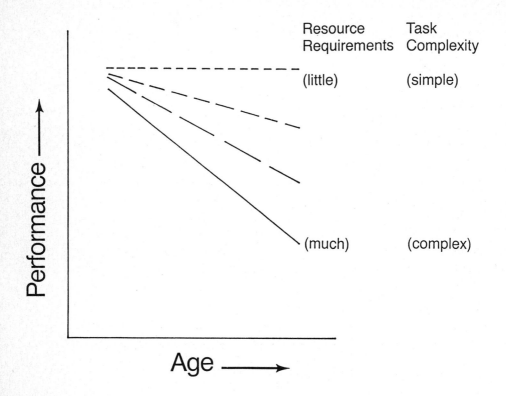

Figure 7.12 Illustration of how the complexity effect may be a consequence of an age-related reduction in the amount of processing resources.

constraints on processing (Craik & Byrd, 1982) implies that
sufficient resources were available at all ages, but they
were not optimally utilized in the elderly without external
guidance.

One means of evaluating the hypothesis that age differences
are attributable to reduced ability to channel or direct available
processing resources to relevant activities is to examine
the performance of young and old adults in divided attention
situations. Subjects can be induced by instructions or incentives
to systematically shift their attentional emphasis (or processing
resources) from one concurrent task to the other, with the
amount of alteration in performance providing an indication
of how effective they are at this selective allocation of
their resources. That is, in one condition the subjects might
be requested to devote 25% emphasis to task A and 75% to task
B, while in other conditions the emphases might be 0%/100%,
50%/50%, 75%/25%, and 100%/0%. This basic procedure, in each
case involving very similar concurrent tasks, has been employed
by Salthouse and Prill (unpublished) with incomplete figure
identification tasks, and by Salthouse, Rogan, and Prill (in
press) with memory span tasks. The results collapsed across
tasks for each emphasis condition are summarized in Table
7.2.

The entries in Table 7.2 reflect performance in each
emphasis condition as a proportion of the performance in the
100% condition for that age group. It is apparent that young
and old adults exhibit a very similar pattern of shifting
attentional emphasis in accordance with task demands. In
particular, both young and old adults performed at comparably
low levels when minimal attention was directed to the task,
and their performances increased in an equivalent fashion
as the amount of attentional emphasis increased. The inefficient
allocation hypothesis is therefore not supported because these
results suggest that young and old adults are equally effective
at selectively allocating their resources from one task to
the other. It could still be argued that the problem is that
more of the resources are needed for executive 'overhead'

Table 7.2

Performance as a Function of Attentional Emphasis

	0%	25%	Emphasis 50%	75%	100%
Memory Span					
Study 1					
Young	45.3	71.0	88.3	94.1	100.0
Old	43.0	64.9	83.4	91.0	100.0
Study 2					
Young	20.1	47.5	72.0	93.4	100.0
Old	18.1	37.2	66.7	94.3	100.0
Study 3					
Young	20.5	60.8	80.0	94.7	100.0
Old	24.4	58.6	75.5	88.2	100.0
Incomplete Figures					
Young	40.2	81.6	97.0	93.3	100.0
Old	33.7	56.6	80.7	88.4	100.0

operations with increased age, but since this would be functionally
equivalent to a reduction in processing resources it may be
incorporated with the interpretation that the age differences
is in the amount of resources available for distribution,
and not in the effectiveness of allocating that which is available.

Objections to Resource Theories

Theories based on the notion of diminished processing
resources are frequently subjected to three criticisms: (1)
the observed differences seem to be qualitative and not quantitative as implied by the resources view; (2) performance on
different tasks should be highly correlated if each is determined
by a common resource; and (3) age differences are frequently
attenuated and sometimes even eliminated by task manipulations
unrelated to the amount of available processing resources.
It is clear that issues such as these need to be resolved
before resource theories of age differences in cognition can
be seriously considered. Although perhaps not leading to
resolution, the following paragraphs discuss how each of these
issues might be addressed from the limited-resources perspective.

First, with respect to the quantitative-qualitative distinction, it can be argued (a) that the dichotomy is sometimes
misleading, and (b) that quantitative differences frequently
are the cause of the qualitative differences. The distinction
can be deceptive because in many cases the processes responsible
for a product are continuous, and hence quantitative, even
if the end products appear to vary qualitatively rather than
quantitatively. Perhaps the best example of this is in the
area of color perception where each hue seems to be a different
quality, and yet all are produced by variations of wavelength,
a quantitative dimension. Whether the differences are considered
to be qualitative or quantitative may therefore depend upon
one's perspective or level of analysis, and does not necessarily
indicate that quantitative variations are not involved.

It also seems reasonable to argue that when qualitative
differences are observed, as for example in the type of strategy
employed in a given task, that quantitative variations in
amount of processing resources may have been at least partially

responsible. In many situations it may be that the particular
strategy employed is the primary determinant of performance,
and thus qualitative factors are clearly important. However,
if it is discovered that older adults tend to use suboptimal
strategies more frequently than older adults, some explanation
is needed to account for the differential strategy use, and
that explanation may well be a quantitative shift in processing
resources. The feasibility of different strategies depends
upon adequate amounts of quantitative entities such as resources,
and therefore qualitative differences may emerge as a function
of quantitative differences.

Detterman (1980) has made a similar argument in the context
of his factory analogy of human information processing. He
suggested that when two factories are observed to differ in
efficiency, it is often assumed that variations in management
effectiveness are responsible. However, this qualitative
interpretation in the form of different executive strategies
is unsatisfactory because no explanation is provided for the
differences presumed to exist at that level. Detterman concluded
his comments with the following recommendation, which succinctly
reflects the present perspective:

> Before postulating higher order principles, parsimony
> dictates that we have a full and complete description
> of the basic units of analysis and their interrelations.
> It may be that higher level units of analysis will
> be required. But it seems to me just as likely
> that principles we reify at higher levels of analysis
> are artifacts of complex systems that are poorly
> understood (Detterman, 1980, p. 589).

The criticism that all resource-dependent activities
should be highly correlated with one another seems based on
a misconception that processing resources are the only determinant
of performance on any given task. This is clearly a radical
position, and one which is probably not held by any serious
adherent of the resources perspective. Instead it is assumed
that there are many determinants of performance, and that
each will continue to contribute to differences across individuals

irrespective of the level of processing resources. Reducing the quantity of resources will tend to lower the average level of performance, but it will not necessarily affect the between-individual variability since other determinants of performance will still be in effect.

The objection that resource theories could not account for the attenuation or elimination of age differences by task manipulations also seems based on the misconception that resources are the only determinant of performance. As Norman and Bobrow (1975a) pointed out, performance may be limited by the availability of resources or by the availability of data, broadly interpreted as the material on which the resource-limited processes operate. It is therefore quite conceivable to have manipulations that shift one out of the resource-limited region of a performance-resource function such that variations in resources are no longer important determinants of performance. (See Chapter 6 for further discussion of the process-variable relationship.)

This argument can be elaborated by a homely example. Assume that you are interested in measuring ability to reach and grasp objects at various heights. Within a certain range of heights, this type of performance will likely be very dependent upon jumping ability, assuming that all individuals being tested are equally tall. A function relating performance (number of objects successfully grasped) to resource (jumping ability) would therefore be reasonably linear in this range. However, an intervention such as providing a ladder will completely eliminate the contribution of jumping ability to performance, and any residual variations in performance would be attributable to other factors such as ability to locate or grasp objects. Note that the introduction of the ladder mimimizes the relevance of jumping ability in that situation, but does not alter jumping ability per se. It is still an open question whether resources once lost could be replenished (e.g., whether jumping ability could be improved), but it is reasonable to expect that numerous situations could be devised in which the importance of the resource for performance is minimized. Only if it could be established that the resource still had the same relative importance in two situations, but one resulted in much greater age differences than the other, would the limited-resources perspective of cognitive aging be seriously threatened. Of course, it is obvious that the reduced age differences should not simply be attributable to measurement artifacts such as a performance ceiling or to weak statistical power due to inadequate sample sizes or unreliable measurement.

What is the Critical Resource?

Although many gerontological researchers have adopted this limited-resources interpretation of age differences in cognitive functioning (e.g., Craik & Byrd, 1982; Craik & Rabinowitz, 1984; Craik & Simon, 1980; Hasher & Zacks, 1979; Light, Zelinski, & Moore, 1982; Rabinowitz, Craik, & Ackerman, 1982), few have been explicit about the nature of these resources, or how they might be measured. This is obviously a major weakness of the resources perspective because there can be little hope for further theoretical progress unless it is possible to provide empirical confirmation of that which has thus far only been assumed -- namely, that the availability of relevant resources actually declines with increased age. Moreover, without such evidence, resource interpretations of age differences are inescapably circular. On the one hand, it is postulated that age-related performance impairments are caused by a reduction in processing resources, and on the other hand, the reduction in resources is inferred on the basis of age-related performance impairments. Explaining a phenomenon by invoking a concept established only in terms of that phenomenon is hardly a means of establishing a sound foundation for a theoretical system.

Clearly what is necessary is a better understanding of the nature of processing resources, and more precision in differentiating among their potential manifestations. Five separate categories of resources were distinguished in the taxonomy of Table 4.1, although this list can be shortened somewhat. For example, the limited-resources interpretation of age differences in cognitive functioning is only meaningful if one assumes that the quantity of resources decreases with

age. Because there is little evidence that the contents of
one's knowledge deteriorate with age, and in fact it might
be expected to increase because of an accumulation over a
greater period of time, the category of knowledge resources
seems unlikely as the primary source of age-related cognitive
impairments. It also appears difficult to distinguish between
the arousal and attentional capacity categories of resources
on empirical grounds, and therefore these categories might
fruitfully be combined into a single composite category.
We are thus left with three major types of resources roughly
corresponding to structure or space, to energy, and to time.

It was suggested in Chapter 4 that limitations of any
of these resources could result in performance impairments
across a wide range of tasks, although detailed arguments
of the sufficiency of the resource limitation have seldom
been stated. At some point, however, it must be established
that an age-related reduction in the relevant resource would
result in the types of age differences typically reported
in memory, perceptual-spatial, and reasoning abilities. Assuming
that one is convinced that a shortage of a given type of resource
could result in the patterns of behavioral impairments one
wishes to explain, how can it be established that it is that
resource and not some other which is reduced with age? Obviously
this requires an independent assessment of the relationship
between age and the quantity of the relevant resource. Only
if it is established that the availability of the critical
resource does in fact decline with increased age would an
explanation of age differences in cognition based on the concept
of resources be plausible.

It is also in this respect that the time, energy, and
space conceptualizations of resources begin to be distinguished
with respect to their credibility for explaining age differences
in cognition. As discussed in Chapter 4, there is still no
generally accepted technique for measuring the amount of attentional capacity or mental energy available to an individual,
and thus it is not yet possible to establish that the quantity
of attentional resources does decline with age. The measurement

problem is only scarcely better with the space version of resources because there is considerable controversy about whether span- or recency-based measures, or even measures from completely different procedures, provide the best estimates of working-memory capacity. Although several researchers (e.g., Light, Zelinski, & Moore, 1982; Spilich, 1983; Wright, 1981) have accounted for their findings in terms of an age-related reduction in working-memory capacity, none have provided independent evidence that this capacity does in fact decline with age. A working-memory interpretation is also complicated because the evidence suggests that the adult age differences are rather slight in measures of short-term or working memory (see Salthouse [1982] for a review), and some reviewers have even claimed that these capacities remain invariant across the adult years (e.g., Craik, 1977; Schonfield & Stones, 1979).

The time conceptualization of processing resources has a distinct advantage over the energy and space conceptualizations in that there is considerable evidence that the speed of most behavioral activities becomes slower with increased age. In fact, the phenomenon of age-related slowing of behavior is often considered the most reliable finding in the gerontological literature (Salthouse, 1985). Many questions still remain concerning the interrelations of various speed measures both within and across age groups, but it is indisputable that the time required to perform nearly all behavioral activities, which is presumably inversely related to the quantity of temporal resources available, increases with increasing age. At least with respect to the measurability of the concept and its relation with age, therefore, speed appears more promising as a candidate for the critical age-related resource than the notions of space and energy.

Two minimum requirements appear necessary to establish the validity of a viable resource theory of cognitive aging phenomena. First, it must be shown that limitations of the relevant resource do in fact produce the types of differences one is trying to explain. And second, it must be demonstrated that the relevant resource does change in the predicted manner across the lifespan. These two issues are the focus of the following two chapters as the next chapter addresses the question of the sufficiency of a resource of time to account for variations in cognitive effectiveness, and the chapter after that examines the evidence concerning the relation of processing speed to age.

Summary

The major conclusions of this chapter can be summarized in terms of the characteristics hypothesized to be necessary in a plausible theory of cognitive aging. First, the theory should acknowledge a substantial contribution of maturational factors in the developmental trends because there appears to be little evidence at the present time that environmental variations markedly influence adult developmental functions in fluid cognitive abilities. Second, the theory should incorporate a competence-based explanation since the available evidence for a larger performance-competence gap with increased age does not appear very convincing. And finally, it seems that a general explanation based on the notion that there is a reduction with age in some type of critical processing resource has several advantages over reliance on many independent explanations. The remaining chapters explore the feasibility of a theory in which time or rate of processing is assumed to be the critical resource responsible for many age-related declines in cognitive functioning.

The Speed Factor in Cognition

Is there evidence that the speed of carrying out basic mental operations is an important factor influencing an individual's cognitive proficiency? In the current chapter this hypothesis will be considered from a general perspective, and in the following chapters the focus will shift to the role of age-related variations in processing speed as a possible determinant of adult age differences in cognitive functioning.

Time and speed measurements have fascinated psychologists since the very beginning of experimental psychology, due at least in part to the unique qualities of time as a dependent variable. Unlike many other variables in psychology, time is clearly objective, yields absolute ratio-scale values rather than arbitrary norm-referenced values, and is inherently meaningful across many different disciplines. In this latter regard it has been hoped that time might function something like the Rosetta Stone in allowing concepts to be linked across the disciplines of psychology, physiology, and neurobiology. That is, the absolute nature of the time scale makes it more likely that interpretations of psychological phenomena expressed in terms of time will be amenable to investigation at more primitive levels of analysis compared to explanations relying upon such arbitrary measures as number of items correctly completed on a given test, or percentage of words recalled five seconds after their presentation.

The fundamental idea to be investigated in this chapter is that the rate at which an individual performs even the most elementary cognitive operations has important implications for both the quantity, and the quality, of mental functioning. This notion is not at all novel since some association between speed and intelligence has long been assumed by both naive and professional observers of intellect. This is reflected by the use of terms such as quick, fast, and efficient as synonyms for bright or intelligent, and even the term 'retarded'

to denote low levels of intelligence has a rate or temporal
connotation. Moreover, test constructors deliberately rely
on timed administrations to incorporate a speed factor in
many tests of ability, and some even allow bonus credit for
the same quality performance produced in a shorter period
of time.

     In the present context, speed is assumed to represent
a fundamental property of an individual's information-processing
system, and not simply a reflection of volitional style, temper-
ament, or preference. In other words, it is not the speed
or tempo at which one typically works that is of concern here,
but rather the maximum speed at which one is capable of performing. It is questionable whether one's typical and maximal
speeds bear a consistent relation to one another across different
individuals, and therefore some deliberate attempt (e.g.,
instructions to work as rapidly as possible) must be made
to ensure that the speeds one is measuring are in some sense
the optimum ones for the individual.

     Because speed is inferred from the duration of observable
responses, it is sometimes assumed that speed is a rather
uninteresting consequence of impaired sensory or motor processes,
or simply an incidental characteristic of responding comparable
to the force or precision with which the response is made.
One indication of this type of perspective is the use of such
phrases as 'perceptual slowing' or 'response slowing' which
imply a discrete, peripheral, origin of the phenomenon. This
viewpoint is rejected here since it is asserted that speed
is an intrinsic, and critically important, property of human
information processing. Furthermore, although it is indisputable
that a variety of manipulations influence the time to make
a response, and for this reason response time has proven a
very useful dependent variable in many types of investigation,
the between-individual variability is always substantial even
when stimuli are easily perceivable by everyone and extremely
simple responses are required that make mimimal demands on
coordination or precision of movement. It is these individual
differences in speed that are of interest in the present context,

particularly with respect to how they may influence effectiveness of functioning in a variety of cognitive tasks. As
Birren (e.g., 1964, 1965, 1970, 1974) has pointed out, this
interpretation views time as an independent or causal variable
rather than as a dependent or consequence variable. Because
this is a somewhat novel perspective to researchers used to
thinking of time as a dependent variable employed to gauge
the effectiveness of one's experimental manipulations, the
next section summarizes the results of a computer simulation
designed to demonstrate the effects of variations in speed
of processing on both time and quality of responses.

The nature of speed as an independent variable in cognitive
functioning has been the subject of speculation for many years.
Two of the earliest statements of this type are as follows:

It is possible that the **quality** of intelligence
may depend upon the number of connections, but also
upon the **speed** with which those connections are
formed. Nerve centers (e.g., association centers)
cannot remain excited indefinitely at maximum intensity;
consequently in the case of a person who forms connections slowly it is possible that the excitation
of the first association centers to be affected
will have diminished and disappeared before the
later centers come into play. Thus only a limited
number of centers are cooperating at any one time.
The person who forms connections quickly, however,
is apt to have more association centers interacting
at once, since the later centers are aroused before
the earlier ones had a chance to lose their effectiveness. But the most intelligent response is, in
general, the one in the determination of which the
greatest number of factors have been taken into
consideration. In neural terms this may well mean
the response in the determination of which the greatest
number of association centers have cooperated, and
the number of simultaneously active centers may
in turn depend to some extent upon the speed with

which nervous impulses are conducted from center
to center and through synapses within the centers
(Lemmon, 1927, p. 35).

Intelligence is probably best defined as the ability
to see relationships and meanings by having access
to as many alternatives or judgments as possible
at approximately the same instant of time. This
would necessitate the reaction patterns which subserve
the judgments to be active within an extremely short
interval of time. The 'feeble-minded' individual
has, relatively speaking, such a slow conduction
rate that one reaction pattern becomes inactive
by the time another becomes active, thus doing away
with the very factor, relative simultaneity of activity,
which makes possible the seeing of a relationship
between ideational elements. Prompt radiation of
the nerve impulse into a large number of associational
systems is probably the neurophysiological basis
of an intelligent response to a complex situation (Travis
& Hunter, 1928, p. 352).

Similar views about how variations in quantity (time) can
translate into differences in quality (represented as accuracy,
goodness or uniqueness of response, etc.) have been expressed
in the literature on aging by Birren (1955a, 1964, 1965),
Bromley (1967), Fozard and Thomas (1975), Heron and Chown
(1967), Jensen (e.g., 1979, 1982a, 1982b), Jones (1956), Rabbitt
(1977), Salthouse (1982), Salthouse and Kail (1983), and Witt
and Cunningham (1979).

A Simple Simulation

These ideas can be made more concrete by examining the
results of a very elementary simulation of the strength of
activation at different levels in a hypothetical network.
Network representations have proven popular in contemporary
cognitive psychology because they are extremely useful for
exploring the consequences of many simultaneous units, often
considered somewhat analogous to neurons, interacting with

one another over limited periods of time. Ideally it would
be desirable to examine the effects of manipulating rate parameters
in a variety of existing simulation models of cognition.
Unfortunately this is not very feasible because of the difficulty
of identifying fairly pervasive rate parameters in the models,
or even obtaining manipulative access to the models. Effects
of varying the time required for elementary processing were
therefore investigated by constructing a new simulation model
based on a very simple network.

The network is illustrated in Figure 8.1. Only a few
nodes are represented at each level, but they are sufficient
to illustrate the basic properties of an interactive system,
and a more realistic portrayal of the actual complexity of
the nervous system would be extremely difficult to conceptualize
and communicate. The operative assumptions of the network
are as follows. First, it is assumed that element nodes are
stimulated by the presentation of a physical stimulus, and
that this activation spreads upward to all connecting nodes.
The level of activation at any given node is the sum of all
of the input activation amounts, and if this sum exceeds a
threshold value, that node will propagate activation to all
nodes to which it is connected. There is no maximum on the
amount of activation at a given node, but the minimum level
cannot be less than zero and there is no provision for inhibition
within the system. These characteristics led to an enormous
range of possible activation levels and hence a logarithmic
transformation was imposed to produce a less extreme dispersion
of values. Activation is assumed to dissipate over time and
thus the activation from connected nodes must converge on
the designated node within a limited time interval in order
for the aggregate activation to exceed the threshold level.

The simulation operates in discrete time cycles, and
hence rate of processing or mental speed can be represented
as the number of time cycles, during which activation is dissi-
pating, between successive propagation from one node to the
next. That is, a faster speed would be associated with a
smaller number of clock cycles between spreading of activation

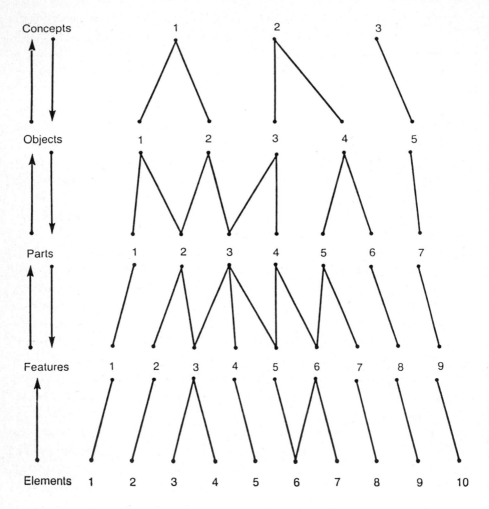

Figure 8.1 Diagram of a simple network containing a hierarchy of processing levels. Higher levels in the network are intended to correspond to progressively more abstract processing.

across nodes in the network. Output of the network is represented as the strength of the activation at any given node in the network, although for ease of description performance is conveniently portrayed as the average across all nodes at a given level. Because amount of activation can be considered the primary determinant of a response, and since the particular response selected is an index of quality of performance, manipulations of rate indicate how quantitative variations can be translated into qualitative effects.

It is recognized that many of the features of this simulation are somewhat arbitrary and that numerous other variations could be proposed. Nevertheless, because a minimal number of assumptions have been made, the results of the current version should be fairly generalizable and not restricted to a large set of highly specific assumptions.

Three variables in addition to propagation rate have been manipulated with the simulation. One of these is the level in the network at which the output is evaluated. That is, average node strength can be examined at the feature level, the part level, the object level, or the concept level, which represent progressively more complex decisions requiring increasing amounts of processing, i.e., more intermediate nodes have to be activated between the initial and final node. Figure 8.2 illustrates that the absolute differences among various rates of propagation increase as the complexity of the decision, i.e., level in the hierarchy, increases. This is essentially the complexity effect discussed in Chapter 7, which was identified as a pervasive phenomenon needing explanation by any satisfactory theory of cognitive aging. The complexity effect is also evident in a latency measure as Figure 8.3 illustrates that the initial time of activation increases across decision levels by a greater amount with slower rates of propagation.

As a matter of curiosity, two manipulations thought to reflect the space and energy conceptualizations of resources were also examined in the simulation. Space limitations were incorporated by reducing the number of nodes in the network that could be activated at any given moment, while variations in energy were introduced by restricting the total level of activation throughout the entire network. The principal results were that limiting the number of nodes or the amount of total activation to 50% or even 25% of the unrestricted levels had no effect on the initial latency functions. There was a slight tendency for the differences in log peak activation strength to be larger at higher levels in the network when the number of active nodes was reduced, but no such trend was apparent when the total activation was reduced. In other words, the complexity effect illustrated in Figures 8.2 and 8.3 was not evident when variables thought to correspond to limitations of space and energy were examined. Of course, these findings should not be interpreted as indicating that the complexity effect pattern cannot be produced by suitable values of the number of active nodes or the total amount of activation, but they do suggest that relative to these variables, the rate of propagating activation is an extremely powerful variable in this particular situation.

The second manipulation examined in the simulation was discriminability or difficulty, defined as the distinctiveness of the nodes at a given level in the network. For example, consider the nodes at the object level in the structure illustrated in Figure 8.1. Nodes 1 and 2 share many lower-level nodes, Nodes 1 and 3 share somewhat fewer nodes, and Nodes 1 and 4 have almost no common nodes at lower levels in the network. These three contrasts can be considered to lie along a continuum of stimulus discriminability, with the 1 versus 4 comparison representing the easiest level and the 1 versus 2 comparison representing the most difficult level. The difference in peak activation strength between the relevant two object nodes when stimulation is selectively directed at Element Nodes 1 through 4 can serve as an index of the ease of distinguishing the stimuli. The discrimination should be easiest when the absolute difference in peak strength is large, but it should become progressively more difficult as the difference in peak strength becomes smaller.

Results from the simulation are illustrated in Figure

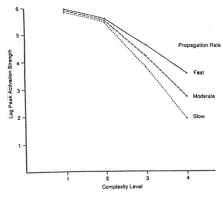

Figure 8.2 Simulation results of activation strength at different levels in the network for three propagation rates. Complexity level 1 refers to the features level in Figure 8.1, while levels 2, 3, and 4 refer to the parts, objects, and concepts levels, respectively.

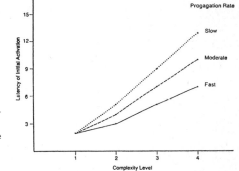

Figure 8.3 Simulation results of number of clock cycles until initial activation at different levels in the network for three propagation rates.

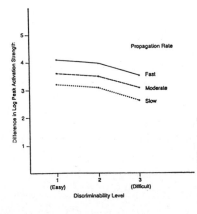

Figure 8.4 Simulation results of activation strength at the object level for three propagation rates. Discriminability level refers to the amount of overlap of lower-level nodes for a particular pair of object nodes.

8.4, where it can be seen that rate of propagation does not interact with level of discriminability. This is an interesting finding because it suggests that the distinction between difficulty or discriminability and complexity may be an important one. The fundamental difference between the two concepts is that complexity refers to the level in the network hierarchy at which the decisions are made, while difficulty indicates the discriminability or distinctiveness of the nodes within a given level. Variations in complexity therefore involve progressively greater amounts of processing or additional numbers of cognitive operations, but variations in difficulty correspond to amount of overlap in the nodes at a given level and therefore do not necessarily involve any different amounts of processing. The simulation results thus suggest that in order to obtain interactive effects with rate of processing one must ensure that the amount of processing is increased, and not merely that the difficulty of making a distinction within the same level of complexity is varied. A confusion between difficulty and complexity in the cognitive aging research literature may have contributed to the failure of earlier workers in the field to have recognized the complexity effect. For example, it is likely that manipulations such as stimulus size, stimulus brightness, and stimulus-response compatibility primarily affect difficulty rather than complexity and therefore results from studies employing these types of manipulations may not be relevant to the complexity effect.

Two further manipulations also resulting in additive effects with the propagation-rate variable were stimulus duration, represented by the number of time cycles during which the element nodes were activated, and the level in the network at which the speed differences were introduced. The effects of stimulus duration on peak activation strength were complex -- first increasing, then decreasing, and finally stabilizing -- but very similar patterns were produced at slow, moderate, and fast rates of propagation. An implication of this result is that consequences of processing rate are largely independent of the duration of external stimulation, at least within a moderately broad range of stimulus durations.

The locus of the processing rate difference was altered by either varying the propagation rate only from the element to the feature nodes, as though it were solely an input phenomenon, or by varying it only after the feature nodes, as though it were solely a central processing phenomenon. Very clear differences were evident across these two conditions as the former, input locus, had virtually no effect since the same level of activation was produced at each propagation rate, while the latter, central locus, resulted in patterns of activation identical to that obtained when the rate was uniform throughout the network. These results suggest that pronounced effects of processing rate may occur only when the speed differences are evident beyond the input phase of processing. Of course there are undoubtedly situations in which transmission speed in the input phase is critical, but the simulation suggests that central speed has greater consequences for most types of processing than input speed.

Taken together, the manipulations of input duration and locus of the speed shift suggest that 'peripheral' factors are fairly unimportant in terms of their effects on 'central' or presumably cognitive, processing. Of course, this is not to say that central processing efficiency is independent of peripheral factors such as stimulus exposure duration or peripheral transmission time, but it does appear unlikely that variations at that level would have widespread effects throughout the system. The simulation suggests that only if the rate variable is operational at higher levels would pronounced effects be expected.

No claim is made that this simulation accurately reflects all of the complexity of human cognition, or even that the manipulation of propagation rate is a completely valid representation of individual differences in speed of information processing. Nevertheless, it is valuable for indicating some of the consequences of varying speeds of processing, and for specifying the nature of the variables that might be expected to interact with rate of processing.

The conclusion from this discussion of the simulation of propagation rate is that speed can be demonstrated to have important consequences for both quantity and quality of responses. It is therefore clear that speed has implications for performance even when there are no explicit timing constraints in either the input or the output. As long as the critical responses require the integration of information from multiple elements or units that each have ebbs and flows of activation, rate of propagation, or its presumed equivalent, speed of mental operation, may be an important determinant of many types of behavior. Naturally if the rate of dissipation of activation was slowed in proportion to the rate of propagation of the activation many of the time effects would disappear, but there will still be external constraints such as growing frustration and societal pressure for rapid responses which may well lead to the abandonment of processing. Time-related effects might therefore be expected with any decrease in processing speed.

The preceding discussion also suggests specific answers to the questions Horn (1980) raised concerning the role of speed in cognitive activity. His questions were:

> Is it possible to think slowly and still think well?
> Is slow performance mainly a reflection of long latency in initiating thought on a problem, or does it indicate slowness in stepping through the stages of solution, or is it mainly a matter of checking and rechecking possible solutions, or does it indicate slowness in making a response after solution has been achieved? (Horn, 1980, p. 308).

Answers suggested by the simulation and the associated discussion are: Yes, slow, quality thinking is possible, but other things being equal it is easier to achieve the same level of quality with fast thinking; No, the slowness is not limited to the initiation of cognitive activity; Yes, it is manifested as a slowness in all stages of solution; No, it does not simply reflect carefulness or compulsive checking; and No, the slowness is not merely a delay in executing the response after the solution is achieved.

Empirical Evidence on the Speed-Intelligence Relationship

One of the few theoretically-based interpretations of the biological basis of intelligence is that variations in intelligence are attributable to individual differences in neural efficiency. Because neural efficiency is thought to be directly related to rate of performing mental operations, it has often been assumed that intelligence should be correlated with certain measures of reaction time. This view can be traced at least to the time of Galton, who hypothesized that brighter individuals had greater sensory acuity and faster reaction times than less intelligent individuals. Galton's reasoning was based on the prevailing associationism views, assuming that keenness of discrimination and judgment, and rapidity of forming and retrieving associations, could be indexed by measures of sensory acuity and quickness of overt action. Most contemporary researchers give little credence to Galton's ideas, although several recent investigators have argued that the proposal about a relation between speed and intelligence was prematurely discarded (e.g., Eysenck, 1967; Jensen, 1982a, 1982b). The following quotations are typical of some of these current perspectives:

> ...consider that the speed-of-processing tests are measuring the efficiency with which persons can perform very basic cognitive operations which are themselves involved in, or which underlie, other kinds of cognitive and intellectual behavior. Further, if it is accepted that these cognitive operations are carried out in some sort of short-term or working memory system, characterized by a limited capacity to hold information, a rapid decay or loss of information in the absence of rehearsal, and a trade-off between the amount of information that can be held and processed simultaneously, then the speed or efficiency with which individuals can execute the cognitive operations involved in a given task or problem might be expected to have a considerable effect on the success of their performance of the task (Vernon, 1983, p. 54).

...even very small individual differences in **rates**
of information processing, when multiplied by days,
weeks, months, or years of interaction with the
myriad opportunities for learning afforded by common
experience, can result in easily noticeable differences
in the amounts of acquired knowledge and developed
intellectual skills. At a moment's glance there
is scarcely a noticeable difference between the
speed of a car averaging 50 and another 51 miles
per hour, but after a few hours on the road they
are completely out of sight of one another (Jensen,
1980, p. 105).

Ideas such as these generated considerable research during
the first quarter of this century, but the results were inconsistent and contradictory, in part because of methodological
flaws in many of the studies. For example, the first major
investigation of the relation between speed measures and intelligence was a study by Wissler (1901) utilizing the test battery
developed by James McKeen Cattell. His primary result, which
has been frequently cited in subsequent years, was that there
was absolutely no correlation (i.e., r = −.02) between reaction
time and intelligence. However, Wissler's measure of reaction
time consisted of the average of only three to five reaction
times for each subject, and intelligence was estimated by
the grades received by the subjects in their college courses.
It is highly unlikely that the reaction time measure based
on only a few trials was reliable, and school performance
has limited validity as an index of intelligence, particularly
in a restricted sample of highly selected college students.

Extremely positive results concerning the relation between
speed and intelligence were reported by Peak and Boring (1926),
but their study also had serious methodological flaws. These
investigators attempted to obtain more reliable estimates
of reaction time by administering 100 reaction time trials,
and more valid measures of intelligence by the use of standardized
objective tests (the Army Alpha and the Otis). A phenomenal

correlation of −.90 was reported between average reaction time and intelligence score, i.e., faster speed was associated with higher intelligence, but the sample consisted of only five individuals, all of whom were either advanced undergraduate or graduate students at Harvard University. Such a small sample of highly select individuals is obviously inadequate as a basis for drawing conclusions about the relationship between speed and intelligence in the general population.

Another study employing a larger sample of 44 subjects also reported an extremely large correlation of −.87 between intelligence score and a measure of neural processing rate, in this case derived from the latency of the patellar reflex (Travis & Hunter, 1928). However, the techniques available for measuring reflex latencies were evidently unreliable because even the original authors were subsequently unable to replicate this result (Travis & Hunter, 1930).

Although not all of the early studies had as severe methodological limitations as those described above, most can be criticized from the perspective of contemporary standards as being deficient in one respect or another. We will therefore restrict the following review to studies published since 1970, when there was a resurgence of interest in the issue of the role of speed in intelligence, and, presumably, greater methodological sophistication on the part of the investigators.

Before discussing studies concerned with the relation between speed and intelligence it is important to point out that this issue should not be confused with the distinction between speed and power tests of a given intellectual ability. Tests with no time constraints, or with very generous time limits, are sometimes considered to assess a rather different aspect of ability than those designed to be performed under speeded conditions. (Although as Peak and Boring [1926] observed, the distinction may be more apparent than real in that the power test may simply not take **account** of speed, but may still **involve** speed.) The evidence for the distinction between speed and power is still rather equivocal because speed and power scores for the same individuals are often highly correlated.

Regardless of its status, however, the distinction is irrelevant in the present context because even the speed tests involve substantial content and thus the score is based not only on speed, but also upon ability in the relevant domain.   The hypothesis under investigation here is that the rate at which an individual performs most processing operations, and not merely those in a specific domain, is causally related to his or her general cognitive effectiveness. The most appropriate measures of speed to test this hypothesis therefore seem to be those derived from simple speeded tasks requiring little or no specific knowledge.

Several different types of speed measures have been examined with respect to the relation between speed and intelligence, but most can be categorized as either reaction time measures, tachistoscopic measures, or one of a variety of psychophysiological measures.   The dominant entry within this latter category are variables based on evoked potentials in electroencephalograms (e.g., Calloway, 1975; Crawford, 1974; Ertl & Schafer, 1969; Shucard & Horn, 1972).   However, because there are still many uncertainties about recording and analysis artifacts with measures of this type (see Calloway [1975] for a brief discussion of several of these issues), it is probably premature to attempt to draw conclusions about the research attempting to relate intelligence to various psychophysiological measures of speed.

Estimates of processing speed derived from tachistoscopic procedures are based on the rationale that time measurements derived from simple perceptual tasks can serve as an index of the duration of the elementary operation of encoding, and thus indirectly as an index of the duration of other fundamental processing operations.   The critical flicker fusion measure representing the rate of oscillation at which a flickering light appears continuous has been used in a number of studies, with some reporting quite positive results (e.g., Colgan, 1954; Loranger & Misiak, 1959; Wilson, 1963).   However, when all of the studies are considered (see Jensen, 1983, for a review), the majority of the evidence suggests that there is little or no correlation between this measure and intelligence, and hence it will be ignored in the present context.

Considerably more success has been reported with tasks requiring that individual stimuli be discriminated or identified. One of the most popular paradigms is the inspection-time or backward-masking procedure in which a stimulus is followed immediately by a visual mask thought to terminate further processing of the stimulus. Much of this research was recently reviewed by Brand and Deary (1982) and Nettelbeck (1982). Nettelbeck's major conclusion was that the inspection time measure is related to intelligence, but that the magnitude of the relation is greatly inflated by the inclusion of retarded individuals in the experimental samples. However, several recent studies (e.g., Smith & Stanley, 1983; Vernon, 1983) have yielded contradictory results, i.e., positive correlations indicating that lower intelligence was associated with faster inspection times, and thus the status of the intelligence-inspection time relation must be considered equivocal at the present time.

By far the greatest number of studies investigating the relation between speed and intelligence have relied upon one or more measures derived from reaction time tasks as the speed variable. Three categories of reaction time measures are commonly used in these studies: measures of central tendency, measures of variability, and some form of difference score thought to provide an index of central processing time independent of input and output processes.

It is sometimes suggested that measures of variability are more fundamental than measures of central tendency because greater variability of underlying processes may lead to increases in the central tendency measure reflecting the sum of the component process durations. However, the causal relationship between measures of variability and central tendency is still ambiguous since increases in the duration of component processes might also be expected to result in greater variability of the aggregate performance, particularly if the variances of the components are independent. Moreover, because of the possibility that variability may additionally, or alternatively,

reflect the consistency of adherence to a strategy, or the
extent to which attention is sustained on the task, the central
tendency measure seems the preferred index for the current
purpose. At any rate, the fact that measures of central tendency
and variability are highly correlated (often above +.8) indicates
that very similar results would generally be expected with
each measure, and therefore only the central tendency measure
will be considered here.

The rationale for obtaining an estimate of central processing
time is based on the assumption, originally introduced by
Donders (1869/1969) in his pioneering studies of mental chronometry, that total reaction time is the sum of the durations
of a number of relatively independent processes. Given this
assumption, one can devise various comparison conditions which
allow the abstraction of a measure presumed to reflect the
duration of only internal processes. For example, the difference
between choice reaction time (two-alternative) and simple
reaction time (one-alternative) can be interpreted as an estimate
of the duration of the choice or discrimination operation.
Slope measures based on the regression line relating reaction
time to some index of task complexity are based on the same
logic, as can be seen by the fact that the slope for a contrast
between two conditions with a separation of one unit on the
abscissa is identical to the difference in reaction times
between those conditions.

Many, although certainly not all, of the recent studies
reporting correlations between a measure of reaction time
and some index of intelligence are summarized in Table 8.1.
Three criteria determined the inclusion of studies in this
table. First, the sample had to include a substantial proportion
of individuals who were of average or above-average intelligence
rather than being dominated by individuals from the sub-normal
range. Second, the people had to be roughly homogeneous with
respect to chronological age in order to avoid confounding
the age effect with the speed-intelligence relation (cf.,
Chapter 6). And third, correlation coefficients had to be
reported between the speed measure and at least one index

Table 8.1A

Reaction Time - Intelligence Correlations

(Mean or Linear Regression Intercept)

Correlation	Source	Sample Size	Population	Intelligence Measure
+.13	Carlson et al., 1983	105	7th Graders	Raven's
-.54	Carlson & Jensen, 1982	20	9th Graders	Raven's
-.28 to -.43	Jenkinson, 1983	60	6th Graders	Fluid Intelligence
-.28 to -.39	Jenkinson, 1983	60	6th Graders	Crystallized Intelligence
+.15	Jensen, 1979	50	College Students	Raven's
-.39	Jensen & Munro, 1979	39	9th Graders	Raven's
+.39	Lally & Nettelbeck, 1977*	32	Non-retarded Adults	WAIS Performance
-.22 to -.28	Lansman, 1981	84	College Students	Fluid Intelligence
+.12 to -.19	Lansman, 1981	84	College Students	Fluid Intelligence
+.08 to -.26	Lansman et al., 1981	91	College Students	Raven's
-.27 to -.49	Lunneborg, 1977	64	High School Students	Miscellaneous
+.10 to -.21	Lunneborg, 1977	63	College Students	Miscellaneous
+.14 to -.31	Lunneborg, 1977	64	High School Students	Miscellaneous
-.36	Nettelbeck & Kirby, 1983	91	Adults, Normal	Raven's/WAIS
-.23 to -.72	Paivio, 1978	16/18	College Students	Visualization
.23 to -.35	Paivio, 1978	16/18	College Students	Verbal Intelligence
-.11	Palmer et al., 1985	91	College Students	Raven's
-.37 to -.53	Seymour & Moir, 1980	120	11-year-olds	Verbal Reasoning
+.05	Smith & Stanley, 1980	45	15-year-olds	Verbal Intelligence
+.07 to -.33	Smith & Stanley, 1983	137	12-year-olds	'g'
+.10 to -.36	Smith & Stanley, 1983	137	12-year-olds	Spatial Ability
-.01 to -.19	Smith & Stanley, 1983	137	12-year-olds	Verbal Ability

*Reported in Nettelbeck & Kirby, 1983

Table 8.1B

Reaction Time - Intelligence Correlations

(Difference Score or Linear Regression Slope)

Correlation	Source	Sample Size	Population	Intelligence Measure
-.20	Carlson & Jensen, 1982	20	9th Graders	Raven's
+.09	Carlson et al., 1983	105	7th Graders	Raven's
+.06 to -.37	Jenkinson, 1983	60	6th Graders	Fluid Intelligence
+.15 to -.32	Jenkinson, 1983	60	6th Graders	Crystallized Intelligence
-.41	Jensen, 1979	50	College Students	Raven's
-.30	Jensen & Munro, 1977	39	9th Graders	Raven's
-.35	Lally & Nettelbeck, 1977*	32	Non-Retarded Adults	WAIS Performance
-.05 to -.11	Lansman, 1981	84	College Students	Fluid Intelligence
+.03 to -.21	Lansman, 1981	84	College Students	Crystallized Intelligence
-.07 to -.55	Lunneborg, 1977	64	High School Students	Miscellaneous
-.41	Nettelbeck & Kirby, 1983	91	Adults, Normal	Raven's/WAIS
-.01 to -.06	Seymour & Moir, 1980	120	11-year-olds	Verbal Reasoning
+.20	Smith & Stanley, 1980	45	15-year-olds	Verbal Intelligence
-.28	Smith & Stanley, 1983	137	12-year-olds	'g'
-.25	Smith & Stanley, 1983	137	12-year-olds	Spatial Ability
-.11	Smith & Stanley, 1983	137	12-year-olds	Verbal Ability
-.47	Spiegel & Bryant, 1978	94	6th Graders	Lorge-Thorndike

*Reported in Nettelbeck & Kirby, 1983

of intelligence in order to express all of the results in terms of a common metric. Obviously many other studies have been conducted that are relevant to the speed-intelligence relation, but adherence to these criteria increases comparability across studies, thus facilitating evaluation of the hypothesis that speed is related to intelligence.

The entries in Table 8.1 are separated into two categories based on whether the speed measure corresponded to average reaction time (or to the intercept of a reaction time regression equation), or to a difference between two reaction times (or to the slope of a reaction time regression equation). It is frequently claimed that derived measures based on slopes of regression equations or differences between two reaction times provide purer measures of mental processing speed, and thus might be expected to yield higher relationships with measures of intelligence. The data of Table 8.1 do not offer much support for this view because the correlations appear to be of comparable magnitude with both types of speed measures.

Although there is considerable variability in the magnitude of the correlations in Table 8.1, and despite few of them being very large, the majority appear to be consistent with the hypothesis that faster speed is associated with higher levels of intelligence. Moreover the magnitudes of the true relationship may have been underestimated in many of these studies because of restricted range of intelligence variation as a result of extremely homogeneous samples, use of measures of unknown validity to represent intelligence, and unreliable measures of reaction time. Jensen (1980, 1982a) seems to have exaggerated when he suggested that the correlations are never in the 'wrong' direction (i.e., positive rather than negative, indicating slower time associated with higher intelligence), but it is the case that negative correlations predominate over positive ones and thus the speed hypothesis appears at least moderately well supported on the basis of existing data.

Criticisms of this Research

Although the results summarized in Table 8.1 are generally consistent with the hypothesis that processing speed is related

to level of intelligence, many of the studies can be criticized
for methodological weaknesses. (Also see Longstreth [1984]
for another methodological critique). Because many of these
same problems could limit the value of research on speed in
the field of aging, it is instructive to examine the nature
of the difficulties in some detail.

One problem with much of the previous research is that
many different speeded measures have been derived from the
experimental tasks, and the hypothesis was considered supported
if any one of the measures exhibited a significant correlation
with intelligence. For example, five measures corresponding
to the mean and standard deviation for both reaction time
and movement time, and the slope of the linear regression
of reaction time on number of stimulus alternatives, were
reported by Jensen and Munro (1979), with sizable negative
correlations (-.30 to -.43) reported for all measures except
the standard deviation of movement time. In a similar study
by Carlson, Jensen, and Widaman (1983) many of the same measures
were again examined but this time only two variables, of which
one was the standard deviation of movement time, were found
to be significantly correlated with intelligence. Replication
of only one out of five outcomes is hardly convincing, and
yet both studies were considered to support the speed-intelligence
hypothesis. Obviously if a large enough number of variables
are included and the investigator is indifferent with respect
to which variable is most relevant, some significant correlations
would be expected simply by chance, even if no true relationship
existed. In order to avoid capitalizing on random variations,
therefore, the one or two speed measures of greatest theoretical
interest should be specified in advance of any analyses, and
the primary conclusions based on the results from only those
measures.

Perhaps the most severe problem in the research on speed
and intelligence is the low or undocumented reliability of
the speed measures. Reliability estimates are sometimes reported,
but they are nearly always assessments of internal consistency
derived from split-half correlations. As discussed in Chapter

6, this type of assessment is insensitive to variations in
strategy or set that are likely to be important determinants
of reaction time, the observable behavior from which processing
speed is inferred. A preferable procedure for assessing reliability in individual differences research is the test-retest
technique in which an interval, during which changes in strategy
or set could conceivably occur, elapses between successive
measurements of the variable. Only if the test-retest correlation
coefficient is reasonably large can one claim that the phenomenon
is stable, and not merely that its measurement is consistent.

Comparisons of split-half (consistency) and test-retest
(stability) estimates of reliability of reaction time measures
nearly always reveal that the former are substantially greater
than the latter (e.g., Barrett, Alexander, Doverspike, Cellar,
& Thomas, 1982; Chiang & Atkinson, 1976). Jensen (1982a)
also reported that the across-session correlations for 100
subjects were only .72 for the reaction time intercept and
.35 for the reaction time slope compared to split-half, within-
session, correlations of .97 and .75, respectively. Jensen
attributed this low stability to the sensitivity of reaction
time parameters to physiological and emotional states which
vary from day to day, but there is clearly a logical difficulty
in attempting to assess a fundamental characteristic of the
nervous system with measures that are not even stable across
an interval as short as a few days. This problem is accentuated
when it is found, as reported by Jensen (1982a), that the
"...parameters that correlate most highly with psychometric
tests of g...also have the lowest stability coefficients (p. 280)."
The lack of stability in the measures of speed is also inconsistent
with the claim that these variables are independent of strategies
and other aspects of knowledge (e.g., Eysenck, 1982; Jensen,
1979, 1982a).

One procedure that might be followed to support the assertion
that the measures are strategy-invariant would be to demonstrate
that nearly identical results are obtained across different
assessment periods, perhaps even when the subjects are encouraged
to approach the task in a different manner during each adminis-

tration of the task.   However, the fact that the test-retest
correlations are not very high even without explicit instructions
to attempt to vary one's strategy indicates that the possibility
that the speed values are influenced by variations in strategy
cannot be ruled out.

Another overstated claim with respect to the 'purity'
of the speed measures is that they directly reflect efficiency
of the nervous system because there are little or no effects
of practice on these measures.   In actuality even the simplest
reaction time and tachistoscopic measures exhibit noticeable
effects of practice across tens, hundreds, and even thousands
of trials.   Many of the relevant studies were reviewed by
Salthouse and Somberg (1982a), who also presented additional
evidence of their own that measures of choice reaction time,
signal detection, and perceptual discrimination all improve
substantially with extensive practice.   It is not clear to
what extent the performance improvement in these tasks can
be attributed to the development of more effective strategies
or to increased efficiency of component processes, but it
is certainly an overstatement to assert that even such presumably
simple measures as reaction time or tachistoscopic discrimination
are direct reflections of unalterable characteristics of the
nervous system.

Seymour and Moir (1980) were so impressed by the possibility
of strategy variations in these types of tasks that they suggested:

> ...it seems likely that qualitative variations in
> the **executive programmes** which schedule and call
> the subordinate routines are more important as cognitive
> determinants of intelligence than differences in
> the speeds of functioning of the individual routines...
> (and)...variations in intelligence have more to
> do with the capacity to determine **what** should be
> compared than with the **speed** with which the comparison
> can be made (Seymour & Moir, 1980, p. 60-61).

While perhaps true in many respects, these statements ignore
the issue of what is responsible for the qualitative differences
in strategy, and, as noted in Chapter 7, it is possible that

differences in speed were the primary causal determinant of
the strategy differences. Regardless of how possible differences
in strategies are to be interpreted, the Seymour and Moir
(1980) quotation does serve to emphasize the need to control
variations in strategy when attempting to examine the relation
between intelligence and speed of elementary processes.

What types of strategies might be involved in tasks such
as reaction time and inspection time? For concreteness we
will simply mention a few that are possible in the two most
popular paradigms used in speed-intelligence studies, the
reaction time - movement time procedure and the inspection
time procedure. (Also see Nettelbeck and Kirby, 1983, and
Smith and Stanley, 1983, for additional discussion of possible
strategies in these tasks.)

The procedure used by Jensen (e.g., 1979, 1982a, 1982b)
and others (e.g., Carlson, Jensen, & Widaman, 1983; Nettelbeck
& Lally, 1983; Vernon, 1983) is based on what is known as
the Hick paradigm because Hick (1952) discovered that reaction
time increased directly with the number of alternative stimuli,
and suggested that the slope of this function could serve
as a measure of information transmission rate. The apparatus
employed to measure reaction time and movement time consists
of a single 'home key' surrounded by a semi-circle of eight
response keys, each adjacent to a different target light.
The task for the subject is hold the home key down and immediately
release it and move the finger to press the key below the
appropriate target light whenever one of the target lights
is illuminated. The two measures obtained from a given trial
are the reaction time to release the home key, and the movement
time to press the target key after the release of the home
key. A problem with this arrangement is that it allows the
subject the option of making the choice decision before releasing
the home key, and thus incorporating decision time into the
initial reaction time, or releasing the key as soon as any
event is detected and then making the choice while the movement
is in progress, thereby including the choice component in
the movement time rather than the reaction time. These two

approaches to the task can be considered different strategies,
and Jensen (1980, 1982a) has reported that what might be an
index of their relative frequency, the ratio of reaction time
to movement time, varies directly with intelligence. Obviously
if people of different levels of intelligence are performing
the task in different ways it is inappropriate to rely on
a single measure as a reflection of basic processing efficiency.

Another indication of possible strategy variation occurs
when there is a high correlation between the slope and intercept
measures derived from the task. A negative relation could
be interpreted as suggesting that some individuals carried
out most of the processing in the components contributing
to the intercept parameter and very little in the component(s)
reflected by the slope parameter, while others apparently
did the opposite.

The inspection-time task also has the potential for a
number of different strategies to influence the magnitude
of the speed estimates. For example, a careful observer may
attend to ostensibly irrelevant, but correlated, aspects of
the display such as apparent movement produced by the replacement
of the target stimulus by the masking stimulus, or to fluctuations
in brightness created by unequal amounts of energy in different
portions of the stimulus field. Even more serious is the
possibility that some subjects develop the technique of synchro-
nizing their eye blinks with the onset of the mask, thereby
blanking out the interfering mask and prolonging the effective
duration of the target stimulus.

While discussing these specific tasks it is also important
to mention two likely artifacts that preclude unambiguous
interpretation of the measures derived from them. First,
in the Jensen reaction time - movement time paradigm, the
target stimuli are generally arranged in a semi-circle with
a 6-inch radius, which at a probable viewing distance of 18
inches results in a visual angle of nearly 34 degrees between
the extreme targets. Such a large stimulus field almost certainly
involves a fairly extensive visual search to locate targets,
and even if responses could be initiated without overt eye

movements, reaction times to extreme targets would be expected
to be delayed because of the distance of the targets from
the fovea. Many studies have reported that reaction time
increases directly with the distance of the target stimulus
from the foveal center of the eye (e.g., Berlucchi, Crea,
DiStefano, & Tassinari, 1977; Sterling & Salthouse, 1981).
Because the more extreme target locations are likely to be
used more frequently in the conditions with the greatest number
of stimulus-response alternatives, a confounding of retinal
location with number of potential stimulus alternatives may
be responsible for at least some of the results reported in
studies employing the Jensen apparatus. In support of this
interpretation is the finding (Jensen, 1982a, 1982b) that
there was a sizable slope (18 milliseconds per bit) even when
subjects only had the reaction time task with no required
movement. In contrast, the typical 'lift-and-move' task yielded
a slope of only 26 milliseconds per bit, indicating that nearly
two-thirds of the effect was independent of the choice requirement,
and perhaps caused by the differential detectability of the
stimuli in the various conditions. Individual differences
in sensitivity to sequential constraints, which are likely
to be more pronounced with a greater number of stimulus alternatives, may also be contributing to some of these slope effects,
and mistakenly interpreted as reflections of additional increments
of pure speed.

A major problem in the inspection time procedure is that
the goal is to obtain an index of the duration required for
initial stimulus processing, and yet by varying the duration
of the target stimulus the energy of the stimulus is confounded
with time available for processing. Strictly speaking, therefore,
one cannot distinguish between time (interstimulus interval)
and energy (the product of illuminance and duration) as the
variable being assessed in this procedure. A more desirable
technique would be to present the target stimulus for a fixed
duration, e.g., 10 milliseconds, and then to have a blank
interval of variable duration between the offset of the stimulus
and the onset of the mask. In this manner the energy of the

stimulus is held constant because the target is always exposed for the same amount of time, and it is only the time allowed for processing that varies.

Another problem with at least some of the research relying on derived measures of reaction time is that the measures are only meaningful if the data on which they are based conform to the task model. This is often not the case with slope measures derived from linear regression analyses of reaction time as a function of some manipulation of complexity because the linear regression equation typically provides a very poor fit to data derived from early stages in practice in individual subjects. There are no absolute criteria for establishing when an equation is considered to be an accurate reflection of the data, but the equation certainly becomes less meaningful as the proportion of variance accounted for drops below about .5. This is equivalent to a correlation of about .7, and yet slopes are sometimes reported when the correlations between the complexity index and reaction time are much less than this, or perhaps even worse, are simply not mentioned.

The Speed-Accuracy Tradeoff   Another often misunderstood confounding in many of the studies of reaction time has to do with the problem of distinguishing between the individual's capacity to perform rapidly on the one hand, and his or her bias towards speed or accuracy on the other hand. If one equates the potential to respond quickly with capacity, and the particular emphasis on accuracy as opposed to speed with strategic bias or cautiousness, this issue can be termed the capacity-audacity confound. The instructions typically given to subjects in reaction time tasks are inherently ambiguous in that they indicate that the subjects should attempt to respond 'as rapidly and as accurately as possible,' but in actuality, speed and accuracy are inversely related and thus these demands are mutually exclusive. At least within certain regions of difficulty, faster speed can only be achieved at the expense of lower accuracy, and higher accuracy is accomplished only by slower speed. It is therefore reasonable to think of a subject in a reaction time task as operating at a particular

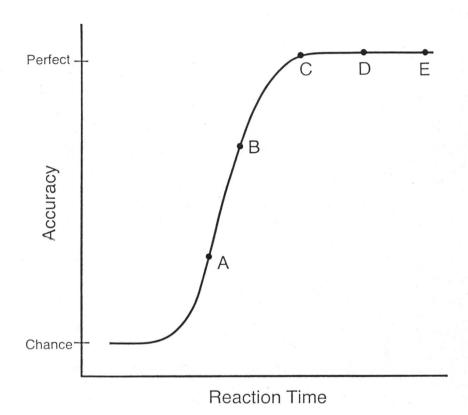

Figure 8.5 Schematic illustration of a speed-accuracy tradeoff. Notice that within a certain range, shorter reaction time (greater speed) is associated with lower accuracy.

point along what has been termed the speed-accuracy operating characteristic. A schematic illustration of such a characteristic is presented in Figure 8.5, along with five points representing different relative emphases on speed and accuracy.

The intent in most reaction time tasks is to measure performance at point C, the minimum reaction time at the maximum level of accuracy. This point might be called the optimum reaction time, but in most situations we have no way of being certain that the subject is operating at this point rather than at any of the other regions along the function. Less than perfect accuracy indicates that the subject is probably operating below this point, e.g., at point A or B, but unless one has complete knowledge about the quantitative relation between speed and accuracy it is impossible to determine exactly how far the subject's performance is from the desired optimum. An even more serious problem occurs when accuracy is nearly perfect because points C, D, and E cannot be distinguished under these conditions, and therefore one cannot be certain that the reaction time truly reflects the maximum speed of which the individual is capable. It is quite possible that certain individuals typically perform farther along the accuracy axis from their optimum reaction time than other individuals, and thus the speed measurements may not reflect the same property in every individual. Indeed, precisely this finding was reported by Salthouse (1979), suggesting that older adults generally place a relatively greater emphasis on accuracy than on speed compared to young adults.

The implication of the speed-accuracy operating characteristic is that single measures of speed or accuracy may not be very meaningful by themselves. Some attempts have been made to deal with the problem of the speed-accuracy tradeoff, but nearly every procedure that has been employed can be severely criticized for one reason or another. For example, it is obviously absurd to ignore the existence of the tradeoff by simply excluding incorrect responses in the computation of average reaction time. To the extent that a speed-accuracy tradeoff is operating, it will affect the latency of all responses, and not merely those which happen to be incorrect.

Another inappropriate procedure is to examine the correlation between speed and accuracy across subjects in an attempt to determine whether the sample as a whole exhibited a speed-accuracy tradeoff. The fallacy in this approach is that it does not address the issue of a speed-accuracy tradeoff within individuals, and it is at that level where there is the greatest concern about obtaining the optimum reaction time. Moreover, even within-subject correlations are unlikely to be very informative since they would merely indicate whether a tradeoff was operative, and not how to identify the individual's optimum speed.

Although often not recognized, comparisons are also flawed when accuracy is perfect in all individuals because, as illustrated in Figure 8.5, they may still differ in their relative distance from the optimum reaction time. That is, both points D and E correspond to error-free performance and yet neither represents the optimum reaction time.

Perhaps the best solution to the speed-accuracy tradeoff problem is to obtain data sufficient to generate the entire speed-accuracy operating characteristic for each individual in each condition (cf., Jackson, 1980; Salthouse, 1979; Salthouse & Somberg, 1982c). In this manner time comparisons can be made at any specified level of accuracy, or conversely, time could be equated and differences examined in terms of accuracy. Without some procedure of this type it must be recognized that the temporal measures are only approximate values, and in fact might best be considered to represent only an ordinal, instead of an interval, or ratio, scale of measurement.

It should also be noted that derived measures of reaction time such as the difference between two reaction times or the slope of a reaction time function are also not immune from speed-accuracy tradeoff contaminations. To illustrate, the slope in the Sternberg memory-scanning paradigm (see Chapter 9 for a description) has been found to vary by up to a factor of five with manipulations of relative emphasis on speed or accuracy (e.g., Banks & Atkinson, 1974; Pachella, 1974).

Conclusions about the Speed-Intelligence Relationship

The preceding sections clearly indicate that there are
a number of methodological flaws in much of the recent research
attempting to establish a relation between speed and intelligence.
It is difficult to determine the extent to which the results
summarized in Table 8.1 were influenced by the flaws, or even
the specific direction of the bias induced by these methodological
characteristics. However, not all of the studies are subject
to these objections and many did report significant negative
correlations. Probably the safest conclusion at the present
time is to suggest that although the evidence is not entirely
convincing, there does seem to be a small negative relationship
between speed and intelligence such that more intelligent
individuals are generally faster on relatively simple speeded
tasks than less intelligent individuals.

It is likely that more compelling evidence for the relation
between speed and cognition will require greater elaboration
of the concept of speed of processing. Although a number
of speed measures have been employed in this area of research,
the choice of a given measure is often rather arbitrary and
there is little understanding of how the different measures
interrelate to one another. In the next section the problem
of identifying a suitable measure of processing speed is discussed
and relevant empirical evidence summarized.

How Should Speed be Measured?

Obtaining an index of an individual's capacity for responding
quickly has been a goal of researchers at least since the
time of the discovery of the 'personal equation' by Maskelyne
in the context of individual differences among astronomers
in timing the positioning of stars and planets (cf. Boring,
1950). As indicated by the attempts described in the preceding
sections, this effort has not yet been very successful because
it has thus far proven difficult to obtain a reliable measure
that can be considered a relatively direct reflection of a
fundamental property of the nervous system such as basic operation
time, clock cycle time, or neural propagation rate.

One variable that has sometimes been proposed as an index

of the rate of an internal clock is a measure of accuracy
of temporal judgments. The reasoning here is that the slope
of the function relating subjective (judged) time to objective
time might serve as a measure of the rate of an internal clock
presumed to be the basis for the time judgments. Unfortunately,
it doesn't appear that the speed of overt, or even covert,
behavioral activities are mediated by the same mechanism(s)
responsible for temporal judgments. For example, several
researchers (e.g., Arenberg, 1968a; Salthouse, Wright, & Ellis,
1979; Surwillo, 1964a) have reported that young and old adults
do not differ in their accuracy of time estimation, despite
the former being much faster in most speeded responses than
the latter. This inconsistency must be resolved before the
time estimation procedure will be useful for estimating the
speed of a hypothesized internal clock.

    Reliance upon direct measures such as reaction time also
has complications because one must still decide whether the
tasks are to be simple or complex, the speed measures direct
or derived, etc. The issue of whether to rely upon simple
or complex tasks in obtaining measures of speed is rather
controversial because plausible arguments can be marshalled
for each position. Advocates of simple tasks suggest that
they minimize the role of other factors such as strategies
or pre-experimental knowledge that complicate the interpretation
of processing speed. On the other hand, proponents of complex
tasks argue that only when the amount of internal processing
is large relative to the duration of input and output processes
does one have a reasonable opportunity to detect variations
in processing rate. There is no easy resolution of this debate,
but it is important to recognize that as tasks become more
complex there is a greater likelihood of the involvement of
many factors besides pure speed. For example, it is probably
unrealistic to expect the speed factor to be very large when
examining average time to solution in different cognitive
tests because the ability specific to the content of each
test will be the major determinant of performance. One possible
compromise is to use tasks that involve a number of different

cognitive operations to perform, thus maximizing the possibility of detecting central speed differences, but which can be performed perfectly in the absence of time limits and hence don't require special abilities.

As noted earlier, many researchers have proposed some form of difference score as the measure of speed because by subtracting the simpler reaction time from the more complex one it is presumed that the duration of input and output processes are eliminated, thus resulting in a pure measure of central processing time. There are several difficulties with this approach, of which the most severe are the generally unverified assumptions about the additive nature of the tasks (Pachella, 1974), and the problem of obtaining reliable and meaningful difference scores (Cronbach & Furby, 1970). The assumption that total reaction time is merely the sum of a number of discrete and independent stages has often been questioned (cf., Pachella, 1976; Sternberg, 1969), and therefore the logical status of the derived score is uncertain. Low reliability of difference scores may be a major reason why the available evidence does not indicate that derived measures are more highly correlated with cognitive measures than direct measures of average reaction time (cf., Table 8.1).

Empirical Evidence of Interrelationships of Speed Measures

If speed of processing is a meaningful task-independent construct, it should be evident in a pattern of high correlations among speeded measures derived from a variety of different types of tasks. In this section the results of two studies will be described in which correlations were computed across measures of speed obtained from several different tasks.

In order to interpret the magnitude of the correlations it is necessary to know the reliability of the measures when reliability is determined in separate administrations of the task. According to the argument advanced earlier, the ideal procedure is probably to obtain the speed measures in different sessions separated by an interval long enough to allow forgetting of any specific strategy used to perform the task. Another acceptable procedure might be to administer each task twice

in a balanced order such that the subject is exposed to all
tasks at least once before being presented with the second
occurrence of a given task. In this manner the subject has
the opportunity to develop a variety of alternative strategies,
and thus the test-retest correlation will indicate the stability
of measurement when there is potential for alternative strategies
to be employed.

For the reason just specified, a counterbalanced sequence
of experimental tasks was employed in these studies. The
studies will be described in considerable detail because they
have not previously been published and the results have important
implications for research on the concept of speed of processing.

Only college-age individuals participated in the project,
thereby avoiding spuriously inflated correlations produced
by including effects of age in the measure of association
(cf., Chapter 6). Furthermore, the experimental procedures
incorporated several features designed to maximize reliability
of the speed measures. First, very similar tasks were used
in the tachistoscopic and reaction time paradigms, and each
task was preceded by several practice trials in order to ensure
complete understanding. Second, the tachistoscopic procedures
relied upon a Parameter Estimation by Sequential Testing (PEST)
adaptive threshold procedure (Taylor & Creelman, 1967) to
determine the interstimulus interval between the target stimulus
and the masking stimulus that resulted in 75% accuracy across
two independent sequences of 20 trials each. The PEST procedure
was considered a much more precise and sensitive method for
assessing temporal thresholds than techniques previously employed
in this area. And third, reaction time measures consisted
of the mean reaction time for a sequence of 50 trials with
an accuracy of at least 90%. This is obviously not an ideal
solution to the problem of the speed-accuracy tradeoff, but
it does minimize some of the problems, particularly if subjects
are strongly encouraged to respond as rapidly as possible
within the specified level of accuracy.

Thirty-eight college students participated in the first
study, which involved four time-stressed paper-and-pencil

tests, two tachistoscopic duration tasks, and six measures
of reaction time. The Digit Symbol test was a modification
of the one used in the Wechsler Adult Intelligence Scale,
while the Finding A's, Identical Pictures, and Number Comparison
tests were from the Kit of Reference Tests for Cognitive Factors
(French, Ekstrom, & Price, 1963). The detection threshold
measure corresponded to the interval between the offset of
a 10-millisecond target stimulus and the onset of a 500-millisecond
masking stimulus sufficient to yield 75% accuracy in decisions
about whether the stimulus was a letter (X or O) or a blank
field. A measure of discrimination threshold was obtained
in the same manner except that the decision was between the
letters X and O rather than the presence or absence of any
letter.

The simple reaction time task consisted of the subject
pressing a designated key as rapidly as possible whenever
either an X or an O appeared. The index finger of the right
hand was used for one 45-trial block, and the index finger
of the left hand for a second 45-trial block. The mean reaction
times for the last 25 trials in each of the two blocks were
averaged to yield the measure of simple reaction time. The
choice reaction time task involved subjects pressing a key
with the left index finger upon the occurrence of an X, and
pressing a key with the right index finger upon the occurrence
of an O. The mean reaction times for the last 25 trials with
an accuracy of 90% or greater after a minimum of 45 trials
served as the measure of choice reaction time.

The matching reaction time task consisted of the presentation
of two pairs of letters, each containing either an upper-
or lower-case X and O (e.g., xO, oX, Xo, or Ox). Subjects
were instructed to press a key with their left index finger
if the letters of the second pair were the same case as those
of the first pair, and to press a key with the right index
finger if the letters were of different cases. Two types
of matches could therefore be distinguished; physical matches
in which both the case and the order of the letters was the
same in the two pairs (e.g., xO - xO, Xo - Xo), and rule matches

in which the order of the letters was different but the cases
were the same (e.g., xO - Ox, Xo - oX). The matching task
continued for a minimum of 75 trials until 50 trials with
an accuracy of 90% or greater was achieved. The mean reaction
times for physical-match (e.g., xO - xO), rule-match (e.g.,
xO - Ox), and different (e.g., xO - Xo) trials within the
criterion set of 50 trials served as the dependent measures.

The major results of this study are summarized in Table
8.2. The values in parentheses are reliability coefficients
computed by correlating the values obtained from the two administrations of each task and boosting this value by the Spearman-
Brown formula to estimate reliability of the composite measure.
All remaining correlations in the table were based on the
average of the scores on the two blocks.

The most interesting result in Table 8.2 is that the
correlations among measures all thought to reflect speed of
processing were fairly low, with a median absolute correlation
of only .29. There are some clusters of moderate to high
correlations among measures from the paper-and-pencil tests,
and among the choice and matching reaction times, but with
these exceptions there was little evidence of substantial
between-task relations in the various measures of speeded
processing. On the whole, then, these data provide little
support for the notion of a unitary, task-independent, construct
of processing speed.

The low reliability of the rule-physical difference score
is also somewhat discouraging in that some theorists might
consider this variable the most promising index of the speed
of mental processing. Like other commonly employed measures
(e.g., name access time in the Posner paradigm, memory scanning
time in the Sternberg paradigm, mental rotation time in the
Shepard paradigm, see Chapter 9 for descriptions of these
procedures), it is based on the time difference obtained in
slightly different reaction time tasks, and therefore could
be assumed to be free of peripheral sensory and motor factors.
Unfortunately, the low reliability of difference scores reduces
the usefulness of this measure despite its theoretical interest.

Table 8.2

Correlation Matrix from Study 1

Variable	Mean	(sd)	1	2	3	4	5	6	7	8	9	10	11	12
1. Digit Symbol	75	12	(.94)	.51	.46	.59	-.18	-.51	-.21	-.27	-.28	-.43	-.36	-.39
2. Finding A's	27	5		(.80)	.32	.50	-.11	-.31	-.13	-.32	-.11	-.12	-.10	-.06
3. Identical Pictures	38	5			(.76)	.57	-.07	-.52	-.24	-.15	-.23	-.33	-.31	-.28
4. Number Comparison	28	5				(.82)	-.12	-.37	.09	-.18	-.28	-.32	-.31	-.20
5. Detection Threshold	43	26					(.28)	.23	.19	.14	.15	.29	.19	.33
6. Discrimination Threshold	39	16						(.67)	.12	.34	.18	.29	.36	.27
7. Simple RT	289	61							(.95)	.34	.20	.32	.24	.31
8. Choice RT	428	53								(.82)	.68	.54	.65	.07
9. Physical Match	625	102									(.83)	.84	.87	.17
10. Rule Match	694	137										(.86)	.89	.68
11. Different	716	129											(.91)	.43
12. Rule-Physical	69	76												(.52)

Note: A correlation with an absolute magnitude of .32 is significant at $p < .05$, and one with an absolute magnitude of .41 is significant at $p < .01$.

The purpose of the second study was to further explore the interrelations of tachistoscopic and reaction time measures of speed of processing in a sample of young adults. As in the first study, the tachistoscopic threshold tasks and the reaction time tasks were designed to involve formally similar decisions in order to maximize the correspondence between the two types of tasks.

Forty-eight college students completed two blocks of each of six tasks in a counterbalanced order. The tachistoscopic and reaction time tasks were designed to be formally identical with decisions concerned with presence/absence (detection threshold, simple reaction time), identity (discrimination threshold, choice reaction time), and recognition (same/different threshold, same/different reaction time).

The tachistoscopic tasks each involved a 10-millisecond presentation of the target stimulus followed after a variable dark interval by a 500-millisecond masking stimulus. The interstimulus interval between the offset of the target and the onset of the mask was adjusted with a PEST procedure to determine the value yielding 75% accuracy in the relevant decision over two independent sequences of 20 trials each. Stimuli in the detection task were either an X, an O, or a blank field, and the subject was instructed to press a key with the left index finger for either an X or an O, and to press a key with the right index finger for a blank. Stimuli in the discrimination task were either an X or an O and the subject was instructed to press a key on the left for an X, and a key on the right for an O. The recognition task involved the presentation of two stimuli; an initial X or O followed shortly later by a 10-millisecond target presentation of an X or an O, the variable blank interval, and the mask. Subjects were instructed to press a key on the left when the two successive stimuli were the same (i.e., X-X or O-O), and to press a key on the right when they were different (i.e., X-O or O-X).

The simple and choice reaction time tasks were identical to those described in the previous study. Each trial involved the presentation of an X or an O, with subjects instructed

to press a specified key as rapidly as possible when either
letter appeared (simple reaction time), or to press a left
key for X and a right key for O (choice reaction time). The
recognition reaction time task was identical to the recognition
tachistoscopic task except that the final stimulus was displayed
until the occurrence of the response and the response was
to be made as quickly as possible.

The dependent variable in the simple reaction time task
was the mean across the two hands of the mean reaction time
for the last 25 trials in blocks of 45 trials for each hand.
Dependent variables in the choice and recognition reaction
time tasks consisted of the mean reaction time for the last
50 trials with an accuracy of at least 90% after a minimum
of 75 trials. The mean thresholds or reaction times across
the two blocks with each tasks served as the primary dependent
variables.

The correlation matrix for the variables of Study 2 is
displayed in Table 8.3. Reliability of the detection threshold
measure was improved relative to Study 1, but it is still
somewhat lower than that for the other measures. As was the
case in the first study, the data in Table 8.3 indicate that
the tachistoscopic threshold measures and the reaction time
measures tended to form separate clusters with correlations
ranging from .59 to .78 within clusters, but only from .24
to .52 between clusters. The median absolute correlation
in Table 8.3 is .35.

It is interesting that the mean durations of the three
thresholds were virtually identical, despite the varying nature
of the decisions. This equivalence is consistent with an
interpretation that the masking procedure terminates an early
stage of processing common to each type of decision. An implication of this finding is that task complexity is probably
not a meaningful dimension with tachistoscopic measures of
processing speed. In view of this result, one may question
the usefulness of tachistoscopic duration measures such as
inspection time for the purpose of investigating relations
between mental speed and measures of complex intellectual

Table 8.3

Correlation Matrix from Study 2

Variable	Mean	(sd)	1	2	3	4	5	6	7
1. Digit Symbol	73	10	--	-.13	-.15	-.23	-.14	-.33	-.27
2. Detection Threshold	60	29		(.63)	.78	.60	.30	.24	.27
3. Discrimination Threshold	60	29			(.86)	.74	.35	.36	.25
4. Recognition Threshold	58	31				(.80)	.52	.39	.41
5. Simple RT	286	49					(.91)	.79	.59
6. Choice RT	433	50						(.85)	.60
7. Recognition RT	569	92							(.82)

Note: A correlation with an absolute magnitude of .28 is significant at $p < .05$, and one with an absolute magnitude of .37 is significant at $p < .01$.

functioning.

Although the correlations in Table 8.3 are somewhat higher than those in Table 8.2, there is still very little evidence to support the claim that the various measures all reflect a common rate of information processing within the nervous system. The low correlations are particularly dramatic in the present study because the tachistoscopic and reaction time tasks were deliberately paired with one another with respect to the nature of the decisions, and the measures appear to have at least moderately high stability. Nevertheless, the correlations across tasks, but presumably involving the same types of processing, are generally lower than those within tasks, and based on different types of decisions.

The correlational results in Tables 8.2 and 8.3 are consistent with the values reported in several other studies in which a number of speeded tasks were administered to the same group of individuals from a relatively homogeneous age range. For example, correlations between different reaction time measures range from .1 to .9, with most between .3 and .6 (e.g., Barrett, Alexander, Doverspike, Cellar & Thomas, 1982; Birren, Riegel, & Morrison, 1962; Chiang & Atkinson, 1976; Jackson, 1980; Jackson & McClelland, 1979; Lanier, 1934; Lansman, Donaldson, Hunt, & Yantis, 1982; Lemmon, 1927; Lunneborg, 1977; Mumaw, Pellegrino, Kail, & Carter, 1984; Palmer, MacLeod, Hunt, & Davidson, 1985; Puckett & Kausler, 1984; Schwartz, Griffin, & Brown, 1983; Vernon, 1983), correlations between reaction time and paper-and-pencil speed measures range between .15 to -.70 (Barrett, et al., 1982; Birren, Botwinick, Weiss, & Morrison, 1963; Lansman, 1981; Lansman, et al., 1982; Lemmon, 1927), and correlations between reaction time and tachistoscopic thresholds from .07 to .25 (Jackson & McClelland, 1979).

It is important to point out that the preceding results are all based on samples that were quite homogeneous with respect to age, and probably intelligence. Much more impressive correlations would therefore be expected with samples containing a greater range of variation on each measure. However, the

present concern is with the degree of interrelation of alternative
measures of speed observed within a relatively homogeneous
group, and consequently increasing the variation by including
individuals with differing characteristics, and thereby incorporating group differences into the correlations, will produce
a misleading indication of these relations.

Now consider the implications of these results for research
attempting to identify a relation between an index of speed
and some aspect of cognition. With suitable care it is evidently
possible to obtain respectable reliabilities in the .8 to
.9 range for most speeded measures, with the possible exception
of difference score measures which will nearly always have
lower reliability than the scores from which they were derived.
This indicates that between 80% and 90% of the variance in
the speed measures is systematic and available for partitioning
into shared components. However, correlations between different
measures from the same type of task, e.g., choice reaction
time with recognition reaction time, are generally in the
.4 to .8 range, indicating that very similar tasks only have
from 16% to 64% common variance. And finally, the correlations
between measures all thought to reflect speed of processing
but derived from different paradigms, e.g., paper-and-pencil
tests versus reaction time or reaction time versus tachistoscopic
interval thresholds, only range from about .15 to .45. Correlations of this magnitude signify that between 2% to 20% of
the variance in each variable is shared with the other variable.
If two measures purporting to reflect the same underlying
concept of speed of processing have such little common variance
it seems unreasonable to expect measures representing quite
different concepts to exhibit any stronger relations. The
explanation for the relatively low correlations between measures
of speed and intelligence may therefore not be that the concepts
are unrelated, but rather that the concept of speed of processing
has yet to be successfully measured.

Is it Possible to Identify a Central Speed Factor?

The lack of high correlations among speeded measures
in the results of speed batteries such as those described

above can be interpreted as an indication that there is no
central speed factor. However, an alternative interpretation
is that central processing speed is only one determinant of
response time (cf., Berger, 1982), and that it may be unrealistic
to expect an accurate characterization of this property in
the face of so many other important determinants of response
time. McFarland (1930) expressed a similar viewpoint many
years ago in distinguishing between the theoretical concept
of speed and the observed characteristic of time:

> One must keep in mind the fact that speed is not
> the same as time in the mental reaction. Time is
> the total length of a reaction with possible distraction,
> fluctuation of attention, or what-not entering into
> the lapse of time. Theoretically speed may be the
> actual length of time required for the response
> free from distractions or anything outside the actual
> striving for the answer. Time, as it is usually
> recorded, then is speed plus disturbing ideas, fluct-
> uations of attention, or any one of many possible
> factors...It is clear from this brief analysis that,
> theoretically, one cannot measure the speed factor
> of a mental response precisely since there is no
> way to control or show objectively what is actually
> taking place during the time consumed by a subject
> (McFarland, 1930, p. 68).

Notice that this view does not deny the existence of some
central speed factor, but merely suggests that the variation
in content across tasks is so great as to make the abstraction
of an index of general processing rate very difficult, if
not impossible.

The difficulty of identifying a common speed factor can
also be illustrated by the following extreme, but possibly
not entirely facetious, example. Imagine that time measures
are available from a sample of individuals for the following
activities: (a) writing one's signature; (b) reading a short
story; (c) making a decision about which movie to see; (d)
getting dressed; and (e) running 50 yards. Even if one could

be assured that the times in each of these activities represented
the individual's maximal performance, it is highly unlikely
that a common speed factor could be isolated because of the
diverse requirements of these activities. The situation with
activities generally acknowledged to be cognitive may not
be too different since little is known about the exact processes
involved in such tasks and it is clear that factors like specific
ability, relevant practice, and motivation will influence
the duration of many, if not all, components of processing.

　　One of the problems with attempting to abstract a general
factor of speed is that time is a property of virtually all
responses and hence it is difficult to identify tasks which
have heavy or light loadings on this factor. In a sense it
may be analogous to trying to infer a general factor of behavioral
quality when nearly all behavior has qualitative aspects.
Traditionally, factors are inferred by varying the nature
of the tests presented to people and determining which dependent
measures are correlated with one another. A prerequisite
for this approach is the availability of tests that require
different amounts of what are thought to be different abilities.
With speed, and perhaps behavioral quality, however, this
may not be possible because they seem to be attributes of
all behavior.

　　This line of reasoning also raises questions about the
most appropriate measures of speed of processing because if
it is centrally determined, and a property of all behavior,
then presumably many variables might be used as a reflection
of processing rate. In other words, such complex and ostensibly
speed-independent tasks as analogical reasoning or free recall
might be just as suitable as choice reaction time to represent
the individual's rate of mental processing. Of course, variables
not measured directly in time are difficult to interpret in
terms of speed or rate, but their performance may be no less
dependent on speed than that of reaction time.

　　The implication of this view is that it is probably naive
to think that the efficiency or rate of information processing
within the nervous system can be accurately assessed by means

of such crude and primitive measures like reaction time or
tachistoscopic encoding time. One strategy might be to administer
a large number of speeded tasks in the hopes of identifying
a speed factor by analysis of the correlational pattern.
The data in Tables 8.2 and 8.3 suggest that more than one
factor might emerge, but a larger battery of tests might provide
information about the precise nature of any factors that are
obtained. Another strategy is to rely on psychophysiological
procedures, perhaps related to well-understood components
of the electroencephalogram, to derive a fairly direct measure
of mental processing speed. At the present time, however,
it must be admitted that lack of a well-accepted measure of
central processing speed is a major obstacle hindering further
understanding of the relation between speed and cognition.

Summary

It has long been proposed that the speed with which an
individual carries out even very simple mental operations
is causally related to his or her efficiency of performing
a great variety of cognitive activities. A very simple computer
simulation of a primitive network illustrated that variations
in speed could have substantial effects on the quality of
information available at various levels in the system, and
that these speed effects were pronounced only when the slowing
was evident throughout the network and not simply at the input
phase. In contrast to the unambiguous results from the simulation,
the empirical evidence relevant to the relation between speed
and intelligence is somewhat equivocal, and at least some
of the studies were discovered to have potentially serious
methodological weaknesses. Results from two studies involving
the administration of batteries of speeded tasks to samples
of college students led to the conclusion that since the available
speeded measures from somewhat different tasks tend to correlate
only about .3 with one another, it is unreasonable to expect
much larger correlations between measures of speed and measures
of cognitive functioning. The concept of a central speed
factor is still poorly understood and needs to be elaborated
before additional progress in this area can be expected.

The Speed Factor in Cognitive Aging

Even though the conclusion of the preceding chapter was
that variations in speed have been found to account for only
a small proportion of the variance in cognitive functioning
among people of the same age, speed might nevertheless be
an important determinant of age-associated differences in
cognition. That is, while the speed factor may be relatively
unimportant among individuals who are all fairly uniform in
their rates of processing, speed may still be the critical
determinant of the cognitive differences between two groups
if the absolute level of speed is drastically reduced from
one group to another. In other words, a speed factor may
emerge from the pattern of speed differences across groups
even if it is not very prominent in the interrelations of
the measures within a given age group.

This point can be illustrated by an analogy to the effects
of oxygen on cognitive performance. In the normal sea-level
environment there are only slight variations in the percentage
of oxygen in the air, and their impact is typically quite
minor relative to many other factors that influence cognitive
performance. As a consequence, amount of oxygen is generally
not considered an important determinant of cognitive functioning.
However, if one were to compare cognitive performance at sea-level
and at high-altitude, or in a hyperbaric chamber where the
only manipulated variable is oxygen pressure, it is quite
likely that a variety of cognitive impairments would be observed
as a function of the amount of oxygen present in the atmosphere
(e.g., McFarland, 1963). The role oxygen percentage plays
in intellectual functioning is therefore revealed only when
it is possible to examine a moderately large range of oxygen
levels.

An assumption of the present perspective is that the
factor of speed may be like oxygen in that its true importance
for cognitive performance is only apparent when groups of

individuals with widely different levels of speed are compared. There are presumed to be many determinants of performance variation at all ages, and consequently within a given age group speed may account for a relatively small proportion of the total variance in cognitive functioning. However, as people become slower with increased age, the speed difference may become progressively more important in accounting for the cognitive differences apparent across people of different ages. The other determinants of performance might still have similar distributions across individuals within each age group, and therefore many sources of individual differences in performance will continue to be important. However, because a reduction in speed is assumed to be the primary behavioral change associated with increased age, it can be hypothesized that the speed differences may be largely responsible for many of the age-related changes in cognitive performance.

To summarize the argument, it is assumed that even if speed has a relatively small effect within a given sample of fairly homogeneous people, it can still be the major cause for cognitive differences across different groups of people if its level is substantially changed across those groups. It was argued in Chapter 7 that two conditions must be satisfied in order for this type of resource-limitation reasoning to be plausible in accounting for age differences in cognition. First, it must be demonstrated that substantial reductions in speed do indeed occur across the adult lifespan, and that they are widespread and not simply restricted to a few unimportant aspects of behavior. And second, the logical status of the speed differences should be clarified, particularly with respect to whether they are causally implicated in the age differences in cognitive functioning. The present chapter addresses this first issue, while the second issue is considered in subsequent chapters.

What slows with age?

In a recent survey of much of the literature on age-related changes in speed of behavior (Salthouse, 1985), it was concluded that nearly every variable examined has been found to exhibit

age differences in speed. In light of the discussion in the
preceding chapter concerning the difficulty of establishing
a central speed factor, the prevalence with which age-related
speed differences are found in measures spanning nearly all
aspects of behavior is particularly impressive. Moreover,
despite the small correlations among the speeds of performing
different types of activities, if each of those speeds is
adversely affected by increased age, it may still be reasonable
to suggest that a shift in speed plays a major role in the
age-related changes in cognitive functioning. This is a central
premise in the current argument, and hence it is important
to be thorough in examining evidence for the generality of
age-related speed effects. The remainder of this section
will therefore focus on the range of variables found to exhibit
age-related differences in speed, and on several reported
exceptions to this general phenomenon.

Before discussing the results from human studies, it
is important to point out that age-related slowing of behavior
has also been reported in other species and thus can be considered
a general phenomenon of aging, and not merely a product of
uniquely human characteristics. Among the animals in which
significant relations between age and speed have been reported
are rats (e.g., Birren, 1955b; Birren & Kay, 1958; Kay & Birren,
1958), and monkeys (e.g., Davis, 1978).

Age differences in speed-related measures are sometimes
reported in the form of correlation coefficients, which provide
an indication of the strength of the relation between age
and speed. Of the studies cited by Salthouse (1985), the
median correlation with adult age was .28 for simple reaction
time, .43 for choice reaction time, and .46 for digit symbol
substitution score. These values, which are typical of those
found with a variety of other speeded measures, indicate that
between 10% and 20% of the variance in speed is associated
with age across the range of from about 18 to 70 years of
age.

Some writers (e.g., Botwinick, 1984) have not been very
impressed with correlations of this magnitude, pointing out

that the age-associated variance is only a small fraction of the total variance. However the important point is whether the relations between age and speed mediate the relations between age and various measures of cognitive functioning, and not the absolute size of the age-speed correlation. A more appropriate comparison is therefore the magnitude of the age-speed correlations relative to the magnitude of the correlations between age and the cognitive variables one is interested in explaining. If the former are small relative to the latter then the plausibility of the speed factor as a determinant of age-related cognitive differences is obviously weakened. On the other hand, a speed-based interpretation would still be reasonable if the correlations between age and speed were as large as, or larger than, the correlations between age and measures of cognitive functioning. We will see in later chapters that the second of these alternatives is generally supported by the empirical evidence, and consequently objections concerning the absolute magnitude of the correlations between age and speed do not seriously threaten the present arguments.

The absolute magnitude of the effects of age on speed vary with the specific dependent variable under investigation (cf., Salthouse, 1976), but for many variables the proportional difference between adults in their 60s and those in their 20s is between 20% and 60%, suggesting that the speed loss ranges from 5% to 15% per decade. Numerous reviews of this literature are available (e.g., Birren, Woods, & Williams, 1979, 1980; Salthouse, 1985; Welford, 1977, 1984), and therefore specific studies reporting age differences in simple speed of behavior will not be discussed here. Instead it will merely be accepted as fact that fairly substantial age differences are nearly always found in elementary tasks such as simple or choice reaction time and a variety of paper-and-pencil measures of perceptual-motor speed, and the reviews or the studies cited in those reviews can be consulted for the details of these results.

Age effects have also been reported in a number of psychophysiological measures thought to be related to speed of neural processing. For example, many studies have examined the relation between chronological age and the latency of various components of the evoked response in the electroencephalogram (EEG), and in nearly all it was reported that increased age was associated with longer latencies (e.g., Beck, Swanson, & Dustman, 1980; Buschbaum, Kenkin, & Christiansen, 1974; Dustman & Beck, 1966, 1969; Ford, Pfefferbaum, Tinklenberg, & Kopell, 1982; Ford, Roth, Mohs, Hopkins, & Kopell, 1979; Goodin, Squires, Henderson, & Starr, 1978). Increased age has also been found to be associated with a slowing of the alpha phase of the EEG, sometimes by as much as nearly 4 milliseconds per decade (Surwillo, 1968).

Effects of age have also been examined on the latency of a variety of reflexes, but with rather mixed results. Significant age-related slowing has been reported with the achilles tendon reflex (Laufer & Schweitz, 1968), and sometimes with the plantar reflex and the superficial abdominal reflex (e.g., Magladery, Teasdall, & Norris, 1958, but not Hugin, Norris & Shock, 1960), and the pupillary reflex (Feinberg & Podolak, 1965; but not Kumnick, 1956). At least one study (Clarkson, 1978) has reported no significant age differences with the patellar reflex. Variations in measurement procedures and inadequate statistical power may be contributing factors to these inconsistencies in the effects of aging on reflex times. However there is a strong tendency for the age differences in speed to increase with the cognitive complexity of the task, and thus it is not unreasonable to expect very slight differences on simple reflex activities.

An implication of the findings with psychophysiological measures, particularly the EEG results, is that the age-related slowing is not merely a peripheral phenomenon only associated with overt responses. The slowness appears to extend to many levels of the central nervous system, and is by no means merely a response phenomenon as implied by the term 'slowness of response' sometimes used to characterize the age-related slowing phenomenon. Further evidence against a primarily motoric locus of age-related slowing comes from studies employing

electromyographic recordings of muscle activity prior to the
overt response. It has consistently been found that age differences are very pronounced in the pre-motor segment of the
reaction time, and not simply in the segment after the appearance
of the muscle activity (e.g., Botwinick & Thompson, 1966;
Clarkson & Kroll, 1978; Onishi, reported in Welford, 1977;
Weiss, 1965).

Measures of Central Processing Time

Of particular interest to many researchers are the effects
of aging on measures derived from various reaction time tasks
in order to reflect the speed of internal processes exclusive
of sensory and motor factors. As discussed in the previous
chapter, measures derived by taking the difference between
two reaction times, or by computing the slope relating reaction
time to some variable of interest, frequently have quite low
reliability. Despite the small amount of systematic variance
available for association with other variables, it is invariably
found that older adults are slower than young or middle-aged
adults in derived measures of this type.

Perhaps the most thoroughly investigated 'central' measure
with respect to its sensitivity to the effects of age is the
slope of the function relating reaction time to size of the
memory set in the Sternberg memory-scanning paradigm (e.g.,
Sternberg, 1969, 1975). This procedure consists of the presentation of a series of unrelated items, typically letters or
digits, followed by the presentation of a single probe item.
The subject's task is to classify the probe item as rapidly
as possible with respect to whether it was a member of the
earlier presented memory set. An extremely robust finding
is that the reaction time to make the classification decision
increases in a linear fashion with the number of items in
the memory set, suggesting that location or scanning of each
additional item in memory requires a fixed amount of time.
Many studies have now been reported in which age comparisons
have been made with respect to the magnitude of the slope
of this function, which is presumed to reflect the duration
of the memory-scanning operation independent of processes

concerned with encoding, decision, and response (cf., Sternberg, 1969, 1975). Substantial age differences in the slope parameter (as well as the intercept parameter representing the duration of all other processes), were reported in most of these studies, with the magnitude of the difference averaging about 60% across the age range from 20 to 70 (e.g., Anders & Fozard, 1973; Anders, Fozard, & Lillyquist, 1972; Eriksen, Hamlin, & Dye, 1973; Ford, Roth, Mohs, Hopkins, & Koppell, 1979; Madden, 1982; Madden & Nebes, 1980; Maniscalco & DeRosa, 1982; Salthouse & Somberg, 1982a, 1982b).

There are some exceptions to this finding (e.g., Ford, Pfefferbaum, Tinklenburg, & Kopell, 1982; Marsh, 1975), but most involved weak tests of the age effects due to small sample sizes, insufficient number of observations to yield stable parameter estimates, or a narrow gap between the extreme age groups. In the face of the very large body of evidence demonstrating the existence of sizable age differences in the magnitude of the slope parameter, the burden of proof clearly rests with those who claim an exception to the general phenomenon. Such proof is unlikely to come from studies with very low power to detect differences if they were to exist, and thus 'exceptions' with these characteristics may reasonably be ignored.

It should be mentioned that the discovery of substantial age differences in the slope parameter from the memory-scanning paradigm applies only to relatively early stages of practice because with moderate practice the slope decreases considerably for people of all ages (e.g., Schneider & Shiffrin, 1977; Salthouse & Somberg, 1982a). The predominant interpretation of this practice-related reduction in the slope parameter is that consistent experience with the same assignment of stimuli to responses results in a gradual replacement of the search or scanning operation by some form of direct connection between target stimuli and their response categories. In effect, therefore, practice is thought to eliminate, or at least greatly reduce, the time-consuming aspects of processing in the scanning phase of the task. To the extent that any form of processing no longer requires much time, one would not expect measures reflecting that processing to exhibit sizable differences as a function of age if the age effects are primarily caused by a slowing of mental operations. Studies reporting that moderate experience reduces or eliminates age differences in the slope parameter from memory-scanning (e.g., Madden, 1983; Madden & Nebes, 1980; Salthouse & Somberg, 1982a) or visual search (e.g., Plude & Hoyer, 1981; Plude, Hoyer, & Lazar, 1982; Plude, Kaye, Hoyer, Post, Saynisch, & Hahn, 1983) paradigms are therefore not inconsistent with the current perspective, and can be interpreted as a special case in which the time requirements of the process are greatly diminished for individuals of all ages. The finding by Thomas, Waugh, and Fozard (1978) that highly familiar letter sequences (e.g., a-b-c-d-e-f) are scanned much faster than unfamiliar sequences, and that the age differences are much smaller in the former case may also be interpreted as an example of this type of practice-mediated exception to the general phenomenon.

Another frequently investigated variable thought to reflect the duration of central processes independent of input and output factors is the slope of the function relating reaction time to angular orientation between two stimuli in the paradigm introduced by Shepard and Metzler (1971). One version of this task consists of the presentation of two adjacent letters, one of which is rotated in the picture plane relative to the other. The subject is required to decide as quickly as possible whether the two letters are identical, or are mirror images (i.e., rotated in the third dimension). Because the decision is easiest when the letters are in congruent orientations, it is assumed that the subject mentally rotates one of the letters to match the orientation of the other. In fact, the function relating decision time to amount of angular deviation between the two letters is typically quite linear, suggesting that this mental rotation process occurs at a fixed rate that can be estimated by the slope of the regression line relating angular deviation to decision time.

Several studies have investigated the effects of aging

on the slope of the mental rotation function, and a consistent
finding is that increased age in adulthood is associated with
a slower rate of mental rotation (e.g., Berg, Hertzog, & Hunt,
1982; Cerella, Poon, & Fozard, 1981; Clarkson-Smith & Halpern,
1983; Gaylord & Marsh, 1975). As with the case of memory
scanning, there are occasional exceptions to this finding
(e.g., Jacewicz & Hartley, 1979), but again they appear to
be explainable on the basis of inadequate statistical power
of the type mentioned above.

A number of studies have also been reported in which
age differences were examined in the slope parameter of the
function relating reaction time to number of stimulus-response
alternatives in a variant of the Hick paradigm described in
the previous chapter. Many of these studies have been reviewed
by Welford (e.g., 1977), who was interested in determining
whether the age differences were primarily evident in the
slope or the intercept of the reaction time function. Welford
argued that the trend was not consistent for the age effects
to be manifested in one or the other of these parameters,
but several of the cited studies involved card-sorting or
reaction time-plus-movement time tasks with substantial motor
components (e.g., Botwinick, Robbin, & Brinley, 1960; Crossman
& Szafran, 1956; Goldfarb, 1941), or consisted of extremely
select subjects (e.g., very healthy airplane pilots in Szafran,
1965). Age differences in the slope measure thought to reflect
the rate of gain of information have been reported in a number
of apparently well-conducted reaction time studies (e.g.,
Griew, 1964; Suci, Davidoff, & Surwillo, 1960; also see Rabbitt,
1980). It is not clear whether the apparent exceptions should
be attributed to weak statistical power for the reasons mentioned
above, or as Welford (1977) suggests, are indications that
other factors such as effective stimulus duration are involved.
However, to the extent that the task emphasizes sensory and
motor factors by requiring fine discriminations or large movements,
the contribution of peripheral factors may tend to overwhelm
that of the central factors presumably responsible for the
slope effects.

Age differences have also been examined in a variety
of difference scores derived by subtracting the reaction time
obtained in one condition from that obtained in another condition.
For example, in a procedure introduced by Posner and his colleagues
(e.g., Posner, Boies, Eichelman, & Taylor, 1969), the subject
is asked to decide whether two simultaneously presented letters
are the same with respect to physical identity (e.g., AA or
aa), the same with respect to name identity (e.g., aA), or
are different (e.g., aB). A measure interpreted as the time
needed to access name information in long-term memory is obtained
by subtracting the reaction time to classify the letters as
physically identical from that needed to classify the letters
as nominally identical. This measure of time to access stored
name codes has been reported to be longer among older adults
than young adults by Hines and Posner (1976), Lindholm and
Parkinson (1983), Poon, Fozard, Vierck, Dailey, Cerella, and
Zeller (1976), and Wright (1981).

Other studies examining age differences in various difference
scores have been reported by Bowles and Poon (1981), Erber,
Botwinick, and Storandt (1978), Mortimer-Tanner & Naylor (1973),
Naylor (1973), Poon and Fozard (1980), Storandt (1976), and
Surwillo (1964b). In each of these studies older adults were
slower than young adults in the difference score measure of
speed. There are occasional exceptions (e.g., Kirsner, 1972),
but most can probably be explained on the basis of low power
due to small sample sizes, differential speed-accuracy tradeoffs
due to variable error rates, unreliable initial measures,
and even less reliable difference score measures.

A variety of studies have also been reported describing
the effects of age on measures presumably reflecting the speed
of a mixture of different cognitive processes. For example,
several psychometric tests have been designed to measure fluency
of some behavior by requesting the individual to generate
as many instances as possible within a limited period of time
which satisfy specific criteria. One particular version of
this type of fluency test involves the individual attempting
to generate words beginning with the letter **'S'** over a period

of 120 seconds. Performance on tests such as these probably reflects a combination of speed factors and experiential factors related to the size and accessibility of one's relevant knowledge, but it is frequently reported that increased age is a disadvantage in performance of fluency tests (e.g., Bilash & Zubek, 1960; Birren, 1955a; Birren, Riegel, & Robbin, 1962; Riegel & Birren, 1966; Schaie, 1958; Schaie, Rosenthal, & Perlman, 1953; Schaie & Strother, 1968; Speakman, in Welford, 1958). The occasional exceptions to this trend (e.g., Horn & Cattell, 1967) may be attributable to the use of tests which placed greater emphasis on stored knowledge (e.g., by employing fairly restrictive criteria for the to-be-generated items), or which allowed sufficient time for the larger amount of stored knowledge of older adults to compensate for their slower rate of access.

[handwritten margin note: What you use in real life.]

The presumably greater experience of older adults with verbal material may also account for the occasional absence of significant age differences in tasks involving the rapid pronunciation of words, i.e., measures of lexical access time (e.g., Cerella & Fozard, 1984; Eysenck, 1975). Another contributing factor in some of these studies may be low statistical power resulting from measures with undocumented reliability (which is probably fairly low because there are often very few observations available from each subject), and generally small sample sizes within each age group. Moreover, variable error rates in many of the studies suggest that a speed-accuracy tradeoff cannot be ruled out. In addition, a number of the studies with verbal material have relied upon vocal reaction times that have been found to yield inconsistent age trends even with very simple tasks (e.g., Nebes, 1978; Salthouse & Somberg, 1982a; see Salthouse, 1985, for further citations and discussion). Possible explanations for the apparent exception of vocal reaction time measures from the age-related slowing phenomenon are: (a) greater experience with vocal output in the form of speech compared to other modes of expression such as manual responses; (b) age-related changes in the acoustic spectrum of speech resulting in earlier triggering of the voice key by older adults; and (c) large variability due to

uncontrolled stammering or stuttering on the part of the subject
resulting in the registration of a response before the appropriate
decision has been reached.

Confirmation of the age-related slowing phenomenon with
continuous activities such as those involved in fluency tests
again suggests that central factors are directly implicated
in the phenomenon. Because these activities typically require
rapid generation of associations and not merely discrete responses
to individual stimuli, peripheral input factors are unlikely
to have a major influence. The discovery of slowing effects
with psychophysiological measures and derived measures of
central processing also indicates that peripheral motor factors,
or factors restricted to discrete tasks such as level of preparation or expectancy, sensitivity to repetition or alternation,
etc., are relatively small determinants of the basic phenomenon.
Although some manifestations of age-related slowing may be
easier to detect with simple discrete tasks such as reaction
time, it seems unlikely that interpretations generated specifically
to account for results with these types of activities will
have the requisite generality to explain the broad phenomenon.
Moreover, the pervasiveness with which age-related slowness
is exhibited across tasks and species suggests that a fundamental
property of the nervous system is involved, and not merely
something restricted to a few particular processes.

Alternative Views of the Nature of Age-Related Slowing

The empirical evidence reviewed in the preceding section,
and examined in greater detail elsewhere (e.g., Birren, Woods,
& Williams, 1979; 1980; Salthouse, 1985; Welford, 1977; 1984),
clearly indicates that increased age is generally associated
with a slower rate of performance on most behavioral variables.
Expressed somewhat abstractly, it appears highly likely that
if young and old adults were to be compared in any set of
four variables, V1 through V4, the older adults would be found
to have longer durations than the young adults for each variable.
While this inference seems quite plausible on the basis of
the well-substantiated slowing phenomenon, the exact nature
of the age effects is still a puzzle. Two possibilities worth

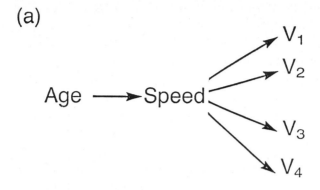

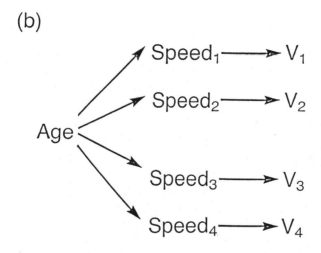

Figure 9.1 Two alternative conceptualizations of the relationship between age and speed.

considering in greater detail are illustrated in Figure 9.1.

Figure 9.1a portrays the possibility that aging affects a single mechanism or process which in turn controls the timing of many behavioral variables. An alternative possibility is represented in Figure 9.1b in which age is presumed to exert similar effects on a number of potentially independent mechanisms or processes which are each responsible for certain behavioral variables. In both cases increased age is accompanied by widespread slowing of many aspects of behavior, but the immediate cause is either a single factor, or a number of factors that are at least conceptually distinct. The single-factor position illustrated in Figure 9.1a implies that the slowing evident across the different variables is attributable to common reliance upon one speed mechanism such as a neural regulator or internal clock. In contrast, the multiple-factor position portrayed in Figure 9.1b suggests that aging has a similar, but not necessarily identical, effect on several different mechanisms each responsible for the rate of one or more variables.

Although it might be expected that distinguishing between the single-factor and the multiple-factor perspectives on age-related slowing would be easy, this has thus far proven surprisingly difficult. It could be argued that the great variety of behavioral measures found to exhibit age-related slowing suggests that a single factor is responsible, but there is no logical reason why the same pattern couldn't be produced by the existence of many factors each separately affected by age. Exceptions to the slowing phenomenon could also be tolerated with both positions since it is possible that one or more variables could be found that were independent of either the single factor or any of the multiple factors.

Two predictions can be derived from the single-factor and multiple-factor perspectives, but in neither case is the available evidence definitive enough to warrant a strong conclusion. One prediction is that because a common speed mechanism is presumed responsible for the slowing of all variables in the single-factor perspective, the correlation among variables

should increase with increased age. That is, if different
people are slowed by different amounts, but all variables
within a given person slowed by the same proportion, then
one might expect that the correlations among variables would
be greater than before the slowing occurred.

One study interpreted as providing strong support for
the prediction that the correlations among speeded variables
should be higher in samples of older adults was reported by
Birren, Riegel, and Morrison (1962). These researchers administered a battery of 22 reaction time tasks to 30 young adults
(age range 18 to 33) and 23 older adults (age range 60 to
80). The old subjects were slower than the young ones, by
an average of nearly 50%, on all variables. Of greatest interest
in the present context is the average correlation between
variables in the two samples of subjects. The median correlation
in the sample of young subjects was .26, while that in the
sample of old subjects was .41 -- results consistent with
the single-factor perspective. However, although the average
correlation was larger within the sample of older adults,
it was still only moderate in magnitude, indicating that the
speed measures do not share a great amount of common variance
even among the older individuals. It is therefore not clear
that these results should be considered very convincing with
respect to the single-factor version of age-related slowing.

Walsh (1982) has also challenged the single-factor position
on the basis of data from tachistoscopic perception tasks.
Older adults were slower than young adults on every measure
of perceptual processing speed, but the correlations among
measures were not universally high as might be expected if
a single factor were responsible. The significance of these
very early stages of perception for later cognitive processes
is still not known, however, and it is possible that measures
reflecting higher-order cognitive functioning might be more
consistent with a single-factor interpretation.

It should be pointed out that there are logical problems
associated with the interpretation of patterns of correlations
regardless of the specific results obtained. For example,

high correlations could be produced simply because older subjects
typically exhibit greater variability than young subjects
and thus have a larger effective range of values. The greater
variability could arise from any number of sources other than
a single slowing factor, and hence a higher average correlation
with increased age is not sufficient to indicate the existence
of a single speed factor. Moreover, a differential pattern
of correlations across age groups may not even be necessary
from the single-factor perspective if there is not much of
a range across individuals in the magnitude of slowing. That
is, if every 65-year old was exactly 50% slower than his or
her speed at age 25, the average correlation among scores
may not differ across age groups because the latencies are
simply shifted by a constant proportion. The two groups would
obviously differ in their absolute values, but the slight
expansion in the range of times for the older subjects may
not result in correlations noticeably different from those
of young subjects. Therefore because a higher average correlation
with increased age is apparently neither necessary nor sufficient
from the single-factor perspective, correlational data should
probably only be considered suggestive, and not definitive,
with respect to the nature of the age-related slowing.

A second potential basis for distinguishing between the
single-factor and multiple-factor interpretations of the slowing-
with-age phenomenon is the magnitude of the slowing across
different behavioral variables. If a single factor is responsible
for the slowing of all variables then the amount of slowing
should be nearly the same proportional amount for each variable.
On the other hand, if slowing is produced by a number of distinct
and potentially independent factors, the pattern of slowing
might be quite different from one variable to another.

Unfortunately, while it is easy to extract an index of
the magnitude of the age difference in speeded performance
by simply dividing the speed of the older adults by that of
the young adults, it is unclear whether these ratios should
be considered equally meaningful across different dependent
variables. That is, even if all of the dependent measures

were expressed in units of time, they should not necessarily be interpreted as having comparable precision for estimating degree of central slowing because of variations in sensory and motor requirements, amount of specific and general experience, level of task complexity, measurement consistency, potential for strategy flexibility, etc. Furthermore, most of the published studies in this area have completely ignored the existence of the speed-accuracy tradeoff and have either reported separate analyses of the speed and accuracy variables, or even worse, have completely failed to describe the levels of accuracy associated with the reported speeds. As noted in the previous chapter, neglecting accuracy when examining time is tantamount to reducing the measurement from a very powerful ratio scale to a weak ordinal scale, or possibly even to a relatively useless nominal scale. These characteristics clearly make quantitative estimates of the degree of age-related slowing rather gross, and consequently it is probably not feasible to attempt to distinguish between the single-factor and multiple-factor perspectives solely on the basis of equivalent or non-equivalent slowing proportions across a variety of speeded variables. Nevertheless, the attempts to quantify the amount of age-related slowing are worth examining, if for no other reason than to document the approximate magnitude of the basic slowing-with-age phenomenon.

The most direct form of comparison is a ratio of the time required by adults of a given age to perform the specified activity relative to the time required by a standard or comparison group (typically young) adults to perform the same activity. It was mentioned earlier that these ratios are typically in the range of 1.2 to 1.6 for adults in their 60s, indicating that on the average, 20-year-olds are between 20% and 60% faster than 65-year-olds.

A much more intriguing comparison, and one which has the potential for providing considerably richer information, consists of simultaneously examining the performance speeds of older adults relative to those of young adults across a variety of different experimental conditions. Brinley (1965) was the first to analyze data in this manner, and the procedure was extended by Salthouse (1978b, 1985; Salthouse & Somberg, 1982b), Cerella, Poon, and Williams (1980), and Madden (1984).

Graphically, the procedure consists of plotting the time for a given activity in a two-dimensional space with the time for the criterion (young) group along the abscissa, and the time for the comparison (old) group along the ordinate. Each temporal measure is then represented by the intersection of the time of the young adults and the time of the older adults. For example, assume that time values are available for both young and old adults across four experimental tasks, A, B, C, and D. Performance in task A would be represented by positioning a point where the time for the young adults (along the horizontal axis) intersected the time for the older adults (along the vertical axis). The points for the other tasks would be determined in a similar fashion, with the final product appearing something like the graphs in Figure 9.2.

Expressing the results of speeded activities in a form like that portrayed in Figure 9.2 allows several different questions to be addressed. These are best described by thinking of the linear regression parameters that could be used to characterize the data points in a graph of this type. First is the correlation coefficient, indicating the extent to which the values from the young and old adults are linearly related to one another. If the data points fall along a single line, the correlation will be quite high and one could infer that both age groups exhibit a similar sensitivity to the experimental manipulations. That is, the task conditions that result in lengthy completion times for the older adults would also have lengthy times for the young adults. Next is the slope of the regression line, which indicates the amount of change in the time of older adults for each unit of time change in the young adults. The slope parameter is roughly equivalent to a slowing factor in that it reflects the relation between a given amount of speed change in the two groups. And finally, one can examine the intercept of the regression line, corresponding to the projected time value of the older adults when the time

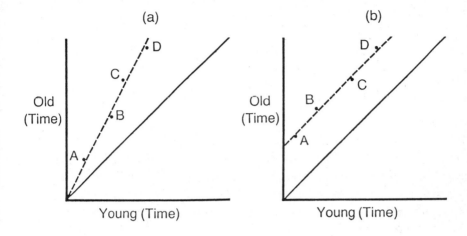

(a)

Old
(Time)

Young (Time)

(b)

Old
(Time)

Young (Time)

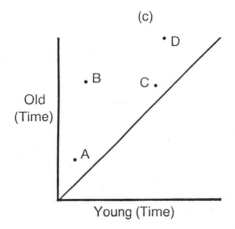

(c)

Old
(Time)

Young (Time)

Figure 9.2 Three plausible alternatives for the
relationship between the speeds of young and old adults.
Each point represents the time of the young adults (along
the abscissa) and the time of the older adults (along the
ordinate) for a particular experimental condition.

of the young adults is assumed to be zero.

The value of this type of analysis is that specific patterns of the parameters lead to quite distinct interpretations of the nature of the slowing process. For example, the data in Figure 9.2a represent a high correlation, a slope much greater than 1.0, and an intercept of approximately zero. This outcome is consistent with a general slowing having nearly proportional effects on all aspects of processing. Generality is implied by the fact that the function is linear, suggesting that there are similar determinants of performance in both groups and consequently that the age differences cannot be traced to a single aspect specific to a particular task or condition. Proportionality is inferred from the intercept of near zero in conjunction with the slope greater than one. When the intercept is exactly zero the slope represents the ratio of performance in older adults relative to young adults, and thus it provides an estimate of the degree of slowing across the dependent measures. A slope of, for example, 1.50, would therefore indicate that the times for the older adults are 50% longer than those for the young adults across all measured activities.

An outcome like that portrayed in Figure 9.2b would lead to a quite different interpretation because the slope of nearly 1.0 indicates that there is a constant absolute, rather than proportional, difference between the times of the two age groups. This pattern is consistent with an age-related slowing of a single component present to the same degree in all tasks, e.g., a sensory or response process involved in each task. The magnitude of this specific slowing can be estimated from the intercept parameter, which because the slope is nearly 1.0, should approximately correspond to the average difference in times between the older and young adults across the various tasks.

The outcome represented in Figure 9.2c is distinguished from the previous ones by a low correlation coefficient indicating a poor fit to a linear equation. In this case one could not conclude that there is much in common across the various speeded

activities because knowing the time required by the young
adults is of little help in predicting the time required by
the older adults. A reasonable inference from this type of
outcome would be that the age differences are attributable
to specific processes found in some, but not all, speeded
activities.

Which of these patterns is most consistent with the empirical
data? Before considering this question, it is important to
mention some criteria that should be satisfied in order to
allow unambiguous interpretation of the parameters. First,
it is clearly necessary that data be available across age
groups for at least three separate conditions or tasks. Correlations are always 1.0 for two data points, and become progressively more meaningful only as the number of pairs is increased.
Second, in order to produce reasonable estimates of the slope
and intercept parameters the time values should span a moderately
large range. Ideally, the minimum and maximum times within
an age group should differ by at least 30%, because it is
difficult to extract an accurate regression equation if the
data points exhibit little range and are clustered closely
together. Third, the various measures should be derived from
tasks with roughly comparable sensory and motor requirements
so as not to introduce confounding peripheral factors. It
would obviously be unreasonable to expect to isolate the contributions of central speed factors if the tasks differ in the
size or discriminability of the stimuli, or in the precision
of the required response. And fourth, the results should
be compared at fairly early stages of practice before specific
experience has altered the mode of performance in a manner
analogous to that found in memory-scanning studies.

Even with these criteria, analyses of the type proposed
suffer from all of the limitations mentioned earlier concerning
inadequacies of the existing data for drawing precise quantitative
conclusions. It is therefore rather surprising that the available
results are fairly consistent in revealing the general nature
of the slowing pattern. Table 9.1 summarizes the results
of several studies which, in addition to the criteria listed

Table 9.1

Regression Parameters for Young and Old Performance Times

Slope	Intercept	Correlation	Source
1.87	-.31	.996	Birren & Botwinick, 1955
1.58	-.04	.961	Birren, Riegel, & Morrison, 1962
1.59	-.27	.975	Botwinick, Brinley, & Robbin, 1958
1.65	-.40	.987	Bowles & Poon, 1981
1.68	-.26	.986	Brinley, 1965
2.01	-.42	.949	Cerella, Poon, & Fozard, 1981
1.51	-.09	.907	Cohen & Faulkner, 1983
1.62	-.30	.982	Petros, Zehr, & Chabot, 1983
2.05	-.33	.958	Rabbitt, 1979c, Exp. 1a
1.23	-.01	.982	Rabbitt, 1979c, Exp. 1b
1.32	-.02	.992	Rabbitt, 1980
1.46	-.10	.982	Rabbitt, 1982b, Exp. 1
1.90	-.30	.984	Rabbitt & Vyas, 1980, Exp. 1
1.60	-.09	.986	Salthouse, 1978a

above, all involved adults from similar age ranges of between
18 and 30 for young adults, and between 55 and 80 for older
adults.

All of the entries in Table 9.1 have high correlations
and slopes greater than 1.0. The intercepts are clustered
around zero, but with more negative values than one might
expect if the true mean were zero. This latter result may
be a consequence of a mixture of peripheral and central determinants of slowing, with the peripheral processes dominating
at brief intervals and thus distorting the function near the
intercept. Regardless of the particular interpretation, negative
intercepts are opposite to the positive intercept effect predicted
from the pattern represented in Figure 9.2b. The empirical
results therefore appear to be quite consistent with the interpretation that the age-related slowing phenomenon is general
and nearly proportional across a variety of activities. An
inference which can be drawn from these data is that adults
in their 60s appear to require about 40% to 60% more time
than adults in their 20s for tasks in which experience is
limited and sensory and motor demands are minimal.

A very similar conclusion has been reached by Cerella,
Poon, and Williams (1980) based on a meta-analysis of results
combined across many different studies. These researchers
also suggested that two different slowing factors were evident,
one of about 1.62 for mental or cognitive tasks, and one of
about 1.14 for sensory-motor tasks. Although it is reasonable
to expect different magnitudes of slowing for peripheral and
central processes, the operational basis for classifying tasks
as sensory or mental in the Cerella, et al. analysis was not
explicitly described, and no statistical confirmation of the
differences in slowing magnitude was provided. Therefore
while it is reassuring to note that the same pattern seems
to be evident in aggregate analyses, the enormous variations
across the studies from which these data are abstracted, and
the lack of statistical verification of the specific inferences,
dictates extreme caution in interpreting possible differences
in quantitative parameters.

It should be noted that the pattern illustrated in Figure 9.2a, and represented by the majority of the data in Table 9.1, is clearly consistent with the complexity effect discussed in Chapters 7 and 8. That is, because the correlation indicates that the functions are linear and the slopes are consistently greater than 1.0, the absolute difference in time between young and old adults increases in proportion to the time of the young adults. These results are also consistent with the findings discussed earlier in which significant age differences are generally reported in measures of 'central processing' derived by subtracting the times in different conditions.

Do the data in Table 9.1 support the single-factor (Figure 9.1a) or the multiple-factor (Figure 9.1b) version of age-related slowing? Unfortunately, they are ambiguous because the precision with which the magnitude of slowing has been determined across different variables is not sufficient to allow an unequivocal conclusion. For many variables the slowness is roughly 50% between the 20s and the 60s, but the range is so great that the possibility of several distinct slowing factors cannot be ruled out. Furthermore, the enormous difficulty of controlling all of the potentially confounding influences in attempting to make quantitative comparisons across variables from different tasks and different samples of subjects may preclude a satisfactory answer to this question from quantitative comparisons of degree of slowing for the forseeable future. Another possible means of examining the single-factor versus multiple-factor interpretations of age-related slowing involves consideration of the hypothesized causes for the slowing phenomenon, and it is that topic which is discussed next.

Is Speed a Cause or a Consequence?

Both psychological and physiological causes for age-related changes in speed can be postulated. The two are distinguished primarily by the level of analysis of the proposed explanation -- if the explanation is at the same level as the phenomenon that it is intended to explain it is considered psychological, while if the explanation is at a lower, more reductionistic, level, it is considered physiological. Another way of viewing this issue is that if the cause of the speed differences is psychological then it is reasonable to think of speed as a consequence of the other psychological factors, while if the cause is physiological then speed might be considered to be the determinant of other psychological phenomena. The empirical literature relevant to these two perspectives will be considered in turn.

Speed as a Consequence of Other Psychological Factors

Because of the widespread usage of reaction time and other speed-related measures as dependent variables to assess the effectiveness of experimental manipulations, most contemporary researchers tend to think of variations in speed as the consequence of some other variables. In the context of aging, it might be postulated that increased age alters one or more factors which in turn result in the widespread slowing of behavior. Among the factors with sufficient generality to account for the slowing-with-age phenomenon are strategy shifts, differential motivation, and varying amounts of familiarity. Ability in a given domain will also influence the speed of performance in that domain, but determinants of this type would likely be specific to a few content areas rather than extending to all of the variables in which speed differences have been reported.

One means of investigating the role of strategy, motivation, and familiarity factors in the relation between age and speed is to manipulate the relevant factor and determine whether it leads to systematic differences in the magnitude of the age differences in speed. An ideal outcome would be complete elimination of the age differences under conditions in which the level of the factor was equivalent across age groups. However, a finding that the age differences are merely substant- ially reduced, after due consideration of the methodological issues discussed in Chapter 6, would at least be consistent with the hypothesis that the manipulated factor functioned as the cause of the age-related speed differences. For the most part, neither of these patterns has been evident in the research literature and thus the 'speed as consequence' inter- pretation has not yet received convincing empirical support.

Two classes of evidence are particularly persuasive in dismissing the differential strategy interpretation. One is that sizable age differences in speed are evident in even the simplest reaction time tasks, and in a variety of presumably 'hardware-determined' psychophysiological measures such as latencies of EEG components. Strategic influences are probably minimal on simple tasks such as these because they seem to allow only one mode of performance, and yet the measures derived from them exhibit pronounced effects of aging.

A second category of evidence against the strategy interpre- tation concerns the most plausible strategy involved in speeded choice tasks -- the individual's relative emphasis on speed as opposed to accuracy. There is some evidence that older adults tend to prefer a greater emphasis on accuracy than young adults (e.g., Salthouse, 1979; Salthouse & Somberg, 1982a; Welford, 1958), but two studies have revealed that large age differences remain even when complete speed-accuracy operating characteristics are generated and comparisons made at the same level of accuracy (e.g., Salthouse, 1979; Salthouse & Somberg, 1982c). It is therefore unlikely that the strategy of preferring accuracy over speed can account for all of the time differences typically found between young and older adults in speeded tasks, although it probably does contribute to the age differences in at least some activities.

Motivation has been manipulated by the administration of electric shock for slow responses (e.g., Botwinick, Brinley, & Robbin, 1958; Weiss, 1965), and special instructions with payoffs for fast responses (e.g., Grant, Storandt, & Botwinick,

1978; Salthouse, 1978a, 1979; Salthouse & Somberg, 1982a).
In no cases did these manipulations eliminate, or even substantially reduce, the age differences in speed and therefore the
differential motivation interpretation of age differences
in speed has not been supported in the available data.

The notion that with increased age people become out
of practice with speeded activities, and consequently perform
slowly because they are less familiar with tasks performed
under rigorous time constraints, is plausible, but the available
evidence suggests that practice has relatively little effect
on the magnitude of overall age differences in speed. One
argument against a lack of practice interpretation is that
the age-related slowing phenomenon is evident in almost every
aspect of behavior, and it is highly unlikely that all activities
would be equally unpracticed. That is, it may be reasonable
to speculate that older adults have had less recent experience
in rapid running, but it is dubious that they are also inexperienced at handwriting, making small finger movements as in
knitting or typing, and generally thinking and remembering.
Because pronounced age differences have been reported in speed
of even very common activities, lack of practice does not
appear to be the major determinant of age-related slowing.

Age differences can be reduced by practice in certain
derived measures, e.g., the slope of the memory scanning function,
but time to perform the overall task still differs across
age groups. Several of the relevant studies have been cited
earlier, and there are now many reports in which age differences
in time to perform a given activity were examined as a function
of practice, with virtually all reporting age differences
persisting throughout at least moderate amounts of practice
(e.g., Baron, Menich, & Perone, 1983; Beres & Baron, 1981;
Berg, Hertzog, & Hunt, 1982; Erber, 1976; Erber, Botwinick,
& Storandt, 1978; Grant, Storandt, & Botwinick, 1978; Leonard
& Newman, 1965; Madden 1983; Madden & Nebes, 1980; Noble,
Baker, & Jones, 1964; Plude & Hoyer, 1981; Plude, Kaye, Hoyer,
Post, Saynisch, & Hahn, 1983; Poon, Fozard, Vierck, Dailey,
Cerella, & Zeller, 1976; Rabbitt, 1964; Salthouse, 1978a;

Salthouse & Somberg, 1982a).

An apparent exception to this generalization occurs when comparisons are made in which amount of relevant experience is positively correlated with age such that older adults have had more practice than young adults. As discussed in Chapter 5, increased experience results in a great number of changes, and it is quite conceivable that some of these serve to counteract the trend towards slower performance with increased age. Specific examples have been provided by LaRiviere and Simonson (1965) and Smith and Greene (1962) who found that the speed of writing did not decline with age among people in occupations that required considerable handwriting, although it did decline in other occupational groups. Salthouse (1984) also reported no age differences in speed of typing in samples of 34 and 40 typists in which age was correlated +.50 and +.55, respectively, with amount of typing experience. The beneficial effects of experience are apparently rather specific, however, because this latter study revealed that typical age effects were evident in other measures of speeded performance such as reaction time, tapping speed, and rate of digit-symbol substitution. There are also limits on the nature of the activities that can be maintained without decrement because studies of age effects in the workplace often find age-related reductions in speed of occupationally-relevant tasks (e.g., Clay, 1956; DeLaMare & Sheperd, 1958; Mark, 1956, 1957).

There are clearly other psychological factors that might be proposed as potential causes of the age differences in speed, but for none is there yet enough evidence to warrant serious consideration (see Salthouse, 1985, for additional discussion of these issues). It therefore seems reasonable to conclude on the basis of the available evidence that the age-related slowing phenomenon is not simply a consequence of age differences in other psychological processes.

Speed as a Consequence of Physiological Factors

If the slowing-with-age phenomenon cannot be explained by processes at the same level of analysis, it is at least possible that the speed differences are in some manner responsible for the differences in cognitive performance observed across age groups. That is, failure to find support for the view that speed is simply a dependent variable allows further consideration of the view that speed functions as an independent variable in the context of age differences in cognition. Before pursuing this hypothesis, it is useful to take a reductionistic perspective and examine possible causes at the level of biology or physiology. No attempt will be made to discuss specific biological processes responsible for the slowing phenomenon, but instead a number of broad speculations about the type of mechanism or mechanisms that might be involved will be briefly summarized.

A variety of possible causes of the age-related slowing phenomenon have been proposed at the physiological level, ranging from hypotheses based on apparently well-established empirical findings to quite vague speculations with little or no relevant evidence. To illustrate the former, it has been reported that there are age-associated declines in the velocity of neural conduction (e.g., LaFratta & Canestrari, 1966; LaFratta & Smith, 1964; Laufer & Schweitz, 1968; Norris, Shock, & Wagman, 1953; Wagman & Lesse, 1952), and in the time to transmit across a synapse in rats (e.g., Waymer & Emmers, 1958). On the basis of these results it could be argued that the cumulative effect of even a very small difference at such an elementary level in the nervous system could be extremely large when multiplied by the tens, hundreds, or even thousands, of individual neurons involved in most cognitive activity. The major difficulty with this interpretation is that it is only conjecture that small differences at the level of individual neurons accumulate to produce the relatively large differences observed across age in many behavioral activities. For example, the difference in choice reaction time between adults in their 20s and adults in their 60s is often 100 milliseconds or more, and yet the differences in conduction velocity across that age range are estimated to be less than 8 milliseconds per meter. If this is the only factor responsible for the differences in reaction time, one would have to infer that the equivalent of nearly 13 meters of neural pathways must be traversed to perform the choice reaction time task. Because this is a difficult if not impossible assertion to verify, the interpretation based on elementary differences at the level of individual neurons has not yet been widely accepted.

An illustration of a more speculative type of proposal is the suggestion that the slowing phenomenon is attributable to reduced levels of activation or arousal, perhaps mediated by the recticular activating system or some other subcortical structure. The basic idea in this perspective (cf., Birren, 1970) is that the older nervous system is somehow 'less lively' than the younger one, although it is not clear exactly what type of physiological or neurological evidence would be directly relevant to this hypothesis.

Another physiologically-based interpretation of the age-related slowing phenomenon is that the timing of mental events is controlled by certain phases of the EEG, which, for still unknown reasons, slows down with age. Surwillo (e.g., 1961, 1963, 1964b, 1968) is the best-known advocate of this position, in support of which he has reported that reaction time and period of the alpha phase in the EEG are highly correlated. This relation appears very tenuous, however, since subsequent attempts to replicate it and to confirm other implications from the timing hypothesis have only been partially successful or unsuccessful (e.g., Birren, 1955a, Obrist, 1963; Woodruff, 1975).

Probably the most discussed hypothesis for the age-related slowing phenomenon in the psychological literature is the idea that with increasing age there is a decrease within the central nervous system in functional signal-to-noise ratio, or equivalently, an increase in the level of neural noise. Numerous variations of this concept have been proposed (e.g., Birren, 1970; Crossman & Szafran, 1957; Gregory, 1957; Kay, 1959; Layton, 1975; Rabbitt, 1980; Szafran, 1965; Welford, 1958, 1963, 1965, 1969, 1977, 1981, 1984), but most assume that with increased age there is either a reduction in signal strength or an increase in background activity such that the

effective ratio of signal to noise decreases with advancing
age.   The reduced signal strength could be produced by diffuse
cell loss or generalized inhibition, while cell loss and greater
persistence of earlier activation have been invoked to account
for the postulated increase in background noise.   Regardless
of the factors responsible for the reduced signal-to-noise
ratio, it has been argued that the existence of such an age
effect might provide an explanation for age differences in
a wide variety of behaviors ranging from sensory thresholds
(e.g., Gregory, 1957), to memory and problem solving (e.g.,
Welford, 1958, 1980, 1981).   In fact, the neural noise concept
has had such wide application that Lindholm and Parkinson
(1983) proposed that:

> ..."noise" is synonymous with processing error:
> It is assumed that the nervous system does not transmit
> information with perfect fidelity and that this
> error occurs at all levels of the nervous system
> and at all stages of information processing (Lindholm
> & Parkinson, 1983, p. 291).

The connection between signal-to-noise ratio and processing
speed is based on the well-accepted statistical principle
that the ease of distinguishing between two distributions
is directly related to the number of relevant observations,
or sample size.   Therefore if the internal distributions of
signal events and noise events overlap, as is the case when
there is a low ratio of signal to noise, a considerable number
of information samples would be needed to allow the distributions
to be distinguished with reasonable confidence.   On the other
hand, if there is a high signal-to-noise ratio, the signal
and noise distributions will have very little overlap and
discriminations could be made on the basis of a small number
of information samples.   Any 'decision' or response of the
system dependent upon a criterion level of confidence will
consequently take longer with the smaller signal-to-noise
ratio because more information samples, each requiring a finite
amount of time, will have to be acquired and integrated to
achieve that criterion degree of confidence.

While the arguments are plausible and the range of phenomena potentially explainable by the hypothesis impressive, there have only been a few attempts to subject the reduced signal-to-noise proposal to empirical investigation, and the results thus far have been contradictory. One attempt to investigate the lowered signal-to-noise hypothesis was reported by Salthouse (1980b). The reasoning in this study was that manipulations of processing time, as controlled by the interval between a target stimulus and a masking stimulus in a tachistoscopic masking paradigm, should be qualitatively equivalent in their effects to manipulations of stimulus discriminability. That is, if the age differences in processing time are produced by the necessity of integrating more samples of information to compensate for a lower signal-to-noise ratio, then a similar pattern of age effects should be produced by directly varying signal-to-noise ratio, in terms of the distinctiveness of the to-be-discriminated stimuli, as by indirectly varying signal-to-noise ratio, by manipulating the effective time allowed for processing. Because the different levels of discriminability were compared at the same interstimulus interval between target and mask, the pattern of age effects observed across discriminability levels could not be attributed to time per se, but instead must be due to the variations in signal-to-noise ratio. A finding of similar age trends across the time and discriminability manipulations would therefore be consistent with the hypothesis that age-related reductions in signal-to-noise ratio are responsible for both sets of results.

The results from one of the two experiments, involving 13 females with a mean age of 24 and 12 females with a mean age of 71 serving as subjects, are illustrated in Figure 9.3. (The second experiment yielded very similar results.) The important point is that the same pattern of age differences can apparently be produced by manipulations of stimulus discriminability, independent of effective processing time, as by manipulations of effective processing time, independent of level of discriminability. It might therefore be inferred

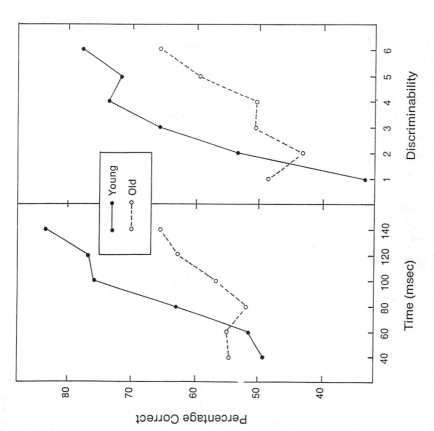

Figure 9.3   Accuracy of making same-different judgments as a function of interstimulus interval and level of discriminability for young and old adults.   Data from Salthouse (1980b).

that the common mechanism for both sets of results is a lower
signal-to-noise ratio in the nervous systems of older adults
compared to young adults.

Although the results of the first study are consistent
with the signal-to-noise hypothesis, a more recent study (Salthouse
& Lichty, 1985) failed to support it. The basic premise in
the Salthouse and Lichty study was that the functional stimulus
representation is more variable in older adults than in young
adults. This fundamental idea, which is equivalent to the
hypothesis that there is a reduction with age in the effective
ratio of signal to noise within the nervous system, led to
two predictions in addition to the basic expectation that
there would be age differences in reaction time.

One hypothesis was that older adults should be able to
tolerate less additional noise in the stimulus display than
young adults because their stimulus representations are:

> ...assumed to be very close to the level of background
> activity with no extra noise in the display, even
> a small amount of added noise will reduce the effective
> signal-to-noise ratio to a level that is no longer
> distinguishable from the normal background activity.
> (However)...(b)ecause the stimulus representation
> in young adults is postulated to have a fairly high
> signal-to-noise ratio, substantial increases in
> extraneous noise presumably could be handled without
> reducing discriminability to the background level
> (Salthouse & Lichty, 1985).

A second hypothesis was that older adults relative to
young adults should be able to tolerate less distortion in
the stimulus patterns because the distortion would weaken
the signal strength and bring it closer to the level of background
activity. In a sense, this manipulation is the converse of
the previous one because while the presence of extraneous
noise can be assumed to increase the total noise from which
signals must be distinguished, increasing the amount of distortion
is thought to reduce the strength of the signal. However,
because both manipulations are presumably dependent upon the

initial signal-to-noise ratio, age differences would be expected in the tolerance thresholds for both extraneous noise and stimulus distortion if age is associated with changes in effective ratio of signal to noise.

The major results from this study, confirmed in two independent experiments, were that young and old adults did not differ significantly in either the threshold for extraneous noise or the threshold for stimulus distortion. Although it might be argued that the manipulations of extraneous noise and stimulus distortion did not appropriately influence the internal determinants of signal and noise, the absence of age differences is clearly inconsistent with the signal-to-noise hypothesis. The reduced signal-to-noise interpretation of the age-related slowing phenomenon must therefore be considered unverified at the present time because the available evidence is equivocal. Nevertheless, it is still a promising perspective because of its generality and plausibility, and hence it probably deserves more thorough investigation before being completely dismissed.

Perhaps the most reasonable conclusion with respect to age-related reductions in speed is that there are many causes of this phenomenon, including psychological factors such as differential accuracy bias and possibly lack of practice, and a variety of physiological factors such as reduced arousal, possibly heightened inhibition, delayed pacing of EEG, impaired circulation, and altered signal-to-noise ratio. The mechanism primarily responsible for the slowing in normal healthy adults cannot yet be identified, but the evidence suggests that it probably has a biological rather than psychological origin.

Active and Passive Processing

Over the last decade an important theoretical distinction has emerged between conscious, controlled, or effortful processing on the one hand, and unconscious, automatic, and effortless processing on the other hand. It is unclear exactly where or when the notion of these different types of processing originated, but the most frequently cited references in connection with this distinction are Hasher and Zacks (1979), Posner and Snyder (1975), and Schneider and Shiffrin (1977; Shiffrin & Schneider, 1977). Although the basic concepts are very similar in all cases, the specific criteria proposed to distinguish between the two types of processing have varied across theorists. For example, Posner and Snyder (1975) suggested that automatic processing could be distinguished from conscious processing because it does not depend upon intentionality, it does not lead to conscious awareness, and it does not result in interference with other concurrent activities. Hasher and Zacks (1979) included invariance across practice and across development as additional criteria, while Schneider and Shiffrin (1977) emphasize the difficulty of suppressing execution once it is underway.

Despite slight variations in specific criteria, a considerable amount of research can be encompassed within the general framework of automatic or passive processing versus effortful or active processing. The distinction has also been very influential in the cognitive aging literature, with much research attempting to investigate the Hasher and Zacks (1979) hypothesis that age differences are minimal in tasks which do not require active or effortful processing.

There is also evidence of different aging patterns on speeded measures involving processes that can be assumed to be passive as opposed to active, and it is this aspect of the active-passive issue which is of primary interest here. One experimental procedure that has generally been interpreted as providing a measure of passive processing is the lexical decision task in which the subject is asked to decide as rapidly as possible whether a string of letters is or is not a word. The time to make the word decisions is generally facilitated when the letter string is preceded by a related word, a phenomenon termed priming because of the assumption that the activation of the initial word spreads activation to closely related words, thus reducing the effective threshold necessary to produce a 'response.' The activation is assumed to spread automatically, and consequently a difference in reaction time between decisions preceded by a related word and decisions preceded by an unrelated word is generally interpreted as a reflection of passive processing.

Conscious expectations could also produce facilitation of related words, and probably inhibition of unrelated words, but most of the studies involving age comparisons have tried to minimize the contribution of this type of active processing by relying on relatively short intervals between prime and target (passive processing is presumably faster than active processing), and including a neutral prime condition (to obtain separate estimates of the amount of facilitation and inhibition of reaction time). Although it is still possible that the results of these studies include a mixture of passive and active processing, we will assume that the difference in reaction time between unrelated and related word pairs (i.e., the priming effect) primarily reflects passive processing.

Results from six separate studies involving 17 distinct comparisons of young and old adults in similar types of lexical decision tasks are summarized in Table 9.2. The studies varied in a number of procedural details, e.g., the Burke and Yee (1984) study used a sentence as the prime instead of a single word, but in all cases the dependent variable was the reaction time to decide whether a letter string was or was not a word. Two sets of data are presented in the table. The related reaction time measures are the mean reaction times to decide that a letter string preceded by a related word or sentence was a word. Notice that the older adults are consistently slower than the young adults on this measure. In fact, when the times of the young and old adults are entered into a regression equation, the correlation is .903, the intercept -.142 seconds, and the slope 1.59. These parameters are very similar to those reported in Table 9.1, and indicate that the overall reaction time results are typical of those reported from other types of studies.

However, the priming data, reflecting the difference in reaction time between unrelated and related primes, does not yield a consistent pattern of age differences. When these values were entered into a regression equation, the parameters

Table 9.2

Data From Lexical Decision Priming Studies

Source	Related Reaction Time		Prime Effect	
	Young	Old	Young	Old
Bowles & Poon, 1985	843	884	81	93
Burke & Yee, 1984	997	1408	-28	19
	907	1365	39	-4
	930	1381	51	106
Cerella & Fozard, 1984	520	555	28	27
	582	608	44	56
Howard, 1983	804	1349	194	87
	865	1435	113	105
Howard, Shaw, &	652	819	15	19
Gillette, 1983	604	802	55	14
(Exp. 1)	570	872	44	42
	636	824	10	-4
	524	724	34	9
(Exp. 2)	494	668	47	45
	478	737	34	57
Howard, McAndrews	1007	1280	63	166
& Lasaga, 1981	912	1446	75	116

Note: Different entries from the same source represent different relations between prime and target, different degrees of degradation, or different interstimulus intervals between prime and target.

were: correlation = .543, intercept = +.027, and slope = 0.554. There is clearly a different pattern evident in the priming measures compared to that in the mean reaction time measures.

Although the priming results could be interpreted as indicating that there are no age differences in the speed of passive processing, it is important to realize that the effect of the prime is really a measure of the product of processing and not a direct reflection of the speed of that processing. This point can be illustrated by considering an analogy to the provision of a clue in a problem solving situation. If the clue is helpful it would most likely result in a faster solution to the problem, and therefore a comparison of decision times with and without the clue provides an indication of whether or not the clue was used in the solution. However, the difference in solution times with and without the clue does not necessarily reflect the time to process the clue. It is legitimate to infer that the clue was influential in the solution on the basis of the solution times, but it is less reasonable to equate the difference in solution times with the duration of clue processing because the clue may have completely altered the manner in which the task was performed. An analogous situation may exist with the priming measures in that the existence of the priming effect can be inferred from the difference in reaction times between related and unrelated primes, but the magnitude of that difference should not necessarily be interpreted as an index of the time to carry out passive processing.

It is difficult to imagine how one might be able to obtain direct estimates of the rate of passive processing, but the manipulation of the interval between prime and target might provide an indirect means of assessing the time course of spreading activation. That is, the rate of passive propagation might be inferred from the minimum interval at which significant priming effects are obtained since this value could be interpreted as the latency to exhibit priming. Howard, Shaw, and Gillette (1983) employed this logic in two studies in which the inter-stimulus interval between the prime and target varied from

50 to 1000 milliseconds. Although the critical interaction
of age by interstimulus interval by trial type (i.e., related
prime vs. unrelated prime) was not statistically significant,
these investigators did report that the priming effect was
significant for the young subjects at an interstimulus interval
of 150 milliseconds, but was not significant for the older
subjects until an interval of 450 milliseconds. This latter
finding could be interpreted as suggesting that the latency
for priming, or the rate at which activation was passively
propagated, was slower with increased age.

A somewhat similar manipulation of prime-target interval
was carried out by Hines and Posner (1976) in a letter classification paradigm in which the subject was required to decide
whether two letters shared the same name. Automatic activation
was inferred from the positive priming effects when a low-validity
prime (i.e., either the same or a different letter) was presented,
and the use of a range of intervals from 65 to 1000 milliseconds
allowed the time course of activation to be determined. Very
similar temporal patterns were evident in young and old age
groups, suggesting that there is no age difference in the
rate at which activation spreads in passive processing. While
the Howard, et al. (1983) and Hines and Posner (1976) studies
appear at first glance to be contradictory, in fact they are
actually consistent in that neither found a significant interaction
of age by interstimulus interval by trial type, indicating
that the temporal patterns of priming effects in young and
old adults could not be reliably distinguished.

A major difficulty with the technique of manipulating
interstimulus intervals to assess the rate of passive processing
is that the inference is based on the absence of a significant
difference in reaction times, and thus it capitalizes on null
results. This is a particularly severe problem in the present
context since the performance of older adults is typically
more variable than that of young adults, and thus a greater
absolute difference on the part of older adults will be needed
to achieve the same level of statistical significance. This
problem could be alleviated by collecting proportionally more

observations from the older adults to ensure comparable statistical power across age groups, but the same number of trials were administered to young and old groups in the Howard et al. (1983) and Hines and Posner (1976) studies.

Another problem, and one which does not seem as easily resolvable, is that more time is apparently needed with increased age simply to register and encode a single stimulus, and therefore older adults might be expected to exhibit delayed priming effects because of a slower registration of the prime stimulus. Many studies employing backward masking procedures in which a second stimulus follows rapidly after an earlier stimulus have found that older adults need a longer interval between the two stimuli than young adults to escape the disrupting effects of the first stimulus (e.g., see Salthouse, 1982, and Walsh, 1982, for reviews). This finding has two implications for the use of priming procedures to infer age differences in speed of passive processing. One is that if the interstimulus interval between the prime and the target is too short, the older adults may not even perceive the target item. There are some reports that significant priming effects occur even with stimuli not consciously perceived (e.g., Fowler, Wolford, Slade, & Tassinary, 1981; Marcel, 1983), but it seems unrealistic to expect that the degree of priming is completely independent of the perceptibility of the stimulus. Therefore because older adults are susceptible to masking at longer intervals than young adults, the quality of the functional stimulus will probably be much lower with increased age and consequently the absence of priming effects in the older age group may simply be attributable to a substantially less perceptible prime stimulus.

Some of the masking effects might be minimized by relying on spatially distinct presentations of prime and target, or upon auditory and visual presentations, but it would still be the case that the time needed to establish an effective encoding of the stimulus is longer for older adults than for younger ones. That is, attempting to determine the speed of activation spreading between S1 and S2 by varying the S1-S2

interval and noting the time to respond to S2 does not eliminate
the contribution of a slower time to establish the initial
activation of S1. If, for example, the time needed to achieve
a comparable level of S1 activation is 50 milliseconds for
young adults but 100 milliseconds for older adults, then one
would expect a difference of at least 50 milliseconds in the
interstimulus interval at which significant priming effects
are first detected regardless of the rate of propagation in
each age group. One could conceivably determine the time
needed to establish equivalent representations in the two
age groups by backward masking procedures, and then subtract
this value from the estimates based on the minimum interstimulus
interval exhibiting priming. However, it would then be necessary
to make the questionable assumption that the rate of propagation
and subsequent activation of the target stimulus is independent
of the time to achieve initial activation, and thus it is
not clear whether these efforts would substantially improve
confidence in the ultimate conclusions.

Another technique that can be employed to assess the
speed of passive processing relies on the Sternberg memory-scanning
paradigm discussed earlier. Schneider and Shiffrin (1977;
Shiffrin & Schneider, 1977) and Salthouse and Somberg (1982a)
have convincingly argued that with extensive practice performance
on this task becomes increasingly automatic and independent
of the limitations on controlled processing. Age differences
in passive processing might therefore be examined by contrasting
young and old adults after extensive practice on memory-scanning
tasks. As noted earlier, several studies have been reported
in which age differences in the slope of the memory-scanning
function were found to be progressively smaller with increased
practice. The results of the Salthouse and Somberg (1982a)
study are perhaps the best illustration of this phenomenon
since their study involved the greatest amount of practice.
The average slopes for setsizes 2 through 4 of that study
were 16.5 and 57.0 milliseconds per item, respectively, for
young and old adults early in practice, but after 40 additional
hours of practice the slopes were 13.5 and 15.0, respectively.

In other words, older adults were significantly slower in the scanning component of the task in the initial sessions of the study, but were no longer distinguishable from the young adults by the end of the study.

A similar discrepancy in the pattern of age differences in the slope parameter under conditions that could be interpreted as requiring active and passive processing is evident in data reported by Madden (1982). His active condition was a typical memory-scanning task involving a mixture of letters and digits in both the positive (targets) and negative (foils) stimulus sets. The condition that can be presumed to involve passive processing involved distinguishing the positive and negative items according to category, with all digits in one stimulus set and all letters in the other stimulus set. No explicit search of memory may be necessary in this condition since the subject could simply rely on his or her knowledge of the category of the item to determine the response. In two separate studies, Madden found that the age differences in slope were much larger in the active processing condition (i.e., 65.8 for older adults vs. 38.9 for young adults in Experiment 1, and 135.5 for older adults vs. 80.1 for young adults in Experiment 2), than in the passive processing condition (i.e., 11.2 vs. 10.5 in Experiment 1, and 16.6 vs. 10.4 in Experiment 2).

The Salthouse and Somberg (1982a) and Madden (1982) studies indicate that under certain circumstances, particularly those involving highly overlearned stimulus categorizations, the absolute magnitude of the age differences are greatly attenuated. What is not yet clear, however, is how this pattern should be interpreted. The major issue is whether these results, and to a lesser extent the results from the lexical access priming studies, should be interpreted as indicating that there are no age differences in the speed of passive or automatic processing. It is certainly true that statistically significant differences are no longer evident in the measures thought to reflect passive processing, but the sensitivity to detect differences is quite poor because of the small magnitude of the relevant durations. Therefore age differences could con-

ceivably have remained proportionally constant, but were not
detected because of the tremendous reduction in absolute level.
It obviously requires considerably more statistical power
to detect a difference of 5 milliseconds than a difference
of 200 milliseconds, and yet no adjustments have been made
to increase the precision of measurement to allow comparable
sensitivity in the two situations.

One could argue that in light of the extremely rapid
nature of passive processing, even if significant age differences
were found they would probably be unimportant because their
magnitude was so small. The difficulty with this argument
is that any differences that might be observed can be presumed
to accumulate across different levels of processing and have
substantial consequences no matter how slight the basic differences
might appear. Unless one can be certain that the effects
are restricted to a particular phase of processing, the possibility
that even what appear to be rather trivial differences have
major consequences cannot be dismissed.

An alternative interpretation of the very small to non-
existent age differences in the lexical access priming measures
and the memory-scanning slope measures with highly familiar
stimuli is that passive processing is unaffected by age.
Salthouse and Somberg (1982a) proposed an explanation of this
type in suggesting that the reduced age differences in the
slope parameter with practice might be attributable to the
introduction of a specialized peripheral processor independent
of the limitations of the central processor responsible for
most other activities.

Although it is not currently possible to reach a definite
conclusion with respect to the meaning of the lack of significant
age differences in measures of passive processing, it is important
to point out that neither interpretation is necessarily inconsistent with the limited-resource theories of age-related
differences in cognitive functioning. If the age differences
are eventually found to be of the same proportional magnitude
in passive processing as in active processing one would conclude
that passive processing differs from active processing simply

in the amount of resources required. On the other hand, if
sensitive measurements reveal that there are no significant
age differences in measures of passive processing, then it
could be claimed that no differences should be expected when
the processing makes no demands on the resource presumed to
decline in quantity with increased age. In other words, if
age differences in cognition are attributable to an age-related
reduction in the availability of a critical processing resource,
the magnitude of the age differences should be proportional
to the demands placed upon that resource by a given task.
Resource theories of cognitive aging would be contradicted
only if no age differences were evident in tasks clearly requiring
the relevant resource, or if age differences were found on
tasks not requiring the relevant resource. The latter outcome
would indicate that the resource was not necessary to produce
age differences, and the former would signify that it was
also not sufficient.

Summary

     The major conclusion from the evidence reviewed in this
chapter is that increased age is associated with a slowing
of a great many behavioral variables. Because the speed with
which activities are carried out can be considered a reflection
of the temporal resources available to an individual, it may
be inferred that time-related resources diminish with age.
It is still unclear whether the age-related slowing is best
characterized as being attributable to one or many factors,
and what the nature of the factor or factors might be. There
are also a few exceptions to the slowing-with-age phenomenon,
but it is indisputable that most aspects of behavior tend
to become slower between 20 and 70 years of age. The situation
is much less clear with respect to passive or automatic processing,
and it is at least plausible that tasks which do not make
demands on processing resources do not exhibit detrimental
effects of aging.

     It therefore appears that any comprehensive theory of
cognitive aging must incorporate an explanation for the extremely
well-documented slowing of nearly all behavior with increased

age.   Because there is remarkable consensus that processes
within the central nervous system and not merely peripheral
sensory or motor processes are responsible for age-related
slowing, it is reasonable to conjecture whether age differences
in aspects of cognitive functioning are independent of the
speed changes, or are in some fashion caused by them.   The
issue to be considered in subsequent chapters is whether the
widespread and well-documented slowing is a major determinant
of the age differences commonly reported in various measures
of cognitive functioning.

The Processing Rate Theory of Cognitive Aging

The preceding chapter clearly documented the existence of a widespread slowing of most behavioral activities with increased age, a phenomenon so pervasive that Birren (e.g., 1964, 1965) has referred to slowing as a primary process of aging. Fozard (1981) claimed that 'the quality of mental performance that most consistently distinguished young and elderly adults is its speed (p. 62),' and Anderson (1955) has even suggested that it might be possible:

> ...to define aging in terms of a loss of speed,
> that is in terms of the rate at which messages pass
> through the communication system which we know as
> the nervous system (Anderson, 1955, p. 117).

Whether the slowing phenomenon should be accorded this lofty status is naturally debatable, and many questions remain concerning the number of factors involved in the phenomenon, the quantitative relations between age and speeded measures, and the physiological causes of the slowing phenomenon. Nevertheless, age-related slowing is certainly well-documented, and thus the phenomenon appears to provide a secure foundation from which to build a theoretical system.

The basic idea in the theory proposed here is that the rate of performing nearly all mental operations slows down with increased age, and that this slowing has important consequences for both the quantity and the quality of performance in many cognitive activities. Although a very simple notion, time as a processing resource appears to satisfy the two major requirements considered necessary for a plausible resource theory of cognitive aging (cf., Chapter 7) -- documented decline across adulthood in the quantity of the resource, and demonstrated sufficiency of differences in the resource to account for differences in cognition. The research surveyed in the previous chapter clearly established that most behavioral activities require more time with increased age, with the bulk of the

evidence suggesting that the slower performance is not attributable
to impaired sensory or motor processes but instead to a central
limitation in the speed of executing cognitive operations.
In this respect, it seems reasonable to infer that there is
a reduction with age in the resource of time, i.e., the rate
of information processing becomes slower with increased age.
It is primarily this feature that distinguishes the time resource
from the resources of energy and space because there is still
little independent evidence that these other resources do
in fact decline with age.

The sufficiency of time limitations to account for variations
in cognitive performance is illustrated by the powerful effects
of propagation rate in the computer simulation, and by the
modest but often statistically significant, relations between
measures of speed and measures of intelligence reviewed in
Chapter 8. These findings, in addition to the plausibility
arguments reflected in the various quotations in Chapter 8,
suggest that differences in speed of processing may indeed
influence the quantity and quality of cognitive functioning.

It is important to point out that while a slower speed
of processing is postulated to be the primary determinant
of age differences in cognition, this change in speed will
likely result in age differences in many other aspects of
processing because of the numerous interdependencies of the
human information processing system. For example, if the
rate of operations is slowed down, many strategies may no
longer be effective and less efficient strategies must be
employed. Or, if the mere performance of the task consumes
nearly all of the available time because of longer durations
of the mental operations, there will be less opportunity to
develop and refine optimal strategies of performance. It
is also possible that a slower rate of mental operation leads
to greater frustration and anxiety about ineffective performance
which in turn may contribute to detrimental performance.
An earlier suggestion that 'the elderly are doing the same
things as the young but merely at a slower rate' (Salthouse,
1980, p. 61) was therefore probably too naive in that it failed

to appreciate the extensive interactions among various aspects
of the information processing system.   Moreover, critiques
of the processing rate perspective based on the assumption
that the only difference between young and old adults is the
speed of carrying out mental operations (e.g., Hartley, Harker,
& Walsh, 1980) may be misleading since it is proposed that
speed differences emerging gradually over a period of several
decades will tend to lead to adjustments or adaptations in
strategy in addition to basic efficiency.

     Age-related changes in peripheral processes such as sensory
ability and muscular mobility which may influence cognitive
performance are likely to occur irrespective of any differences
in rate of central processing.   Information obviously cannot
be processed if it never enters the system, and the results
of any processing that is carried out cannot be communicated
if it is impossible to execute the necessary responses.   Disease-
related pathologies, which tend to increase with age, probably
also contribute to both general and specific impairments in
cognition and may be difficult to distinguish from processes
of 'normal' aging.   And finally, although not well documented
at the present time, it is still reasonable to speculate that
socio-cultural factors have at least some influence in age-related
differences in fluid cognitive functioning.

     Speed of processing is therefore viewed as a major determinant
of age differences in cognition, but certainly not as the
dominant factor in all types of individual differences.   In
other words, while faster is not always better, it is suggested
that other things being equal, an individual with the capability
for fast processing will have distinct advantages over one
only able to process information at a slow rate.   In a sample
homogeneous with respect to age, it is likely that other factors
are probably responsible for more of the variance in cognitive
performance than the rate of processing.   However as that
rate slows with age, it may emerge as the principal factor
responsible for differences in performance associated with
increased age.   In this context it is useful to realize that
speed and time are considered processing resources, which,

although desirable and frequently advantageous, are not sufficient by themselves to ensure competent performance. As with all resources, they must be efficiently allocated in order to fully realize their potential. An impulsive individual who attempts to act before deliberating on the consequences of those actions will thus tend to be less successful in many situations than a more reflective individual, regardless of his or her capacity for rapid processing. In the same manner that the resource of working memory capacity can be squandered by retaining task-irrelevant material, so can the resource of time be wasted by inappropriate use of that time. Therefore while efficient allocation of one's resources is necessary to capitalize upon their existence, unless there is sufficient quantity of resources one's cognitive potential will be limited because there is an inadequate amount of resources to be allocated.

A schematic illustration of the proposed relations among the major variables in the processing rate theory is presented in Figure 10.1. (Because the concern in this monograph is with fluid abilities thought to be largely independent of specific experience, cf., Chapter 5, no arrow is drawn between age and experience, although such a linkage probably does exist for crystallized abilities.) Notice that while many variables are assumed to influence cognitive performance, speed is the major one postulated to be directly related to age. It is this postulate that is the essence of the processing rate theory. However, Figure 10.1 clearly indicates that even if a slower rate of processing with increased age is the major determinant of age-related differences in cognition, it is unreasonable to expect that it will be the only determinant. Even those variables indirectly attributable to the slower rate of processing may be difficult to relate to the factor of speed because of the subtle and intricate adjustments postulated to have taken place over the decades during which the changes in speed were occurring. That is, a decline in speed may have been the precursor of, or the primary factor in, the cognitive decline, but it might no longer be represented in any particular expression of cognition because of the extensive

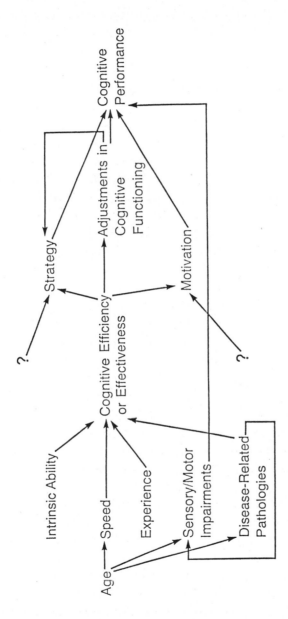

Figure 10.1 Hypothesized relations among factors contributing to cognitive performance according to the processing rate theory of cognitive aging.

adaptations and compensations that have occurred. One should therefore not be surprised to find little evidence for a monolithic determinant of cognitive aging phenomena, or any cognitive phenomena for that matter, because the human processing system is so complex and interrelated that even if such a factor did exist, it would be difficult to identify from limited behavioral observations of the type obtained in most psychological experiments.

Researchers in the field of intelligence face a similar problem when attempting to explain why, if there is a common g factor in intelligence, it accounts for such a small part of the total variance in any given activity. Simon's (1976) answer to this question is relevant in the present context because many of his explanations can also be applied to the question of why speed influences are not more pronounced in many cognitive tasks. His suggested reasons were:

> First, we have seen that, while there is a great commonality of process, most tasks require also some very specific knowledge (words, perceptual tests, familiar chunks), and expert performance of some tasks calls for an enormous amount of such knowledge. Second, while the same basic processes show up in many different tasks, a given process may be employed more or less frequently in different task environments. Third, the basic processes may be combined in more than one way to produce a program for performing a particular task...Proficiency in a task may depend on how the basic processes and relevant knowledge have been organized into the program for task performance...Finally, it is not certain to what extent **g** is to be attributed to common processes among performance programs, or to what extent it derives from individual differences in the efficacy of the learning programs that assemble the performance programs (Simon, 1976, p. 96).

Some critics might argue that allowing for the possibility of indirect effects of speed and not ruling out the influence

of other determinants of age differences considerably weakens
the power of the processing rate theory. Although these considerations undoubtedly do make it more difficult to obtain evidence
which unequivocally rejects the theory, it seems very unrealistic
to expect that a difference with such profound implications
for the efficiency of many aspects of information processing
would not be accompanied by gradual adjustments in the manner
of performing cognitive activities. Moreover, the complexity
of human cognition ensures that cognitive performance has
many important determinants, even when steps are taken to
minimize the influence of many variables suspected to affect
performance. We will see that is still possible to test predictions from the processing rate perspective by making several
rather strong assumptions, but the naive view that the **only**
difference between young adults and older adults is the speed
of carrying out mental operations is considered highly unlikely
in light of the complex and interactive nature of human information
processing. It is important to emphasize that the processing
rate theory does assume that the principal causal factor responsible for age differences in cognition is a slower rate of
processing with increased age. What it does not assume, however,
is that the difference in processing rate occurred in a vacuum
with no adjustments of modifications in other aspects of processing.

Comparison with Alternative Interpretations

The processing rate position can be clarified by contrasting
it with alternative views of the role of speed in age differences
in cognition. First, it should be obvious from the discussion
of the preceding chapters that the current perspective asserts
that age-related speed differences are the cause, and not
merely the consequence, of age differences in cognition.
A popular interpretation is just the opposite, as reflected
in the following passage by Arenberg (1980):

> Speed would seem to be an outcome rather than an
> explanation. It is more likely that a procedure
> which induces proficient encoding leading to improved
> performance **results in rather than from** faster encoding,

search, and retrieval (Arenberg, 1980, p. 69).
This issue obviously cannot be resolved simply from arguments
based on which interpretation seems more likely, but it is
important to point out that the age-related differences that
are assumed to result in altered efficiency also need to be
explained. In other words, if the speed differences are attributed
to differences in the proficiency of encoding, or to other
unspecified variations in strategy, etc., we would still need
an explanation of why those processes were affected by age.
As noted above, it is at least conceivable that age-related
changes in the speed of processing are largely responsible
for age differences in strategy or quality, as well as efficiency
or quantity, and thus speed factors may be the cause of these
other differences as well.

Another interpretation of the relations among age, speed,
and cognition is that speed influences cognitive performance,
but only for relatively uninteresting, peripheral, reasons.
This might be called the 'hearing aid' perspective since it
assumes that, just as is the case with vision and hearing,
increased age leads to certain peripheral (i.e., not in the
central nervous system) impairments, but that they can be
eliminated by suitable adjustment of the testing environment
such as the provision of hearing aids, spectacles, or the
elimination of temporal limits for responding.   According
to Lorge (1936), one of the early advocates of this position,
'speed obscures sheer mental power in older adults,' and consequently should be eliminated from the process of evaluating
intellectual ability.

A third view is that speed is not important in producing
age differences in cognitive performance because the elimination of time limits frequently does not alter the magnitude
of the age differences (e.g., Doppelt & Wallace, 1955; Gilbert,
1935; Klodin, 1976; Miles, 1934; Schaie, Rosenthal, & Perlman,
1953; Storandt, 1977). That is, according to this interpretation,
removing time limits presumably minimizes the effects of speed,
and because this manipulation does not eliminate the age differences, it is suggested that speed has little effect on the

age differences observed in cognitive ability.

Both of these latter interpretations are based on the assumption that age-related slowing is a peripheral phenomenon, with little or no central consequences. That is, they either claim that the speed effects are large but irrelevant to central cognitive processing (the second position), or are apparently unimportant in central cognitive processing (the third position), but in both cases the assumption is that the speed effects are restricted to peripheral mechanisms. This is clearly contrary to the current position, in which speed is assumed to be a central factor affecting nearly all mental operations, and is consequently an intrinsic property of cognition. Attempting to remove the influence of speed from tests of cognitive ability might therefore be considered equivalent to throwing the baby out with the bath water: either the attempt would be successful and all age differences would be eliminated, or the attempt would fail by only minimizing peripheral influences and a substantial age effect would remain.

Paradoxical mixtures of inconsistent interpretations of age-related speed effects also exist in the literature. For example, the following two passages appeared on the same page in a recent article by Schaie and Hertzog (1983):

> ...it is tempting to speculate that much of the decline in PMA performance is a function of age changes in the speed of encoding cognitive operations required by different subtests.

> ...Does age-related slowing in cognitive speed lead us to overestimate the loss of intellectual ability -- the ability to reason, image a visual rotation, and so forth -- when assessing performance in speeded tests of intelligence? (Schaie & Hertzog, 1983, p. 541).

The co-occurrence of these statements is puzzling because in both passages speed is apparently acknowledged as a potential causal factor in cognitive functioning, and yet in the second passage it is discussed as though it were not an intrinsic

feature of intellectual ability. Admitting that speed is
cognitive and yet suggesting that it might be separable from
cognitive ability seems analogous to stating that a person's
skeletal structure distorts the assessment of the individual's
size. Of course, the authors may not have intended to imply
that cognitive speed was an intrinsic feature of cognitive
functioning, but to the extent that the speed is cognitive
or central rather than sensory or peripheral, it is difficult
to imagine how it could be distinguished from ability per
se.

Establishing Realistic Expectations

Before turning to a discussion of methods that might
be used to investigate the processing rate theory, it is desirable
to have a clear understanding of what should be expected from
a successful theory of cognitive aging. Perhaps because most
theoretical perspectives employed in research investigating
the effects of aging on cognitive functioning have been borrowed
from those originally applied in research with young adults,
there sometimes seems to be an assumption that a satisfactory
theory of age differences in cognition must also account for
other types of individual differences, and for variations
in performance produced by within-task manipulations. From
the present perspective this may be asking for too much in
that the factors responsible for age differences in a particular
activity could be only a subset of those contributing to total
performance.

This argument can be elaborated by thinking of the total
variance on the relevant performance measure as being partitioned
into several different components. For example, one important
subset of the total variance is that which reflects the reliable
variance, as indexed by the reliability coefficient. Obviously,
one cannot hope to provide an explanation for all of the variance
in a task if only a portion of it is systematic from one measurement occasion to the next. In a similar manner, it seems
unrealistic for a theory of aging to be expected to account
for a greater proportion of the variance than that found to
be associated with aging. If the correlation between age

and the dependent variable of interest is, say .5, then only 25% (.5 X .5) of the total variance is predictable on the basis of age and therefore it is that amount rather than the entire variance which needs to be explained. Moreover, just as a task-oriented theory would be considered successful if it was found to account for a substantial proportion of the reliable across-item variance, so should an aging theory be considered successful if it was found to account for a substantial proportion of the age-associated variance. A theory able to account for all individual differences in performance rather than simply those attributable to age would obviously be preferred, but the importance of explaining the age-related differences should not be underestimated.

How Can the Processing Rate Theory be Investigated?

The evidence reviewed in Chapters 8 and 9, and the arguments in earlier sections of the current chapter, suggest that the processing rate theory offers a promising perspective on the reasons for adult age differences in cognition. However, but the viability of the theory clearly depends on the amount and type of evidence which can be found to support it. Some means must therefore be found of testing these still vague speculations with respect to empirical data.

Three distinct approaches appear useful in investigating the hypothesis that age differences in cognition are determined, at least in part, by age-related differences in speed of processing. One is to follow the lead of the research on the relation between speed and intelligence summarized in Chapter 8, and focus on task-independent measures of processing speed. A second possible approach is to switch to task-dependent measures of processing rate in the hopes of obtaining measures with demonstrated validity for the task of interest. The third strategy for investigating the processing rate theory is to carry out manipulations thought to simulate the effects of an altered rate of processing and then to determine their effects on cognitive functioning. Each of these tactics will be examined in the following sections.

Task-Independent Measures of Processing Speed

As discussed in Chapter 8, there have been many attempts to identify a measure that might serve as an index of an individual's general rate of information processing. It was concluded that while these efforts have not yet proven very successful, more promising measures might eventually be identified, perhaps based on a composite of several behavioral variables, or derived from some type of psychophysiological recordings.

Until the time that an optimal index of speed is identified, it might still be possible to investigate the processing rate theory by selecting a compromise speed measure possessing several desirable characteristics. Of course, the paramount consideration is that the measure accurately reflect the average speed of information processing within the nervous system. However the possibility that active and passive processing are carried out at different rates, and the difficulty of assessing either rate with a single measure may make it impossible to satisfy this criterion at the present time. It does seem likely that relatively complex tasks involving familiar content might be more appropriate than either very simple tasks or tests dependent upon specific ability, but which tasks those might be, and why, cannot yet be answered.

A second criterion for selection of a speed measure is the degree to which the measure is sensitive to the effects of age. If it is assumed that rate of processing declines with increased age, the measure selected to represent processing rate should exhibit moderately high correlations with age. In effect, this criterion is designed to maximize the possibility that the speed measure is tightly coupled with age, and not indirectly related through mechanisms which might partially compensate for the hypothesized age-related slowing in processing.

The third criterion is that the index of speed should be highly reliable, because the relationship between speed and cognition can be meaningfully investigated only if the measure of speed is both consistent and stable. Inadequate reliability was implicated as a probable contributor to the low correlations between speed and intelligence reviewed in

Chapter 8, and it is important that this weakness be avoided by employing measures with high test-retest (and not merely split-half) reliability. Finally, the fourth desirable characteristic is that the speed measure should be relatively easy to obtain without time-consuming procedures and complex equipment.

A measure that appears to possess most of these characteristics is the score on the Digit Symbol Substitution Test from the Wechsler Adult Intelligence Scale. Actually, the fact that this test is incorporated in several omnibus intelligence test batteries can be interpreted as support for the importance of speed factors in cognition because the task appears to have little in common with other tests of intelligence and yet the scores are moderately correlated with those from other tests. Matarazzo (1972) expressed this view, in addition to reiterating the importance of speed in age differences in cognition, in the following passage:

> ...when the Digit Symbol is administered over a wide adult age range, scores on the test begin to decline earlier and to drop off more rapidly with age than other tests of intelligence. At the same time, however, the test's correlation with Full Scale scores at different ages remains consistently high. This suggests that older persons may be penalized by speed, the penalty being "deserved" since resulting reduction in test performance is on the whole proportional to the subject's overall capacity at the time he is tested. There is strong evidence that the older person is not only slower but also "slowed" up mentally (Matarazzo, 1972, p. 215).

The digit symbol test is a paper-and-pencil test consisting of a code table containing pairs of digits and symbols, and a series of randomly ordered digits below each of which is an empty box. The task for the subject is to write the appropriate symbol below each digit and to complete as many of these substitutions as possible in 90 seconds. Many studies have documented that score in digit symbol tests exhibits among the largest age relationships of any behavioral variables that have been investigated. The mean performance decline in cross-sectional age samples is nearly 10% per decade (see Figure 4.12 in Salthouse, 1982), and correlations with age in samples of people between 20 and 70 years of age typically range between .4 and .6 (e.g., Birren & Morrison, 1961; Birren & Spieth, 1962; Goldfarb, 1941; Heikkinen, Kiiskinen, Kayhty, Rimpela, & Vuori, 1974; Heron & Chown, 1967; Weisenburg, Roe, & McBride, 1936). In fact, the age effects are so pronounced with the digit symbol measure that a consistent finding in many experiments is that the score at the 75th percentile for the sample in their 60s and 70s is only at about the 5th percentile for the sample in their late teens and early 20s.

Digit symbol score is quite reliable, with test-retest correlations in samples homogeneous with respect to age ranging from about .8 to .9 (cf., Table 8.1; Derner, Aborn, & Canter, 1950; Lemmon, 1927; Wechsler, 1958). The digit symbol substitution test is also very short and easy to administer without complex apparatus. It is therefore ideal as a supplemental task to be administered in addition to the primary tasks of interest.

A concern one might have about this test is that it appears to involve factors other than pure speed of mental operations. In particular, writing of symbols involves a motor factor and associating digit-symbol pairs involves a memory factor. Obviously if there are marked age differences in either of these components, then the age differences on the digit symbol measure cannot be attributed entirely to central speed factors. However, the measure might still be useful if it could be established that sizable age differences remain after taking the motor and memory factors into account. Any residual age difference could presumably be interpreted as a reflection of the central speed factor (or factors), and particularly if it is large relative to the contribution of other factors, the aggregate score might still provide a meaningful index of overall processing speed.

Two different approaches have been taken to examine the role of the motor handwriting component in the age differences in digit symbol substitution score, and the results of both suggest that it cannot account for a very large proportion of the age differences in performance. One approach has involved comparison of the age functions on the standard task with those obtained on a simplified copying task in which the digits are replaced by symbols that are merely to be copied as rapidly as possible. Because this manipulation involves the same handwriting components as the original task, it is possible to subtract the copying score from the score on the original digit symbol test to obtain a motor-free measure of coding speed. Although there are age differences in the copying speed measure, it has been reported that they are more pronounced with the standard digit symbol measure (e.g., Lachman, Lachman, & Taylor, 1982), and are still evident in the motor-free measure of coding speed (e.g., Erber, Botwinick, & Storandt, 1981; Storandt, 1976).

The second technique used to minimize the motor component in the digit symbol test involved changing the test to require the examinee to cross out incorrect symbols rather than write all symbols. That is, symbols were supplied in each of the boxes, with 50% of them correct and 50% incorrect, and the task for the subject was simply to draw a slash through the incorrect symbols. This obviously reduces the motor component considerably, but Salthouse (1978a) found very similar age differences in the standard version and this minimal-motor version of the digit symbol task.

Because it seems reasonable to expect that an individual able to remember more of the digit symbol associations than another individual will perform faster since fewer glances at the code table are necessary, the digit symbol test is sometimes thought to involve a strong memory component. However, several analyses indicate that the memory involvement is apparently no greater for older adults than for young adults because the age patterns are nearly identical with modified versions of the task designed to minimize the role of memory. In two studies, simplifying the task either by pretraining the young and old adults to the same accuracy criterion of associating the digit symbol pairs (e.g., Erber, Botwinick, & Storandt, 1981), or by reducing the number of digit symbol pairs (Salthouse, 1978a), resulted in very similar age trends to those obtained with the standard task. Moreover, while memory of an increased number of digit symbol pairs is probably a major factor in practice-related improvement on the digit symbol test, several studies have indicated that practice effects are comparable across subjects in young and old age groups (e.g., Beres & Baron, 1981; Erber, 1976; Erber, Botwinick, & Storandt, 1981; Grant, Storandt, & Botwinick, 1978; Salthouse, 1978a). Salthouse (1978a) also inferred on the basis of an analysis of error frequencies that the young and older adults relied on approximately the same number of pairs in their functional working memory while performing the task. It has been reported (e.g., Erber, 1976; Thorndike, Bregman, Tilton, & Woodyard, 1928; Willoughby, 1929) that older adults recall fewer of the digit symbol associations on a subsequent test, but as Jerome (1959) and Welford (1958) noted, some of this difference may be attributable to decreased opportunity to learn because of the slower rate of substitution.

On the basis of the evidence just reviewed, it seems reasonable to suggest that although the digit symbol substitution test clearly involves motor and memory components, these factors are probably not major contributors to the age differences in digit symbol score. This conclusion is also consistent with introspective analyses of the processing operations seemingly involved in the digit symbol task. For example, Bromley (1974) suggested that the following steps are required in this task:

> ...attend to the first digit, store it in short-term memory, shift attention to the code, find the same digit, translate it into the equivalent symbol, store it in short-term memory, shift attention back to the first digit, retrieve symbol from store, write in the symbol; attend to the next digit, and so on (Bromley, 1974, p. 191).

To the extent that all of these operations are performed and each is slowed with age, the influence of additional age differ-

ences in the size of the short-term memory or the speed of
writing might be expected to be fairly small in comparison.

Therefore, because a slower rate of performing nearly
all mental operations may be hypothesized to be primarily
responsible for the age-related declines in digit symbol performance, score on the digit symbol substitution test might provide
a plausible index of the rate of information processing.
It must be viewed as a provisional measure, however, because
it correlates only moderately with other measures presumed
to reflect rate of processing (cf., Tables 8.1 and 8.2), and
consequently its status as an index of the average time to
perform mental operations is still somewhat questionable.
Processing on the digit symbol test also seems to be active
rather than passive, and hence the best one could hope is
that it reflects the rate of active processing but not passive
processing. A measure that might function as an index of
passive processing rate has not yet been identified.

Once a suitable measure of processing speed is available,
several predictions from the processing rate perspective can
be derived and contrasted with those from alternative views
of the interrelations of age, speed, and cognition. The processing
rate position is summarized in Equation 10.1, with two rival
interpretations represented in Equations 10.2 (the position
that speed is an irrelevant concomitant of aging) and 10.3
(the speed-as-consequence position). These are obviously
extreme simplifications since many more correlates of each
variable could be included, as well as numerous manifestations
of speed and cognition. For example, Equation 10.1 may be
contrasted with Figure 10.1 in order to illustrate the abstractness with which the actual relations are portrayed in these
summary equations. Nevertheless, the equations are useful
for emphasizing major issues in this area, and to serve as
a basis for deriving predictions which might allow them to
be distinguished on empirical grounds.

$$(10.1) \quad \text{Age} \; \longrightarrow \; \text{Speed} \; \longrightarrow \; \text{Cognition}$$
$$(10.2) \quad \text{Speed} \; \longleftarrow \; \text{Age} \; \longrightarrow \; \text{Cognition}$$
$$(10.3) \quad \text{Age} \; \longrightarrow \; \text{Cognition} \; \longrightarrow \; \text{Speed}$$

One of the important issues concerning the interrelations of age, speed, and cognition is whether the correlation between speed and cognition is mediated by the age variable, as suggested by Equation 10.2, or is independent of age, as suggested by Equations 10.1 and 10.3. If the speed-cognition correlation is produced by the common influence of age on both variables (i.e., Equation 10.2), then partialling out the effects of age should result in the elimination of the correlation. However, if age only exerts its effects by influencing the level of speed (i.e., Equation 10.1), or by influencing the level of cognition (i.e., Equation 10.3), then the speed-cognition correlation should remain unchanged by partialling out the effects of age. An examination of the magnitude of speed-cognition correlations with and without control of the age variable should therefore allow the viability of Equation 10.2 to be determined.

A second set of predictions from Equations 10.1, 10.2, and 10.3 concerns the correlation between age and cognition with, and without, control of the level of speed. Equation 10.1 implies that speed mediates the age-cognition relation, and therefore partialling speed out of the correlation between age and cognition should result in elimination of the correlation. On the other hand, if the relation among these variables is as indicated in Equation 10.2 or Equation 10.3, there should be no difference in the magnitude of the correlation between age and cognition with, and without, control of speed because speed is either assumed to be another, largely irrelevant, concomitant of aging (Equation 10.2), or to be a consequence of the differences in cognition (Equation 10.3).

Table 10.1 summarizes these predictions concerning the expected relations between zero-order and partialled correlations from each of the perspectives represented in Equations 10.1, 10.2,

Table 10.1

Predictions from Different Conceptualizations
of the Relations Among Age, Speed, and Cognition

Correlations

Relationship	Age-Cognition	Age-Cognition .Speed	Speed-Cognition	Speed-Cognition .Age
Age → Speed → Cognition		>		=
Speed ← Age → Cognition		=		>
Age → Cognition → Speed		=		=

and 10.3. Notice that while the speed-cognition comparison
is sufficient to determine the plausibility of Equation 10.2,
the age-cognition comparison is necessary to distinguish between
Equations 10.1 and 10.3. That is, only the view that age
effects in cognition are mediated by speed would predict substantial differences in the age-cognition correlation by partialling out speed, and only the view that cognition and speed
are relatively independent consequences of aging would predict
a large reduction in the speed-cognition correlation by partialling
out age.

     There is some debate about the most appropriate method
for partialling out the effects of one variable in examining
the relation between two other variables. Partial correlation
procedures remove the variance of the controlled variable
from both variables, while semi-partial or part correlation
procedures remove the variance from only one variable (cf.,
Cohen & Cohen, 1983). The difference in the present context
is that the partial correlation reflects the residual correlation
between age and the cognitive measure after removing the effects
of speed from the relation, i.e., (Age - Cognition).Speed,
while the semi-partial correlation represents the correlation
between age and the residual cognitive measure after removing
the effects of speed from that measure, i.e., Age - (Cogni-
tion.Speed). Although Horn and his colleagues (e.g., 1982a;
Horn, Donaldson, & Engstrom, 1981) have advocated the use
of semi-partial correlations on the grounds that it is illogical
to remove behavioral (speed) variance from the status variable
of age, partial correlations seem preferable from a dynamic
perspective. That is, the semi-partial procedure removes
the effects of speed from the cognitive measure, but it does
not remove the **relation** between age and speed from the relation between age and cognition. This latter goal is accomplished by partial correlations, and thus they seem preferable
for these analyses.

     Some evidence relevant to the predictions summarized
in Table 10.2 is available in the studies reviewed in Chapter
8 concerning the relation between speed and intelligence in

samples of individuals relatively homogeneous with respect
to age. Slight, but frequently statistically significant,
correlations are often reported between these two types of
variables, thus suggesting that the speed-cognition relation
is not completely mediated by the influence of age.

Additional evidence relevant to the predictions in Table
10.2 can be obtained from studies involving a range of ages
so that the zero-order and partial correlations can be compared
directly. In order to be relevant the studies must have involved
the collection of cognitive and speed measures from adults
throughout a wide age range, and have reported correlations
between age and the speed measure, between age and the cognitive
measure, and between the speed and cognitive measures. The
predictions from the processing rate theory would be supported
by findings that the correlation between age and the cognitive
measure was greatly reduced by partialling speed out of the
relation, but that the correlation between speed and the cognitive
measure was largely unaffected by partialling out age.

In subsequent chapters these types of analyses will be
applied to performance measures derived from memory, perceptual-
spatial, and reasoning tests administered to adults of varying
ages. For the reasons discussed earlier, the digit symbol
score will be used as the index of speed whenever possible,
but alternative measures will be employed where necessary
in order to subject the predictions to the broadest possible
examination.

The correlational approach described above is very crude
in that it deliberately ignores all determinants of cognition
except speed. Furthermore, one must not only assume that
the speed variable selected accurately reflects the rate of
nearly all forms of information processing, but also that
the slowness resulting from a progressive biological change
over 40 or more years of adulthood is functionally equivalent
to the slowness found in certain young individuals. In light
of an extensive literature concerning a large number of non-speed
determinants of cognitive performance, in combination with
an almost complete absence of empirical information about

the best means of measuring internal processing speed and
of the compensatory adjustments to a gradually evolving loss
of speed, it is clear that the proposed procedures represent
gross and imprecise tests of the role of speed in age-related
differences in cognition.

Task-Dependent Measures of Processing Speed

The tactic of relying on task-dependent measures of processing
speed eliminates the necessity of obtaining a single, abstract,
index of rate of processing, and instead uses measures derived
from specific tasks in the domain of interest. An advantage
of this approach is that the measure can be directly related
to proficiency in the criterion task, and thus the correlation
with overall performance provides an indication of the validity
of the speed measure.

The difference between the task-independent and task-dependent
research strategies is roughly analogous to the distinction
Pellegrino and Glaser (1979) have drawn between the cognitive
correlates and the cognitive components approaches to characterizing the processes responsible for various aptitude constructs.
Task-independent measures can be considered similar to the
correlates method, but the focus on task-dependent measures
of speed relies on the decomposition of complex performance
into simpler components each with its own measurable properties,
and thus corresponds to the cognitive components approach.

One means by which the task-dependent research strategy
might be implemented is to obtain measures of the duration
of several components in a complex task, and then to enter
the measures into a multiple regression equation attempting
to predict composite performance. It may not even be necessary
to obtain independent assessments of the times of the relevant
components because multiple regression techniques might be
employed to generate simultaneous estimates from several relevant
components. Similar procedures have been used with considerable
success in the area of reading comprehension by extracting
duration estimates from the regression parameters relating
reading time to variables of interest (e.g., Graesser, Hoffman,
& Clark, 1980; Just & Carpenter, 1980; Kieras, 1981). That

is, the total reading time is measured for material that varies along relevant dimensions such as number of distinct propositions, thematic relatedness, etc., and then these dimensions are entered into the regression equation as predictor variables for the dependent variable of reading time. The resulting unstandardized regression weights thus serve as an estimate of the temporal contribution of each variable to overall reading time. Riegel (1968) applied a similar procedure in which parameters associated with objective characteristics of words were used to predict word recognition thresholds in young and old adults. Although no statistical analyses were reported with respect to age differences in the regression parameters, older adults, as would be expected, had considerably larger regression parameters for each variable than young adults.

Regardless of the manner in which the component duration estimates are derived, however, the strong expectation from the processing rate theory is that every parameter related to criterion performance should exhibit significant age differences in the direction of longer times with increased age. The possibility of compensatory adjustments to the slower rate of processing cannot be ignored, however, and thus a weaker expectation, that increased age should be associated with longer durations of most components accompanied by indications of an altered mode of processing, may be more justified for many situations.

Simulation of Altered Processing Speed

Another potentially useful technique for investigating the processing rate theory is to attempt to manipulate experimental variables thought to be functionally equivalent to a difference in speed of processing. A critical consideration in this approach is that the manipulation accurately mimics an alteration in the rate of nearly all aspects of information processing. Many researchers have apparently assumed that the effects of processing rate could be simulated by manipulating the time to encode stimuli, execute responses, or generally perform the task. For example, in the context of a review of age effects on memory, Burke and Light (1981) claimed that:

The cognitive slowing position predicts that age
differences should be eliminated by slow or self-paced
learning conditions (Burke & Light, 1981, p. 519).
However, this prediction is unwarranted if, as is postulated
from the processing rate theory, that the age-related differences
in processing speed are distributed throughout the central
nervous system, and not merely localized in peripheral components
concerned with initial registration or execution of a response.
Manipulations of stimulus duration or response pacing are
therefore probably inadequate for the purpose of simulating
different rates of processing since it can be assumed that
they primarily affect peripheral processes. In fact, the
results of the computer simulation of the simple network model
described in Chapter 8 suggest that the rate of peripheral
processes may be much less important than the rate of more
central processes. Therefore, only if the manipulation can
be assumed to alter the rate at which all internal processing
operations are performed, and not merely the time available
for executing those concerned with input or output, would
the processing rate differences be faithfully represented
in the simulation.

Despite the substantial practical problems of identifying
a manipulation that truly affects internal processing rate,
which quite frankly may be insurmountable from a psychological
perspective, the simulation technique is, at least in principle,
quite simple. To the extent that the processing rate theory
is correct and the manipulation accurately simulates the effects
of a different rate of processing, performance should systematically vary with the magnitude of the manipulated variable
in the same manner as it varies across the adult lifespan.
Therefore while the simulation technique may be quite difficult
to implement, it does provide another means of evaluating
the hypothesis that age differences in cognition are largely
attributable to a slower rate of processing with increased
age.

Summary

The processing rate theory of cognitive aging maintains

that effectiveness of cognitive functioning is influenced
by the availability of temporal resources, and that the quantity
of these resources decline throughout adulthood.   Unlike other
limitedresource theories, there is considerable evidence that
temporal resources do decline with age because older adults
have been found to be slower than young adults on most measures
of speeded performance.   Three research strategies are proposed
to investigate implications of the processing rate theory.
One relies on correlational analyses of the relations among
age, speed, and cognition, with the score on the digit symbol
test recommended as the preferred measure of speed.   The second
strategy involves direct examination of the speed of component
processes in specific cognitive tasks.   Simulation of the
effects of an altered rate of processing is the third strategy
proposed for examining the theory.   The following three chapters
discuss the application of these three research strategies
to the empirical literature concerned with memory abilities,
perceptual/spatial abilities, and reasoning and problem solving
abilities.

Memory Abilities

Before attempting to examine the role of speed in age differences in memory it is desirable to document the existence and magnitude of the effects of age in various measures of memory performance. Two sets of data are relevant in this connection. One is the mean performance of older adults (typically with an average age in the 60s) expressed in units of standard deviations of the young adults (typically with an average age of about 20), i.e., (Mean[Old] − Mean[Young])/SD(Young). Results of this type are useful for indicating where the average performance of the older adults falls with respect to the distribution of young adults. Moreover, by assuming that the distributions are normal, this measure allows one to derive estimates of the percentage of young individuals performing above the level of the average older adult.

A second measure of the magnitude of the age effects is the Pearson product-moment correlation between chronological age (in the range from about 18 to 70) and score on the relevant variable. It might be objected that the correlations are based on a linear relation between age and the performance measure, and consequently misleading results would be obtained if the actual function is not linear. There are two replies to this argument. One is that the available data from studies employing large numbers of individuals across the adult life span seem reasonably well characterized by linear functions (e.g., see Figures 4.1 through 4.14 in Salthouse, 1982). The second reply is that even if the relationship is non-linear, the product-moment correlation will tend to underestimate, rather than overestimate, the degree of age sensitivity, and thus provide a relatively conservative assessment of the influence of age.

Table 11.1 contains the standard score and correlational data for a variety of memory measures. The median correlations ranged from −.21 for forward digit span to −.48 for sentence/par-

Table 11.1

Magnitude of Age Relations in Measures of Memory

Measure	Correlation	SD from Young	Source
Digit Span (Forwards)			
	-.31/-.34		Botwinick & Storandt, 1974
	-.13		Dirken, 1972
	-.31		Hayslip & Kennelly, 1982
	-.27		Heron & Chown, 1967
	-.14		Kriauciunas, 1968
	-.12		Robertson-Tchabo & Arenberg, 1976
		-.67	Burke & Yee, 1984
		-.35	Caird, 1966
		-.08	Ferris, et al., 1980
		-.51	Friedman, 1974
		-.63/-.70	Gilbert, 1941
		-.21	Inglis & Ankus, 1965
		-.45	Kriauciunas, 1968
		-1.21	Schneider, et al., 1975
Digit Span (Backwards)			
	-.33/-.40/-.29		Botwinick & Storandt, 1974
	-.40		Hayslip & Kennelly, 1982
		-.58	Burke & Yee, 1984
		-.15	Ferris, et al., 1980
		-.87	Gilbert, 1941
		-.96	Schneider, et al., 1975

Table 11.1 (Continued)

Free Recall

-.20/-.22	Horn, et al., 1981
-.35	Hulicka, 1982
-.45	Robertson-Tchabo & Arenberg, 1976
-.91/-1.70	Craik & Masani, 1967
-1.05	Erber, 1974
-1.30	Erber, et al., 1980
-2.76	Eysenck, 1974
-.94	Harwood & Naylor, 1969
-1.35	Howard, 1983
-1.01/-1.34	Howard, et al., 1981
-.80	Pavur, et al., 1984
-.91/-1.09	Rabinowitz, 1984

Sentence/Paragraph Recall

-.42/-.53	Botwinick & Storandt, 1974
-.45/-.61	Ferris, et al., 1980
-1.28/-1.41	Gilbert, 1941
-1.28/-1.92	Gordon, 1975
-.84	Gordon & Clark, 1974
-.63	Hulicka, 1982
-.73/-1.34	Kausler & Puckett, 1981
-1.41	Meyer & Rice, 1981
-.05/-1.12/-1.93	Taub, 1979
-2.39/-3.57/-3.90	Whitbourne & Slevin, 1978
-1.24/-1.91/-2.48	

Paired Associate Learning/Memory

-.90/-1.45/-2.18	Canestrari, 1968
-1.11/-1.26	Ferris, et al., 1980
-1.93/-2.61	Gilbert, 1941
-1.35	Hulicka, 1966
-1.12	Kausler & Puckett, 1980
-2.75/-4.34	Ross, 1968
-4.05/-2.00/-6.67/-4.57	Rowe & Schnore, 1971
-2.22	Wittels, 1972
-1.77	Yesavage & Rose, 1984

Table 11.1 (Continued)

Visual/Spatial Memory

−.47/−.47/−.51	Arenberg, 1978
−.21	Botwinick & Storandt, 1974
−.56	Riege & Inman, 1981
−1.13	Ferris, et al., 1980
−2.35	Gilbert, 1941
−1.76	Murphy, et al., 1981
−.65	Perlmutter, et al., 1981
−3.92	Riege, et al., 1981

agraph recall, with intermediate values of -.29 for free recall, -.37 for backwards digit span, and -.47 for visual-spatial memory. Median standard scores ranged from -.51 for forward digit span to -2.00 for paired associate learning and memory, with intermediate values of -.73 for backwards digit span, -1.07 for free recall, -1.32 for sentence/paragraph recall, and -1.76 for visual-spatial memory. These values indicate that age is responsible for between 4% and 24% of the total variance on assorted measures of memory performance, and that the average 65-year-old performs at between the 3rd and the 31st percentile of the distribution of 20-year-old adults.

There can be little doubt from these data that increased age is generally associated with poorer performance in a variety of measures of memory functioning. The remainder of the chapter examines evidence relevant to the hypothesis that many of these age differences are attributable to a slower rate of processing information with increased age.

Correlational Analyses of the Age-Speed Relationship

A series of studies conducted in my laboratory provided data that can be used to examine predictions concerning correlations among age, speed, and memory. Each study involved the administration of the digit symbol substitution test to provide an index of speed, and one or more memory tasks to samples of 16 to 34 young adults (aged 17 to 30) and a comparable number of older adults (aged 55 to 84).

Two of the memory tasks assessed digit span and letter span by determining the largest sequence of unrelated digits or consonants that could be correctly repeated on two independent trials. A dual-span task involved the presentation of 75% of an individual's digit span together with 75% of his or her letter span. In other words, if the digit span was eight and the letter span four, the dual-span task consisted of the presentation of six digits concurrent with three letters. Another task, designated supra-span, involved the presentation of eight trials of seven pairs of letters or seven pairs of digits. Standard free recall and paired associates tasks were also administered with either 16 or 20 words in each

of four free recall lists, and four trials each with 12 word
pairs in the paired associates task. A final task consisted
of the presentation of eight trials of seven locations in
a spatial array with the subject requested to recall the locations
by marking positions on a blank array. In all tasks the performance measure was the average number of items correctly recalled.

The correlational results from these studies are presented
in Table 11.2. Notice first that the point-biserial correlations
between age (young = 0, old = 1) and memory performance are
higher than the product-moment correlations reported in Table
11.1, most likely because the latter are based on complete
age distributions. Next consider the correlations relevant
to the predictions from the processing rate theory. One of
the predictions was that the correlation with age should be
greatly attenuated by controlling speed, while the other was
that the correlation with speed should be unaffected by controlling
age. In terms of the arrangement in Table 11.2, the values
in the second column should be close to zero, while the values
in the third and fourth columns should be nearly equivalent.

It is obvious that the results are mixed with respect
to these predictions. The digit span, letter span, dual span,
and supra-span measures appear reasonably consistent with
the predictions, the free recall measures were partially consistent, but the paired associates and spatial recall measures
were completely incompatible with the expectations from the
processing rate hypothesis.

Since the paired associates and spatial recall measures
are clearly inconsistent with the processing rate hypothesis,
it is instructive to examine them first. One possible explanation
of the failure of the processing rate predictions with the
spatial recall task is that the information processing in
this task may have been more passive than active, and consequently
processing speed inadequately assessed with the digit symbol
score. Introspective reports support this interpretation
since many subjects·claim that it is impossible to rehearse,
or otherwise actively remember, spatial locations. If there
are no active or effortful mental operations involved in remember-

Table 11.2

Age, Speed Correlations with Memory Measures

	Age	Age.Speed	Speed	Speed.Age
(Predictions)		>		=
Digit Span	−.17	+.10	+.30	+.27
	−.10	+.10	+.26	+.26
Letter Span	−.24	+.13	+.41	+.37
	−.41	−.12	+.49	+.32
Dual Span	−.42	−.04	+.51	+.33
	−.45	−.17	+.53	+.34
Supra-Span	−.51	+.07	+.67	+.50
Free Recall				
(16 items)	−.71	−.43	+.68	+.35
(20 items)	−.73	−.46	+.70	+.39
Paired Associates	−.81	−.65	+.67	+.23
Spatial Recall	−.58	−.45	+.43	−.10

Note: Correlations between Age and Speed
(Digit Symbol Score) ranged from −.67
to −.82 across samples.

ing spatial material then the rate of performing active mental operations should not be expected to be related to performance. Further support for this interpretation is available in a study by Hunt and Lansman (1982) involving only young adults. These investigators found that performance on an auditory reaction time task varied only slightly when subjects were concurrently remembering spatial information. This result was interpreted as indicating that the spatial memory task was not resource limited, just as is postulated in the present context on the basis of the absence of a sizable correlation with the digit symbol measure of speed.

The failure of the paired associates measure to conform to the predictions of the processing rate hypothesis represents something of a paradox because it can be interpreted as providing support for a critical assumption, while at the same time falsifying a basic prediction. It was argued in Chapter 10 that age differences in digit symbol performance are primarily determined by speed of mental operations, but it is still possible that memory factors played a role in the age effects on digit symbol score. This is obviously a crucial concern in the present studies because the processing rate theory would not be fairly tested if the digit symbol measure is a reflection of memory instead of, or in addition to, speed. However, to the extent that the digit symbol task involves memory, it is most likely a paired associates form of memory in that pairs of digits and symbols have to be associated. The discovery that the measure of paired associates memory was only slightly correlated with digit symbol score after controlling for age (and actually negatively correlated in the sample of young adults, $r = -.07$), can therefore be interpreted as confirming the assumption that age differences in digit symbol performance are not primarily attributable to varying efficiency of associative processes.

Despite this optimistic interpretation, the failure of speed to be related to paired associate performance is puzzling from the processing rate perspective, and only speculative explanations can be offered for this finding. One is that subjects often remember paired associates with some type of interacting visual or spatial imagery and thus the processing rate predictions might fail for the same reasons proposed in the case of spatial recall, i.e., because the digit symbol score is an inappropriate measure of speed. Indeed, imaginal mediation is often considered a major factor in successful paired associates performance, and Baddeley, Grant, Wight, and Thomson (1975) found that a concurrent visual-motor tracking task impaired performance on a paired associates task but not on a verbal free recall task, suggesting that the former but not the latter had a spatial component. However, Hunt and Lansman (1982), in the study cited earlier, found that a paired associates task, but not the spatial memory task, was associated with substantial slowing of a concurrently performed reaction time task. This suggests that the paired associates task was resource limited, and that different mechanisms need to be invoked to account for the results with the spatial memory and paired associates tasks.

A second speculative interpretation of the finding that paired associates performance was unrelated to the digit symbol measure of speed is that the variance in effectiveness of alternative performance strategies was so large that it overwhelmed the influence of speed. This interpretation would suggest that the speed influence would be more noticeable if it could be ensured that all subjects were employing exactly the same strategy.

Neither of these speculations is very satisfying since both are admittedly post-hoc. At the present time the failure of the processing rate predictions in the paired associates task must be considered a definite embarrassment for the perspective that age effects in cognition are mediated by speed.

Now consider the remaining entries in Tables 11.2, from the digit span to the free recall measures. The age effect on the digit span and letter span measures was rather small and thus there appears to be little to be explained with these measures. It is nonetheless interesting to note that the correlational pattern with these measures was consistent with

the predictions from the processing rate perspective. With
the remaining measures the accuracy of the processing rate
predictions appears to decrease with an increase in the amount
of material to be remembered. This trend is evident in a
contrast of the variance in memory performance attributable
to age before and after the control of speed (i.e., column
1 vs. column 2 in Table 11.2). Age accounted for 17.6, 20.3,
and 26.0 percent of the variance in the dual span and supra-span
measures without control of speed, but for only 0.2, 2.9,
and 0.5 percent of the variance after partialling out speed.
On the other hand, age accounted for 50.4 and 53.3 percent
of the variance on the free recall measures, with a reduction
to 18.5 and 21.2 percent after controlling speed.

One interpretation of these results is that speed is
a major factor in the age differences with relatively simple
tasks, but as the complexity of the task increases other influences
account for progressively more of the variance in performance.
For example, differences in the strategies of mediation, elaboration, or organization are likely to be present in the recall
tasks involving 16 or 20 words, and uncontrolled variation
in these factors may tend to overshadow the effects of speed.

The preceding proposal is graphically illustrated in
Figure 11.1. Notice that the age-associated reductions in
speed are postulated to reduce the efficiency of implementing
any given sequence of processing operations, but that variations
in strategy are more important than sheer speed as the amount
of material to be remembered is increased. With low information
levels it is assumed that speed factors dominate, but as the
information load increases more effective strategies need
to be employed, with the particular strategy selected serving
as an important determinant of the amount of material that
can be successfully remembered.

In keeping with the present interpretation is the finding
with young adult subjects of substantial relations between
measures of speed and the size of one's memory span. For
example, Mackworth (1963), and Standing, Bond, Smith, and
Isley (1980) found that the material named the fastest had

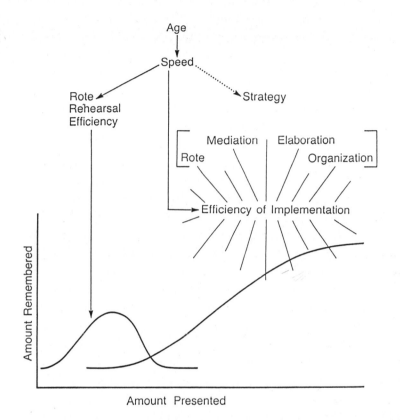

Figure 11.1 Proposed role of speed in tasks involving different amounts of presented material. Notice that while speed is postulated to exert only an indirect influence on the choice of strategy, it is hypothesized to directly affect the efficiency of implementing whatever strategy is adopted.

the greatest memory spans, and Cavanaugh (1972), Brown and
Kirsner (1980), and Puckett and Kausler (1984) found the same
type of relation with the slope of the memory scanning function
(cf. Chapter 9) serving as the measure of speed. Baddeley
and Hitch (e.g., 1974; Baddeley, Thomson, & Buchanan, 1975;
Hitch, 1980; Hitch & Baddeley, 1976) offered an explanation
for how speed might affect performance on certain memory tasks.
Their proposal was that speed was important in what they termed
the articulatory output buffer of working memory. This component,
which is assumed to be a major determinant of performance
in memory span tasks, is postulated to consist of the cycling
of speech-coded verbal information in an articulatory loop.
The evidence for this inference is that memory span is reduced:
(a) with phonemically similar material; (b) when articulation
is suppressed by concurrent vocalization; and (c) with longer
words. With respect to the last finding, it was reported
that, across words of one to five syllables, the span is approximately equal to the number of words that could be vocalized
in two seconds. Moreover, on the average, subjects with faster
rates of vocalization had larger spans. Vocalization rate
is likely to be important only when the amount of to-be-remembered
material is not excessively large, however, and as the material
to be remembered exceeds the capacity of the articulatory
rehearsal buffer other strategies of remembering can be expected
to become progressively more important.

It is important to clarify the distinction between the
complexity effect discussed in earlier chapters in which age
differences are found to increase as the task becomes more
complex, and the trend in the current studies for the role
of speed to decrease as the information requirements of the
task increase. Although seemingly contradictory, these phenomena
are really quite consistent with one another. The resolution
of this apparent paradox is that as the complexity or information
load of a task increases, so also does the variety of approaches
one could adopt to perform the task. In fact, a number of
mental operations are apparently needed simply to extend memory
beyond the immediate memory span, and the quality of those

operations (e.g., organization, elaboration, 'deep' processing, etc.) seems to be an important determinant of how much additional information can be retained. Performance variation attributable to different strategies may therefore be much larger than that directly attributable to different rates of processing. In general, the more opportunity a task provides for alternative strategies of performance, the smaller will be the direct contribution of any single factor, including the factor of speed. However, as noted above, some strategies are probably difficult if not impossible to implement effectively with a slow rate of processing, and consequently there may be speed-determined constraints on the specific strategies that can be employed in a given situation.

Additional evidence pertinent to the predictions concerning the correlations among age, speed, and memory is available from other studies in the literature. Relevant correlations from several such studies are summarized in Table 11.3, where it can be seen that the previously discussed results are largely confirmed. In particular, the majority of the age correlations are greatly attenuated by controlling for level of speed, while the speed correlations change only slightly when age is controlled.

An objective evaluation of the correlational evidence relevant to the processing rate predictions would have to conclude that the results described above provide mixed support, at best, for the processing rate theory. Many of the inconsistent results were attributed to the growing importance of alternative mnemonic strategies as the amount of to-be-remembered material increased, and to the unavailability of a measure of rate of passive processing. However, these interpretations are admittedly post-hoc, and it is clearly necessary to obtain additional evidence before they can be taken too seriously. In particular, it is highly desirable that considerable more information be acquired about the nature of the processing in different memory tasks so that the influence of rate variations could be better understood.

Table 11.3

Further Correlations Among Age, Speed, and Memory

	Age	Age.Speed	Speed	Speed.Age	Source
(Predictions)		>		=	
Digit Span					
	−.19	+.02	+.45	+.42	Birren & Morrison, 1961
	−.18	−.04	+.29	+.23	Goldfarb, 1941
	−.12	−.10	+.07	+.02	Robertson-Tchabo & Arenberg, 1976
Primary Memory					
	−.15	−.04	+.28	+.24	Horn, et al., 1981
	−.09	−.03	+.26	+.25	" "
	−.24	−.18	+.19	+.10	Robertson-Tchabo & Arenberg, 1976
Secondary Memory					
	−.12	−.03	+.23	+.20	Horn, et al., 1981
	−.13	−.11	+.12	+.09	" "
	−.45	−.38	+.29	+.13	Robertson-Tchabo & Arenberg, 1976
Free Recall					
	−.20	+.02	+.52	+.49	Horn, et al., 1981
	−.22	−.03	+.48	+.44	" "
Delayed Recall					
	−.45	−.37	+.33	+.18	Robertson-Tchabo & Arenberg, 1976
Delayed Recognition					
	−.26	−.15	+.31	+.23	Robertson-Tchabo & Arenberg, 1976
Incidental Memory					
	−.19	−.14	+.27	+.24	Horn, et al., 1981

Note: Correlation signs have been converted
such that faster speed is indicated by
higher numbers, i.e., slowing with age
should lead to a positive correlation.

Direct Measurement of Durations

Some of the most compelling evidence for the processing rate theory in the domain of memory derives from studies attempting to measure the time required to perform specific processing components presumed relevant to memory effectiveness. Of course such measurement is always somewhat tentative because the identification of a processing component requires the adoption of a fairly specific theoretical model of the task which may later prove to be invalid or unrealistic. Nevertheless, measurement of this type is valuable because an implication of the processing rate theory is that all memory-relevant aspects of processing should exhibit age-related slowing, and consequently contribute to the poorer performance on memory tasks. A finding that certain processes are clearly involved in efficient memory and yet do not exhibit substantial slowing with increased age would therefore provide contradictory evidence for this perspective, and an accumulation of such evidence would obviously render the theory invalid.

Memory Scanning

A number of distinct memory components have been measured with respect to their temporal efficiency in samples of young and old adults, and in most cases older adults were found to have longer durations of the relevant operation than the young adults. One example of a slower memory operation among older adults is the memory-scanning component discussed in Chapter 9. It will be remembered that the speed of scanning or searching memory is estimated from the slope of the function relating probe reaction time to the number of previously presented memory set items. As noted in Chapter 9, a very consistent finding in the research literature is that the slope of the function relating reaction time to number of memory items increases, indicating that the rate of scanning memory decreases, with increased age. Anders and Fozard (1973) pointed out that this slower time to access stored information may have important consequences for memory functioning:

Since most conventional tests of short-term memory
are designed so that the quality of a subject's

performance (i.e., the amount recalled) is, at least
in part, the result of a race between the speed
of the retrieval mechanism and the speed of forgetting,
the disadvantage of the old person's slowed retrieval
search is clear. The additional time they require
to search for...the first few items in memory increases
the probability that items as yet not searched for
or reported will be forgotten before they can be
retrieved (Anders & Fozard, 1973, p. 415).

A study combining features of the memory scanning task
with probes of visual, phonemic, and semantic information
was reported by Lorsbach and Simpson (1984). As would be
expected from previous research, visual information was retrieved
quickest, semantic information slowest, and phonemic information
at intermediate speeds. Of greater relevance in the present
context was that older adults were slower than young adults
at retrieving each type of information, with the absolute
differences greatest with semantic information retrieved from
secondary memory. This result is clearly consistent with
the interpretation that age differences in memory occur because
with increased age there is less time to perform important
mnemonic operations, and that the age differences tend to
be largest with the most time-consuming operations. Waugh,
Fozard, and Thomas (1978) also found that age differences
were greatest when information had to be retrieved from secondary
memory than from primary memory. Because these same individuals
did not differ very much in the sensory and motor aspects
of the task, it seems reasonable to conclude that it was the
process of accessing and retrieving stored information that
was primarily responsible for the observed age differences.

Rehearsal Speed

Two studies have also been reported in which the speed
of mnemonic rehearsal was measured in groups of young and
old adults. Although quite different procedures were employed,
very similar results indicating slower rehearsal among older
adults were obtained. Salthouse (1980a) measured rehearsal
rate indirectly by requesting subjects to repeat words either

one, two, or three times as fast as possible, and then used
the slope of the function relating vocalization time to number
of repetitions as the measure of rehearsal rate. This index
averaged about 345 milliseconds per word for adults with a
mean age of 22.8, but 440 milliseconds per word for adults
with a mean age of 71.1, a difference of nearly 28%. The
proportional age difference in amount of words recalled in
a free recall task was very similar, with the elderly adults
recalling 20% fewer words than the young adults.

    The second study investigating the rate of rehearsal
in young and old adults (Sanders, Murphy, Schmitt, & Walsh,
1980) employed an overt rehearsal procedure in which the subjects
were instructed to "verbalize aloud whatever they thought
of as they studied a list."   These verbalizations were tape
recorded, with subsequent analyses then allowing an examination
of the number and type of rehearsals within individual subjects.
As expected from the processing rate perspective, older adults
(mean age 73.9 years) were found to have fewer rehearsals
than the young adults (mean age 23.9 years). It was also
reported that:

       ...the probability of recall increased with number
       of rehearsals...(and)...recall of the older adults
       is as strongly related to rehearsal level as it
       is with the younger subjects, at least for those
       few older subjects who did produce higher levels
       of rehearsal (Sanders, et al., 1980, p. 556).

Because number of rehearsals, and consequently speed of rehearsal,
is related to better recall, these results clearly suggest
that the slower speed of rehearsal associated with increased
age is implicated in the poorer memory performance of older
adults compared to young adults. The primary focus of the
Sanders, et al. study was on age differences in organizational
strategies, and indeed, it was found that the sample of young
adults relied more on categorical organization of the to-be-
remembered items than did the sample of old adults. However,
the question remains as to why this age difference in mnemonic
organization occurs. The processing rate interpretation,

of course, is that the lowered organization is a consequence of the slower rate of processing, and not simply that the slower processing is a consequence of the poorer organization.

Apparent Contradictions

Several studies have been reported in which little or no age differences were found in measures thought to reflect the duration of memory-related processes, but all can be criticized on methodological grounds. For example, Macht and Buschke (1984) claimed that:

> ...this study showed that certain kinds of complex mental processes do not show age-related slowing because the present data indicate that there are no age differences in the speed of verbal control under appropriately controlled conditions (Macht & Bushke, 1984, p. 442).

However, the statistical power for being able to detect an age difference was probably quite low in the Macht and Buschke study since only 12 young and 12 old individuals participated for a single recall trial each. Moreover, the measures of speed were very gross and consisted of cued-recall latencies assessed with a stop watch (a procedure which includes the experimenter's reaction time in the measurement), and free-recall rate derived from an analysis of the number of items recalled in successive temporal intervals. Both measures undoubtedly include many processes besides retrieval, and it is unlikely that relatively small differences in retrieval speed could be detected with such a coarse index of rate. To illustrate, in the cumulative free recall task both age groups recalled approximately seven to eight items in the first 30 seconds, which corresponds to a duration of about 4 seconds per item. Estimates of the time needed to retrieve an item from secondary memory derived from memory scanning tasks are generally less than 150 milliseconds (e.g., Anders & Fozard, 1973; Sternberg, 1969), suggesting that the Macht and Bushke (1984) measures included much more than simple memory retrieval. One wouldn't expect to be able to obtain accurate measures of paper thickness with a yardstick, but it may be that attempting to assess retrieval speed in seconds constitutes a comparable type of coarseness.

Two studies by Nebes and his colleagues (1976; Nebes & Andrews-Kulis, 1976) are sometimes cited as indicating that there are no age differences in the speed of performing relevant mnemonic operations, but upon close analysis neither study appears very convincing. The Nebes (1976) study employed a paradigm in which subjects were to decide as rapidly as possible whether two stimuli were the same or different, with the stimuli consisting either of a verbal description and a picture, or two pictures, and the interval between stimuli ranging from zero to three seconds. It was assumed that the interstimulus interval at which the reaction times to the description-picture pairs matched that of the picture-picture pairs could be interpreted as the time needed to recode the verbal information into a pictorial form. Both young and older adults were slower at the description-picture pairs when the stimuli were presented simultaneously, but were equally fast at description-picture pairs and picture-picture pairs at interstimulus intervals of one second or more. Nebes interpreted this result as demonstrating:

> ...that the elderly are not excessively slower in performing such a transformation. If the pictorial representations formed in this experiment are equivalent to an "image," as it is traditionally conceived of in memory mediation work, then these results make it unlikely that the relative neglect of imagery by the elderly is due to an excessive slowness in the generation of images (Nebes, 1976, p. 426).

Unfortunately, the design of the study precluded a very sensitive test of this hypothesis since no intervals between zero and one second were examined. It is conceivable that age differences in the speed of recoding would have been apparent at briefer intervals, particularly since both groups of subjects exhibited evidence that the recoding was completed by one second. Because the study failed to include intervals in the range where differences might be expected, the results cannot be considered

very informative for the purpose of determining the speed
of forming mnemonic mediators in different age groups.

The study by Nebes and Andrews-Kulis (1976) attempted
to investigate possible age differences in the speed of generating
verbal mediators by measuring the time needed to form a sentence
incorporating a specified pair of nouns. The primary conclusion
of the study was that:

> The present results clearly demonstrate that older
> subjects can generate a sentence incorporating a
> given pair of nouns just as rapidly as younger subjects
> (Nebes & Andrews-Kulis, 1976, p. 324)

However, the mean sentence generation times indicated that
the older subjects took an average of 3.68 seconds compared
to only 2.60 seconds for the young subjects. This difference
of nearly 42% is very similar to that found in many other
speeded tasks (cf., Chapter 9), and the failure to achieve
an acceptable level of statistical significance is probably
attributable to low power due to only 24 responses from each
of 16 young and 16 older subjects. Hulicka, Sterns, and Grossman
(1967) also failed to find a significant age difference in
the time to form a mediator between two words, but speed was
apparently not stressed in their task and consequently this
particular finding is not easily interpreted.

It is unfortunate that these studies are flawed in the
manner indicated because the procedures offer a promising
means of investigating the role of age-related speed differences
in memory functioning. However the severity of the problems
precludes a definite interpretation, and thus the studies
cannot be considered directly relevant in the present context.

With the exception of the studies argued to be flawed
for the purpose of providing sensitive measurements, the results
of comparisons of the duration of important memory components
reveal that increased age is generally associated with slower
processing. In only a few cases has there been a direct relationship established between component processing time and overall
task performance, and the number of components whose durations
have been examined in samples of young and old adults is still

quite limited. These restrictions notwithstanding, the processing rate theory receives moderately strong support since age-related slowing has been documented in important aspects of processing relevant to memory functioning such as encoding, search, and rehearsal.

Simulations of Reduced Processing Rate

The logic of the simulation procedure is to attempt to manipulate a variable in one or more groups of adults that has the same effect as an altered rate of processing presumed to be responsible for the observed age differences in memory. It is important to realize that the simulation procedure is essentially based on a metaphor or analogy, and thus may be inappropriate because of an inadequate conceptualization of the basic mechanism. That is, the simulation may differ from the actual mechanism in many ways, ranging from incomplete representation of the critical characteristic to inclusion of irrelevant features, and to the extent that the simulation is faulty the results may be irrelevant and meaningless. Nevertheless, the simulation procedure has the potential for providing valuable evidence relevant to the processing rate perspective and thus it is worth examining attempts to simulate the effects of an altered rate of processing on memory performance.

A number of manipulations have been investigated in the context of a speed-based interpretation of age-related memory differences, but perhaps the most frequent has involved varying stimulus presentation time to determine its effects on memory performance of young and old adults. The reasoning seems to have been that if the original performance differences were a result of the inability of the older adults to encode or register the to-be-remembered stimuli because of a limited amount of time, then increasing the presentation time should prove more beneficial to older adults than to young adults. In effect, then, reducing the rate of stimulus presentation by allowing a longer duration for each stimulus is postulated to simulate the youthful condition in older adults. Notice that this procedure is based on the assumption that the temporal limitation of older adults is confined to the input or encoding stage of mnemonic processing since altering presentation time is likely to affect only the initial stage of processing. It was argued in Chapter 9 that the bulk of the experimental evidence indicates that the age effects on speed are not consistent with a localization only in the input stage, and therefore such a limited or incomplete representation of the rate of processing effect is probably defective in many respects. Nevertheless, it is reassuring to note that most studies manipulating the time available for peripheral processing did find that the age differences were generally smaller with additional time (e.g., Arenberg, 1965, 1967; Arenberg & Robertson-Tchabo, 1977; Canestrari, 1963, 1968; Eisdorfer, 1968; Eisdorfer, Axelrod, & Wilkie, 1963; Kinsbourne, 1973; Taub, 1967). Simon (1979) also found that reducing stimulus duration in young adults resulted in a pattern of performance across different memory conditions qualitatively similar to that exhibited by older adults at a longer stimulus duration.

A study by Rabinowitz, Craik, and Ackerman (1982) is also consistent with the processing rate theory, although the authors interpreted their results in terms of age differences in an unspecified form of attentional resource. The study, their Experiment II, involved a comparison of older adults with young adults whose time for processing was limited by the requirement to attend to auditory digits and write targeted pairs on a sheet of paper. It is unclear exactly how much this manipulation reduced the available time (or attention, or memory space) of the young adults for performing the primary task, but the pattern of memory performance under these conditions was nearly identical to that of older adults. The digit-monitoring manipulation can therefore be considered successful in simulating the effects of aging, but the exact mechanism is ambiguous because it is likely that the resources of time, working memory space, and attentional energy were all reduced by having to perform the concurrent task.

A more direct attempt at simulating the effects of a slower rate of processing on the memory performance of young and old adults was reported in a study by Salthouse (1980a).

The rationale for this study was described as follows:

> ...if the age difference in memory was indeed produced by a slower rehearsal in older adults, then another factor that also affected speed of rehearsal should produce the same pattern of results as the age factor. We selected number of syllables per item as our other factor, believing that three-syllable items would take longer to say or rehearse than one-syllable items. If rehearsal speed is the mechanism common to both the age and syllable factors, then the difference between three- and one-syllable words should be qualitatively similar...to the difference between old and young adults (Salthouse, 1980a, p. 56-57).

Results of the study were in general agreement with the predictions in that across three segments of the serial position curve the differences between 'slow' (three-syllable) and 'fast' (one-syllable) items were comparable to the differences between old and young adults.

However, as with the manipulation of presentation time, there are limitations of this method of attempting to simulate a slower rate of processing. For example, increasing the length of the words may have introduced an irrelevant, but nonetheless important, perceptual component in that three-syllable words may tend to take more time to register than one-syllable words. A difference of this type may well lead to performance differences in memory tasks, but for reasons distinct from those one is attempting to simulate. That is, the difference between young and old adults may originate as a slower rate of processing, but not simply as a longer duration of perceptual encoding as produced by the increased length of the words. A second limitation of the number-of-syllables technique of simulating an altered rate of processing is that word length may not be a salient characteristic at all stages of mnemonic processing. In fact, Chase (1977) and Clifton and Tash (1973) failed to find differences in memory-scanning rates across words of different syllabic length, and thus even at the stage of search or scanning there seems to have been some type of recoding of the initial material.

It is probably premature to attempt a realistic appraisal of the simulation evidence relevant to the processing rate theory at this time. Manipulations of stimulus presentation time or word length have generally resulted in outcomes consistent with the processing rate predictions, but there are reasons to question whether the manipulations accurately mimicked the effects of an altered rate of processing information instead of merely influencing the duration of a single processing component. The difficulty of identifying a manipulation which successfully shifts the speed of all aspects of information processing is clearly the greatest obstacle to further progress with the simulation procedure.

Summary

The three classes of evidence reviewed in the present chapter indicate that the processing rate theory provides at least a plausible interpretation of the age differences in memory performance. Controlling for the effects of speed tended to reduce the effects of age, although the amount of reduction diminished as the opportunity for alternative strategies increased. Several theoretically important memory operations were found to have longer durations with increased age, and apparent exceptions were discovered to have had methodological weaknesses which limit their value. Results from the simulation procedure were also consistent with the processing rate predictions, despite reservations about the fidelity of simulating rate of processing by manipulations such as stimulus presentation duration and number of syllables in the to-be-remembered words.

Perceptual-Spatial Abilities

The topic of the present chapter is the effects of aging on perceptual-spatial abilities closely related to higher-order cognitive processes. These abilities are sometimes assessed by tests of performance as opposed to tests of verbal ability or acquired knowledge in general intelligence batteries, and they are often categorized in the psychometric literature with labels such as visualization, orientation, mechanical aptitude, and imagery. Sensory processes, perceptual illusions, and most of what would normally be called sensation and perception will therefore not be of concern here. All of the tasks of interest in the current context have involved stimuli with intensities, discriminabilities, and durations sufficiently large that it can be safely assumed that performance was not limited by these factors in any age group.

A sizable literature exists on tachistoscopic-based measures of processing speed across the adult lifespan, but that material will not be considered here because reviews are available in other sources (e.g., Salthouse, 1982; Walsh, 1982). The major findings from this tachistoscopic literature can be briefly summarized with the statement that nearly all measures of duration thresholds or processing effectiveness with limited intervals exhibit poorer performance with increased age, indicating that older adults require more time than young adults to achieve a comparable level of accuracy. These results are consistent with the processing rate theory, but because the significance of very early phases of processing for higher cognitive functioning is still not clear, this area of research will not be considered further.

The types of tasks that will be examined typically require various combinations of analysis, integration, and manipulation. These can be distinguished as follows:

    Analysis operations are required when the individual
    is expected to locate a specific component within

a large configuration, or to identify a missing
or unusual component within a scene or complex figure.
Integration skills are needed to synthesize complete
figures from jumbled or partial segments. And finally,
manipulation or transformation abilities are implicated
in the performance of tasks involving the comparison
of different perspectives of an object or environment
(Salthouse, 1982, p. 156).

Prototypical analysis tasks are miscellaneous embedded figure
tasks, the Hidden Figures test, and the Wechsler Picture Completion
test. The Gestalt Closure test, the Wechsler Block Design
and Object Assembly tests, the Hooper Visual Organization
Test, and the Minnesota Paper Form Board test all seem to
be dependent upon some type of synthesis or integration, and
mental manipulations such as rotating, reflecting, or folding
appear to be involved in the Primary Mental Abilities Space
test, the Paper Folding test, the Cube Comparisons test, the
Surface Development test, and the Guilford-Zimmerman Spatial
Orientation test.

Table 12.1 was prepared to summarize the results of a
number of studies investigating age effects in tasks requiring
one or more of these types of perceptual-spatial abilities.
The format of this table is similar to that of Table 11.1,
with age relations expressed both in terms of correlation
coefficients, and with respect to the mean performance of
the older adults in standard deviation units of the young
adults.

The major point to be noted from the entries in Table
12.1 is that the age effects in perceptual-spatial ability
are pronounced with both types of analyses. The median correlation
across all tasks in the table is -.40, which indicates that
age accounts for nearly 16% of the total variance among individuals
in these measures. The median standard score is -1.28, suggesting
that the average performance of adults in their 60s is at
about the 10th percentile of the distribution of performance
of adults in their early 20s. The remainder of this chapter
examines the role of speed in accounting for these age differences

Table 12.1

Magnitude of Age Relations in Measures of Perceptual/Spatial Ability

Measure	Correlation	SD from Young	Source
WAIS Picture Completion			
	-.28		Birren & Morrison, 1961
	-.23		Goldfarb, 1941
		-1.08	Berkowitz, 1953
WAIS Block Design			
	-.32		Birren & Morrison, 1961
	-.17		Goldfarb, 1941
	-.51		Riege & Inman, 1981
		-1.56	Berkowitz, 1953
		-.83/-1.20	Hines, 1979
		-1.61	Riege, et al., 1981
WAIS Object Assembly			
	-.28		Birren & Morrison, 1961
	-.16		Goldfarb, 1941
		-1.38	Berkowitz, 1953
WAIS Picture Arrangement			
	-.37		Birren & Morrison, 1961
	-.43		Goldfarb, 1941
		-1.76	Berkowitz, 1953
PMA Space			
	-.42		Clark, 1960
		-1.35	Adamowicz & Hudson, 1978
		-.83	Schaie, 1958

Table 12.1 (Continued)

Embedded Figures

-.40		Botwinick & Storandt, 1974
-.37		Chown, 1961
-.20		Crosson, 1984
-.43		Lee & Pollack, 1978
	-1.59	Panek, et al., 1978

Hooper Visual Organization Test

-.59		Botwinick & Storandt, 1974
-.45		Mason & Ganzler, 1964

'Spatial Aptitude'

-.56		Hirt, 1959
	-.73/-.99	Fozard & Nuttall, 1972
	-1.03/-1.06	
	-.56/-.65/-1.96	Prohaska, et al., 1984
	-2.56/-.85/-1.91	
	-1.96/-2.53	"

Incomplete Figure Identification

-.49		Dirken, 1972

in perceptual-spatial ability.

Task-Independent Speed Measures

One of the research strategies proposed in Chapter 10 for investigating the hypothesis that reductions in the speed of processing are responsible for age-related decrements in cognitive functioning is based on an analysis of correlations among the measure of cognitive performance, a general index of speed of processing, and chronological age. The argument was also advanced that score on the digit symbol substitution test provides a useful, although certainly not ideal, measure of general processing speed. It is therefore possible to examine the pattern of correlations among age, digit symbol score, and measures of performance on specific perceptual-spatial tasks to investigate predictions from the processing rate theory. Specifically, it is expected that the correlation between age and the performance measure should be greatly reduced by partialling out speed (digit symbol score), while the correlation between speed (digit symbol score) and the performance measure should be relatively unaffected by partialling out age.

Several studies recently conducted in my laboratory provide data pertinent to these predictions. Two different perceptual closure tasks were used, the Gestalt Closure Test (French, Ekstrom, & Price, 1963), and a task involving the identification of computer-generated incomplete figures. In both cases the subject attempts to identify the object represented by a mutilated, or incomplete, drawing. Only two extreme age groups were employed in these studies, and therefore the correlations with the age variable are point-biserial correlations with the young group (between 18 and 30 years of age) coded as 0 and the older group (between 55 and 80 years of age) coded as 1.

The relevant correlations are displayed in Table 12.2. Notice that substantial age differences are evident in both measures of perceptual closure, although the use of only two extreme age groups exaggerates the magnitude of the correlations relative to those in Table 12.1 based on a complete distribution

Table 12.2

Correlations with Perceptual Closure Score

	Age	Age.Speed	Speed	Speed.Age
(Predictions)	>			=
Gestalt Closure Test				
	−.65	−.49	.49	.08
	−.77	−.60	.60	.11
Incomplete Figures				
	−.65	−.48	.51	.01
	−.68	−.57	.46	.07

Note: Correlations between Age and Speed (Digit Symbol Score) ranged from −.62 to −.72 across samples.

of ages. The most interesting results in this table are that, contrary to the predictions of the processing rate theory, the correlations between age and perceptual-spatial performance are not markedly reduced by controlling for level of speed, while the correlations between speed and perceptual-spatial performance are virtually eliminated by controlling for age. There can be no doubt that these findings are completely inconsistent with the predictions, and offer absolutely no support for the idea that speed factors as reflected in the digit symbol substitution score are responsible for the age differences in perceptual closure. Instead the results are more consistent with the view that closure ability and speed are independent correlates of age with no causal relation to one another.

Why was there such a convincing failure of the predictions from the processing rate hypothesis? Of course, one possibility is that the fundamental premise is incorrect and that loss of speed is simply a relatively unimportant correlate of age, with no causal role in cognitive functioning. However, an alternative interpretation is that the digit symbol score only reflects the speed of deliberate, effortful cognitive operations, and not the speed with which activation is passively propagated throughout the cognitive system. In other words, digit symbol score may be a reasonable index of the speed of active processing, but it may be completely insensitive to the speed of passive processing, and perceptual closure could be more dependent upon passive rather than active processing.

There are two implications of the interpretation that age differences in perceptual closure may be attributable to differences in the speed of passive rather than active processing. One is that independent sources of evidence should reveal that closure tasks are largely performed in a passive rather than an active manner. The second implication is that the correlational predictions should be supported with a speed measure that reflects the rate of passive processing. Some support is available for the first implication, but no suitable measure of passive processing rate has yet been identified and thus the second implication cannot be evaluated at the present time.

Three additional research findings from these studies (Salthouse & Prill, 1985) are relevant to the speculation that perceptual closure is based on passive instead of active processing. The first is that variations in presentation time have been found to have relatively little effect on the accuracy of identifying the incomplete drawings, suggesting that the relevant processing takes place fairly rapidly. This seems more consistent with some form of passive processing than an active sequence of generating and testing successive hypotheses, although speed per se is probably not a defining characteristic of active or passive processing. A second finding is that performance on closure tests is only minimally impaired by the requirement of performing another concurrent activity -- in this case another identical task. According to the dual-task logic outlined in Chapter 4, this result suggests that the tasks made few demands on the resources necessary for active deliberate processing. And finally, a third result suggesting that perceptual closure is achieved via a relatively passive processing mode is that there appears to be little general transfer to novel stimuli after practice identifying specific stimuli. What seems to be acquired with practice is not more effective strategies or greater efficiency of active and deliberate processing, but rather increased knowledge of the properties of specific stimuli.

Still another reason for believing that passive processing is sufficient to account for performance on perceptual closure tasks is that a computer simulation similar to that described in Chapter 7 was found to provide a reasonable account of several findings by representing the age variable in terms of the rate of propagation through the network. That is, not only were the absolute differences in accuracy predicted, but so also were the observed additive, rather than interactive, effects of stimulus duration and stimulus completeness. Because activation in the network propagates without any conscious control or effort, it can be considered a passive form of processing.

The preceding interpretation is admittedly quite speculative, although it appears plausible on the basis of the available pattern of results. A more direct assessment of this view requires a measure of speed of passive processing that would allow the correlational predictions to be investigated. Unfortunately such a measure is not yet available and thus further exploration of this issue is probably not immediately forthcoming.

Results from other perceptual-spatial tasks administered to adults of varying ages from whom an index of speed was derived are displayed in Table 12.3. Notice that the pattern with the Closure and Visual Organization tasks is very similar to that summarized in Table 12.2. In both cases the data fail to conform to the processing rate predictions. However, for several of the other tasks the pattern is consistent with that expected from the processing rate interpretation.

One possible interpretation of the diversity of patterns across different perceptual-spatial abilities is that familiar, meaningful stimuli tend to be processed passively while unfamiliar and abstract stimuli are processed actively. The contrast is perhaps most apparent between closure tasks and the block Design test because the stimuli used in perceptual closure tasks are generally drawings of easily recognized objects, while the block design stimuli are abstract designs composed of solid or diagonally divided colored blocks. It is conceivable that meaningless stimuli are processed in a deliberate and conscious manner in which speed of active processing plays an important role. This interpretation is supported by the generally better fit of the processing rate predictions to the data from the Block Design tests compared to the closure tests. However, other results are not as consistent, e.g., the Object Assembly test involves meaningful stimuli like the Hooper Visual Organization test and yet is reasonably well fit by the processing rate predictions, and thus the suggestion must be considered quite speculative at the current time.

Another possible factor contributing to the variation in results across different spatial tasks is that the tests

Table 12.3

Further Correlations Among Age, Speed
and Perceptual/Spatial Ability

	Age	Age.Speed	Speed	Speed.Age	Source
(Predictions)	>		=		
WAIS Picture Completion					
	-.28	-.07	+.50	+.43	Birren & Morrison, 1961
	-.23	-.09	+.32	+.25	Goldfarb, 1941
WAIS Block Design					
	-.32	-.12	+.50	+.42	Birren & Morrison, 1961
	-.17	+.02	+.37	+.34	Goldfarb, 1941
WAIS Object Assembly					
	-.28	-.09	+.46	+.39	Birren & Morrison, 1961
	-.16	-.14	+.08	-.01	Goldfarb, 1941
WAIS Picture Arrangement					
	-.37	-.17	+.52	+.42	Birren & Morrison, 1961
	-.43	-.34	+.30	+.11	Goldfarb, 1941
PMA Space					
	-.42	-.19	+.54	+.41	Clark, 1960
Hooper Visual Organization Test					
	-.59	-.44	+.45	+.13	Botwinick & Storandt, 1974
Closure	-.49	-.38	+.38	+.18	Dirken, 1972

probably varied in complexity, and speed effects may have
been most pronounced in tasks at certain levels of complexity.
Zimmerman (1954a,b) has speculated that the loadings of a
test change from perceptual speed to reasoning as it is made
progressively more complex by adding required operations,
but it could also be argued that the importance of speed increases
as the number of time-consuming operations increases.   It
is not clear which of these alternatives is more likely, but
it should be recognized that as the complexity of a task increases
so also does the number of alternative strategies for performing
the task.   As was the case with memory abilities, therefore,
one might expect speed effects to be more pronounced if some
means could be devised for ensuring that all subjects performed
the task in an identical fashion.

The correlational evidence for the processing rate perspective
is definitely mixed, with some moderately convincing results
and other results completely contradictory to the predictions.
One intriguing speculation is that several perceptual-spatial
tasks are performed passively rather than actively, and therefore
better fits to the processing rate predictions might be expected
if a measure of speed of passive processing were available.

Task-Specific Measurements of Speed

It was reported in Chapter 9 that older adults are generally
found to be slower than young adults in both the intercept
and the slope of the function relating reaction time to angular
deviation between two visual stimuli in the mental rotation
paradigm (Shepard & Metzler, 1971). These results have important
implications for explaining age differences in certain spatial
ability tests because several researchers have reported that
mental rotation parameters are significantly correlated with
performance on tests of spatial ability (e.g., Lansman, 1981;
Lansman, Donaldson, Hunt, & Yantis, 1982; Mumaw, Pellegrino,
Kail, & Carter, 1984; Poltrock & Brown, 1984; Snyder, 1972).
For example, Mumaw, et al. (1984) found that both intercept
and slope parameters were smaller (i.e., faster) among college
students with higher scores on the Primary Mental Abilities
Space test.

In a very extensive study involving adults ranging from 18 to 69 years of age, Berg, Hertzog, and Hunt (1982) found that increased age was associated with markedly slower performance on the mental rotation task, and with lower scores on the Primary Mental Abilities Space test. Of particular interest were the correlations between the mental rotation parameters and the scores on the psychometric spatial ability test in the young (age 18 to 35) and middle-aged (age 44 to 69) groups. The median correlations across the four sessions of the study were -.29 and -.22 for the slope and intercept, respectively, in the young adults, and -.58 and -.50, for these parameters in the middle-aged adults. These findings indicate that the speed of mental rotation, and the speed of the processes reflected in the intercept parameter of the mental rotation function, are important determinants of performance on at least this particular psychometric test of spatial ability. Moreover, the tendency for the correlations to be larger in the older group suggests that speed factors may increase in importance with increased age, just as one might expect from the processing rate perspective.

At least one study has reported age differences in time measures of component processes in a task requiring integration or synthesis. Ludwig (1982) recorded the time young and older adults took to visualize a pattern composed of two separate fragments, and also the time required to decide whether a new design matched the composite pattern. In two separate experiments the older adults were found to be slower than the young adults on both measures. These results are clearly consistent with the processing rate theory, although they would have been even more convincing if the component durations were then demonstrated to be correlated with quality of performance. Unfortunately, no correlations of this type were reported in the article.

Possible Process Models

Unlike the situation with memory, relatively little research has been conducted in which age differences have been examined in processes contributing to performance on perceptual-spatial

tasks. However, a number of information-processing models
have now been proposed to account for performance variations
across items in tests of perceptual-spatial ability (e.g.,
Egan, 1979, 1981; Mumaw & Pellegrino, 1984; Mumaw, Pellegrino,
Kail, & Carter, 1984; Pellegrino, Alderton, & Shute, 1984;
Royer, 1981; Snow, 1980), and hence it should be possible
to adopt an analytical approach to the nature of age differences
in spatial ability. The prediction from the processing rate
theory is that older adults should be slower than young adults
in each parameter found to be related to overall task proficiency,
and that other age-related differences would be expected to
emerge as a consequence of this reduced efficiency.

The usefulness of a process approach can be illustrated
by considering the speculative process model of the Wechsler
Block Design test represented in Figure 12.1. This is a par-
ticulary interesting test for the current purpose because
it appears to involve components of analysis, manipulation,
and integration. Materials in the Block Design task consist
of nine colored blocks, each having two red sides, two white
sides, and two sides with one-half colored red and one-half
colored white. The examinee is shown a design on a card and
asked to arrange the blocks in a configuration that will reproduce
the design. Either one or two minutes are allowed for each
of 10 designs, with bonus points awarded for rapid completion
of the most complex designs.

Although the task appears quite simple, many people experience
considerable difficulty with it, and performance has been
found to decrease by nearly 40% between the 20s and 70s (cf.,
Table 12.1; Figures 7.5 and 7.6; Figure 4.10 in Salthouse,
1982). The process model in Figure 12.1 suggests several
possible sources of difficulty in this task.

One likely determinant of poor performance is inefficiency
of analyzing or segmenting the to-be-matched pattern into
discrete blocks. Results from embedded figures tasks indicate
that older adults experience great difficulties in trying
to segregate the complex configuration into simpler elements,
and thus the second box in Figure 12.1 may be a major source

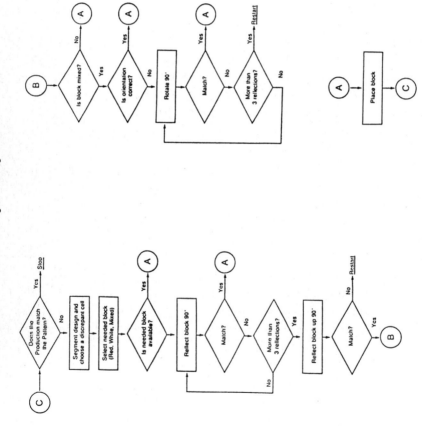

Figure 12.1 Proposed processing model for the Block Design task.

of age differences in block design tasks.

The third box in Figure 12.1 is another possible source of the age differences on the Block Design task because selection of an appropriate block requires an ability to imagine an integrated or synthesized configuration. Since older adults have been found to experience considerable difficulty with integration tasks such as the Gestalt Closure task, the Hooper Visual Organization Test, and the Wechsler Object Assembly Test (also see Ludwig, 1982), it is plausible that this particular component is a major factor hampering their performance.

From the processing rate perspective, what may be the greatest source of difficulty for older adults on the Block Design task is the number of operations that need to be carried out before a meaningful placement of a block can occur. That is, if the block is not readily available, as many as seven discrete rotation and reflection (3-d rotation) operations may intervene between the determination of the desired block and its actual placement. If each of these operations requires a little bit more time with increased age, then it is likely that the subject could lose track of the purpose of the manipulations and become confused. This confusion might even result in abandoning systematic solution strategies, and simply attempting to fit a particular block in whatever space it seems to fit with little or no concern about the pattern one is ostensibly trying to reproduce.

The process model in Figure 12.1 is only speculative, but it does indicate that there are many possible components that may contribute to success or failure in the Block Design task. Moreover, measures of their efficiency and effectiveness should be obtainable through clever experimental manipulations. If the model is valid, total time to perform the task should be predictable from the sum of the component durations. Accuracy is not as easily interpreted since a failure in any processing component may be propagated to all subsequent components, but the pattern of errors would be expected to mirror the pattern of latencies if longer time contributes to error proneness.

The expectation from the processing rate perspective

is that many of the important components in this task will
be slower with increased age, and that this slowness is a
major factor contributing to the poorer performance of older
adults. Age differences in the strategy of performance would
also be expected as certain strategies become less feasible
because of a slower rate of executing the relevant operations.

A lack of relevant research prevents a definitive conclusion
about the status of the processing rate theory on the basis
of evidence from the duration of specific processing components.
Older adults have consistently been found to be slower than
young adults at mental rotation, and this process has been
demonstrated to be strongly related to performance on several
tests of spatial ability. However, there has been very little
evidence concerning the duration of other processing components,
in part because of the lack, until quite recently, of detailed
processing models of spatial ability tasks. This situation
may be changing with the emergence of several alternative
models of a variety of tasks, one of which is briefly described
here.

<u>Summary</u>

Although there has been very little experimental research
concerned with age differences in perceptual-spatial abilities,
pronounced effects of aging are evident in a variety of measures
of perceptual-spatial performance. A speed-based interpretation
can only account for a portion of these results, perhaps because
no measure is currently available to reflect speed of passive
processing. A slower speed of performing manipulative operations
such as mental rotation is almost certainly a major factor
in the poorer performance of older adults on some tests of
spatial ability since moderate to substantial correlations
have been reported between manipulation speed and overall
ability score even in groups with a very restricted range
of ages. More research derived from explicit process models
of specific tasks is needed, and manipulations which might
simulate the effects of a slower rate of processing on perceptual-
spatial tasks would also be very desirable.

Reasoning Abilities

There are many reports of age-related declines in the efficiency of reasoning, problem-solving, and decision making (see Chapter 5 in Salthouse, 1982, for a brief review), but only a small fraction has relied upon analytical process models that might be helpful in identifying the exact nature of those deficits. For this reason the present chapter will be rather short, and much of it frankly quite speculative.

The existence and magnitude of the age differences in reasoning and problem solving tasks are documented in Table 13.1 which contains information similar to that of Tables 11.1 and 12.1 for the current domain. Notice that the correlations range from -.12 to -.64 with a median of about -.36, and that the median standard score of the older adults is -1.60, corresponding to approximately the 5th percentile of the distribution of young adults. These results clearly indicate that substantial effects of aging are evident in a number of measures reflecting effectiveness of reasoning and problem solving.

The possible role of speed factors in contributing to these age differences has been discussed by several earlier researchers. For example, Welford (1958), in the context of a discussion of an experiment involving electrical circuit problems conducted by Bernadelli, suggested that:

> The solution of a problem of the type used in this experiment appears to demand the bringing together of information, some of which is used at once, while the rest is being 'carried' in some form of short-term memory ready to be brought into play when required. Slowness in dealing with any part of the problem will place a strain upon the short-term memory and will cause pieces of information such as meter-readings to be forgotten so that they have to be taken again. On the other hand, any failure to carry information satisfactorily will have the effect of reducing

Table 13.1

Magnitude of Age Relations in Measures of Reasoning Ability

Measure	Correlation	SD from Young	Source
Raven's			
	-.27		Burke, 1972
	-.62		Davies & Leytham, 1964
	-.64/-.51		Heron & Chown, 1967
		-2.73/-2.93	Botwinick & Birren, 1963
		-2.84	Clayton & Overton, 1976
		-3.31	Panek & Stoner, 1980
Series Completion			
	-.49		Clark, 1960
	-.42		Cornelius, 1984
		-1.14/-2.31	Prohaska, et al., 1984
		-2.53/-3.18	
		-1.61	Schaie, 1958
Figural Relations			
	-.27		Cornelius, 1984
		-.93	Kausler & Puckett, 1980
		-1.60	Kausler, et al., 1981
		-1.50	Kausler, et al., 1982
Concept Identification			
	-.44		Hoyer, Rebok, & Sved, 1979
		-1.29	Arenberg, 1968b
		-1.28/-2.03	Hayslip & Sterns, 1979
Efficient Inquiries			
	-.15		Horn, et al., 1981
	-.12/-.17/-.20		Arenberg, 1974
		-1.50	Denney & Palmer, 1981
		-1.51	Denney, et al., 1982
		-1.16/-1.52	Hartley & Anderson, 1983
		-2.06/-1.57	

Table 13.1 (Continued)

Shaw Test

          -.52   -1.96   Bromley, 1956

Shipley Abstraction

          -.29   Mason & Ganzler, 1964

the quantity of data that can be applied simultaneously
to the part of the problem being dealt with, and
at least slow down a solution if not prevent it
altogether. It seems therefore that any slowness
in organizing data will produce an apparent inefficiency
of short-term memory, and any deficiency in short-term
memory will impair the ability to organize data
(Welford, 1958, p. 204-205).

Bromley (1967) also emphasized the importance of speed in
accounting for age-related differences in high-quality intellectual
output.

Intellectual achievements of merit require a number
of preliminary formulations with successive transformations to a final superior conceptual product,
e.g., searching for a solution to a scientific problem.
The number of such transformations is reduced as
age advances because of the slower rate of mental
work and the impairment of unspeeded cognitive capacity.
The serial order of appearance of a number of such
transformations is associated with a property variously
described as difficulty, ingenuity, originality,
and rarity - all of which help to define the term
"quality." Since older Ss make fewer conceptual
transformations, they do not achieve the higher
levels of quality associated with intellectual achievements appearing as the end result of a long series
of preliminary formulations. Older Ss, moreover,
have a slower rate of intellectual output, so they
make fewer cognitive transformations in a given
period (Bromley, 1967, p. 41).

These speculations are obviously consistent with the
processing rate theory, but they have little direct support
because experimentally oriented research on age differences
in reasoning abilities is very scarce, and even less is available
on the role of speed in producing the differences that have
been observed. Nevertheless, there are a few studies in which
speed and reasoning measures were obtained across the adult

age range, and therefore it is possible to examine at least some of the processing rate predictions.

Task-Independent Speed Measures

Only three studies could be located with the appropriate data to allow the correlational predictions to be examined. The relevant results are displayed in Table 13.2. It is difficult to interpret the Horn, et al. (1981) findings since the age effects on both the reasoning ($r = -.15$, $r = -.22$) and speed ($r = -.23$) measures were much smaller than generally reported. The values in the Clark (1960) study are more typical, but are ambiguous with respect to the processing rate predictions. The age correlation was reduced by partialling out speed, but the reduction was rather small and an even greater reduction occurred by partialling age out of the correlation with speed. These latter correlations are predicted to be equivalent, and thus this finding is inconsistent with the processing rate perspective.

At the present time it appears that no real conclusion can be derived with respect to the correlational predictions about the role of speed in age differences in reasoning. Very little relevant data are available, and none of the existing studies employed the digit symbol measure of speed, which has been advocated as the best available index of rate of active processing.

Process Models of Reasoning

In the last several years a number of similar process models have been proposed to account for performance on inductive reasoning tasks such as analogies, series completion, and classification (e.g., Holzman, Pellegrino, & Glaser, 1982, 1983; Mulholland, Pellegrino, & Glaser, 1980; Pellegrino & Glaser, 1980; Sternberg, 1977; Sternberg & Gardner, 1983; also see Spearman, 1923). Because rule induction plays such an important role in many aspects of reasoning and problem solving, it will be used as the prototype ability to illustrate the usefulness of a process model in this domain. A composite model applicable to a variety of inductive reasoning tasks is illustrated in Figure 13.1.

Table 13.2

Correlations Among Age, Speed, and Reasoning

	Age	Age.Speed	Speed	Speed.Age	Source
(Predictions)	>			=	
PMA Reasoning	-.49	-.34	+.45	+.26	Clark, 1960
Efficient Hypotheses	-.15	-.12	+.13	+.10	Horn, et al., 1981
	-.22	-.11	+.57	+.55	" "

Figure 13.1 is represented in abstract terms because the content material for inductive reasoning tasks has ranged from words, to numbers, to geometric forms. However, in order to minimize the role of cumulative knowledge in tasks of this type, only nonverbal material will be emphasized in the following discussion. Analogy tasks typically involve the presentation of three terms, with the subject instructed to produce (or select) a fourth term that bears the same relationship to the third term as the second does to the first. Matrix tasks are essentially two-dimensional analogy tasks in that the missing term must satisfy relations on both vertical and horizontal dimensions. Series completion tasks generally consist of a sequence of letters or digits with the subject required to select the item that provides the best continuation of the sequence. Classification tasks exist in a variety of forms, but most require that the subject discover how certain items are related in order to determine which additional item belongs in the same grouping.

Notice that the flow chart in Figure 13.1 suggests that a key component in all tasks is the abstraction and inference of the relation between the initial two terms in the problem. This relation is then applied to the C term to generate the D term in analogy tasks, it is integrated with the A-C relation and used to identify the D term by extension from the B (vertical) and C (horizontal) terms in matrix tasks, it is confirmed in the B-C relation and then applied to the C term to generate the D term in series completion tasks, and it is confirmed in all possible pairs to establish the basis for grouping in classification tasks.

Prior research with young adult subjects indicates that the efficiency and effectiveness of the infer relation component is inversely related to the number of elements, and to the number and type of transformations associated with each element (e.g., Holzman, Pellegrino, & Glaser, 1982; 1983; Mulholland, Pellegrino, & Glaser, 1980; Sternberg, 1977). For example, Mulholland, et al. (1980) found that the solution latency for analogies composed of geometric patterns could be accurately

Analogies	A–B:C–?
Series Completion	A–B–C–?
Classification	A B C: D₁ D₂...
Matrices	A–B
	C–?

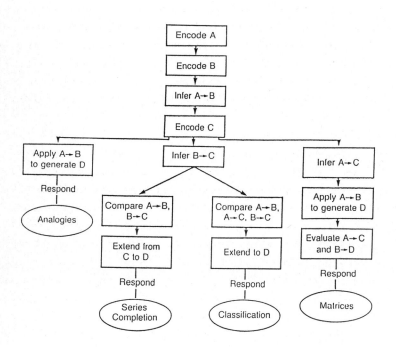

Figure 13.1 Possible processing model for four common inductive reasoning tasks.

predicted by assuming that each discrete element required approximately 358 milliseconds, and that each additional transformation required about 425 milliseconds. If each of these operations takes more time with increased age, it is reasonable to expect there to be sizable age differences in the total time for that operation.

The processing rate theory predicts longer durations with increased age for each of the components portrayed in Figure 13.1, and to the extent that the component contributes to overall performance, it would also lead to the an expectation of age differences in global measures of proficiency. However, there might additionally be effects attributable to slower time relations among components above and beyond those associated with longer component durations. For example, if the components in Figure 13.1 were carried out at a slow rate, the A-B relation may no longer be available when it is needed to generate the D term, or to be contrasted with other relations. Hypotheses of this type allow a fairly direct means of assessing the viability of the processing rate theory, but there have not yet been studies contrasting adults of different ages in relevant measures.

In the two studies by Holzman, et al. (1982, 1983) it was suggested that working memory played a major role in handling the mental bookkeeping needed to retain and update the products of intermediate processing operations. Moreover, young adults differed from children both in their performance on the experimental reasoning tasks and on measures of backward memory span (which served as an index of working memory capacity), thereby providing correlational support for the working memory interpretation. Although it is reasonable to expect a similar pattern to be evident in comparisons of young and older adults, it is important to point out that this would not necessarily indicate that the critical resource is related to space or working memory capacity. As discussed in Chapter 4, the concepts of attentional energy, working memory capacity, and rate of processing are probably interchangeable in many respects. In particular, if working memory is viewed as a dynamic rather than static entity, the rate at which refresh or rehearsal operations can be performed will be an important determinant of overall capacity.

Whether because of limitations of memory space, attentional energy, or processing time, unsuccessful processing in tasks of inductive reasoning is likely to result in a number of symptoms of failure. For example, some relevant information may be ignored, certain inquiries may be made redundantly, and generally unsystematic solution strategies may be pursued. Characteristics such as these have been found to be associated with increased age (see Chapter 5 in Salthouse [1982] for a review), but they are important from the current perspective because they are viewed as a consequence, rather than a cause, of the age-related impairments. That is, each of these qualities is assumed to be a manifestation of the failure of successful processing, and not the reason for the initial inability to perform successfully.

Summary

Although age differences are pronounced and well-documented in various measures of reasoning ability, there has been remarkably little analytical investigation of the reasons for these differences. A consequence of this lack of systematic research exploring the nature of age-related differences in reasoning is that all theories of these phenomena must be considered primarily speculation. The processing rate theory is not exception since there are only a few relevant correlational studies, virtually no age-comparative data on the duration of important processing components, and absolutely no attempts at simulating the effects of a slower rate of processing. Nevertheless, an interpretation based on the idea that increased age is associated with a slower rate of carrying out relevant processing operations and that this altered speed detrimentally affects reasoning performance seems to provide a plausible and integrated hypothesis for age-related deficiencies in reasoning abilities.

Implications and Future Directions

The preceding chapters have attempted to outline a theoretical perspective towards cognitive aging phenomena, but I hope that readers recognize that the area is exceedingly complicated and that any formulations at the present time must necessarily be tentative and highly speculative. The processing rate perspective represents only one of many possible sets of proposals about cognitive aging, but it is presented at this time because of a belief that theoretical issues in this area need to be addressed and one means of encouraging advocates of different perspectives to communicate their positions is to describe one view as explicitly as possible. Alternative views might be described at least in part by contrasting them, and their accompanying assumptions, with the already articulated positions. The ultimate goal of this focus on theoretical issues should be greater structure and more direction in the empirical research, and eventually better understanding of the true nature of cognitive aging.

Methodological Issues

Weaknesses in the methodology employed in much current research may be one reason for the relative lack of interest in integrative theoretical issues because little confidence is warranted in empirical results obtained with procedures that are methodologically suspect. One methodological concern has to do with measurement reliability. Since few researchers have been sensitive to the issue of whether the same individuals would produce similar results on a subsequent occasion, it is possible to question the stability of many of the phenomena investigated in cognitive aging laboratories. Failure to recognize the importance of adequate statistical power is also a shortcoming of many studies in adult cognition since the small sample sizes and imprecise measurement may lead to the conclusion that no age differences existed when in fact the probability of detecting a real difference was extremely

small. Both the reliability and power issues are easily addressed
by slight modifications of existing procedures, but the problem
of interpreting statistical interactions when one group performs
at a different level than the other group does not appear
readily resolvable. However, recognition of the problems
associated with attempting to localize age deficits in a specific
processing component based on patterns of statistical interactions
should at least make researchers more cautious in drawing
inferences from their results, and possibly encourage the
adoption of procedures involving several converging operations.
At any rate, it is highly desirable that future research address
methodological concerns such as these since there is little
point in attempting to generate theoretical interpretations
of phenomena that may not even exist.

Empirical Generalizations

    A number of descriptive generalizations that appear to
apply to empirical results in the area of cognitive aging
can be abstracted from the discussion in earlier chapters.
One of these is simply that the cognitive system is highly
complex and interdependent, and consequently a difference
in one aspect of processing is likely lead to differences
in other aspects as the system adapts to the initial alteration.
It may be difficult to specify the causal priority of various
processing characteristics observed to be associated with
increased age, but awareness of the possibility that differences
in one aspect may have partially caused differences in other
aspects should minimize the tendency to treat each phenomenon
as independent and unrelated to other aging phenomena.

    A second broad generalization is that experience nearly
always improves performance, and that aging is associated
with increased experience in at least certain domains. These
assertions imply that experience needs to be considered in
evaluating the effects of age either in laboratory tasks,
or in real-world situations. The confounding of age and experience
should be eliminated if one wants to draw conclusions about
the effects of aging on basic abilities, but it should be
specifically acknowledged in attempts to generalize to real-world

settings from results with unfamiliar laboratory tasks.

A third empirical generalization is that age differences tend to increase in magnitude as the cognitive task is made more complex. This complexity effect appears to be evident across many types of activity, and is important for both methodological and theoretical reasons. The methodological issue has to do with attempts to localize the effects of aging in a specific processing component by contrasting performance on tasks with, and without, that component. Because the version of the task with the critical component will often be more complex than the version without that component, the existence of the complexity effect leads to the expectation that the age differences would be greater in the more complex version of the task **regardless of the nature of the added component.** In other words, many interpretations of a localized aging effect may be spurious because they are based on the discovery of a statistical interaction that may simply be a manifestation of the complexity effect. The complexity effect is also relevant to theoretical interpretations of aging phenomena since it seems to imply that something like a general processing resource is responsible for many of the age differences in cognition.

The fourth and final empirical generalization from the literature on aging and cognition is that most aspects of behavior require more time with increased age. Few, if any, other empirical results are as well-documented and pervasive as this one, and thus it should play an important role in any reasonably comprehensive theory of cognitive aging.

Examination of evidence relevant to the three dimensions considered critical for distinguishing among possible theories of adult development led to the inferences that a satisfactory theory should (a) emphasize maturational determinants that (b) limit competence in a (c) rather general fashion. Some type of processing resource therefore seems to be implicated in many of the age differences in cognition, and the three most likely resources are related to the concepts of space, energy, and time. The well-established reduction in rate of processing associated with increased age, in conjunction with plausible arguments and empirical data demonstrating the sufficiency of limited temporal resources for producing performance impairments in cognitive performance, led to the hypothesis that the critical resource responsible for age differences in cognition was related to time.

Limitations of the Processing Rate Theory

The processing rate perspective has a number of obvious limitations. One major weakness is that there is no consideration of the role of motivation and emotion in cognition, and particularly in age differences in cognition. These factors have generally been neglected in information-processing approaches to cognition, and a complete theory should deal with issues of motivation and emotion even if they are not presumed to be major determinants of the age differences in cognitive functioning. Another limitation of the current approach, and of most other information-processing approaches to cognition, is that the interconnectedness of the processing system means that it will likely be very difficult to obtain evidence for a single specific deficit. If a deficiency in one processing component leads to adjustments and compensations in other components, precise localization of the 'critical' factor responsible for group differences in performance will be difficult if not impossible. This has clear implications for the testability of hypotheses since many predictions may not be easily falsified if one believes that the initial differences in one aspect of processing led to a variety of 'secondary' differences in other aspects of processing. In particular, if, as is postulated here, variations in the rate of processing often lead to alterations in the mode or quality of processing, it may be nearly impossible to isolate the true cause of the observed phenomena.

The processing rate theory also suffers from a lack of convincing evidence for a central speed factor. It is obviously not very compelling to suggest that speed is responsible for a variety of age-related cognitive deficits, and yet not be able to provide an operational definition of speed. A first approximation was suggested with the Digit Symbol Substitution score, but it is still only weakly related to other measures, and even at best only provides an index of active processing speed and not speed of passive processing. The situation might be improved if an adequate physiological basis for the slowing-with-age phenomenon were available, but the existing evidence is not very promising in this respect.

Perhaps because of the preceding characteristics, the processing rate theory also suffers from a paucity of convincing empirical evidence at the current time. Durations of what are postulated to be relevant processing components have consistently been found to be longer in older adults than in young adults, but results from the correlational analyses have been rather mixed, and attempts to simulate an altered rate of processing have not yet been very successful.

Despite these clear weaknesses, it is still believed that the processing rate theory provides the best characterization of the nature of cognitive aging currently available. The arguments proposed in Chapter 7 suggest that some form of a limited-resource theory is apparently needed to account for the empirical findings, particularly the complexity effect in which the magnitude of age differences increases directly with task complexity. The exact nature of that critical resource is more uncertain, and it would be highly desirable to have operational definitions of each of the space, energy, and time conceptualizations in order that their explanatory potential be fully investigated. However, the existence of such a vast amount of evidence documenting a slowing of nearly all aspects of behavior with increased age suggests that temporal factors are intrinsically related to the declining resource, whatever its specific manifestation.

Future Directions

At least six distinct directions can be identified for further investigation. Each of these research directions emanates from the processing rate perspective, although results would likely be relevant to more than this specific theory.

One promising direction for future research is to extend the investigations of the correlational predictions from the

processing rate theory. The digit symbol substitution test,
and possibly other tasks yielding additional measures of speed
of processing, could be administered along with a variety
of memory, perceptual-spatial, and reasoning tasks. The results
summarized in Chapters 11, 12, and 13 provide an intriguing,
but incomplete, picture of the potential of the processing
rate theory, and it is highly desirable to obtain additional
data that would allow a more conclusive evaluation of the
predictions.

A second direction for future research is to attempt
to identify a suitable measure of passive processing speed
that would allow a test of the hypothesis that age differences
in certain aspects of cognition are attributable to a slower
rate of passive processing. Tasks such as spatial memory
and perceptual closure seem particularly likely to involve
passive rather than active processing, and an index of speed
of passive processing is needed to provide a fair test of
the processing rate predictions.

Another issue deserving serious investigation is whether
or not age differences in efficiency are evident when all
individuals are employing exactly the same strategy. The
outcome of this type of research would be informative with
respect to the role of qualitative factors such as strategy
choice or meta-cognitive abilities in producing age differences
in cognitive performance. In many cases older adults have
been found to use less efficient strategies than young adults,
but reasons for those suboptimal strategies have never been
clearly specified. A discovery that age differences were
completely eliminated when subjects of all ages were using
the same strategy would constitute impressive support for
a 'qualitative' interpretation of age differences. On the
other hand, if performance differences still remain when there
is no variation in strategy, it would have to be concluded
that strategy differences were not responsible for all age
differences in performance. This is a departure from the
approach employed by many contemporary investigators, who
seem mainly interested in demonstrating the existence of differ-

ences in strategy, but it may have greater potential for the ultimate understanding of cognitive aging.

A fourth direction for future research is to obtain operational definitions of alternative conceptualizations of processing resources such as working memory capacity and attentional energy, and then to examine the pattern of correlations in multivariate test batteries administered to samples of young and old adults. It has thus far proven difficult to identify suitable measures of each of the types of processing resources, but once such measures are available it should be possible to determine the predictive power of each in accounting for age differences in a variety of tasks, and also to examine the interrelations of the various measures of processing resources. A possible outcome from this type of investigation is the discovery that certain measures of processing resources either do not differ significantly across adulthood, or that they are unrelated to performance on a large number of cognitive tasks. Results such as these would clearly present a major problem for explanations based on that particular type of processing resource.

Greater clarification of the concept of complexity is also necessary in future research if the 'complexity effect' is to continue to play an important role in determining the nature of theories of cognitive aging. It seems reasonable to assume that something in addition to the processes specific to particular tasks is involved in across-task variations in performance, but the exact nature of that something is still quite mysterious. Although useful in the preliminary conceptualizations, the notion that tasks vary in the number of relevant processing operations, or in the space, energy, or time required by those operations, is unsatisfactory in the long run unless there is an independent means of verifying those speculations. Moreover, it may be desirable to incorporate skill-dependent qualifications in the ultimate definition of complexity because the same task may become less complex as the individual achieves greater skill in the relevant domain.

A final direction worth pursuing in future research is

to increase the reliance upon formal modelling procedures
in attempting to determine the sufficiency of different mechanisms
in specific task domains.   Successful implementation of this
strategy will require considerably more information than that
currently available, both about possible mechanisms such as
processing resources and about the processing involved in
specific tasks.   However, the potential value of this approach
is enormous because precise specification of the relevant
information processing in a form like a computer simulation
allows explicit predictions in advance of actual empirical
data.   Only relatively weak expectations are currently possible
because of very limited understanding of important mechanisms
and their consequences for performance in a complex and highly
interactive processing system.

References

Adamowicz, J.K. & Hudson, B.R. 1978. Visual short-term memory, response delay, and age. **Perceptual and Motor Skills, 46,** 267-270.

Adelson, B. 1981. Problem solving and the development of abstract categories in programming languages. **Memory & Cognition, 9,** 422-433.

Adelson, B. 1984. When novices surpass experts: The difficulty of a task may increase with expertise. **Journal of Experimental Psychology: Learning, Memory and Cognition, 10,** 483-495.

Ahearn, S. & Beatty, J. 1979. Pupillary responses during information processing vary with scholastic aptitude scores. **Science, 205,** 1289-1292.

Allport, D.A. 1980. Attention and performance. In G. Claxton (Ed.), **Cognitive Psychology: New Directions.** London: Routledge & Kegan-Paul, (pp. 112-153).

Anastasi, A. 1973. Preface. In C. Eisdorfer & M.P. Lawton (Eds.), **The Psychology of Adult Development and Aging.** Washington, D.C.: American Psychological Association, (pp. vvi).

Anders, T.R. & Fozard, J.L. 1973. Effects of age upon retrieval from primary and secondary memory. **Developmental Psychology, 9,** 411-416.

Anders, T.R., Fozard, J.L., & Lillyquist, T.D. 1972. Effects of age upon retrieval from short-term memory. **Developmental Psychology, 6,** 214-217.

Anderson, J.E. 1955. The assessment of aging. In J.E. Anderson (Ed.), **Psychological Aspects of Aging.** Washington, D.C.: American Psychological Association, (pp. 75-80).

Anderson, J.R. 1982. Acquisition of cognitive skill. **Psychological Review, 89,** 369-406.

Anderson, J.R. 1983. **The Architecture of Cognition.** Cambridge, Ma.: Harvard University Press.

Arenberg, D. 1965. Anticipation interval and age differences in verbal learning. **Journal of Abnormal Psychology, 70,** 419-425.

Arenberg, D. 1967. Age differences in retroaction. **Journal of Gerontology, 22,** 88-91.

Arenberg, D. 1968a. Retention of time judgment in young and old adults. **Journal of Gerontology, 23,** 35-40.

Arenberg, D. 1968b. Concept problem solving in young and old adults. **Journal of Gerontology, 23,** 279-282.

Arenberg, D. 1974. A longitudinal study of problem solving. **Journal of Gerontology, 29,** 650-658.

Arenberg, D. 1978. Differences and changes with age in the Benton Visual Retention Test. **Journal of Gerontology, 33,** 534-540.

Arenberg, D. 1980. Comments on the processes that account for memory declines with age. In L.W. Poon, J.L. Fozard, L. Cermak, D. Arenberg, & L.W. Thompson (Eds.), **New Directions in Memory and Aging.** Hillsdale, N.J.: Erlbaum, (pp. 67-71).

Arenberg, D. 1982. Learning from our mistakes in aging research. **Experimental Aging Research, 8,** 73-76.

Arenberg, D. & Robertson-Tchabo, E.A. 1977. Learning and aging. In J.E. Birren & K.W. Schaie (Eds.), **Handbook of the Psychology of Aging.** New York: Van Nostrand Reinhold, (pp. 421-449).

Atkinson, R.C. & Shiffrin, R.M. 1968. Human memory: A proposed system and its control processes. In K.W. Spence & J.T. Spence (Eds.), **The Psychology of Learning and Motivation, Vol. 2.** New York: Academic Press, (pp. 90-195).

Baddeley, A.D. 1981. The concept of working memory: A view of its current state and probable future development. **Cognition, 10,** 17-23.

Baddeley, A.D., Grant, S., Wight, E., & Thomson, N. 1975. Imagery and working memory. In P.M.A. Rabbitt & S. Dornic (Eds.), **Attention and Performance V,** New York: Academic Press, (205-217).

Baddeley, A.D. & Hitch, G.J. 1974. Working memory. In G. Bower (Ed.), **The Psychology of Learning and Motivation, Vol. 8.** New York: Academic Press, (pp. 47-89).

Baddeley, A.D., Thomson, N., & Buchanan, M. 1975. Word length and the structure of short-term memory. **Journal of Verbal Learning and Verbal Behavior, 14,** 575-589.

Bahrick, H.P., Noble, M., & Fitts, P.M. 1954. Extra-task performance as a measure of learning a primary task. **Journal of Experimental Psychology, 48,** 298-302.

Baltes, P.B. 1968. Longitudinal and cross-sectional sequences in the study of age and generation effects. **Human Development, 11,** 145-171.

Baltes, P.B., Dittmann-Kohli, F., & Dixon, R.A. 1984. New perspectives on the development of intelligence in adulthood: Toward a dual-process conception and a model of selective optimization with compensation. In P.B. Baltes & O.G. Brim, Jr. (Eds.), **Life-Span Development and Behavior, Vol. 6.** New York: Academic Press, (33-76).

Baltes, P.B. & Labouvie, G.V. 1973. Adult development of intellectual performance: Description, explanation, and modification. In C. Eisdorfer & M.P. Lawton (Eds.), **The Psychology of Adult Development and Aging.** Washington, D.C.: American Psychological Association, (pp. 157-219).

Baltes, P.B., Reese, H.W., & Lipsitt, L.P. 1980. Life-span developmental psychology. **Annual Review of Psychology, 31,** 65-110.

Baltes, P.B., Reese, H.W., & Nesselroade, J.R. 1977. **Life-Span Developmental Psychology: Introduction to Research Methods.** Belmont, Ca.: Wadsworth.

Baltes, P.B. & Willis, S.L. 1977. Toward psychological theories of aging and development. In J.E. Birren & K.W. Schaie (Eds.), **Handbook of the Psychology of Aging.** New York: Van Nostrand Reinhold, Inc., (pp. 128-154).

Baltes, P.B. & Willis, S.L. 1982. Plasticity and enhancement of intellectual functioning in old age: Penn State's Adult Development and Enrichment Project (ADEPT). In F.I.M. Craik & S.H. Trehub (Eds.), **Aging and Cognitive Processes.** New York: Plenum, (pp. 353-389).

Banks, W.P. & Atkinson, R.C. 1974. Accuracy and speed strategies in scanning active memory. **Memory & Cognition, 2,** 629-636.

Baron, A., Menich, S.R., & Perone, M. 1983. Reaction times of younger and older men and temporal contingencies of reinforcement. **Journal of the Experimental Analysis of Behavior, 40,** 275-287.

Baron, J. 1978. Intelligence and general strategies. In G. Underwood (Ed.), **Strategies of Information Processing.** London: Academic Press, (pp. 403-450).

Baron, J. & Treiman, R. 1980. Some problems in the study of differences in cognitive processes. **Memory & Cognition, 8,** 313-321.

Barrett, G.V., Alexander, R.A., Doverspike, D., Cellar, D., & Thomas, J.C. 1982. The development and application of a computerized information-processing test battery. **Applied Psychological Measurement, 6,** 13-29.

Bartus, R.T. 1980. Cholinergic drug effects on memory and cognition in animals. In L.W. Poon (Ed.), **Aging in the 1980s.** Washington, D.C.: American Psychological Association, (pp. 163-180).

Bartus, R.T., Dean, R.L., Goas, J.A., & Lippa, A.S. 1980. Agerelated changes in passive avoidance retention: Modulation with dietary choline. **Science, 209,** 301-303.

Basowitz, H. & Korchin, S.J. 1957. Age differences in the perception of closure. **Journal of Abnormal and Social Psychology, 54,** 93-97.

Beck, E., Swanson, C., & Dustman, R.E. 1980. Long latency components of the visually evoked potential in man: Effects of aging. **Experimental Aging Research, 6,** 523-545.

Beres, C.A. & Baron, A. 1981. Improved digit symbol substitution by older women as a result of extended practice. **Journal of Gerontology, 36,** 591-597.

Berg, C., Hertzog, C., & Hunt, E. 1982. Age differences in the speed of mental rotation. **Developmental Psychology, 18,** 95-107.

Berger, M. 1982. The "scientific approach" to intelligence: An overview of its history with special reference to mental speed. In H.J. Eysenck (Ed.), **A Model for Intelligence.** New York: Springer-Verlag, (pp. 13-43).

Berkowitz, B. 1953. The Wechsler-Bellevue performance of white males past age 50. **Journal of Gerontology, 8,** 76-80.

Berlucchi, G., Crea, F., DiStefano, M., & Tassinari, G. 1977. Influence of spatial stimulus-response compatibility on response time of ipsilateral and contralateral hand to lateralized light stimuli. **Journal of Experimental Psychology: Human Perception and Performance, 3,** 505-517.

Bilash, I. & Zubek, J.P. 1960. The effects of age on factorially "pure" mental abilities. **Journal of Gerontology, 15,** 175-182.

Birren, J.E. 1952. A factorial analysis of the Wechsler-Bellevue scale given to an elderly population. **Journal of Consulting Psychology, 16,** 399-405.

Birren, J.E. 1955a. Age changes in speed of responses and perception and their significance for complex behavior. In **Old Age in the Modern World.** Edinburgh: Livingstone, (pp. 235-247).

Birren, J.E. 1955b. Age differences in startle reaction time of the rat to noise and electric shock. **Journal of Gerontology, 10,** 437-440.

Birren, J.E. 1956. The significance of age changes in speed of perception and psychomotor skills. In J.E. Anderson (Ed.), **Psychological Aspects of Aging.** Washington, D.C.: American Psychological Association, (pp. 97-104).

Birren, J.E. 1960a. Behavioral theories of aging. In N.W. Shock (Ed.), **Aging: Some Social and Biological Aspects.** Washington, D.C.: American Association for the Advancement of Science, (pp. 305-332).

Birren, J.E. 1960b. Psychological aspects of aging. **Annual Review of Psychology, 11,** 161-198.

Birren, J.E. 1964. **The Psychology of Aging.** Englewood Cliffs, N.J.: Prentice-Hall.

Birren, J.E. 1965. Age changes in speed of behavior: Its central nature and physiological correlates. In A.T. Welford & J.E. Birren, (Eds.), **Behavior, Aging, and the Nervous System.** Springfield, Il.: Charles C Thomas, (pp. 191-216).

Birren, J.E. 1970. Toward an experimental psychology of aging. **American Psychologist, 25,** 124-135.

Birren, J.E. 1974. Translations in Gerontology: From Lab to Life: Psychophysiology and speed of response. **American Psychologist, 29,** 808-815.

Birren, J.E., Allen, W.R., & Landau, H.G. 1954. The relation of problem length in simple addition to time required, probability of success, and age. **Journal of Gerontology, 9,** 150-161.

Birren, J.E. & Botwinick, J. 1955. Speed of response as a function of perceptual difficulty and age. **Journal of Gerontology, 10,** 433-436.

Birren, J.E., Botwinick, J., Weiss, A.D., & Morrison, D.F. 1963. Interrelations of mental and perceptual tests given to healthy elderly men. In J.E. Birren, R.N. Butler, S.W. Greenhouse, L. Sokoloff, & M.R. Yarrow (Eds.), **Human Aging: A Biological and Behavioral Study.** Bethesda, MD: National Institute of Mental Health, (pp. 143-156).

Birren, J.E., Cunningham, W.R., & Yamamoto, K. 1983. Psychology of adult development and aging. **Annual Review of Psychology, 34,** 543-575.

Birren, J.E. & Kay, H. 1958. Swimming speed of the albino rat: I. Age and sex differences. **Journal of Gerontology, 13,** 374-377.

Birren, J.E. & Morrison, D.F. 1961. Analysis of the WAIS subtests in relation to age and education. **Journal of Gerontology, 16,** 363-369.

Birren, J.E. & Renner, V.J. 1977. Research on the psychology of aging: Principles and experimentation. In J.E. Birren & K.W. Schaie (Eds.), **Handbook of the Psychology of Aging,** New York: Van Nostrand Reinhold, (pp. 3-38).

Birren, J.E., Riegel, K.F., & Morrison, D.F. 1962. Age differences in response speed as a function of controlled variations of stimulus conditions: Evidence of a general speed factor. **Gerontologia, 6,** 1-18.

Birren, J.E., Riegel, K.F., & Robbin, J.S. 1962. Age differences in continuous word associations measured by speed recordings. **Journal of Gerontology, 17,** 95-96.

Birren, J.E. & Spieth, W. 1962. Age, response speed, and cardiovascular functions. **Journal of Gerontology, 17,** 390-391.

Birren, J.E., Woods, A.M., & Williams, M.V. 1979. Speed of behavior as an indicator of age changes and the integrity of the nervous system. In F. Hoffmeister & C. Mueller (Eds.), **Brain Function in Old Age.** Berlin: Springer-Verlag, (pp. 10-44).

Birren, J.E., Woods, A.M., & Williams, M.V. 1980. Behavioral slowing with age: Causes, organization and consequences. In L.W. Poon (Ed.), **Aging in the 1980's.** Washington, D.C.: American Psychological Association, (pp. 293-308).

Book, W.F. 1908. **The Psychology of Skill.** Missoula, MT.: University of Montana Press.

Boring, E.G. 1950. **The History of Experimental Psychology.** New York: Appleton-Century Crofts.

Botwinick, J. 1966. Cautiousness in advanced age. **Journal of Gerontology, 21,** 347-353.

Botwinick, J. 1967. **Cognitive Processes in Maturity and Old Age.** New York: Springer.

Botwinick, J. 1975. Behavioral processes. In S. Gershon & A. Raskin (Eds.), **Aging, Vol 2.** New York: Raven Press, (pp. 1-18).

Botwinick, J. 1984. **Aging and Behavior.** (3rd Ed.), New York: Springer.

Botwinick, J. & Arenberg, D. 1976. Disparate time spans in sequential studies of aging. **Experimental Aging Research, 2,** 55-61.

Botwinick, J. & Birren, J.E. 1963. Mental abilities and psychomotor responses in healthy aged men. In J.E. Birren, R.N. Butler, S.W. Greenhouse, L. Sokoloff, & M.R. Yarrow (Eds.), **Human Aging: A Biological and Behavioral Study.** Bethesda, MD: National Institute of Mental Health, (pp. 97-108).

Botwinick, J., Brinley, J.F., & Robbin, J.S. 1958. The effect of motivation by electric shocks on reaction in relation to age. **American Journal of Psychology, 71,** 408-411

Botwinick, J., Brinley, J.F., & Robbin, J.S. 1958b. Task alternation time in relation to problem difficulty and age. **Journal of Gerontology, 13,** 414-417.

Botwinick, J., Robbin, J.S., & Brinley, J.F. 1959. Reorganization of perceptions with age. **Journal of Gerontology, 14,** 85-88.

Botwinick, J., Robbin, J.S., & Brinley, J.F. 1960. Age differences in card sorting performance in relation to task difficulty, task set, and practice. **Journal of Experimental Psychology, 59,** 10-18.

Botwinick, J. & Storandt, M. 1974. **Memory, Related Functions, and Age.** Springfield, IL: Charles C Thomas.

Botwinick, J. & Thompson, L.W. 1966. Components of reaction time in relation to age and sex. **Journal of Genetic Psychology, 108,** 175-183.

Bowles, N.L. & Poon, L.W. 1981. The effect of age on speed of lexical access. **Experimental Aging Research, 7,** 417-425.

Bowles, N.L. & Poon, L.W. 1985. Aging and retrieval of words in semantic memory. **Journal of Gerontology, 40,** 71-77.

Brand, C.R. & Deary, I.J. 1982. Intelligence and 'inspection time'. In H.J. Eysenck (Ed.), **A Model for Intelligence.** New York: Springer-Verlag, (pp. 133-148).

Brinley, J.F. 1965. Cognitive sets, speed and accuracy of performance in the elderly. In A.T. Welford & J.E. Birren (Eds.), **Behavior, Aging, and the Nervous System.** Springfield, IL: Charles C Thomas, (pp. 114-149).

Brinley, J.F. & Fichter, J. 1970. Performance deficits in the elderly in relation to memory load and set. **Journal of Gerontology, 25,** 30-35.

Broadbent, D.E. 1958. **Perception and Communication.** London: Pergamon.

Broadbent, D.E. & Gregory, M. 1965. Some confirmation results on age differences in memory for simultaneous stimulation. **British Journal of Psychology, 56,** 77-80.

Broadbent, D.E. & Heron, A. 1962. Effects of a subsidiary task on performance involving immediate memory by younger and older men. **British Journal of Psychology, 53,** 189-198.

Bromley, D.B. 1956. Some experimental tests of the effect of age on creative intellectual output. **Journal of Gerontology, 11,** 74-82.

Bromley, D.B. 1958. Some effects of age on short-term learning and remembering. **Journal of Gerontology, 13,** 398-406.

Bromley, D.B. 1963. Age differences in conceptual abilities. In R.H. Williams, C. Tibbitts, & W. Donahue (Eds.), **Processes of Aging, Volume I.** New York: Atherton, (pp. 96-112).

Bromley, D.B. 1967. Age and sex differences in the serial production of creative conceptual responses. **Journal of Gerontology, 22,** 32-42.

Bromley, D.B. 1974. **The Psychology of Human Ageing.** Middlesex, England: Penguin.

Brown, H.L. & Kirsner, K. 1980. A within-subjects analysis of the relationship between memory span and processing rate in short-term memory. **Cognitive Psychology, 12,** 177-187.

Bryan, W.L. & Harter, N. 1899. Studies on the telegraphic language: The acquisition of a hierarchy of habits. **Psychological Review, 6,** 345-375.

Burke, D.M. & Light, L.L. 1981. Memory and aging: The role of retrieval processes. **Psychological Bulletin, 90,** 513-546.

Burke, D.M. & Yee, P.L. 1984. Semantic priming during sentence processing by young and older adults. **Developmental Psychology, 20,** 903-910.

Burke, H.R. 1972. Raven's progressive matrices: Validity, reliability, and norms. **Journal of Psychology, 82,** 253-257.

Buschbaum, M., Kenkin, R., & Christiansen, R. 1974. Age and sex differences in average evoked responses in a normal population, with observations on patients with gonadal dysgenesis. **Electroencephalography and Clinical Neurophysiology, 37,** 137-144.

Butterfield, E.C. 1981. Testing process theories of intelligence. In M.P. Friedman, J.P. Das, & N. O'Connor (Eds.), **Intelligence and Learning,** New York: Plenum, (pp. 277-295).

Caird, W.K. 1966. Aging and short-term memory. **Journal of Gerontology, 21,** 295-299.

Calfee, R.C. & Hedges, L.V. 1980. Independent process analyses of aptitude-treatment interactions. In R.E. Snow, P. Federico, & W.E. Montague (Eds.), **Aptitude, Learning and Instruction, Vol. I.** Hillsdale, N.J.: Erlbaum, (pp. 293-313).

Calloway, E. 1975. **Brain Electrical Potentials and Individual Psychological Differences.** New York: Grune & Stratton.

Campbell, B.A, Krauter, E.E., & Wallace, J.E. 1980. Animal models of aging: Sensory-motor and cognitive function in the aged rat. In D.G. Stein (Ed.), **The Psychobiology of Aging.** Amsterdam: Elsevier/North Holland, (pp. 201-226).

Canestrari, R.E. 1963. Paced and self-paced learning in young and elderly adults. **Journal of Gerontology, 18,** 165-168.

Canestrari, R.E. 1966. The effects of commonality on paired-associate learning in two age groups. **Journal of Genetic Psychology, 108,** 3-7.

Canestrari, R.E. 1968. Age changes in acquisition. In G.A. Talland (Ed.), **Human Aging and Behavior.** New York: Academic Press, (pp. 169-188).

Carlson, J.S. & Jensen, C.M. 1982. Reaction time, movement time, and intelligence: A replication and extension. **Intelligence, 6,** 265-274.

Carlson, J.S., Jensen, C.M., & Widaman, K.F. 1983. Reaction time, intelligence, and attention. **Intelligence, 7,** 329-344.

Carroll, J.B. 1976. Psychometric tests as cognitive tasks: A new "structure of intellect". In L.B. Resnick (Ed.), **The Nature of Intelligence.** Hillsdale, N.J.: Erlbaum, (pp. 27-56).

Carroll, J.B. 1980. **Individual Difference Relations in Psychometric and Experimental Cognitive Tasks.** Technical Report No. 163, Thurstone Psychometric Laboratory, University of North Carolina, Chapel Hill.

Carroll, J.B. & Maxwell, S.E. 1979. Individual differences in cognitive abilities. **Annual Review of Psychology, 30,** 603-640.

Cattell, R.B. 1963. Theory of fluid and crystallized intelligence: A critical experiment. **Journal of Educational Psychology, 54,** 1-22.

Cattell, R.B. 1971. **Abilities: Their Structure, Growth and Action.** New York: Houghton Mifflin.

Cavanaugh, J.P. 1972. Relation between the immediate memory span and the memory search rate. **Psychological Review, 79,** 525-530.

Cerella, J. & Fozard, J.L. 1984. Lexical access and age. **Developmental Psychology, 20,** 235-243.

Cerella, J., Poon, L.W., & Fozard, J.L. 1981. Mental rotation and age reconsidered. **Journal of Gerontology, 36,** 620-624.

Cerella, J., Poon, L.W., & Williams, D.M. 1980. Age and the complexity hypothesis. In L.W. Poon (Ed.), **Aging in the 1980's.** Washington, D.C.: American Psychological Association, (pp. 332-340).

Charles, D.C. 1973. Comments on the papers of Labouvie, Hoyer, and Gottesman. **Gerontologist, 13,** 36-38.

Charness, N. 1979. Components of skill in bridge. **Canadian Journal of Psychology, 33,** 1-16.

Charness, N. 1981. Aging and skilled problem solving. **Journal of Experimental Psychology: General, 110,** 21-38.

Charness, N. 1982. Problem solving and aging: Evidence from semantically rich domains. **Canadian Journal of Aging, 1,** 21-28.

Charness, N. 1983. Age, skill, and bridge bidding: A chronometric analysis. **Journal of Verbal Learning and Verbal Behavior, 22,** 406-416.

Chase, W.G. 1977. Does memory scanning involve implicit speech? In S. Dornic (Ed.), **Attention and Performance, VI.** Hillsdale, N.J.: Erlbaum, (pp. 607-628).

Chase, W.G. & Chi, M.T.H. 1981. Cognitive skill: Implications for spatial skill in large-scale environments. In J.H. Harvey (Ed.), **Cognition, Social Behavior, and the Environment.** Hillsdale, N.J.: Erlbaum, (pp. X-Y).

Chase, W.G. & Simon, H.A. 1973. Perception in chess. **Cognitive Psychology, 4,** 55-81.

Chi, M.T.H. 1978. Knowledge structures and memory development. In R.C. Siegler (Eds.), **Children's Thinking: What Develops?** Hillsdale, N.J.: Erlbaum, (pp. 73-96).

Chi, M.T.H., Feltovich, P.J. & Glaser, R. 1981. Categorization and representation of physics problems by experts and novices. **Cognitive Science, 5,** 121-152.

Chi, M.T.H. & Glaser, R. 1980. The measurement of expertise: Analysis of the development of knowledge and skill as a basis for assessing achievement. In E.L. Baker & E.S. Quellmalz (Eds.), **Educational Testing and Evaluation: Design Analysis and Policy.** Beverly Hills, Ca.: Sage, (pp. 37-47).

Chiang, A. & Atkinson, R.C. 1976. Individual differences and interrelationships among a select set of cognitive skills. **Memory & Cognition, 4,** 661-672.

Chiesi, H.L., Spilich, G.J., & Voss, J.F. 1979. Acquisition of domain-related information in relation to high and low domain knowledge. **Journal of Verbal Learning and Verbal Behavior, 18,** 257-273.

Chown, S.M. 1961. Age and the rigidities. **Journal of Gerontology,
16,** 353-362.

Clark, S.W. 1960. The aging dimension: A factorial analysis
of individual differences with age on psychological and
physiological measurements. **Journal of Gerontology,
15,** 183 187.

Clarkson, P.M. 1978. The relationship of age and level of
physical activity with the fractionated components of
patellar reflex time. **Journal of Gerontology, 33,** 650-656.

Clarkson, P.M. & Kroll, W. 1978. Practice effects on fractionated
response time related to age and activity level. **Journal
of Motor Behavior, 10,** 275-286.

Clarkson-Smith, L. & Halpern, D.F. 1983. Can age-related
deficits in spatial memory be attenuated through the
use of verbal coding? **Experimental Aging Research, 9,**
179-184.

Clay, H.M. 1954. Changes of performance with age on similar
tasks of varying complexity. **British Journal of Psychology,
45,** 7-13.

Clay, H.M. 1956. A study of performance in relation to age
at two printing works. **Journal of Gerontology, 11,** 417-424.

Clay, H.M. 1957. The relationship between time, accuracy
and age on simlar tasks of varying complexity. **Gerontologia,
1,** 41-49.

Clayton, V. & Overton, W.F. 1976. Concrete and formal operational
thought processes in young adulthood and old age. **International Journal of Aging and Human Development, 7,** 237-245.

Clifton, C., Jr. & Tash, J. 1973. Effect of syllabic word
length on memory-search rate. **Journal of Experimental
Psychology, 99,** 231-235.

Cohen, G. 1979. Language comprehension in old age. **Cognitive
Psychology, 11,** 412-429.

Cohen, G. 1981. Inferential reasoning in old age. **Cognition,
9,** 59-72.

Cohen, G. & Faulkner, D. 1981. Memory for discourse in old
age. **Discourse Processes, 4,** 253-265.

Cohen, G. & Faulkner, D. 1983. Age differenes in performance
     of two information-processing tasks: Strategy selection
     and processing efficiency. **Journal of Gerontology, 38,**
     447-454.

Cohen, G. & Faulkner, D. 1984. Memory for text: Some age
     differences in the nature of the information that is
     retrieved after listening to texts. In H. Bouma & D.G.
     Bouwhuis (Eds.), **Attention and Performance, X.** Hillsdale,
     N.J.: Erlbaum, (pp. 501-514).

Cohen, J. & Cohen, P. 1983. **Applied Multiple Regression/Corre-**
     lation Analysis for the Behavioral Sciences. Hillsdale,
     N.J.: Erlbaum.

Colgan, C.M. 1954. Critical flicker frequency, age, and intelli-
     gence. **American Journal of Psychology, 67,** 711-713.

Coover, J.E. 1923. A method of teaching typewriting based
     upon a psychological analysis of expert typing. **National**
     Education Association: Addresses and Proceedings, 61,
     561-567.

Cornelius, S.W. 1984. Classic pattern of intellectual aging:
     Test familiarity, difficulty, and performance. **Journal**
     of Gerontology, 39, 201-206.

Craik, F.I.M. 1965. The nature of the age decrement in performance
     on dichotic listening tasks. **Quarterly Journal of Experi-**
     mental Psychology, 17, 227-240.

Craik, F.I.M. 1968. Short-term memory and the aging process.
     In G.A. Talland (Ed.), **Human Aging and Behavior.** New
     York: Academic Press, (pp. 131-168).

Craik, F.I.M. 1977. Age differences in human memory. In
     J.E. Birren & K.W. Schaie (Eds.), **Handbook of the Psychology**
     of Aging. New York: Van Nostrand Reinhold, (pp. 384-420).

Craik, F.I.M. & Byrd, M. 1982. Aging and cognitive deficits:
     The role of attentional resources. In F.I.M. Craik &
     S.E. Trehub (Eds.), **Aging and Cognitive Processes.** New
     York: Plenum, (pp. 191-211).

Craik, F.I.M. & Masani, P.A. 1967. Age differences in the
     temporal integration of language. **British Journal of**
     Psychology, 58, 291-299.

Craik, F.I.M. & Masani, P.A. 1969. Age and intelligence differ-
    ences in coding and retrieval of word lists. **British
    Journal of Psychology, 60,** 315-319.
Craik, F.I.M. & Rabinowitz, J.C. 1984. Age differences in
    the acquisition and use of verbal information: A tutorial
    review. In J. Bouma & D.G. Bouwhuis (Eds.), **Attention
    and Performance, X.** Hillsdale, N.J.: Erlbaum, (pp. 471-499).
Craik, F.I.M. & Simon, E. 1980. Age differences in memory:
    The roles of attention and depth of processing. In L.W. Poon,
    J.L. Fozard, L.S. Cermak, D. Arenberg, & L.W. Thompson
    (Eds.), **New Directions in Memory and Aging.** Hillsdale,
    N.J.: Erlbaum, (pp. 95-112).
Crawford, C.B. 1974. A canonical correlation analysis of
    cortical evoked response and intelligence test data.
    Canadian Journal of Psychology, 28, 319-332.
Cronbach, L.J. & Furby, L. 1970. How we should measure "change"
    - or should we? **Psychological Bulletin, 74,** 68-80.
Crosby, J.V. & Parkinson, S.R. 1979. A dual-task investigation
    of pilots' skill level. **Ergonomics, 22,** 1301-1313.
Crossman, E.R.F.W. & Szafran, J. 1956. Changes with age in
    the speed of information-intake and discrimination.
    **Experientia Supplementum, IV: Symposium on Experimental
    Gerontology,** Basel: Birkhauser, (pp. 128-135).
Crosson, C.W. 1984. Age and field independence among women.
    Experimental Aging Research, 10, 165-170.
Crowder, R.G. 1980. Echoic memory and the study of aging
    memory systems. In L.W. Poon, J.L. Fozard, L.S. Cermak,
    D. Arenberg, & L.W. Thompson (Eds.), **New Directions in
    Memory and Aging.** Hillsdale, NJ: Erlbaum, (pp. 181-204).
Daneman, M. & Carpenter, P.A. 1980. Individual differenes
    in working memory and reading. **Journal of Verbal Learning
    and Verbal Behavior, 19,** 450-466.
Davies, A.D.M. & Leytham, G.W.H. 1964. Perception of verticality
    in adult life. **British Journal of Psychology, 55,** 315-320.
Davies, D.R. & Griew, S. 1965. Age and vigilance. In A.T. Welford
    & J.E. Birren (Eds.), **Behavior, Aging, and the Nervous
    System.** Springfield, IL: Charles C Thomas, (pp. 54-59).

Davis, R.T. 1978. Old monkey behavior. **Experimental Gerontology,
13,** 237–250.

Dean, R.L., Scozzafava, J., Goas, J.A., Regan, B., Beer, B.,
& Bartus, R.T. 1981. Age-related differences in behavior
across the life span of the C57BL/6J mouse. **Experimental
Aging Research, 7,** 427–451.

DeGroot, A.D. 1978. **Thought and Choice in Chess.** (2nd Edition). The Hague: Mouton.

DeLaMare, G.C. & Sheperd, R.D. 1958. Ageing: Changes in speed
and quality of work among leather cutters. **Occupational
Psychology, 32,** 204–209.

Denney, D.R. & Denney, N.W. 1973. The use of classification
for problem solving: A comparison of middle and old age.
Developmental Psychology, 9, 275–278.

Denney, N.W. 1974. Clustering in middle and old age. **Developmental Psychology, 10,** 471–475.

Denney, N.W. 1984. A model of cognitive development across
the life span. **Developmental Review, 4,** 171–191.

Denney, N.W. & Palmer, A.M. 1981. Adult age differences on
traditional and practical problem-solving measures.
Journal of Gerontology, 36, 323–328.

Denney, N.W., Pearce, K.A., & Palmer, A.M. 1982. A developmental
study of adults' performance on traditional and practical
problem-solving tasks. **Experimental Aging Research,
8,** 115–118.

Derner, G.F., Aborn, M., & Canter, A.H. 1950. The reliability
of the Wechsler-Bellevue subtests and scales. **Journal
of Consulting Psychology, 14,** 172–179.

Detterman, D.K. 1980. Understand cognitive components before
postulating metacomponents. **Behavioral and Brain Sciences,
3,** 589.

Diehl, M.J. & Siebel, R. 1962. The relative importance of
visual and auditory feedback in speed typewriting. **Journal
of Applied Psychology, 5,** 365–369.

Dirken, J.M. 1972. **Functional Age of Industrial Workers.**
Groningen: Wolters-Noordhoff.

Dixon, R.A., Simon, E.W., Nowak, C.A., & Hultsch, D.F. 1982. Text recall in adulthood as a function of level of information, input modality, and delay interval. **Journal of Gerontology, 37,** 358–364.

Donaldson, G. 1981. Letter to the Editor. **Journal of Gerontology, 36,** 634–636.

Donders, F.C. 1869/1969. On the speed of mental processes. (English translation of original article). **Acta Psychologica, 30,** 412–431.

Doppelt, J.E. & Wallace, W.L. 1955. Standardization of the Wechsler Adult Intelligence Scale for older persons. **Journal of Abnormal and Social Psychology, 51,** 312–330.

Drachman, D.A. & Leavitt, J. 1972. Memory impairment in the aged: Storage versus retrieval deficit. **Journal of Experimental Psychology, 93,** 302–308.

Dustman, R. & Beck, E. 1966. Visually evoked potentials: Amplitude changes with age. **Science, 151,** 1013–1015.

Dustman, R. & Beck, E. 1969. The effects of motivation and aging on the wave form of visually evoked potentials. **Electroencephalography and Clinical Neurophysiology, 26,** 2–11.

Eccles, J.D. 1978. The Dentist. In W.T. Singleton (Ed.), **The Study of Real Skills. Vol. 1: The Analysis of Practical Skills.** Lancaster, England: MTP Press, (pp. 127–150).

Egan, D.E. 1979. Testing based on understanding: Implications from studies of spatial ability. **Intelligence, 3,** 1–15.

Egan, D.E. 1981. An analysis of spatial orientation test performance. **Intelligence, 5,** 85–100.

Egan, D.E. & Schwartz, B.J. 1979. Chunking in recall of symbolic drawings. **Memory & Cognition, 7,** 149–158.

Eisdorfer, C. 1968. Arousal and performance: Experiments in verbal learning and a tentative theory. In G.A. Talland (Ed.), **Human Aging and Behavior.** New York: Academic Press, (pp. 189–216).

Eisdorfer, C., Axelrod, S., & Wilkie, F.L. 1963. Stimulus exposure time as a factor in serial learning in an aged sample. **Journal of Abmormal and Social Behavior, 67,** 594-600.

Eisdorfer, C. & Lawton, M.P. (Eds.), **The Psychology of Adult Development and Aging.** Washington, D.C.: American Psychological Association.

Elstein, A.S., Shulman, L.S., & Sprafka, S.A. 1978. **Medical Problem Solving: An Analysis of Clinical Expertise.** Cambridge, MA.: Harvard University Press.

Engle, R.W. & Bukstel, L. 1978. Memory processes among bridge players of differing expertise. **American Journal of Psychology, 91,** 673-689.

Erber, J.T. 1974. Age differences in recognition memory. **Journal of Gerontology, 29,** 177-181.

Erber, J.T. 1976. Age differences in learning and memory on a digit symbol substitution task. **Experimental Aging Research, 2,** 45-53.

Erber, J.T., Botwinick, J., & Storandt, M. 1981. The impact of memory on age differences in digit symbol performance. **Journal of Gerontology, 36,** 586-590.

Erber, J., Herman, T.G., & Botwinick, J. 1980. Age differences in memory as a function of depth of processing. **Experimental Aging Research, 6,** 341-348.

Eriksen, C.W., Hamlin, R.M., & Dye, C. 1973. Aging adults and rate of memory scan. **Bulletin of the Psychonomic Society, 1,** 259-260.

Ertl, J.P. & Schafer, E.W.P. 1969. Brain response correlates of psychometric intelligence. **Nature, 223,** 421-422.

Estes, W.K. 1978. The information-processing approach to cognition: A confluence of metaphors and methods. In W.K. Estes (Ed.), **Handbook of Learning and Cognitive Processes: Vol. 5: Human Information Processing.** Hillsdale, N.J.: Erlbaum, (pp. 1-18).

Eysenck, H.J. 1967. Intelligence assessment: A theoretical and experimental approach. **British Journal of Psychology, 37,** 81-98.

Eysenck, H.J. 1982. Introduction. In H.J. Eysenck (Ed.), **A Model for Intelligence.** New York: Springer-Verlag, (pp. 1-10).

Eysenck, M.W. 1974. Age differences in incidental learning. **Developmental Psychology, 10,** 936-941.

Eysenck, M.W. 1975. Retrieval from semantic memory as a function of age. **Journal of Gerontology, 30,** 174-180.

Feinberg, R. & Podolak, E. 1965. Latency of pupillary reflex to light stimulation and its relationship to aging. In A.T. Welford & J.E. Birren (Eds.), **Behavior, Aging, and the Nervous System.** Springfield, IL: Charles C Thomas, (pp. 326-339).

Ferris, S.H., Crook, T., Clark, E., McCarthy, M., & Rae, D. 1980. Facial recognition memory deficits in normal aging and senile dementia. **Journal of Gerontology, 35,** 707-714.

Fitts, P.M. 1964. Perceptual-motor skill learning. In A.W. Melton (Ed.), **Categories of Human Learning.** New York: Academic Press, (243-283).

Fitts, P.M. & Posner, M.I. 1967. **Human Performamce.** Belmont, CA.: Brooks/Cole.

Flavell, J.H. 1970. Cognitive changes in adulthood. In L.R. Goulet & P.B. Baltes (Eds.), **Life-Span Developmental Psychology: Research and Theory.** New York: Academic Press, (pp. 247-253).

Ford, J.M., Pfefferbaum, A., Tinklenberg, J.R., Kopell, B.S. 1982. Effects of perceptual and cognitive difficulty on P3 and RT in young and old adults. **Electroencephalography and Clinical Neurophysiology, 54,** 311-321.

Ford, J.M., Roth, W.T., Mohs, R.C., Hopkins, W.F., & Kopell, B.S. 1979. Event-related potentials recorded from young and old adults during a memory retrieval task. **Electroencephalography and Clinical Neurophysiology, 47,** 450-459.

Foster, J.C. & Taylor, G.A. 1920. The applicability of mental tests to persons over 50. **Journal of Applied Psychology, 4,** 39-58.

Foulds, G.A. & Raven, J.C. 1948. Normal changes in the mental abilities of adults as age advances. **Journal of Mental Science, 94,** 133–142.

Fowler, C.A., Wolford, G., Slade, R., & Tassinary, L. 1981. Lexical access with and without awareness. **Journal of Experimental Psychology: General, 110,** 341–362.

Fozard, J.L. 1981. Speed of mental performance and aging: Costs of age and benefits of wisdom. In F.J. Pirozzolo & G.J. Maletta (Eds.), **Behavioral Assessment and Psychopharmacology.** New York: Praeger, (pp. 59–94).

Fozard, J.L. & Nuttall, R.L. 1971. General aptitude test battery scores for men differing in age and socioeconomic status. **Journal of Applied Psychology, 55,** 372–379.

Fozard, J.L. & Thomas, J.C. 1975. Psychology of Aging: Basic findings and some psychiatric applications. In J.G. Howells (Ed.), **Modern Perspectives in the Psychiatry of Old Age.** New York: Brunner/Masel, (pp. 107–169).

Fraser, D.C. 1958. Decay of immediate memory with age. **Nature, 182,** 1163.

Friedman, H. 1974. Interrelation of two types of immediate memory in the aged. **Journal of Psychology, 87,** 177–181.

Friend, C.M. & Zubek, J.P. 1958. The effects of age on critical thinking ability. **Journal of Gerontology, 13,** 407–413.

French, J.W., Ekstrom, R.B., & Price, R.B. 1963. **Manual for Kit of Reference Tests for Cognitive Factors.** Princeton, N.J.: Educational Testing Service.

Frey, P.W. & Adesman, P. 1976. Recall memory for visually presented chess positions. **Memory & Cognition, 4,** 541–547.

Ganzler, H. 1964. Motivation as a factor in the psychological
    deficit of aging. **Journal of Gerontology, 19,** 425-429.

Gaylord, S.A. & Marsh, G.R. 1975. Age differences in the
    speed of a spatial cognitive process. **Journal of Gerontology,
    30,** 674-678.

Giambra, L.M. & Arenberg, D. 1980. Problem-solving, concept
    learning, and aging. In L.W. Poon (Ed.), **Aging in the
    1980s.** Washington, D.C.: American Psychological Association,
    (pp. 253-259).

Gilbert, J.G. 1935. Memory efficiency in senescence. **Archives
    of Psychology, 27,** Whole No. 188.

Gilbert, J.G. 1941. Memory loss in senescence. **Journal of
    Abnormal and Social Psychology, 36,** 73-86.

Gilbert, J.G. & Levee, R.T. 1971. Patterns of declining memory.
    Journal of Gerontology, 26, 70-75.

Gilbert, L.C. 1959. Saccadic movements as a factor in visual
    perception in reading. **Journal of Educational Psychology,
    50,** 15-19.

Glaser, R. 1980. General discussion: Relationships between
    aptitude, learning, and instruction. In R. Snow, P. Federico,
    & W.E. Montague (Eds.), **Aptitude, Learning, and Instruction
    Vol. 2.** Hillsdale, N.J.: Erlbaum, (pp. 309-326).

Gold, P.E., McGaugh, J.L., Hankins, L.L., Rose, R.P., & Vasquez,
    B.J. 1981. Age dependent changes in retention in rats.
    Experimental Aging Research, 8, 53-58.

Goldfarb, W. 1941. **An Investigation of Reaction Time in Older
    Adults.** New York: Columbia Teachers College, Contributions
    to Education, No. 831.

Goodin, D., Squires, K., Henderson, B., & Starr, A. 1978.
    Agerelated variations in evoked potentials to auditory
    stimuli in normal human subjects. **Electroencephalography
    and Clinical Neurophysiology, 44,** 447-458.

Goodrick, C.L. 1972. Learning by mature young and age Wistar
    rats as a function of test complexity. **Journal of Geron-
    tology, 27,** 353-357.

Goodrick, C.L. 1980. Problem solving and age: A critique of rodent research. In R.L. Sprott (Ed.), **Age, Learning Ability and Intelligence.** New York: Van Nostrand Reinhold, (pp. 5-25).

Gordon, S.K. 1975. Organization and recall of related sentences by elderly and young adults. **Experimental Aging Research, 1,** 71-80.

Gordon, S.K. & Clark, W.C. 1974. Application of signal detection theory to prose recall and recognition in elderly and young adults. **Journal of Gerontology, 29,** 64-72.

Graesser, A.C., Hoffman, N.L., & Clark, L.F. 1980. Structural components of reading time. **Journal of Verbal Learning and Verbal Behavior, 19,** 134-151.

Grant, E.A., Storandt, M., & Botwinick, J. 1978. Incentive and practice in the psychomotor performance of the elderly. **Journal of Gerontology, 33,** 413-415.

Green, R.F. 1969. Age-intelligence relationship between ages sixteen and sixty-four: A rising trend. **Developmental Psychology, 1,** 618-627.

Greeno, J.G. 1980. Some examples of cognitive task analysis with instructional implications. In R.E. Snow, P. Federico, & W.E. Montague (Eds.), **Aptitude, Learning and Instruction, Vol. 2.** Hillsdale, N.J.: Erlbaum, (pp. 1-21).

Gregory, R.L. 1957. Increase in "Neurological Noise" as a factor in ageing. **Proceedings of the 4th Congress of the International Association of Gerontology,** Merano, Italy, (pp. 314-324).

Griew, S. 1964. Age, information transmission and the positional relationship between signals and responses in the performance of a choice task. **Ergonomics, 7,** 267-277.

Halpern, A.R. & Bower, G.H. 1982. Musical expertise and melodic structure in memory for musical notation. **American Journal of Psychology, 95,** 31-50.

Hartley, A.A. 1981. Adult age differences in deductive reasoning processes. **Journal of Gerontology, 36,** 700-706.

Hartley, A.A. & Anderson, J.W. 1983. Task complexity and problem-solving performance in younger and older adults. **Journal of Gerontology, 38,** 72-77.

Hartley, J.T., Harker, J.O., & Walsh, D.A. 1980. Contemporary issues and new directions in adult development of learning and memory. In L.W. Poon (Ed.), **Aging in the 1980s.** Washington, D.C.: American Psychological Association, (pp. 239-252).

Hartley, J.T. & Walsh, D.A. 1980. The effect of monetary incentive on amount and rate of free recall in older and younger adults. **Journal of Gerontology, 35,** 899-905.

Harwood, E. & Naylor, G.F.K. 1969. Recall and recognition in elderly and young subjects. **Australian Journal of Psychology, 21,** 251-257.

Hasher, L. & Zacks, R.T. 1979. Automatic and effortful processes in memory. **Journal of Experimental Psychology: General, 108,** 356-388.

Hatano, G. & Osawa, K. 1983. Digit memory of grand experts in abacus-derived mental calculation. **Cognition, 15,** 95-110.

Hayslip, B. & Kennelly, K.J. 1982. Short-term memory and crystallized-fluid intelligence in adulthood. **Research on Aging, 4,** 314-332.

Hayslip, B. & Sterns, H.L. 1979. Age differences in relationships between crystallized and fluid intelligences and problem solving. **Journal of Gerontology, 34,** 404-414.

Heglin, H.J. 1956. Problem solving set in different age groups. **Journal of Gerontology, 11,** 310-317.

Heikkinen, E., Kiiskinen, A., Kayhty, B., Rimpela, M., & Vuori, I. 1974. Assessment of biological age. **Gerontologia, 20,** 33-43.

Heron, A. & Chown, S.M. 1967. **Age and Function.** London: Churchill.

Hess, T.M. & Higgins, J.N. 1983. Context utilization in young and old adults. **Journal of Gerontology, 38,** 65-71.

Hick, W.E. 1952. On the rate of gain of information. **Quarterly Journal of Experimental Psychology, 4,** 11-26.

Hines, T. 1979. Information feedback, reaction time, and error rates in young and old subjects. **Experimental Aging Research, 5,** 207-215.

Hines, T.M. & Posner, M.I. 1976. Slow but sure: A chronometric analysis of the process of aging. In L.W. Poon & J.L. Fozard (Eds.), **Design Conference on Decision Making and Aging.** Boston: Boston Geriatric Research, Educational and Clinical Center, Technical Report 76-01, (pp. 82-97).

Hirt, M. 1959. General Aptitude Test Battery to determine aptitude changes with age and to predict job performance. **Journal of Applied Psychology, 43,** 36-39.

Hirst, W., Spelke, E.S., Reaves, C.C., Caharack, G. & Neisser, U. 1980. Divided attention without alternation or automaticity. **Journal of Experimental Psychology: General, 109,** 98-117.

Hitch, G.J. 1980. Developing the concept of working memory. In G. Claxton (Ed.), **Cognitive Psychology: New Directions.** London: Routledge & Kegan-Paul, (pp. 154-196).

Hitch, G.J. & Baddeley, A.D. 1976. Verbal reasoning and working memory. **Quarterly Journal of Experimental Psychology, 28,** 603-621.

Holding, D.H. & Reynolds, R.I. 1982. Recall or evaluation of chess positions as determinants of chess skill. **Memory & Cognition, 10,** 237-242.

Holzman, T.G., Pellegrino, J.W., & Glaser, R. 1982. Cognitive dimensions of numerical rule induction. **Journal of Educational Psychology, 74,** 360-373.

Holzman, T.G., Pellegrino, J.W., & Glaser, R. 1983. Cognitive variables in series completion. **Journal of Educational Psychology, 75,** 603-618.

Horn, J.L. 1970. Organization of data on life-span development of human abilities. In L.R. Goulet & P.B. Baltes (Eds.), **Life-Span Developmental Psychology: Research and Theory.** New York: Academic Press, (pp. 423-466).

Horn, J.L. 1975. Psychometric studies of aging and intelligence. In S. Gershon & A. Raskin (Eds.), **Aging, Vol. 2: Genesis and Treatment of Psychologic Disorders in the Elderly.** New York: Raven Press, (pp. 19-43).

Horn, J.L. 1978. Human ability systems. In P.B. Baltes (Ed.), **Life-Span Development and Behavior: Vol. 1.** New York: Academic Press, (pp. 211-256).

Horn, J.L. 1980. Concepts of intellect in relation to learning and adult development. **Intelligence, 4,** 285-317.

Horn, J.L. 1982a. The theory of fluid and crystallized intelligence in relation to concepts of cognitive psychology and aging in adulthood. In F.I.M. Craik & S. Trehub (Eds.), **Aging and Cognitive Processes.** New York: Plenum, (pp. 237-278).

Horn, J.L. 1982b. The aging of human abilities. In B.B. Wolman (Ed.), **Handbook of Developmental Psychology.** Englewood Cliffs, NJ: Prentice-Hall, (pp. 847-870).

Horn, J.L. & Cattell, R.B. 1966. Age differences in primary mental ability factors. **Journal of Gerontology, 21,** 210-220.

Horn, J.L. & Cattell, R.B. 1967. Age differences in fluid and crystallized intelligence. **Acta Psychologica, 26,** 107-129.

Horn, J.L. & Donaldson, G. 1976. On the myth of intellectual decline in adulthood. **American Psychologist, 31,** 701-709.

Horn, J.L. & Donaldson, G. 1980. Cognitive development in adulthood. In O.G. Brim & J. Kagan (Eds.), **Constancy and Change in Human Development.** Cambridge, MA: Harvard University Press, (pp. 445-529).

Horn, J.L., Donaldson, G., & Engstrom, R. 1981. Apprehension, memory, and fluid intelligence decline in adulthood. **Research on Aging, 3,** 33-84.

Howard, D.V. 1983. The effects of aging and degree of association on the semantic priming of lexical decisions. **Experimental Aging Research, 9,** 145-151.

Howard, D.V., McAndrews, M.P., & Lasaga, M.I. 1981. Semantic priming of lexical decisions in young and old adults. **Journal of Gerontology, 36,** 707-714.

Howard, D.V., Shaw, R., & Gillette, J. 1983. **Aging and the Time Course of Semantic Activation.** Technical Report NIA-83-7, Department of Psychology, Georgetown University, Washington, D.C.

Hoyer, W.J., Rebok, G.W., & Sved, S.M. 1979. Effects of varying irrelevant information on adult age differences in problem solving. **Journal of Gerontology, 34,** 553-560.

Hugin, F., Norris, A.H., & Shock, N.W. 1960. Skin reflex and voluntary reaction times in young and old males. **Journal of Gerontology, 15,** 388-391.

Hulicka, I.M. 1966. Age differences in Wechsler Memory Scale scores. **Journal of Genetic Psychology, 109,** 135-145.

Hulicka, I.M. 1982. Memory functioning in late adulthood. In F.I.M. Craik & S. Trehub (Eds.), **Aging and Cognitive Processes.** New York: Plenum, (pp. 331-351).

Hulicka, I.M., Sterns, H., & Grossman, J. 1967. Age-group comparisons of paired-associate learning as a function of paced and self-paced association and response times. **Journal of Gerontology, 22,** 274-280.

Hultsch, D.F. 1971. Organization and memory in adulthood. **Human Development, 14,** 16-29.

Hultsch, D.F. & Hickey, T. 1978. External validity in the study of human development: Theoretical and methodological issues. **Human Development, 21,** 76-91.

Hunt, E. 1976. Varieties of cognitive power. In L.B. Resnick (Ed.), **The Nature of Intelligence.** Hillsdale, N.J.: Erlbaum, (pp. 237-259).

Hunt, E. 1978. Mechanics of verbal ability. **Psychological Review, 85,** 109-130.

Hunt, E. 1980a. The foundations of verbal comprehension. In R. Snow, P. Federico, & W.E. Montague (Eds.), **Aptitude, Learning and Instruction, Vol. 1.** Hillsdale, N.J.: Erlbaum, (pp. 87-104).

Hunt, E. 1980b.   Intelligence as an information-processing concept. **British Journal of Psychology, 71,** 449-474.

Hunt, E. 1983.   On the nature of intelligence. **Science, 219,** 141-146.

Hunt, E., Frost, N., & Lunneborg, C.E. 1973.   Individual differences in cognition: A new approach to intelligence. In G. Bower (Ed.), **The Psychology of Learning and Motivation, Vol. 7.** New York: Academic Press, (pp. 87-122).

Hunt, E. & Lansman, M. 1982.   Individual differences in attention. In R.J. Sternberg (Ed.), **Advances in the Psychology of Human Intelligence: Vol. I.** Hillsdale, N.J.: Erlbaum, (pp. 207254).

Hunt, E. & MacLeod, C. 1979.   The sentence-verification paradigm: A case study of two conflicting approaches to individual differences.   In R.J. Sternberg & D.K. Detterman (Eds.), **Human Intelligence: Perspectives on its Theory and Measurement.** Norwood, N.J.: Ablex, (pp. 89-104).

Inglis, J. & Ankus, M.N. 1965.   Effects of age on short-term storage and serial rote learning. **British Journal of Psychology, 56,** 183-195.

Jacewicz, M.M. & Hartley, A.A. 1979.   Rotation of mental images by young and old college students: The effects of familiarity. **Journal of Gerontology, 34,** 396-403.

Jackson, M.D. 1980.   Further evidence for a relationship between memory access and reading ability. **Journal of Verbal Learning and Verbal Behavior, 19,** 683-694.

Jackson, M.D. & McClelland, J.L. 1975.   Sensory and cognitive determinants of reading speed. **Journal of Verbal Learning and Verbal Behavior, 14,** 565-574.

Jackson, M.D. & McClelland, J.L. 1979.   Processing determinants of reading speed. **Journal of Experimental Psychology: General, 108,** 151-181.

Jenkinson, J.C. 1983.   Is speed of information processing related to fluid or crystallized intelligence? **Intelligence, 7,** 91-106.

Jensen, A.R. 1979. **g:** Outmoded theory or unconquered frontier? **Creative Science & Technology, 2,** 16-29.

Jensen, A.R. 1980. Chronometric analysis of intelligence. **Journal of Social and Biological Structures, 3,** 103-122.

Jensen, A.R. 1982a. The chronometry of intelligence. In R.J. Sternberg (Ed.), **Advances in the Psychology of Human Intelligence, Vol. I.** Hillsdale, N.J.: Erlbaum, (pp. 255-310).

Jensen, A.R. 1982b. Reaction time and psychometric g. In H.J. Eysenck (Ed.), **A Model for Intelligence.** New York: Springer-Verlag, (pp. 93-132).

Jensen, A.R. 1983. Critical flicker frequency and intelligence. **Intelligence, 7,** 217-225.

Jensen, A.R. & Munro, E. 1979. Reaction time, movement time, and intelligence. **Intelligence, 3,** 121-126.

Jerome, E.A. 1962. Decay of heuristic processes in the aged. In C. Tibbitts & W. Donahue (Eds.), **Social and Psychological Aspects of Aging.** New York: Columbia University Press.

Johnson, P.E., Duran, A.S., Hassebrock, F., Moller, J., Prietula, M., Feltovich, P.J., & Swanson, D.B. 1981. Expertise and error in diagnostic reasoning. **Cognitive Science, 5,** 235-283.

Johnston, W.A., Wagstaff, R.R., & Griffith, D. 1972. Information-processing analysis of verbal learning. **Journal of Experimental Psychology, 96,** 307-314.

Jones, H.E. 1955. Age changes in mental abilities. In **Old Age and the Modern World.** Edinburgh: Livingstone, (pp. 267-274).

Jones, H.E. 1956. Problems of aging in perceptual and intellective functions. In J.E. Anderson (Ed.), **Psychological Aspects of Aging.** Washington, D.C.: American Psychological Association, (pp. 135-139).

Jones, H.E. 1959. Intelligence and problem solving. In J.E. Birren (Ed.), **Handbook of Aging and the Individual.** Chicago: University of Chicago Press, (pp. 700-738).

Jones, H.E. & Conrad, H.S. 1933. The growth and decline of intelligence: A study of a homogeneous group between the ages of ten and sixty. **Genetic Psychology Monographs, 13,** 223-298.

Jones, H.E., Conrad, H., & Horn, A. 1928. Psychological studies of motion pictures: Observation and recall as a function of age. **University of California Publications in Psychology, 3,** 225-243.

Just, M.A. & Carpenter, P.A. 1980. A theory of reading: From eye fixations to comprehension. **Psychological Review, 87,** 329-354.

Kahneman, D. 1973. **Attention and Effort.** Englewood Cliffs, N.J.: Prentice-Hall.

Kamin, L.J. 1957. Differential changes in mental abilities in old age. **Journal of Gerontology, 12,** 66-70.

Kaplan, O.J. 1951. The place of psychology in gerontology. **Geriatrics, 6,** 298-303.

Kastenbaum, R. 1968. Perspectives on the development and modification of behavior in the aged: A developmental-field perspective. **Gerontologist, 8,** 280-283.

Kausler, D.H. 1982. **Experimental Psychology and Human Aging.** New York: Wiley.

Kausler, D.H. & Hakami, M. 1983. Memory for activities: Adult age differences and intentionality. **Developmental Psychology, 19,** 889-894.

Kausler, D.H., Hakami, M.K., & Wright, R.E. 1982. Adult age differences in frequency judgments of categorical represent-ations. **Journal of Gerontology, 37,** 365-371.

Kausler, D.H. & Lair, C.J. 1966. Associative strength and paired associate learning in elderly subjects. **Journal of Gerontology, 21,** 278-280.

Kausler, D.H. & Puckett, J.M. 1979. Effects of word frequency on adult age differences in word memory span. **Experimental Aging Research, 5,** 161-169.

Kausler, D.H. & Puckett, J.M. 1980. Frequency judgments and correlated cognitive abilities in young and elderly adults. **Journal of Gerontology, 35,** 376-392.

Kausler, D.H. & Puckett, J.M. 1981. Adult age differences in memory for sex of voice. **Journal of Gerontology, 36,** 44-50.

Kausler, D.H., Wright, R.E., & Hakami, M.K. 1981. Variation
    in task complexity and adult age differences in frequency-
    of-occurrence judgments. **Bulletin of the Psychonomic
    Society, 18,** 195-197.

Kay, H. 1959. Theories of learning and aging. In J.E. Birren
    (Ed.), **Handbook of Aging and the Individual.** Chicago:
    University of Chicago Press, (pp. 614-654).

Kay, H. & Birren, J.E. 1958. Swimming speed of the albino
    rat: II. Fatigue, practice, and drug effects on age and
    sex differences. **Journal of Gerontology, 13,** 378-385.

Kelley, C.R. 1968. **Manual and Automatic Control.** New York:
    Wiley.

Kieras, D.E. 1981. Component processes in the comprehension
    of simple prose. **Journal of Verbal Learning and Verbal
    Behavior, 20,** 1-23.

Kinsbourne, M. 1973. Age effects on letter span related to
    rate and sequential dependency. **Journal of Gerontology,
    28,** 317-319.

Kirchner, W.K. 1958. Age differences in short-term retention
    of rapidly changing information. **Journal of Experimental
    Psychology, 55,** 352-358.

Kirsner, K. 1972. Developmental changes in short-term recognition
    memory. **British Journal of Psychology, 63,** 109-117.

Klatzky, R.L. 1980. **Human Memory: Structures and Processes.**
    San Francisco: W.H. Freeman.

Kleinmuntz, B. 1968. The processing of clinical information
    by man and machine. In B. Kleinmuntz (Ed.), **Formal Repre-
    sentation of Human Judgment.** New York: Wiley, (pp. 149-186).

Klodin, V.M. 1976. The relationship of scoring treatment
    and age in perceptual-integrative performance. **Experimental
    Aging Research, 2,** 303-313.

Korchin, S.J. & Basowitz, H. 1957. Age differences in verbal
    learning. **Journal of Abnormal and Social Behavior, 54,**
    64-69.

Kriauciunas, R. 1968. The relationship of age and retention-
    interval activity in short-term memory. **Journal of Geron-
    tology, 23,** 169-173.

Kuhlen, R.G. 1963. Age and intelligence: The significance of cultural change in longitudinal vs. cross-sectional findings. **Vita Humana, 6,** 113-124.

Kuhn, T.S. 1962. **The Structure of Scientific Revolutions.** Chicago: University of Chicago Press.

Kumnick, L. 1956. Aging and the latency and duration of pupil constriction in response to light and sound stimuli. **Journal of Gerontology, 11,** 391-396.

Labouvie, E.W. 1980. Identity versus equivalence of psychological measures and constructs. In L.W. Poon (Ed.), **Aging in the 1980s.** Washington, D.C.: American Psychological Association, (pp. 493-502).

Lachman, M.E. & Jelalian, E. 1984. Self-efficacy and attributions for intellectual performance in young and elderly adults. **Journal of Gerontology, 39,** 577-582.

Lachman, R., Lachman, J.L., & Butterfield, E.C. 1979. **Cognitive Psychology and Information Processing: An Introduction.** Hillsdale, N.J.: Erlbaum.

Lachman, R., Lachman, J.L., & Taylor, D.W. 1982. Reallocation of mental resources over the productive lifespan: Assumptions and task analyses. In F.I.M. Craik & S. Trehub (Eds.), **Aging and Cognitive Processes.** New York: Plenum, (pp. 279-308).

LaFratta, C.W. & Canestrari, R.E. 1966. A comparison of sensory and motor nerve conduction velocities in relation to age. **Archives of Physical Medicine and Rehabilitation, 47,** 286-290.

LaFratta, C.W. & Smith, O.H. 1964. A study of the relationship of motor nerve conduction velocity in the adult to age, sex, and handedness. **Archives of Physical Medicine and Rehabilitation, 45,** 407-412.

Lally, M. & Nettelbeck, T. 1977. Intelligence, reaction time, and inspection time. **American Journal of Mental Deficiency, 82,** 273-281.

Lane, D.M. & Robertson, L. 1979. The generality of the levels of processing hypothesis: An application to memory for chess positions. **Memory & Cognition, 7,** 253-256.

Lanier, L.H. 1934. The interrelationships of speed of reaction
    measurements. **Journal of Experimental Psychology, 17,**
    371-399.

Lansman, M. 1981. Ability factors and speed of information
    processing. In M.P. Friedman, J.P. Das, & N. O'Connor
    (Eds.), **Intelligence and Learning.** New York: Plenum,
    (pp. 441-457).

Lansman, M., Donaldson, G., Hunt, E., & Yantis, S. 1982. Ability
    factors and cognitive processes. **Intelligence, 6,** 347-386.

Larkin, J.H., McDermott, J., Simon, D.P., & Simon, H.A. 1980.
    Models of competence in solving physics problems. **Cognitive
    Science, 4,** 317-345.

LaRiviere, J.E. & Simonson, E. 1965. The effect of age and
    occupation on speed of writing. **Journal of Gerontology,
    20,** 415-416.

Laufer, A.C. & Schweitz, B. 1968. Neuromuscular response
    tests as predictors of sensory-motor performance in aging
    individuals. **American Journal of Physical Medicine,
    47,** 250-263.

Layton, B. 1975. Perceptual noise and aging. **Psychological
    Bulletin, 82,** 875-883.

Leaper, D.J., Gill, P.W., Staniland, J.R., Horrocks, J.C.,
    & deDombal, F.T. 1973. Clinical diagnostic process:
    An analysis. **British Medical Journal, 3,** 569-574.

Lee, J.A. & Pollack, R.H. 1978. The effects of age on perceptual
    problem-solving strategies. **Experimental Aging Research,
    4,** 37-54.

Lehman, H.C. 1953. **Age and Achievement.** Princeton, N.J.:
    Princeton University Press.

Lemmon, V.W. 1927. The relation of reaction time to measures
    of intelligence, memory, and learning. **Archives of Psych-
    ology,** Whole No. 94.

Leonard, J.A. & Newman, R.C. 1965. On the acquistion and
    maintenance of high speed and high accuracy in a keyboard
    task. **Ergonomics, 8,** 281-304.

Lesgold, A.M. 1984. Acquiring expertise. In J.R. Anderson & S.M. Kosslyn (Eds.), **Tutorials in Learning and Memory.** San Francisco: Freeman, (pp. 31-60).

Light, L.L., Zelinski, E.M., & Moore, M. 1982. Adult age differences in reasoning from new information. **Journal of Experimental Psychology: Learning, Memory, and Cognition, 8,** 435-447.

Lindholm, J.M. & Parkinson, S.R. 1983. An interpretation of age-related differences in letter-matching performance. **Perception & Psychophysics, 33,** 283-294.

Loftus, G.R. 1978. On the interpretation of interactions. **Memory & Cognition, 6,** 312-319.

Logan, G.D. 1978. Attention in character-classification tasks: Evidence for the automaticity of component stages. **Journal of Experimental Psychology: General, 107,** 32-63.

Logan, G.D. 1979. On the use of a concurrent memory load to measure attention and automaticity. **Journal of Experimental Psychology: Human Perception and Performance, 5,** 189-207.

Long, G.M. 1984. The pre-treatment weighting technique. **Journal of Experimental Psychology: Human Perception and Performance, 10,** 140-143.

Longstreth, L.E. 1984. Jensen's reaction time investigations of intelligence: A critique. **Intelligence, 8,** 139-160.

Loranger, N.W. & Misiak, H. 1959. Critical flicker frequency and some intellectual functions in old age. **Journal of Gerontology, 14,** 323-327.

Lorge, I. 1936. The influence of the test upon the nature of the mental decline as a function of age. **Journal of Educational Psychology, 27,** 100-110.

Lorsbach, T.C. & Simpson, G.B. 1984. Age differences in the rate of processing in short-term memory. **Journal of Gerontology, 39,** 315-321.

Ludwig, T.E. 1982. Age differences in mental synthesis. **Journal of Gerontology, 37,** 182-189.

Lunneborg, C.E. 1977. Choice reaction time: What role in ability measurement? **Applied Psychological Measurement, 1,** 309-330.

Macht, M.L. & Buschke, H. 1984. Speed of recall in aging. **Journal of Gerontology, 39,** 439-443.

Mackworth, J. 1963. The relation between the visual image and post-perceptual immediate memory. **Journal of Verbal Learning and Verbal Behavior, 2,** 75-85.

Madden, D.J. 1982. Age differences and similarities in the improvement of controlled search. **Experimental Aging Research, 8,** 91-98.

Madden, D.J. 1983. Aging and distraction by highly familiar stimuli during visual search. **Developmental Psychology, 19,** 499-507.

Madden, D.J. 1984. Data-driven and memory-driven selective attention in visual search. **Journal of Gerontology, 39,** 72-78.

Madden, D.J. & Nebes, R.D. 1980. Aging and the development of automaticity in visual search. **Developmental Psychology, 16,** 377-384.

Magladery, J.W., Teasdall, R.D., & Norris, A.H. 1958. Effect of aging on plantar flexor and superficial abdominal reflexes in man. **Journal of Gerontology, 13,** 282-288.

Mandler, G. & Kessen, W. 1959. **The Language of Psychology.** New York: Wiley.

Maniscalco, C.I. & DeRosa, D.V. 1983. Memory scanning of young and old adults: The influence of rate of presentation and delay interval on recognition memory performance. **Bulletin of the Psychonomic Society, 21,** 7-10.

Marcel, A.J. 1983. Conscious and unconscious perception: Experiments on visual masking and recognition. **Cognitive Psychology, 15,** 197-237.

Mark, J.A. 1956. Measurement of job performance and age. **Monthly Labor Review, 79,** 1410-1414.

Mark, J.A. 1957. Comparative job performance by age. **Monthly Labor Review, 80,** 1467-1471.

Marsh, G.R. 1975. Age differences in evoked potential correlates of a memory scanning process. **Experimental Aging Research, 1,** 3-16.

Marx, M.H. 1970. Observation, discovery, confirmation, and theory building. In A.R. Gilgen (Ed.), **Contemporary Scientific Psychology.** New York: Academic Press, (pp. 13-42).

Mason, C.F. & Ganzler, H. 1964. Adult norms for the Shipley Institute of Living Scale and Hooper Visual Organization Test based on age and education. **Journal of Gerontology, 19,** 419-424.

Mason, M. 1978. From print to sound in mature readers as a function of reader ability and two forms of orthographic regularity. **Memory & Cognition, 6,** 568-581.

Mason, S.E. 1979. Effects of orienting tasks on the recall and recognition performance of subjects differing in age. **Developmental Psychology, 15,** 467-469.

Matarazzo, J.D. 1972. **Wechsler's Measurement and Appraisal of Adult Intelligence.** Baltimore: The Williams & Wilkins Co.

McCarthy, M., Ferris, S.H., Clark, E., & Crook, T. 1981. Acquisition and retention of categorized material in normal aging and senile dementia. **Experimental Aging Research, 7,** 127-135.

McClelland, J.L. & Rumelhart, D.E. 1981. An interactive activation model of context effects in letter perception: Part I: An account of basic findings. **Psychological Review, 88,** 375-407.

McFarland, R.A. 1930. An experimental study of the relationship between speed and mental ability. **Journal of General Psychology, 3,** 67-97.

McFarland, R.A. 1956. Functional efficiency, skills, and employment. In J.E. Anderson (Ed.), **Psychological Aspects of Aging.** Washington, D.C.: American Psychological Association, (pp. 227-235).

McFarland, R.A. 1963. Experimental evidence of the relationship between aging and oxygen want: In search of a theory of aging. **Ergonomics, 6,** 339-366.

McNulty, J.A. & Caird, W. 1967. Memory loss with age: An unsolved problem. **Psychological Reports, 20,** 283-288.

Meyer, B.J.F. & Rice, G.E. 1981. Information recalled from prose by young, middle, and old adult readers. **Experimental Aging Research, 7,** 253-268.

Miles, C.C. 1934. Influence of speed and age on intelligence scores of adults. **Journal of Genetic Psychology, 10,** 208-210.

Miles, W.R. 1933. Age and human ability. **Psychological Review, 40,** 99-123.

Miles, W.R. 1935. Training, practice, and mental longevity. **Science, 81,** 79-87.

Miller, G.A., Galanter, E., & Pribram, K.H. 1960. **Plans and the Structure of Behavior.** New York: Holt, Rinehart & Winston.

Moenster, P.A. 1972. Learning and memory in relation to age. **Journal of Gerontology, 27,** 361-363.

Mortimer-Tanner, R.S. & Naylor, G.F.K. 1973. Rates of information acceptance and executive response in youthful and elderly subjects. **Australian Journal of Psychology, 25,** 139-145.

Mueller, J.H., Kausler, D.H., & Faherty, A. 1980. Age and access time for different memory codes. **Experimental Aging Research, 6,** 445-450.

Mueller, J.H., Kausler, D.H., Faherty, A. & Olivieri, M. 1980. Reaction time as a function of age, anxiety, and typicality. **Bulletin of the Psychonomic Society, 16,** 473-476.

Mueller, J.H., Rankin, J.L., & Carlomusto, M. 1979. Adult age differences in free recall as a function of basis of organization and method of presentation. **Journal of Gerontology, 34,** 375-380.

Mulholland, T.M., Pellegrino, J.W., & Glaser, R. 1980. Components of geometric analogy solution. **Cognitive Psychology, 12,** 252-284.

Mumaw, R.J. & Pellegrino, J.W. 1984. Individual differences in complex spatial processing. **Journal of Educational Psychology, 76,** 920-939.

Mumaw, R.J., Pellegrino, J.W., Kail, R.V., & Carter, P. 1984. Different slopes for different folks: Process analysis of spatial aptitude. **Memory & Cognition, 12,** 515-521.

Murphy, M.D., Sanders, R.E., Gabriesheski, A.S., & Schmitt, F.A. 1981. Metamemory in the aged. **Journal of Gerontology, 36,** 185-193.

Mursell, G.R. 1929. Decrease in intelligence with increase in age among inmates of penal institutions. **Journal of Juvenile Research, 13,** 199-203.

Navon, D. 1984. Resources: A theoretical soup stone? **Psychological Review, 91,** 216-234.

Naylor, G.F.K. 1973. The anatomy of reaction time and its relation to mental function in the elderly. **Proceedings of the Australian Association of Gerontology, 2,** 17-19.

Nebes, R.D. 1976. Verbal-pictorial recoding in the elderly. **Journal of Gerontology, 31,** 421-427.

Nebes, R.D. 1978. Vocal versus manual response as a determinant of age difference in simple reaction time. **Journal of Gerontology, 33,** 884-889.

Nebes, R.D. & Andrews-Kulis, M.E. 1976. The effect of age on the speed of sentence formation and incidental learning. **Experimental Aging Research, 2,** 315-331.

Nesselroade, J.R. 1977. Issues in studying developmental change in adults from a multivariate perspective. In J.E. Birren & K.W. Schaie (Eds.), **Handbook of the Psychology of Aging.** New York: Van Nostrand Reinhold, (pp. 59-69).

Nettelbeck, T. 1982. Inspection time: An index for intelligence? **Quarterly Journal of Experimental Psychology, 34A,** 299-312.

Nettelbeck, T. & Kirby, N.H. 1983. Measures of timed performance and intelligence. **Intelligence, 7,** 39-52.

Newell, A. 1973. You can't play 20 questions with nature and win: Projective comments on the papers of this symposium. In W.G. Chase (Ed.), **Visual Information Processing.** New York: Academic Press, (pp. 283-308).

Newell, A. & Simon, H.A. 1972. **Human Problem Solving.** Englewood Cliffs, N.J.: Prentice-Hall.

Noble, C.E., Baker, B.L., & Jones, T.A. 1964. Age and sex parameters in psychomotor learning. **Perceptual and Motor Skills, 19,** 935-945.

Norman, D.A. 1980. Twelve issues for cognitive science. **Cognitive Science, 4,** 1-32.

Norman, D.A. & Bobrow, D.G. 1975a. On data limited and resource limited processes. **Cognitive Psychology, 7,** 44-64.

Norman, D.A. & Bobrow, D.G. 1975b. On the role of active memory processes in perception and cognition. In C.N. Cofer (Ed.), **The Structure of Human Memory.** San Francisco, Ca.: Freeman, (pp. 114-132).

Norris, A.H., Shock, N.W., & Wagman, I.H. 1953. Age changes in the maximum conduction velocity of motor fibers in human ulnar nerves. **Journal of Applied Physiology, 5,** 589-593.

Obrist, W.D. 1963. The electroencephalogram of healthy aged males. In J.E. Birren, R.N. Butler, S.W. Greenhouse, L. Sokoloff, & M.R. Yarrow (Eds.), **Human Aging: A Biological and Behavioral Study.** Washington, D.C.: U.S. Public Health Service, (pp. 79-93).

Overton, W.F. & Reese, H.W. 1973. Models of development: Methodological implications. In J.R. Nesselroade & H.W. Reese (Eds.), **Life-Span Developmental Psychology: Methodological Issues.** New York: Academic Press, (pp. 65-86).

Pachella, R.G. 1974. The interpretation of reaction time in information processing research. In B. Kantowitz (Ed.), **Human Information Processing: Tutorials in Performance and Cognition.** Hillsdale, N.J.: Erlbaum, (pp. 41-82).

Paivio, A. 1978. Mental comparisons involving abstract attributes. **Memory & Cognition, 6,** 199-208.

Palmer, J., MacLeod, C.M., Hunt, E., & Davidson, J.E. 1985. Information processing correlates of reading. **Journal of Memory and Language, 24,** 59-88.

Panek, P.E., Barrett, G.V., Sterns, H.L., & Alexander, R.A. 1978. Age differences in perceptual style, selective attention, and perceptual-motor reaction time. **Experimental Aging Research, 4,** 377-387.

Panek, P.E. & Stoner, S.B. 1980.   Age differences on Raven's Coloured Progressive Matrices.   **Perceptual and Motor Skills, 50,** 977-978.

Parkinson, S.R., Lindholm, J.M., & Inman, V.W. 1982. An analysis of age differences in immediate recall.   **Journal of Gerontology, 37,** 425-431.

Pavur, E.J., Comeaux, J.M., & Zeringue, J.A. 1984.   Younger and older adults' attention to relevant and irrelevant stimuli in free recall.   **Experimental Aging Research, 10,** 59-60.

Peak, D.T. 1968.   Changes in short-term memory in a group of aging community residents.   **Journal of Gerontology, 23,** 9-16.

Peak, D.T. 1970.   A replication study of changes in short-term memory in a group of aging community residents.   **Journal of Gerontology, 25,** 316-319.

Peak, H. & Boring, E.G. 1926.   The factor of speed in intelligence.   **Journal of Experimental Psychology, 9,** 71-94.

Pellegrino, J.W., Alderton, D.L., & Shute, V.J. 1984.   Understanding spatial ability.   **Educational Psychologist, 19,** 239-253.

Pellegrino, J.W. & Glaser, R. 1979.   Cognitive correlates and components in the analysis of individual differences. In R.J. Sternberg & D.K. Detterman (Eds.), **Human Intelligence: Perspectives on Its Theory and Measurement.**   Norwood, N.J.: Ablex, (pp. 61-88).

Pellegrino, J.W. & Glaser, R. 1980.   Components of inductive reasoning.   In R.E. Snow, P.A. Federico, & W.E. Montague (Eds.), **Aptitude, Learning, and Instruction, Vol. 1.** Hillsdale, N.J.: Erlbaum, (pp. 177-217).

Pepper, S.C. 1942.   **World Hypotheses: A Study in Evidence.** Berkeley, Ca.: University of California Press.

Perfetti, C.A. & Lesgold, A.M. 1977.   Discourse comprehension and sources of individual differences.   In M.A. Just & P.A. Carpenter (Eds.), **Cognitive Processes in Comprehension.** Hillsdale, N.J.: Erlbaum, (pp. 141-183).

Perlmutter, M. 1978. What is memory aging the aging of?
  Developmental Psychology, 14, 330-345.

Perlmutter, M. 1979. Age differences in adults' free recall,
  cued recall, and recognition. **Journal of Gerontology,
  34,** 533-539.

Perlmutter, M., Metzger, R., Nezworski, T., & Miller, K. 1981.
  Spatial and temporal memory in 20 and 60 year olds.
  Journal of Gerontology, 36, 59-65.

Perlmutter, M. & Mitchell, D.B. 1982. The appearance and
  disappearance of age differences in memory. In F.I.M. Craik
  & S. Trehub (Eds.), **Aging and Cognitive Processes.** New
  York: Plenum, (pp. 127-144).

Petros, T.V., Zehr, H.D., & Chabot, R.J. 1983. Adult age
  differences in accessing and retrieving information from
  long-term memory. **Journal of Gerontology, 38,** 589-592.

Plude, D.J. & Hoyer, W.J. 1981. Adult age differences in
  visual search as a function of stimulus mapping and processing
  load. **Journal of Gerontology, 36,** 598-604.

Plude, D.J., Hoyer, W.J., & Lazar, J. 1982. Age, response
  complexity and target consistency in visual search.
  Experimental Aging Research, 8, 99-102.

Plude, D.J., Kaye, D.B., Hoyer, W.J., Post, T.A., Saynisch,
  M.J., & Hahn, M.V. 1983. Aging and visual search under
  consistent and varied mapping. **Developmental Psychology,
  19,** 508-512.

Poltrock, S.E. & Brown, P. 1984. Individual differences in
  visual imagery and spatial ability. **Intelligence, 8,**
  93-138.

Poon, L.W. & Fozard, J.L. 1980. Age and word frequency effects
  in continuous recognition memory. **Journal of Gerontology,
  35,** 77-86.

Poon, L.W., Fozard, J.L., Vierck, B., Dailey, B.F., Cerella, J., & Zeller, P. 1976. The effects of practice and information feedback on age-related differences in performance speed, variability and error rates in a two-choice decision task. In L.W. Poon & J.L. Fozard (Eds.), **Design Conference on Decision Making and Aging.** Boston: Boston Geriatric Research, Educational and Clinical Center, Technical Report 76-01, (pp. 65-81).

Posner, M.I., Boies, S.J., Eichelman, W.H., & Taylor, R.L. 1969. Retention of visual and name codes of single letters. **Journal of Experimental Psychology, (Monograph), 79,** 1-16.

Posner, M.I. & MacLeod, P. 1982. Information processing models: In search of elementary operations. **Annual Review of Psychology, 33,** 477-514.

Posner, M.I. & Snyder, C.R.R. 1975. Attention and cognitive control. In R.L. Solso (Ed.), **Information Processing and Cognition: The Loyola Symposium.** Hillsdale, N.J.: Erlbaum, (pp. 55-85).

Prohaska, T.R., Parham, I.A., & Teitelman, J. 1984. Age differences in attributions to causality: Implications for intellectual assessment. **Experimental Aging Research, 10,** 111-117.

Puckett, J.M. & Kausler, D.H. 1984. Individual differences and models of memory span: A role for memory search rate? **Journal of Experimental Psychology: Learning, Memory and Cognition, 10,** 72-82.

Quetelet, M.A. 1842. **A Treatise on Man and the Development of His Faculties.** Edinburgh: Chambers.

Rabbitt, P.M.A. 1964. Set and age in a choice response task. **Journal of Gerontology, 19,** 301-306.

Rabbitt, P.M.A. 1965. Age and discrimination between complex stimuli. In A.T. Welford & J.E. Birren (Eds.), **Behavior, Aging, and the Nervous System.** Springfield, IL: Charles C Thomas, (pp. 35-53).

Rabbitt, P.M.A. 1968. Age and the use of structure in transmitted
    information. In G.A. Talland (Ed.), **Human Aging and
    Behavior.** New York: Academic Press, (pp. 75-92).

Rabbitt, P.M.A. 1977. Changes in problem solving ability
    in old age. In J.E. Birren & K.W. Schaie (Eds.), **Handbook
    of the Psychology of Aging.** New York: Van Nostrand Reinhold,
    (pp. 606-625).

Rabbitt, P.M.A. 1979a. Current paradigms and models in human
    information processing. In V. Hamilton & D.M. Warburton
    (Eds.), **Human Stress and Cognition.** Chichester, England:
    Wiley, (pp. 115-140).

Rabbitt, P.M.A. 1979b. Some experiments and a model for changes
    in attentional selectivity with old age. In F. Hoffmeister
    & C. Muller (Eds.), **Brain Function in Old Age.** Berlin:
    Springer-Verlag, (pp. 82-94).

Rabbitt, P.M.A. 1979c. How old and young subjects monitor
    and control responses for accuracy and speed. **British
    Journal of Psychology, 70,** 305-311.

Rabbitt, P.M.A. 1980. A fresh look at changes in reaction
    times in old age. In D.G. Stein (Ed.), **The Psychobiology
    of Old Age.** Amsterdam: Elsevier/North Holland, (pp. 425-442).

Rabbitt, P.M.A. 1981a. Cognitive psychology needs models
    for changes in performance with old age. In J. Long
    & A. Baddeley (Eds.), **Attention and Performance, IX.**
    Hillsdale, N.J.: Erlbaum, (pp. 555-573).

Rabbitt, P.M.A. 1981b. Sequential reactions. In D. Holding
    (Ed.), **Human Skills.** New York: Wiley, (pp. 153-175).

Rabbitt, P.M.A. 1982a. Breakdown of control processes in
    old age. In T.M. Field, A. Huston, H.C. Quay, L. Troll,
    & G.E. Finley (Eds.), **Review of Human Development.**
    New York: Wiley, (pp. 540-550).

Rabbitt, P.M.A. 1982b. How do old people know what to do
    next? In F.I.M. Craik & S. Trehub (Eds.), **Aging and
    Cognitive Processes.** New York: Plenum, (pp. 79-98).

Rabbitt, P.M.A. & Vyas, S.M. 1980. Selective anticipation
    for events in old age. **Journal of Gerontology, 35,** 913-919.

Rabinowitz, J.C. 1984. Aging and recognition failure. **Journal of Gerontology, 39,** 65-71.

Rabinowitz, J.C., Craik, F.I.M., & Ackerman, B.P. 1982. A processing resource account of age differences in recall. **Canadian Journal of Psychology, 36,** 325-344.

Ramalingaswami, P. 1975. **Measurement of Intelligence among Adult Indians.** New Delhi: National Council of Educational Research and Training.

Reed, H.B.C. & Reitan, R.M. 1963. Changes in psychological test performance associated with the normal aging process. **Journal of Gerontology, 18,** 271-274.

Reese, H.W. 1976. Models of memory development. **Human Development, 19,** 291-303.

Reisberg, D. 1983. General mental resources and perceptual judgments. **Journal of Experimental Psychology: Human Perception and Performance, 9,** 966-979.

Reitman, J.S. 1976. Skilled perception in GO: Deducing memory structures from inter-response times. **Cognitive Psychology, 8,** 336-356.

Ridgway, J. 1981. Towards a symbiosis of cognitive psychology and psychometrics. In M.P. Friedman, J.P. Das, & N. O'Connor (Eds.), **Intelligence and Learning.** New York: Plenum, (pp. 163-167).

Riege, W.H. & Inman, V. 1981. Age differences in nonverbal memory tasks. **Journal of Gerontology, 36,** 51-58.

Riege, W.H., Kelly, K., & Klane, L.T. 1981. Age and error differences on memory for designs. **Perceptual and Motor Skills, 52,** 507-513.

Riegel, K.F. 1968. Changes in psycholinguistic performance with age. In G.A. Talland (Ed.), **Human Aging and Behavior.** New York: Academic Press, (pp. 239-279).

Riegel, K.F. 1973. On the history of psychological gerontology. In C. Eisdorfer, M.P. Lawton (Eds.), **The Psychology of Adult Development and Aging.** Washington, D.C.: American Psychological Association, (pp. 37-68).

Riegel, K.F. 1976. **Psychology of Development and History.** New York: Plenum.

Riegel, K.F. & Birren, J.E. 1966. Age differences in verbal associations. **Journal of Genetic Psychology, 108,** 153-170.

Robertson-Tchabo, E.A. & Arenberg, D. 1976. Age differences in cognition in healthy educated men: A factor analysis of experimental measures. **Experimental Aging Research, 2,** 75-79.

Roediger, J.L. 1980. Memory metaphors in cognitive psychology. **Memory & Cognition, 8,** 231-246.

Rose, A.M. 1980. Information-processing abilities. In R.E. Snow, P. Federico, & W.E. Montague (Eds.), **Aptitude, Learning and Instruction, Vol. 1.** Hillsdale, N.J.: Erlbaum, (pp. 65-86).

Ross, E. 1968. Effects of challenging and supportive instructions on verbal learning in older persons. **Journal of Educational Psychology, 59,** 261-266.

Rowe, E.J. & Schnore, M.M. 1971. Item concreteness and reported strategies in paired-associate learning as a function of age. **Journal of Gerontology, 26,** 470-475.

Royer, F.L. 1977. Information processing in the Block Design task. **Intelligence, 1,** 32-50.

Rumelhart, D.E. 1977. Toward an interactive model of reading. In S. Dornic (Ed.), **Attention and Performance, VI.** Hillsdale, N.J.: Erlbaum, (pp. 573-603).

Salthouse, T.A. 1976. Speed and age: Multiple rates of age decline. **Experimental Aging Research, 2,** 349-359.

Salthouse, T.A. 1978a. The role of memory in the age decline in digit symbol substitution performance. **Journal of Gerontology, 33,** 232-238.

Salthouse, T.A. 1978b. **Age and Speed: The Nature of the Relationship.** Unpublished Manuscript.

Salthouse, T.A. 1979. Adult age and the speed-accuracy tradeoff. **Ergonomics, 22,** 811-821.

Salthouse, T.A. 1980a. Age and Memory: Strategies for localizing the loss. In L.W. Poon, J.L. Fozard, L. Cermak, D. Arenberg, & L.W. Thompson (Eds.), **New Directions in Memory and Aging.** Hillsdale, N.J.: Erlbaum, (pp. 47-65).

Salthouse, T.A. 1980b. Age differences in visual masking: A manifestation of decline in signal/noise ratio? Paper presented at the 33rd Annual Meeting of the Gerontological Society of America, San Diego, CA.

Salthouse, T.A. 1982. **Adult Cognition: An Experimental Psychology of Human Aging.** New York: Springer-Verlag.

Salthouse, T.A. 1984. Effects of age and skill in typing. **Journal of Experimental Psychology: General, 113,** 345-371.

Salthouse, T.A. 1985. Speed of behavior and its implications for cognition. In J.E. Birren & K.W. Schaie (Eds.), **Handbook of the Psychology of Aging.** (2nd Edition), New York: Van Nostrand Reinhold, (pp. 400-426).

Salthouse, T.A. & Kail, R. 1983. The role of processing rate in memory development. In P.B. Baltes & O.G. Brim (Eds.), **Life-Span Development and Behavior, Vol. 5.** New York: Academic Press, (pp. 89-116).

Salthouse, T.A. & Kausler, D.H. 1985. Memory methodology in maturity. In C.J. Brainerd & M. Pressley (Eds.), **Basic Processes in Memory Development.** New York: Springer--Verlag, (pp. 279-311).

Salthouse, T.A. & Lichty, W. (1985). Tests of the neural noise hypothesis of age-related cognitive change. **Journal of Gerontology.**

Salthouse, T.A. & Prill, K. 1983. Analysis of a perceptual skill. **Journal of Experimental Psychology: Human Perception and Performance, 9,** 607-621.

Salthouse, T.A. & Prill, K. 1985. **Effects of Aging on Perceptual Closure.** Manuscript in preparation.

Salthouse, T.A., Rogan, J.D., & Prill, K. 1984. Division of attention: Age differences on a visually presented memory task. **Memory & Cognition, 12,** 613-620.

Salthouse, T.A. & Somberg, B.L. 1982a. Skilled performance: Effects of adult age and experience on elementary processes. **Journal of Experimental Psychology: General, 111,** 176-207.

Salthouse, T.A. & Somberg, B.L. 1982b. Isolating the age deficit in speeded performance. **Journal of Gerontology, 37,** 59-63.

Salthouse, T.A. & Somberg, B.L. 1982c. Time-accuracy relationships
    in young and old adults. **Journal of Gerontology, 37,**
    349-353.

Salthouse, T.A., Wright, R. & Ellis, C.L. 1979. Adult age
    and the rate of an internal clock. **Journal of Gerontology,**
    34, 53-57.

Sanders, R.E., Murphy, M.D., Schmitt, F.A., & Walsh, K.K. 1980.
    Age differences in free rehearsal strategies. **Journal**
    of Gerontology, 35, 550-558.

Sarason, S.B. 1984. If it can be studied or developed, should
    it be? **American Psychologist, 39,** 477-485.

Schaie, K.W. 1958. Rigidity-flexibility and intelligence:
    A cross-sectional study of the adult lifespan from 20
    to 70. **Psychological Monographs, 72,** 462, Whole No. 9.

Schaie, K.W. 1965. A general model for the study of developmental
    problems. **Psychological Bulletin, 64,** 92-107.

Schaie, K.W. 1967. Age changes and age differences. **Geronto-**
    logist, 7, 128-132.

Schaie, K.W. 1973. Methodological problems in descriptive
    developmental research on adulthood and aging. In J.R.
    Nesselroade & H.W. Reese (Eds.), **Life-Span Developmental**
    Psychology: Methodological Issues. New York: Academic
    Press, (pp. 253-280).

Schaie, K.W. 1975. Age changes in adult intelligence. In
    D.S. Woodruff & J.E. Birren (Eds.), **Aging: Scientific**
    Perspectives and Social Issues. New York: Van Nostrand,
    (pp. 111-124).

Schaie, K.W. 1983. The Seattle Longitudinal Study: A 21-year
    exploration of psychometric intelligence in adulthood.
    In K.W. Schaie (Ed.), **Longitudinal Studies of Adult Psycho-**
    logical Development. New York: Guilford, (pp. 64-135).

Schaie, K.W. & Hertzog, C. 1983. Fourteen-year cohort-sequential
    analyses of adult intellectual development. **Developmental**
    Psychology, 19, 531-543.

Schaie, K.W., Rosenthal, F., & Perlman, R.M. 1953. Differential
    mental deterioration of factorially "pure" functions
    in later maturity. **Journal of Gerontology, 8,** 191-196.

Schaie, K.W. & Strother, C.R. 1968. Cognitive and personality variables in college graduates of advanced age. In G.A. Talland (Ed.), **Human Behavior and Aging.** New York: Academic Press, (pp. 281-308).

Schneider, N.G., Gritz, E.R., & Jarvik, M.E. 1975. Age differences in learning, immediate and one-week delayed recall. **Gerontologia, 21,** 10-20.

Schneider, W. & Shiffrin, R.M. 1977. Controlled and automatic human information processing: I. Detection, search, and attention. **Psychological Review, 84,** 1-66.

Schoenfeld, A.H. & Herrmann, D.J. 1982. Problem perception and knowledge structure in expert and novice mathematical problem solvers. **Journal of Experimental Psychology: Learning, Memory and Cognition, 8,** 484-494.

Schonfield, A.D. & Robertson, B. 1966. Memory storage and aging. **Canadian Journal of Psychology, 20,** 228-236.

Schonfield, A.D. & Stones, M.J. 1979. Remembering and aging. In J.F. Kihlstrom & F.J. Evans (Eds.), **Functional Disorders of Memory.** Hillsdale, NJ: Erlbaum, (pp. 103-139).

Schwartz, S., Griffin, T.M., & Brown, J. 1983. Power and speed components of individual differences in letter matching. **Intelligence, 7,** 369-378.

Seymour, P.H.K. & Moir, W.L.N. 1980. Intelligence and semantic judgment time. **British Journal of Psychology, 71,** 53-61.

Shaps, L.P. & Nilsson, L. 1980. Encoding and retrieval operations in relation to age. **Developmental Psychology, 16,** 636-643.

Shepard, R.N. & Metzler, J. 1971. Mental rotation of three-dimensional objects. **Science, 171,** 701-703.

Shiffrin, R.M. & Atkinson, R.C. 1969. Storage and retrieval processes in long-term memory. **Psychological Review, 76,** 179-193.

Shiffrin, R.M. & Schneider, W. 1977. Controlled and automatic human information processing: II. Perceptual learning, automatic attending, and a general theory. **Psychological Review, 84,** 127-190.

Shucard, D. & Horn, J.L. 1972. Evoked cortical potentials and measurement of human abilities. **Journal of Comparative and Physiological Psychology, 78,** 59-68.

Shuell, T.J. 1980. Learning theory, instructional theory, and adaptation. In R.E. Snow, P. Federico, & W.E. Montague (Eds.), **Aptitude, Learning and Instruction, Vol. 2.** Hillsdale, N.J.: Erlbaum, (pp. 277-302).

Simon, D.P. & Simon, H.A. 1980. Individual differences in solving physics problems. In R.S. Siegler (Ed.), **Children's Thinking: What Develops?** Hillsdale, N.J.: Erlbaum, (pp. 325-348).

Simon, E. 1979. Depth and elaboration of processing in relation to age. **Journal of Experimental Psychology: Human Learning and Memory, 5,** 115-124.

Simon, H.A. 1976. Identifying basic abilities underlying intelligent performance of complex tasks. In L.B. Resnick (Ed.), **The Nature of Intelligence.** Hillsdale, N.J.: Erlbaum, (pp. 65-98).

Simon, H.A. 1979. Information processing models of cognition. **Annual Review of Psychology, 30,** 363-396.

Singleton, W.T. 1978. Laboratory studies of skill. In W.T. Singleton (Ed.), **The Study of Real Skills: Vol. I: The Analysis of Practical Skills.** Lancaster, England, MTP Press, (pp. 1643).

Smith, G.A. & Stanley, G. 1980. Relationships between measures of intelligence and choice reaction time. **Bulletin of the Psychonomic Society, 16,** 8-10.

Smith, G.A. & Stanley, G. 1983. Clocking g: Relating intelligence and measures of timed performance. **Intelligence, 7,** 353-368.

Smith, K.U. & Greene, D. 1962. Scientific motion study and ageing processes in performance. **Ergonomics, 5,** 155-164.

Snow, R.E. 1979. Theory and method for research on aptitude processes. In R.J. Sternberg & D.K. Detterman (Eds.), **Human Intelligence: Perspectives on its Theory and Measurement.** Norwood, N.J.: Ablex, (pp. 105-137).

Snow, R.E. 1980. Aptitude processes. In R.E. Snow, P.A. Federico, & W.E. Montague (Eds.), **Aptitude, Learning, and Instruction, Vol. 1.** Hillsdale, N.J.: Erlbaum, (pp. 27-63).

Snow, R.E. 1981. Toward a theory of aptitude for learning: I. Fluid and crystallized abilities and their correlates. In M.P. Friedman, J.P. Das, & N. O'Connor (Eds.), **Intelligence and Learning.** New York: Plenum, (pp. 345-362).

Snyder, C.R.R. 1972. **Individual Differences in Imagery and Thought.** Unpublished Dissertation, University of Oregon, Eugene, Oregon.

Somberg, B.L. & Salthouse, T.A. 1982. Divided attention abilities in young and old adults. **Journal of Experimental Psychology: Human Perception and Performance, 8,** 651-663.

Spearman, C. 1923. **The Nature of Intelligence and the Principles of Cognition.** London: McMillan & Co.

Spearman, C. 1927. **The Abilities of Man.** London: McMillan & Co.

Spiegel, M.R. & Bryant, N.D. 1978. Is speed of information processing related to intelligence and achievement? **Journal of Educational Psychology, 70,** 904-910.

Spilich, G.J. 1983. Life-span components of text processing: Structural and procedural differences. **Journal of Verbal Learning and Verbal Behavior, 22,** 231-244.

Spilich, G.J., Vesonder, G.T., Chiesi, H.L., & Voss, J.F. 1979. Text processing of domain-related information for individuals with high and low domain knowledge. **Journal of Verbal Learning and Verbal Behavior, 18,** 275-290.

Standing, L., Bond, B., Smith, P., & Isley, C. 1980. Is the immediate memory span determined by subvocalization rate? **British Journal of Psychology, 71,** 525-539.

Sterling, J.J. 1982. **The Utilization of Sign Information by Radiologists Diagnosing Bone Tumors.** Ph.D. Dissertation, University of Missouri, Columbia.

Sterling, J.J. & Salthouse, T.A. 1981. Retinal location and visual processing rate. **Perception & Psychophysics, 30,** 114-118.

Sternberg, R.J. 1977. **Intelligence, Information Processing, and Analogical Reasoning.** Hillsdale, N.J.: Erlbaum.

Sternberg, R.J. 1978. Intelligence research at the interface between differential and cognitive psychology: Prospects and proposals. **Intelligence, 2,** 195-222.

Sternberg, R.J. 1980. Sketch of a componential subtheory of human intelligence. **Behavioral and Brain Sciences, 3,** 573-614.

Sternberg, R.J. & Gardner, M.K. 1983. Unities in inductive reasoning. **Journal of Experimental Psychology: General, 112,** 80-116.

Sternberg, S. 1969. Memory scanning: Mental processes revealed by reaction-time experiments. **American Scientist, 57,** 421-457.

Sternberg, S. 1975. Memory scanning: New findings and current controversies. **Quarterly Journal of Experimental Psychology, 27,** 1-32.

Storandt, M. 1976. Speed and coding effects in relation to age and ability level. **Developmental Psychology, 12,** 177-178.

Storandt, M. 1977. Age, ability level, and method of administering and scoring the WAIS. **Journal of Gerontology, 32,** 175-178.

Suci, G.J., Davidoff, M.D., & Surwillo, W.W. 1960. Reaction time as a function of stimulus information and age. **Journal of Experimental Psychology, 60,** 242-244.

Summers, J.J. 1981. Motor programs. In D. Holding (Ed.), **Human Skills.** New York: Wiley, (pp. 41-64).

Surwillo, W.W. 1961. Frequency of the "alpha" rhythm, reaction time, and age. **Nature, 191,** 823-824.

Surwillo, W.W. 1963. The relation of simple response time to brain-wave frequency and the effects of age. **Electroencephalography and Clinical Neurophysiology, 15,** 105-114.

Surwillo, W.W. 1964a. Age and the perception of short intervals of time. **Journal of Gerontology, 19,** 322-324.

Surwillo, W.W. 1964b. The relation of decision time to brain wave frequency and to age. **Electroencephalography and Clinical Neurophysiology, 17,** 194-198.

Surwillo, W.W. 1968. Timing of behavior in senescence and the role of the central nervous system. In G.A. Talland (Ed.), **Human Aging and Behavior.** New York: Academic Press, (pp. 1-35).

Sward, K. 1945. Age and mental ability in superior men. **American Journal of Psychology, 58,** 443-479.

Szafran, J. 1965. Decision processes and ageing. In A.T. Welford & J.E. Birren (Eds.), **Behavior, Aging, and the Nervous System.** Springfield, IL: Charles C Thomas, (pp. 21-34).

Talland, G.A. 1962. The effect of age on speed of simple manual skill. **Journal of Genetic Psychology, 100,** 69-76.

Talland, G.A. 1968. Age and the span of immediate recall. In G.A. Talland (Ed.), **Human Aging amd Behavior.** New York: Academic Press, (pp. 93-129).

Taub, H.A. 1967. Paired-associates learning as a function of age, rate, and instructions. **Journal of Genetic Psychology, 111,** 41-46.

Taub, H.A. 1973. Memory span, practice, and aging. **Journal of Gerontology, 28,** 335-338.

Taub, H.A. 1974. Coding for short-term memory as a function of age. **Journal of Genetic Psychology, 125,** 309-314.

Taub, H.A. 1975. Mode of presentation, age, and short-term memory. **Journal of Gerontology, 30,** 56-59.

Taub, H.A. 1979. Comprehension and memory of prose materials by young and old adults. **Experimental Aging Research, 5,** 3-13.

Taub, H.A. & Long, M.K. 1972. The effects of practice on short-term memory of young and old subjects. **Journal of Geromtology, 27,** 494-499.

Taylor, M.M. & Creelman, C.D. 1967. PEST: Efficient estimates on probability functions. **Journal of the Acoustical Society of America, 41,** 782-787.

Thomas, J.C., Waugh, N.C., & Fozard, J.L. 1978. Age and familiarity in memory scanning. **Journal of Gerontology, 33,** 528-533.

Thorndike, E.L., Bregman, E.O., Tilton, J.W., & Woodyard, E. 1928. **Adult Learning.** New York: MacMillan.

Till, R.E. & Walsh, D.A. 1980. Encoding and retrieval factors in adult memory for implicational sentences. **Journal of Verbal Learning and Verbal Behavior, 19,** 1-16.

Travis, L.E. & Hunter, T.A. 1928. The relation between 'intelligence' and reflex conduction rate. **Journal of Experimental Psychology, 11,** 342-354.

Travis, L.E. & Hunter, T.A. 1930. The relations of electromyographically measured reflex times in the patellar and achilles reflexes to certain physical measurements and to intelligence. **Journal of General Psychology, 3,** 374-400.

Underwood, G. 1976. **Attention and Memory.** New York: Pergamon.

Vernon, P.A. 1983. Speed of information processing and general intelligence. **Intelligence, 7,** 53-70.

Voss, J.F., Tyler, S.W., & Yengo, L.A. 1983. Individual differences in the solving of social science problems. In R.F. Dillon & R.R. Schmeck (Eds.), **Individual Differences in Cognition, Vol. 1.** New York: Academic Press, (pp. 205-232).

Voss, J.F., Vesonder, G.T., & Spilich, G.J. 1980. Text generation and recall by high-knowledge and low-knowledge individuals. **Journal of Verbal Learning and Verbal Behavior, 19,** 651-667.

Wagman, I.H. & Lesse, H. 1952. Maximum conduction velocities of motor fibers of ulnar nerves in human subjects of various ages and sizes. **Journal of Neurophysiology, 15,** 235-244.

Wallace, J.G. 1956. Some studies of perception in relation to age. **British Journal of Psychology, 47,** 283-297.

Walsh, D.A. 1982. The development of visual information processes in adulthood and old age. In R. Sekuler, D. Kline, & K. Dismukes (Eds.), **Aging and Human Visual Function.** New York: Alan R. Liss, (pp. 203-230).

Waugh, N.C., Fozard, J.L., & Thomas, J.C. 1978. Retrieval time from different memory stores. **Journal of Gerontology, 33,** 718-724.

Waymer, M.J. & Emmers, R. 1958. Spinal synaptic delay in young and aged rats. **American Journal of Physiology, 194,** 403-405.

Wechsler, D. 1939/1955/1981. **Manual for the Wechsler Adult Intelligence Scale.** New York: The Psychological Corporation.

Wechsler, D. 1958. **Measurement of Adult Intelligence.** 4th Edition, Baltimore, MD: The Williams & Wilkins Co.

Weisenburg, T., Roe, A., & McBride, K.E. 1936. **Adult Intelligence.** New York: The Commonwealth Fund.

Weiss, A.D. 1965. The locus of reaction time change with set, motivation, and age. **Journal of Gerontology, 20,** 60-64.

Welford, A.T. 1957. Methodological problems in the study of changes in human performance with age. In G.E.W. Wolstenholme & C.M. O'Connor (Eds.), **Ciba Colloquia on Ageing.** London: Churchill, (pp. 149-169).

Welford, A.T. 1958. **Ageing and Human Skill.** London: Oxford University Press.

Welford, A.T. 1962. On changes of performance with age. **Lancet,** (Feb. 17), 335-339.

Welford, A.T. 1963. Social, psychological, and physiological gerontology - An experimental gerontologist's approach. In R.H. Williams, C. Tibbits, & W. Donahue (Eds.), **Processes of Aging, Volume I.** New York: Atherton, (pp. 115-131).

Welford, A.T. 1965. Performance, biological mechanisms and age: A theoretical sketch. In A.T. Welford & J.E. Birren (Eds.), **Behavior, Aging, and the Nervous System.** Springfield, IL: Charles C Thomas, (pp. 3-20).

Welford, A.T. 1969. Age and skill: Motor, intellectual and social. In A.T. Welford (Ed.), **Interdisciplinary Topics in Gerontology, 4.** Basel: S. Karger, (pp. 1-22).

Welford, A.T. 1977. Motor performance. In J.E. Birren & K.W. Schaie (Eds.), **Handbook of the Psychology of Aging.** New York: Van Nostrand Reinhold, (pp. 450-496).

Welford, A.T. 1980. On the nature of higher-order skills. **Journal of Occupational Psychology, 53,** 107-110.

Welford, A.T. 1981. Signal, noise, performance and age. **Human Factors, 23,** 97-109.

Welford, A.T. 1984. Between bodily changes and performance: Some possible reasons for slowing with age. **Experimental Aging Research, 10,** 73-88.

Wessels, M.G. 1982. **Cognitive Psychology.** New York: Harper & Row.

West, L.J. 1967. Vision and kinaesthesis in the acquisition of typewriting skill. **Journal of Applied Psychology, 51,** 161-166.

Whitbourne, S.K. & Slevin, A.E. 1978. Imagery and sentence retention in elderly and young adults. **Journal of Genetic Psychology, 133,** 287-298.

Willoughby, R.R. 1929. Incidental learning. **Journal of Educational Psychology, 20,** 671-682.

Wilson, T.R. 1963. Flicker fusion frequency, age and intelligence. **Gerontologia, 7,** 200-208.

Wissler, C. 1901. The correlation of mental and physical tests. **Psychological Review Monographs,** Whole No. 3.

Witt, S.J. & Cunningham, W.R. 1979. Cognitive speed and subsequent intellectual development: A longitudinal investigation. **Journal of Gerontology, 34,** 540-546.

Wittels, I. 1972. Age and stimulus meaningfulness in paired-associate learning. **Journal of Gerontology, 27,** 372-375.

Woodruff, D.S. 1975. Relationships among EEG alpha frequency, reaction time, and age: A biofeedback study. **Psychophysiology, 12,** 673-681.

Wright, R.E. 1981. Aging, divided attention, and processing capacity. **Journal of Gerontology, 36,** 605-614.

Yerkes, R.M. 1921. Psychological examining in the United States Army. **Memoirs of the National Academy of Sciences, 15,** 1-877.

Yesavage, J.A. & Rose, T.L. 1984. The effects of a face-name mnemonic in young, middle-aged, and elderly adults. **Experimental Aging Research, 10,** 55-57.

Zimmerman, W.S. 1954a.   The influence of item complexity upon
    the factor composition of a spatial visualization test.
    Educational and Psychological Measurement, 14, 106–119.
Zimmerman, W.S. 1954b.   Hypotheses concerning the nature of
    the spatial factors.   **Educational and Psychological Measure-
    ment, 14,** 396–400.

Name Index